Northampton County Area Community College
Learning Resources Center
Bethlehem, PA   18017

JOHN WILLIS

SCREEN WORLD

1983

Volume 34

CROWN PUBLISHERS, INC.

ONE PARK AVENUE

NEW YORK, NEW YORK 10016

TO

MARLENE DIETRICH

whose talent, fabulous face and figure, and ageless charm brought her international celebrity and adoration as one of the world's most elegant and glamorous stars.

BEN KINGSLEY AS MAHATMA GANDHI

© Columbia Pictures

1982 ACADEMY AWARDS FOR BEST ACTOR AND BEST FILM

CONTENTS

EDITOR: JOHN WILLIS

Assistant Editor: Stanley Reeves

Staff: Joe Baltake, Marco Starr Boyajian, Mark Cohen, Mark Gladstone,
Miles Kreuger, John Sala, Van Williams

Acknowledgments: This volume would not be possible without the cooperation of Tom Allen, Chris Anderson, Jane Alsobrook, Pamela Austin, Fred Baker, Henry Baker, Nina Baron, Sharon Behn, Mike Berman, Ian Bernie, Jim Bertges, Denice Brassard, Joseph Brenner, Susan Brockman, Mike Brox, Barry Cahn, John Calhoun, Fabiano Canosa, Karen Capen, Philip Castanza, Jerry Clark, Sandy Cobe, Bill Coleman, Karen Cooper, Alberta D'Angelo, Francene Davidoff, Cindy DePaula, Donna Dickman, Ira Deutchman, Dennis Doph, Robert Dorfman, Helen Eisenman, Bill Elsor, Steve Fagan, Suzanne Fedak, Lynn Fischoff, Tim Fisher, Andrew Fox, Don Vrancella, Dore Freeman, Renee Furst, Kathryn Galan, Roul Gatchalian, Joseph Green, Elisa Greer, Elizabeth Hager, Allison Hanau, Ron Harvey, Tom Haskins, Richard Hassanein, Dennis Higgins, Chuck Jones, Stephen Jones, Peggy Kirton, Richard Kraft, Don Krim, Jack Kurnes, Christene LaMont, Clare Larson, Jack Leff, Lloyd Leipzig, Wynn Lowenthal, Peter Lowy, Arlene Ludwig, William Lustig, Jeff Mackler, Kathy Madden, Howard Mahler, Leonard Maltin, Harold Marenstein, Louis Marino, Priscilla McDonald, Peter Meyer, John Miller, Susan Mills, Barbara Mudge, Eileen Nad, Joanna Ney, Kim Noe, Lillie Padell, Tom Patricia, Janet Perlberg, Paula Pevzner, Jerry Pickman, John Pierson, John Quinn, Jerald Rappoport, Jackie Raynal, Reid Rosefelt, Ed Russell, Suzanne Salter, Les Schecter, Richard Schwarz, Barbara Schwei, Mike Scrimenti, Eve Segal, Jacqueline Sigmund, John Skouras, Stephen Soba, Fran Speelman, Alicia Springer, John Springer, Laurence Steinfeld, Stuart Strutin, Ken Stutz, Deborah Taylor-Bellman, Maureen Tolsdorf, Bruce Trinz, Mark Urman, Don Velde, Sherrie Wallace, Bob Winestein, Christopher Wood, Stuart Zakim, Mindy Zepp, Wendy Zimmerman, Michael Zuker, Paul Zul

1. Burt Reynolds

2. Clint Eastwood

3. Sylvester Stallone

4. Dudley Moore

5. Richard Pryor

6. Dolly Parton

7. Jane Fonda

8. Richard Gere

9. Paul Newman

10. Harrison Ford

11. Goldie Hawn

12. Katharine Hepburn

13. Alan Alda

14. Sally Field

15. Cheech & Chong

16. Meryl Streep

6

TOP 25 BOX OFFICE STARS OF 1982
(Tabulated by Quigley Publications)

17. Robert Redford

18. Christopher Reeve

19. Dustin Hoffman

20. Timothy Hutton

1982 RELEASES

January 1 through December 31, 1982

21. Roger Moore

22. Chuck Norris

23. Bo Derek

24. Brooke Shields

25. Al Pacino

Julie Andrews

Jack Lemmon

Sissy Spacek

SHOOT THE MOON

(MGM) Director, Alan Parker; Screenplay, Bo Goldman; Producer, Alan Marshall; Photography, Michael Seresin; Designer, Geoffrey Kirkland; Editor, Gerry Hambling; Executive Producers, Edgar J. Scherick, Stuart Millar; Costumes, Kristi Zea; Assistant Directors, Raymond L. Greenfield, Francois X. Moullin; Art Director, Stu Campbell; In Metrocolor; 124 minutes; Rated R; January release.

CAST

George Dunlap	Albert Finney
Faith Dunlap	Diane Keaton
Sandy	Karen Allen
Frank Henderson	Peter Weller
Sherry	Dana Hill
Jill	Viveka Davis
Marianne	Tracey Gold
Molly	Tina Yothers
French DeVoe	George Murdock
Charlotte DeVoe	Leora Dana
Howard Katz	Irving Metzman
Maitre D'	Kenneth Kimmins
Officer Knudson	Michael Aldredge
Leo Spinelli	Robert Costanzo
Scott Gruber	David Landsberg
Willard	Lou Cutell
Harold	James Cranna
Joanne	Nancy Fish
Timmy	Jeremy Schoenberg
Rick	Stephen Morrell
M. C.	Jim Lange
Isabel	Georgann Johnson
Countergirl	O-Lan Shepard
Singer	Helen Slayton-Hughes
Waiter	Robert Ackerman
Mexican Woman	Eunice Suarez
Mexican Man	Hector M. Morales
Photographer	Morgan Upton
Reporter	Edwina Moore
Nurse	Kathryn Trask
Priest	Bill Reddick
Mourners	Bonnie Carpenter, Margaret Clark, Jan Dunn, Rob Glover

Albert Finney, Diane Keaton, and above with (middle row) Dana Hill, Viveka Davis, (front) Tracy Gold, Tina Yothers

Diane Keaton, Peter Weller Top: Karen Allen, Albert Finney

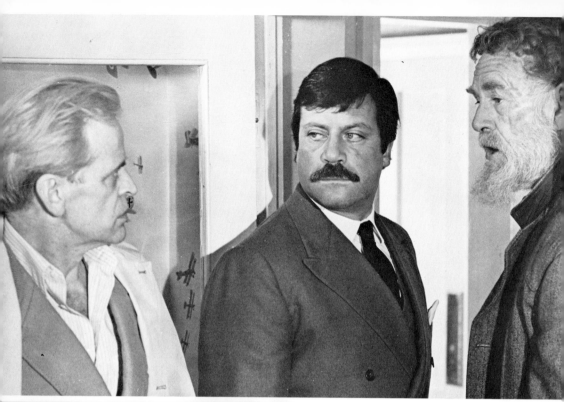

VENOM

(PARAMOUNT) Producer, Martin Bregman; Director, Piers Haggard; Screenplay, Robert Carrington; Based on novel by Alan Scholefield; Executive Producers, Louis A. Stroller, Richard R. St. Johns; Music, Michael Kamen; Photography, Gilbert Taylor, Denys Coop; Art Director, Tony Curtis; Associate Producer, Harry Benn; Assistant Directors, Dominic Fulford, Nick Daubeny; In Technicolor and Dolby Stereo; 93 minutes; Rated R; January release.

CAST

Jacmel	Klaus Kinski
Dave	Oliver Reed
Cmdr. William Bulloch	Nicol Williamson
Dr. Marion Stowe	Sarah Miles
Howard Anderson	Sterling Hayden
Ruth Hopkins	Cornelia Sharpe
Philip Hopkins	Lance Holcomb
Louise	Susan George
Det. Constable Dan Spencer	Mike Gwilym
Det. Sgt. Glazer	Paul Williamson
David Ball	Michael Gough
Taxi Driver	Hugh Lloyd
Mrs. Loewenthal	Rita Webb
Lord Dunning	Edward Hardwicke
Sgt. Nash	John Forbes-Robertson
Constable in police station	Ian Brimble
Hodges	Peter Porteous
Sampson	Maurice Colbourne
Police Superintendent	Nicholas Donnelly
Man in 17	Cyril Conway
Woman in 17	Sally Lahee
Driver	David Sterne
Driver's Mate	Charles Cork
Constable	Howard Bell
Peters	Alan Ford
Williams	Norman Mann
Martin	Tony Meyer
Rogers	Michael Watkins
Smith	Gerard Ryder
Murkerjee	Moti Makan
Susan Stowe	Katherine Wilkinson
Airline Clerk	Eric Richard
Head Waiter	Arnold Diamond

Klaus Kinski, Lance Holcomb Top: Klaus Kinski, Oliver Reed, Sterling Hayden
© *Paramount*

Klaus Kinski, Sarah Miles Top: Kinski, Susan George, Lance
Holcomb

Nicol Williamson

PERSONAL BEST

(WARNER BROTHERS) Executive Producer, David Geffen; Produced, Directed and Written by Robert Towne; Photography, Michael Chapman; Designer, Ron Hobbs; Editor, Bud Smith; Music, Jack Nitzsche, Jill Fraser; Associate Producer, Peter Peyton; Assistant Directors, Jerry Grandy, Bill Beasley, Robert Doherty, Daniel Jason Heffner; In Technicolor; 124 minutes; Rated R; February release.

CAST

Chris Cahill	Mariel Hemingway
Terry Tingloff	Scott Glenn
Tory Skinner	Patrice Donnelly
Denny Stites	Kenny Moore
Roscoe Travis	Jim Moody
Penny Brill	Kari Gosswiller
Nadia "Pooch" Anderson	Jodi Anderson
Tanya	Maren Seidler
Sheila	Martha Watson
Maureen	Emily Dole
Jan	Pam Spencer
Trish	Deby LaPlante
Laura	Mitzi McMillin
Karen	Jan Glotzer
Yelovitch	Jan Van Reenen
Zenk	Allan Feverbach
Fern Wadkins	Jane Frederick
Charlene Benveniste	Cindy Gilbert
Pam Burnside	Marlene Harmon
Debbie Floyd	Linda Waltman
Kim Stone	Cindy Banks
Willie Lee	Milan Tiff
Randy Van Zile	Earl Bell
Rick Cahill	Larry Pennell
Rita Cahill	Luana Anders
Raoul	George de la Pena

and Robert Patten (Colin), Margaret Ellison (Nellie), Charlie Jones, Frank Shorter (tv announcers), Jim Tracy (Duane), Janet Hake (Waitress), Sharon Brazell (Hostess), Chuck Debus (Coach), Gregory Clayton (Trainer), David Edington (Waiter), Robert Horn (Polo Coach), Christopher Vargas (Polo Player), Wendell Ray (Announcer), Richard Martini (Manager), Len Dawson (Announcer), Clim Jackson, John Smith (Team Members), Anna Biller, Susan Brownell, Desiree Gauthier, Sharon Hatfield, Linda Hightower, Joan Russell, Themis Zambrzycki (Women's Team Members)

Left: Patrice Donnelly, Jodi Anderson, Mariel Hemingway
Top: Mariel Hemingway, Scott Glenn
© Warner Bros

Mariel Hemingway, Kenny Moore

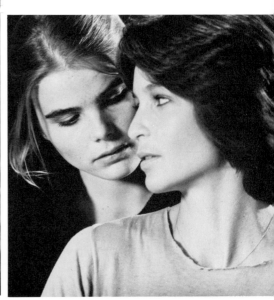

Mariel Hemingway, Patrice Donnelly

DEATH WISH II

(FILMWAYS) Producers, Manahem Golan, Yoram Globus; Executive Producers, Hal Landers, Bobby Roberts; Director, Michael Winner; Screenplay, David Engelbach; Based on characters created by Brian Garfield; Photography, Richard H. Kline, Tom Del Ruth; Music, Jimmy Page; Editors, Arnold Crust, Julian Semilian; Designer, William Hiney; Assistant Director, Russell Vreeland; In color; 93 minutes; Rated R; February release.

CAST

Paul Kersey	Charles Bronson
Geri Nichols	Jill Ireland
Frank Ochoa	Vincent Gardenia
New York D. A.	J. D. Cannon
L. A. Police Commissioner	Anthony Franciosa
Lt. Mankiewicz	Ben Frank
Carol Kersey	Robin Sherwood
Rosario	Silvana Gillardo
Fred McKenzie	Robert F. Lyons
Elliott Cass	Michael Prince
Deputy Commissioner Hawkins	Drew Synder
N.Y. Police Commissioner	Paul Lambert
Nirvana	Thomas Duffy
Stomper	Kevyn Major Howard
Jiver	Stuart K. Robinson
Cutter	Laurence Fishburne III
Punkcut	E. Lamont Johnson

Top: Charles Bronson, Robin Sherwood, Jill Ireland Below:
Stuart K. Robinson, Sherwood, Kevyn Major Howard
©*Filmways*

Jill Ireland, Charles Bronson (also above)

ONE FROM THE HEART

(COLUMBIA) Producers, Gray Frederickson, Fred Roos; Executive Producer, Bernard Gersten; Co-Producer, Armyan Bernstein; Director, Francis Coppola; Screenplay, Armyan Bernstein, Francis Coppola; Story, Armyan Bernstein; Special Effects, Robert Swarthe; Editors, Anne Goursaud, Rudi Fehr, Randy Roberts; Costumes, Ruth Morley; Songs and Music, Tom Waits; Sung by Crystal Gayle, Tom Waits; Designer, Dean Tavoularis; Photography, Vittorio Storaro, Ronald V. Garcia; Associate Producer, Mona Skager; Assistant Director, Arne Schmidt; Art Director, Angelo Graham; Choreographer, Kenny Ortega; A Zoetrope Film in Metrocolor, Dolby Stereo; 101 minutes; Rated R; February release.

CAST

Hank	Frederic Forrest
Frannie	Teri Garr
Ray	Raul Julia
Leila	Nastassia Kinski
Maggie	Lainie Kazan
Moe	Harry Dean Stanton
Restaurant Owner	Allan Goorwitz
Airline Ticket Agent	Jeff Hamlin
Couple in elevator	Italia Coppola, Carmine Coppola

Nastassia Kinski, Frederic Forrest
Above: Teri Garr, Raul Julia

Top Left: Teri Garr, Harry Dean Stanton, Frederic Forrest,
Lainie Kazan Right: Raul Julia, Teri Garr
©Columbia

14

CANNERY ROW

(UNITED ARTISTS/MGM) Producer, Michael Phillips; Direction and Screenplay, David S. Ward; Based on John Steinbeck's "Cannery Row" and "Sweet Thursday"; Photography, Sven Nykvist; Designer, Richard MacDonald; Music, Jack Nitzsche; Editor, David Bretherton; Associate Producer, Kurt Neumann; Costumes, Ruth Myers; Narrated by John Huston; Assistant Directors, Jerry Sobul, Ross Brown; Art Director, William F. O'Brien; Choreographer, Lou Wills; In Metrocolor; 120 minutes; Rated PG; February release.

CAST

Doc	Nick Nolte
Suzy	Debra Winger
Fauna	Audra Lindley
Hazel	Frank McRae
Mack	M. Emmet Walsh
Hughie	Tom Mahoney
Jones	John Malloy
Eddie	James Keane
The Seer	Sunshine Parker
Joseph and Mary	Santos Morales
Wisteria	Ellen Blake
Agnes	Sharon Ernster
Violet	Kathleen Doyle
Lola	Mary Margaret Amato
Martha	Brenda Hillhouse
Blossom	Mariko Tse
Pitcher	Colleen O'Grady
Golden Poppy Waitress	Tona Dodd
Beer Milkshake Waitress	Judy Kerr
Doctor	Tom Pletts
Suzy's Trick	William Bronder
Ellen Sedgewick	Rosana DiSoto
Sonny	Walter Mathews
Doorman	Art LaFleur
Boy	Joshua Lawrence
Tucker	Joe Terry

Fraternity Boys: Carl Ciarfalio, Reid Rondell, John Meier, Tim Culbertson, Scott Wilder, Gilbert B. Combs, Christopher Doyle, Gary McLarty, Bobby Sargent, Bill Cross, Ted Duncan

Right: John Malloy, M. Emmet Walsh, Frank McRae

Top: Debra Winger
©MGM

Debra Winger, Nick Nolte

Nick Nolte, Debra Winger

MISSING

(UNIVERSAL) Producers, Edward Lewis, Mildred Lewis; Director, Costa-Gavras; Screenplay, Costa-Gavras, Donald Stewart; Executive Producers, Peter Guber, Jon Peters; Photography, Ricardo Aronovich; Designer, Joe I. Tompkins; Music, Vangelis; Associate Producer, Terry Nelson; Based on book by Thomas Hauser; Special Effects, Albert Whitlock; Art Directors, Agustin Ytuarte, Lucero Isaac; Assistant Directors, Elie Cohn, Anna Roth; Editor, Francoise Bonnot; A Polygram presentation in Technicolor; 122 minutes; Rated PG; February release.

CAST

Ed Horman	Jack Lemmon
Beth Horman	Sissy Spacek
Terry Simon	Melanie Mayron
Charles Horman	John Shea
Capt. Ray Tower	Charles Cioffi
Consul Phil Putnam	David Clennon
U. S. Ambassador	Richard Venture
Colonel Sean Patrick	Jerry Hardin
Carter Babcock	Richard Bradford
Frank Teruggi	Joe Regalbuto
David Holloway	Keith Szarabajka
David McGeary	John Doolittle
Kate Newman	Janice Rule
Congressman	Ward Costello
Senator	Hansford Rowe
Maria	Tina Romero
Statesman	Richard Whiting
Paris	Martin Lasalle
Colonel Clay	Terry Nelson
Peter Chernin	Robert Hitt
Rojas	Felix Gonzalez
Mrs. Duran	M. E. Rios
Espinoza	Jorge Russek
Pia	Edna Nochoechea
Samuel Roth	Alan Penwrith
Silvio	Alex Camacho

and M. Avilla Camacho (Doctor), Kimberly Farr (Young Woman), Elizabeth Cross (Ann), Piero Cross (Hotel Manager), Gary Richardson (Embassy Operator), Josefina Echanove (Doctor), Robert Johnstreet (Bob), Lynda Spheeris (Woman in U.S. Embassy), Jorge Mancilla (Airport Captain), Gerardo Vigil (Sexy Soldier), Mario Valdez (Laundry Officer), Jaime Garza (Young Man at Stadium), Joe Tompkins (Marine Officer), John Fenton (Carlos), Jacqueline Evans, Jorge Santoyo, Juan Vazquez, Antonio Medellin, Albert Cates

Left: John Shea, and top with Sissy Spacek
© *Universal*

1982 Academy Award for Best Screenplay Adaptation

John Shea, Sissy Spacek, Melanie Mayron

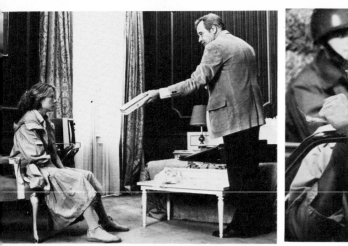

Sissy Spacek, Jack Lemmon (also at top)
Above: Janice Rule

Sissy Spacek, Jack Lemmon
Above: John Shea
Top: Keith Szarabajka, Joe Regalbuto

THE BORDER

(UNIVERSAL) Producer, Edgar Bronfman, Jr.; Executive Producer, Neil Hartley; Director, Tony Richardson; Screenplay, Deric Washburn, Walon Green, David Freeman; Photography, Ric Waite; Designer, Toby Rafelson; Editor, Robert K. Lambert; Music, Ry Cooder; Art Director, Richard Sawyer; Costumes, Vicki Sanchez; Assistant Director, Irby Smith; In Panavision and Technicolor; 107 minutes; Rated R; February release.

CAST

Charlie .... Jack Nicholson
Cat .... Harvey Keitel
Marcy.. Valerie Perrine
Red.. Warren Oates
Maria ....Elpidia Carrillo
Savannah .... Shannon Wilcox
Juan ....Manuel Viescas
J. J. ....Jeff Morris
Manuel .... Mike Gomez
Beef .... Dirk Blocker
Andy .... Lonny Chapman
Hooker .... Stacey Pickren
Lou...Floyd Levine
Frank .... James Jeter
Hawker .... Alan Fudge
Jimbo .... William Russ
Honk ....Gary Grubbs
Slim .... Gary Sexton
George .... Billy Silva
Donny .... William McLaughlin
Kevin .... David Beecroft
and Esther Sylvey (Secretary), Luis Mejia, Roberto Rivera (Sweepers), Jay Thurman (Timmy), Craig Terry (Salesman), Juan Ramirez (Angel), Adalberto Cortez (Doper), Concepcion Palmares (Old Woman), Juan Salas (Boy), Norma Mayo (Woman at party), Paula Ruiz (Matron), Carlos Bruno Villanueva (Trustee), Ronne Drummond (El Scorcho), Richard Watts, Bernice E. Shamaley, Kenna Esperson, Glenda Meadows, Joe Zizik, Maria Delgado, Lupe Ontiveros, Francisco Farias, Edmundo Alonzo, Alan Gibbs, James W. Gavin, Ross Reynolds

Right: Harvey Keitel, Jack Nicholson
Top: Warren Oates (C)
© Universal

Manuel Viescas, Elpidia Carillo

Jack Nicholson, Adalberto Cortez

LOVE AND MONEY

(PARAMOUNT) Produced, Directed and Written by James To-
back; Photography, Fred Schuler; Art Director, Lee Fischer; Editor,
Dennis Hill; Associate Producer, Richard McWhorter; Assistant
Directors, Kim Friese, Scott Ira Thaler; In Metrocolor; 93 minutes;
Rated R; February release.

CAST

Byron Levin	Ray Sharkey
Catherine Stockheinz	Ornella Muti
Frederick Stockheinz	Klaus Kinski
Lorenzo Prado	Armand Assante
Walter Klein	King Vidor
Vicky	Susan Heldfond
Ambassador Paultz	William Prince
Raoul	Tony Sirico
Mrs. Paultz	Jacqueline Brookes
Hector	Daniel Faraldo
General Sanzer	Rodolfo Hoyos
Clem Dixon	Terry Jastrow
Blair	Tom McFadden
Newscaster	Cynthia Allison
Bodyguard	Sonny Gibson
National Guard General	Tony Plana
Youth Counselor	Nick Powers
Hankland	Stephen Keep
Melanie Dixon	Kathy Spring
Sandy	Susan Welsh
Hotel Doorman	Breck Costin
Adela	Laura Grayson
Hotel Waiter	Gene Rutherford

Top: Susan Heldfond, King Vidor, Ray Sharkey Right: Klaus
Kinski, Ornella Muti Center: Ray Sharkey and (R) with
Ornella Muti
©*Paramount*

Klaus Kinski, Armand Assante

MAKING LOVE

(20th CENTURY-FOX) Producers, Allen Adler, Daniel Melnick; Director, Arthur Hiller; Screenplay, Barry Sandler; Story, A. Scott Berg; Photography, David M. Walsh; Designer, James D. Vance; Editor, William H. Reynolds; Music, Leonard Rosenman; Associate Producers, Barry Sandler, Dorothy Wilde; Assistant Director, Jack Roe; In DeLuxe Color; 113 minutes; Rated R; February release.

CAST

Zack	Michael Ontkean
Claire	Kate Jackson
Bart	Harry Hamlin
Winnie	Wendy Hiller
Henry	Arthur Hill
Christine	Nancy Olson
Tim	John Dukakis
Harrington	Terry Kiser
Larry	Dennis Howard
Ted	Asher Brauner
David	John Calvin
Arlene	Gwen Arner
Ken	Gary Swanson
Lila	Ann Harvey
Charlie	Stanley Kamel
Chip	Chip Lucia
Doug	Doug Johnson
Ben	Ben Mittleman
Cowboy Musician	Mickey Jones

and Joe Medalis (Announcer), Erica Hiller (Lucie), Michael Shannon (Marty), Arthur Taxier (Don), Phoebe Dorin (Jenny), Mark Schubb (Josh), Carol King (Pam), Camilla Carr (Susan), Lili Haydn (Little Sister), Paul Sanderson (Bill), David Knell (Michael), David Murphy, Michael Dudikoff, John Starr, Charles Zukow, Scott Ryder, Joanne Hicks, Stacey Kuhne, Stephanie Segal, Kedren Jones, Alexander Lockwood, Andrew Harris, Michael Harris, Robert Mikels, Jason Mikels

Michael Ontkean, Harry Hamlin Above: Ontkean, Kate Jackson

Top: Kate Jackson, Michael Ontkean Left: Ontkean, Harry Hamlin
©*20th Century-Fox*

DEAD MEN DON'T WEAR PLAID

(UNIVERSAL) Producers, David V. Picker, William E. McEuen; Director, Carl Reiner; Screenplay, Carl Reiner, George Gipe, Steve Martin; Special Effects, Glen Robinson; Photography, Michael Chapman; Designer, John DeCuir; Editor, Bud Molin; Associate Producer, Richard F. McWhorter; Assistant Directors, Newton Arnold, Mitchell Bock; Costumes, Edith Head; Music, Miklos Rozsa; In black and white; 89 minutes; Rated PG; March release.

CAST

Rigby Reardon	Steve Martin
Juliet Forrest	Rachel Ward
Field Marshall VonKluck	Carl Reiner
Carlos Rodriguez	Reni Santoni
Dr. Forrest	George Gaynes
Waiter	Frank McCarthy
Mildred	Adrian Ricard
Hoods	Charles Picerni, Gene Labell, George Sawaya
Puppy Secretary	Britt Nilsson
Duty Secretary	Jean Beaudine
German Henchman	John "Easton" Stuart

and Ronald Spivey, Bob Hevelone, Dieter Curt, Phil Kearns, Kent Deigaard, Eugene Brezany, Brad Baird

Right: Reni Santoni, Steve Martin Below: Steve Martin Top: Rachel Ward, Steve Martin
©*Universal*

Rachel Ward, Steve Martin

Steve Martin, Carl Reiner

21

VICTOR/VICTORIA

(MGM) Producers, Blake Edwards, Tony Adams; Direction and Screenplay, Blake Edwards; Photography, Dick Bush; Designer, Rodger Maus; Music, Henry Mancini; Lyrics, Leslie Bricusse; Editor, Ralph E. Winters; Choreographer, Paddy Stone; Costumes, Patricia Norris; Associate Producers, Gerald T. Nutting, Buckhantz-NMC Co. Inc.; Art Directors, Tim Hutchinson, William Craig Smith; Assistant Directors, Richard Hoult, Peter Kohn, Paul Tivers; Editor, Alan Killick; Based on the 1933 UFA-Film "Viktor und Viktoria" conceived by Hans Hoemburg with direction and Screenplay by Rheinhold Schuenzel; In Metrocolor, Panavision, Dolby Stereo; 133 minutes; Rated PG; March release.

CAST

Victor/Victoria	Julie Andrews
King	James Garner
Toddy	Robert Preston
Norma	Lesley Ann Warren
Squash	Alex Karras
Cassell	John Rhys-Davies
Waiter	Graham Stark
Labisse	Peter Arne
Bovin	Sherloque Tanney
Hotel Manager	Michael Robbins
Sal	Norman Chancer
Restaurant Manager	David Gant
Madame President	Maria Charles
Richard	Malcolm Jamieson
Juke	John Cassady
Clam	Mike Tezcan
Stage Manager	Christopher Good
Cassell's Receptionist	Matyelock Gibbs
Guy Langois	Jay Benedict
Langois' Companion	Olivier Pierre
Concierge	Martin Rayner
Fat Man with Eclair	George Silver
Large Lady in restaurant	Joanna Dickens
Deviant Husband	Terence Skelton
Simone Kallisto	Ina Skriver
Boyfriend to actress	Stuart Turton
Police Inspector	Geoffrey Beevers
Chorus Boys	Sam Williams, Simon Chandler
Nightclub M. C.	Neil Cunningham
Chambermaid	Vivienne Chandler
LeClou	Bill Monks
Balancing Man	Perry Davey
Opera Singer	Elizabeth Vaughan
Photographer	Paddy Ward
Desk Clerk	Tim Stern

Left: Robert Preston, Julie Andrews

Top: Julie Andrews
©*MGM/UA*

1982 Academy Award for Best Original Song Score

James Garner, Lesley Ann Warren

Robert Preston, Julie Andrews

22

Julie Andrews (also top) Above: Robert Preston, Andrews, James Garner, Alex Karras

James Garner, Julie Andrews
Top: Lesley Ann Warren

I'M DANCING AS FAST AS I CAN

(PARAMOUNT) Producers, Edgar J. Scherick, Scott Rudin; Director, Jack Hofsiss; Screenplay, David Rabe; Based on book by Barbara Gordon; Executive Producer, David Rabe; Photography, Jan DeBont; Editor, Michael Bradsell; Associate Producer, David A. Nicksay; Music, Stanley Silverman; Designer, David Jenkins; Costumes, Julie Weiss; Assistant Directors, Jerry C. G. Grandey, Robert Doherty; Art Director, Fred Kolo; In Movielab Color; 107 minutes; Rated R; March release.

CAST

Barbara Gordon	Jill Clayburgh
Derek Bauer	Nicol Williamson
Julie Addison	Dianne Wiest
Roger	Joe Pesci
Jean Martin	Geraldine Page
Sam Mulligan	James Sutorius
Karen Mulligan	Ellen Greene
Fran	Cordis Heard
Alan Newman	Richard Masur
Sound Woman	Kasey Connors
Bartender	Charles Stavola
Waiter	Roger Etienne
Passerby	Gregory Osborne
Emmy Presenter	Eleanor Zee
Emmy Official	John Shearin
Stage Manager	David Polk
Dr. Kalman	Joe Maher
Nurse	Ann Weldon
Delivery Boy	Angel Ferreira
Dr. Roberts	Jeffrey DeMunn
Dr. Morgan	Thomas Hill
Debbie	Toni Kalem
Teddy	Robert Doqui
Jim	Daniel Stern
Anne	C. C. H. Pounder
Iris	Anne DeSalvo

and Richard Hamilton (Joe), Dan Hedaya (Dr. Klein), Margaret Ladd (Lara), Ebbe Roe Smith (Chet), Kathleen Widdoes (Dr. Rawlings), Debbie Lynn Foreman (Cindy), Erin Halligan (Denise), Beatrice Lynch (Patient), Eddie Donno, Glenn R. Wilder, Harold Jones (Orderlies), Andrew Winner (Greg), Edward Betz (Assistant Editor), John Lithgow (Brunner), Lara Cody (Newscaster), Wendy Cutler (Crew Member), Malcolm Groome (Talent Coordinator), Devera Marcus (Therapist), Paul Willson, Gloria Irrizzary (Patients), Andy Goldberg (Disc Jockey), Dennis Lee, Lawrence Sellars, Jordan Derwin (Doctors)

Cordis Heard, Jill Clayburgh Above: Nicol Williamson, Clayburgh, Richard Masur Top: Williamson, Clayburgh

Top: Dianne Wiest, Jill Clayburgh
Below: Geraldine Page, Clayburgh
©*Paramount*

I OUGHT TO BE IN PICTURES

(20th CENTURY-FOX) Producers, Herbert Toss, Neil Simon; Director, Herbert Ross; Screenplay, Neil Simon from his play of same title; Executive Producer, Roger M. Rothstein; Photography, David M. Walsh; Designer, Albert Brenner; Editor, Sidney Levin; Music, Marvin Hamlisch; Lyrics, Carole Bayer Sager; Costumes, Ruth Morley; Associate Producer, Rick McCallum; Assistant Directors, Jack Roe, John Kretchmer; Associate Producer, Charles Matthau; In DeLuxe Color; 108 minutes; Rated PG; March release.

CAST

Herbert Tucker	Walter Matthau
Stephanie	Ann-Margret
Libby	Dinah Manoff
Gordon	Lance Guest
Soldier	Lewis Smith
Monte Del Rey	Martin Ferrero
Marty	Eugene Butler
Larane	Samantha Harper
Mexican Truck Driver	Santos Morales
Martin	David Faustino
Shelley	Shelby Balik
Truck Driver	Bill Cross
Auto Cashier	Virginia Wing
Boy on the bus	Michael Dudikoff
Waitress	Gillian Farrell
Groundskeepers	Jose Rabelo, Norberto Kerner
Rabbi	Calvin Ander
Motel Cashier	Muni Zano
Baseball Fans	Allan Graf, Art LaFleur, Nomi Mitty, Charles Parks, Wayne Woodson, Tom Wright

Right: Dinah Manoff, Walter Matthau Top: Ann-Margret, Walter Matthau
© 20th Century-Fox

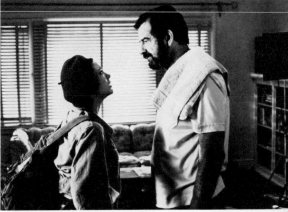

Ann-Margret

Dinah Manoff, Walter Matthau

DEATHTRAP

(WARNER BROTHERS) Producer, Burtt Harris; Director, Sidney Lumet; Executive Producer-Screenplay, Jay Presson Allen; Based on stage play by Ira Levin; Photography, Andrzej Bartkowiak; Production and Costume Design, Tony Walton; Editor, John J. Fitzstephens; Music, Johnny Mandel; Associate Producer, Alfred deLiagre, Jr.; Assistant Directors, Burtt Harris, Mark McGann; Art Director, Edward Pisoni; In Technicolor; 116 minutes; Rated PG: March release.

CAST

Sidney Bruhl	Michael Caine
Clifford Anderson	Christopher Reeve
Myra Bruhl	Dyan Cannon
Helga ten Dorp	Irene Worth
Porter Milgrim	Henry Jones
Seymour Starger	Joe Silver
Burt the bartender	Tony DiBenedetto
Handsome Actor	Al LeBreton
Minister	Francis B. Creamer, Jr.
Stewart Klein	Stewart Klein
Jeffrey Lyons	Jeffrey Lyons
Joel Siegel	Joel Siegel
Stage Newsboy	Jenny Lumet
Stage Actress	Jayne Heller
Stage Actors	George Peck, Perry Rosen

Left: Michael Caine
© *Warner Bros.*

Dyan Cannon

Michael Caine, Christopher Reeve Above: Caine, Irene Worth

26

Christopher Reeve, Michael Caine Above: Irene Worth, Michael Caine

Christopher Reeve, Michael Caine Top: Caine, Dyan Cannon

PARTNERS

(PARAMOUNT) Producer, Aaron Russo; Director, James Burrows; Executive Producer-Screenplay, Francis Veber; Photography, Victor J. Kemper; Designer, Richard Sylbert; Editor, Danford B. Greene; Associate Producer, Mitchell L. Gamson; Music, Georges Delerue; Assistant Director, Thomas Lofaro, David Valdes; Costumes, Wayne Finkelman; In Movielab Color; 98 minutes; Rated R; April release.

CAST

Benson	Ryan O'Neal
Kerwin	John Hurt
Chief Wilkens	Kenneth McMillan
Jill	Robyn Douglass
Halderstam	Jay Robinson
Clara	Denise Galik
Walter	Joseph R. Sicari
Monroe	Michael McGuire
Douglas	Rick Jason
Edward K. Petersen	James Remar
Secretary	Jennifer Ashley
AL	Darrell Larson
Second Aide	Tony March
Gillis	Seamon Glass
Counter Boy	Steve Reisch
First Aide	Carl Kraines
Detective	Bob Ozman
Officer	Carol Williard
Jogger	Iris Alhanti
Man on balcony	Bob Bigelow
Body Builder	John Garber
Telephone Operator	Sherrie Lessard
Doorman	Ed McCready
Photo Assistant	Jackie Millines
Muscle Man	Ray Sanders
Pablo	Luis Torres
Cops	Gene Ross, Douglas Bruce, Bill Cross, Craig Shreeve, Gregory L. Hodal

Right: Robyn Douglass, Ryan O'Neal Top: John Hurt, O'Neal, Kenneth McMillan
©*Paramount*

John Hurt, Ryan O'Neal

Ryan O'Neal, John Hurt

A LITTLE SEX

(UNIVERSAL) Producers, Robert DeLaurentis, Bruce Paltrow; Director, Bruce Paltrow; Screenplay, Robert DeLaurentis; Photography, Ralf D. Bode; Editor, Bill Butler; Designer, Stephen Hendrickson; Costumes, Patrizia von Brandenstein; Music, Georges Delerue; Associate Producer, Stephen F. Kesten; Assistant Directors, Victor Hsu, Joseph Reidy, Howie Horowitz; In Panavision and Technicolor; 97 minutes; Rated R; April release.

CAST

Michael Donovan	Tim Matheson
Katherine	Kate Capshaw
Tommy	Edward Herrmann
Walter	John Glover
Mrs. Harrison	Joan Copeland
Nancy Barwood	Susanna Dalton
Philomena	Wendie Malick
Oliver	Wallace Shawn
Passerby	Betsy Aidem
Theresa Donovan	Sharon Bamber
Joyce	Tanya Berezin
Wedding Photographer	Michael Bias
Bubble Girl	Kim von Brandenstein
Office Girl	Barbara Bratt
Mindy	Christy Brown
Joe Donovan	Robert Burr
Betty	Melinda Culea
Marie Donovan	Leigh Curran
Lucy	Lisa Dunsheath
Electrician	Frankie Faison
Old Lady	Sara Felcher
Salesgirl	Sharon Foote

and Donna R. Fowler, Jennine Marie Gourine, Sam Gray, James Greene, Delphi Harrington, Frances Helm, Carolyn Houlihan, Elva Josephson, Wayne Kell, Ann Lange, Sagan Lewis, Renee Lippin, Merry Lommis, Jim Lovelett, J. Frank Lucas, Ron Maccone, P. J. Mann, Winston May, Patricia Mertens, Joshua Michaels, Sharron Miller, Linda G. Miller, Carolyn Perry, Nick Petron, Don Philips, Isabel Price, Kathleen Purrman, Eric Ratcliff, Mary Ritter, Janine Robbins, Lauren Sautner, Sara Schedeen, Carol Lee Shahid, Bill Smitrovich, Kimberly Stern, Alex Stevens, Melanie Strauss, John Tillinger, Victoria Vanderkloot, Chris Westwood, David Wilkins.

Right: John Glover, Kate Capshaw Top: Edward Herrmann, Tim Matheson
© *Universal*

Kate Capshaw, Joan Copeland

Tim Matheson, Kate Capshaw

DINER

(MGM/SLM) Producer, Jerry Weintraub; Direction and Screenplay, Barry Levinson; Photography, Peter Sova; Editor, Stu Linder; Music, Joe Tuley; In color; 110 minutes; Rated R; April release

CAST

Eddie	Steve Guttenberg
Shrevie	Daniel Stern
Boogie	Mickey Rourke
Fenwick	Kevin Bacon
Billy	Timothy Daly
Beth	Ellen Barkin
Modell	Paul Reiser
Barbara	Kathryn Dowling
Bagel	Michael Tucker
Mrs. Simmons	Jessica James
Carol Heathrow	Colette Blonigan
Diane	Kelle Kipp
Tank	John Aquino
David Frazer	Richard Pierson
Jane Chisholm	Claudia Cron

Left: Ellen Barkin, Daniel Stern
©MGM/SLM

Seated: Daniel Stern, Kevin Bacon, Timothy Daly
Standing: Mickey Rourke, Steve Guttenberg

Kevin Bacon, Mickey Rourke, Daniel Stern, Paul Reiser Top:
(L) Timothy Daly, Kathryn Dowling (R) Mickey Rourke,
Colette Blonigan

SOME KIND OF HERO

(PARAMOUNT) Producer, Howard W. Koch; Director, Michael Pressman; Screenplay, James Kirkwood, Robert Boris; Based on novel by James Kirkwood; Photography, King Baggot; Art Director, James L. Schoppe; Editor, Christopher Greenbury; Music, Patrick Williams; Co-Producer, James Kirkwood; Associate Producer, Robert Boris; Assistant Directors, Kim Kurumada, Marty Ewing; In Movielab Color; 116 minutes; Rated R; April release.

CAST

Eddie Keller	Richard Pryor
Toni	Margot Kidder
Vinnie	Ray Sharkey
Col. Powers	Ronny Cox
Lisa	Lynne Moody
Jesse	Olivia Cole
Leon	Paul Benjamin
The Kid	David Adams
Tank	Martin Azarow
Olivia	Shelly Batt
Jeanette	Susan Berlin
Cal	Tim Thomerson

and Mary Betten (Teller), Herb Braha, Peter Jason (Honchos), Anthony R. Charnota (Commander), Matt Clark (Mickey), Jude Farese (Bandit), Elizabeth Farley (Secretary), John Fujioka (Captain), Raymond Guth (Motel Clerk), Anne Haney (Monica), Mary Jackson (Frances), Caren Kaye (Sheila), Enid Kent (Reporter), Nan Martin (Hilda), Bill Morey (Major), Warren Munson (Bank President), Kenneth O'Brien (Bartender), Antony Ponzini (Sal), Kario Salem (Young Soldier), Pearl Shear (Customer), Sara Simmons (Nurse), Jon Van Ness (Aide), Sandy Ward (Colonel), Aka, Danny Wong (Guards), David Banks (Disc Jockey), David Byrd (Doorman), Mathew Clark (Bandit), Kenneth S. Eiland, Alberto Isaac, Leigh Kim (V. C. Guards), Stephen Kurumada (Dentist), Richard McKenzie (Psychiatrist), Nicholas Mele (Officer), Harvey Parry (Old Drunk), Bill M. Ryusaki (Basketball Player), William Schoneberger (Technician), Hayward Soo Hoo (Soldier)

Richard Pryor, and above with Margot Kidder Top: Pryor, Ray Sharkey

Top: Richard Pryor, Lynne Moody Below: Herb Braha, Pryor, Margot Kidder, Peter Jason

WRONG IS RIGHT

(COLUMBIA) Produced, Directed and Written by Richard Brooks; Executive Producer, Andrew Fogelson; Photography, Fred J. Koenekamp; Designer, Edward Carfagno; Associate Producer-Editor, George Grenville; Based on novel "The Better Angels" by Charles McCarry; Music, Artie Kane; Assistant Directors, Steve H. Perry, R. Anthony Brown, B. Thomas Seidman; Costumes, Ray Summers; Art Director, Karl Hueglin; In Metrocolor; 117 minutes; Rated R; April release.

CAST

Patrick Hale	Sean Connery
President Lockwood	George Grizzard
General Wombat	Robert Conrad
Sally Blake	Katharine Ross
Philindros	G. D. Spradlin
Homer Hubbard	John Saxon
Rafeeq	Henry Silva
Mallory	Leslie Nielsen
Harvey	Robert Webber
Mrs. Ford	Rosalind Cash
Helmut Unger	Hardy Kruger
Hacker	Dean Stockwell
King Awad	Ron Moody
Erika	Cherie Michan
Abu	Tony March
Suzy	Marianne Marks
Mike	Jeffrey Wheat
John Brown	Joseph Whipp
Billy Bob Harper	Tom McFadden
Housewife	Ivy Bethune
Young Girl	Jennifer Jason Leigh

and Kiva Lawrence (Receptionist), Barry Cahill (Husband), Angelo Bertolini (Cardinal), Keith McConnell (Smythe), Alexander Zale (Faheem), Donald Bishop (Congressman), Dianne Lynn Wilson (Woman with dog), George Skaff (Qadee), Denis Hoppe (Hagreb Officer), Milt Jamin (Hagreb Doctor), Edward L. Moskowitz (Technician), Myron Natwick (Admiral), Paul Lambert (Defense Secretary), Suzanne Reynolds (TV Reporter), David Frankham (British Reporter), Ed Pennybacker (U.S. Reporter), Ken Bibeau (Marcus), Art Evans, Mio Polo (Guards), Charles Hutchins (Cabbie), Robert Alan Browne (Motorist), Mickey Jones (Gunman), Dawna O'Brien (President's Secretary), Pamela V. Kobbe (Hale's Secretary), Claire Grenville (Campaigner), Merrill M. Mazuer, Ken Gale, Kerry Sullivan, Melanie Stensland, Ray Conners, Melinda Ann Casey, Don Dunwell, Don Worsham (News Staff)

Right: Sean Connery Top: G. D. Spradlin, George Grizzard
©*Columbia*

Katharine Ross

Robert Conrad

CHAN IS MISSING

(NEW YORKER) Producer-Director, Wayne Wang; Screenplay, Wayne Wang, Isaac Cronin, Terrel Seltzer; Photography, Michael Chin; Editor, Wayne Wang; Music, Robert Kikuchi; In black and white; 80 minutes; Not rated; April release.

CAST

Jo	Wood Moy
Steve	Marc Hayashi
Amy	Laureen Chew
Lawyer	Judi Nihei
Henry the cook	Peter Wang
Presco	Presco Tabios
Frankie	Frankie Alarcon
Mrs. Chan	Ellen Yeung
Jenny	Emily Yamasaki
George	George Woo
Jenny's Friend	Virginia Cerenio
Mr. Lee	Roy Chan
Mr. Fong	Leung Pui Chee

Left: Peter Wang
©*New Yorker*

Marc Hayashi, Wayne Wang, Wood Moy

THE ESCAPE ARTIST

(ORION) Producers, Doug Claybourne, Buck Houghton; Director, Caleb Deschanel; Executive Producers, Francis Coppola, Fred Roos; Screenplay, Mellissa Mathison, Stephen Zito; Based on novel by David Wagoner; Photography, Stephen H. Burum; Designer, Dean Tavoulsris; Editor, Arthur Schmidt; Music, Georges Delerue; Art Directors, Angelo Graham, James Murakami; Assistant Directors, Michael Haley, Andy Anderson, Mark Radcliffe; Costumes, Gloria Gresham; A Zoetrope Studios production in Technicolor and Dolby Stereo; 104 minutes; Rated PG; May release.

CAST

Stu Quinones	Raul Julia
Danny Masters	Griffin O'Neal
Mayor Quinones	Desiderio Arnaz
Arlene	Teri Garr
Aunt Sibyl	Joan Hackett
Uncle Burke	Gabriel Dell
Vernon	John P. Ryan
Sandra	Elizabeth Daily
Fritz	M. Emmet Walsh
Magic Shop Owner	Jackie Coogan
Cop at mayor's office	Hal Williams
Neighbor	Helen Page Camp
Newspaper Editor	David Clennon
Sax Player	Harry Caesar
Turnkey	Huntz Hall
Harry Masters	Harry Anderson
Water Commissioner	George Brengel
Treasurer's Secretary	Carlin Glynn
Secretary at newspaper office	Isabel Cooley
Mailbox Cop	Tom Signorelli
Jail Trustee	George Cantero
Jailmate	Harry Cohn
Cop at bridal shop	James Howard
Reporters	R. Wayne Kruse, Margaret Ladd
M.C	Tom Mahoney
Drummer	G. K. Marshall
Photographer	Doug McGrath
Woman at club	Susi Sherman

Top: Desiderio Arnaz, Raul Julia Below: Julia, Teri Garr
Top Right: Jackie Coogan, Griffin O'Neal, Teri Garr
©*Zoetrope*

Griffin O'Neal, and above with Joan Hackett

ROCKY III

(MGM/UA) Producers, Irwin Winkler, Robert Chartoff; Direction and Screenplay, Sylvester Stallone; Photography, Bill Butler; Editors, Don Zimmerman, Mark Warner; Art Director, Ronald Kent Forman; Assistant Director, Cliff Coleman; Design, William J. Cassidy; Music, Bill Conti; In Technicolor and Dolby Stereo; 99 minutes; Rated PG: May release

CAST

Rocky Balboa	Sylvester Stallone
Apollo Creed	Carl Weathers
Adrian	Talia Shire
Paulie	Burt Young
Mickey	Burgess Meredith
Clubber Lang	Mr. T
Rocky Junior	Ian Fried
Al	Al Silvani
Clubber's Manager	Wally Taylor
Duke	Tony Burton
Thunderlips	Hulk Hogan

Left: Sylvester Stallone, Talia Shire
© *United Artists*

Sylvester Stallone, Burgess Meredith

Carl Weathers, Sylvester Stallone, and at top

ANNIE

(COLUMBIA) Producer, Ray Stark; Director, John Huston; Associate Producer and Screenplay, Carol Sobieski; Based on stage production that was based on the comic strip "Little Orphan Annie"; Executive Producer and Musical Sequences Created by Joe Layton; Photography, Richard Moore; Designer, Dale Hennesy; Costumes, Theoni V. Aldredge; Editor, Margaret Booth; Music, Charles Strouse; Lyrics, Martin Charnin; Musical Staging/Choreography, Arlene Phillips; Assistant Directors, Jerry Ziesmer, Chris Soldo, Phil Morini; Art Directors, Robert Guerra, Diane Wager; Original Soundtrack Album on Columbia Records and Tapes; In Metrocolor, Panavision and Dolby Stereo; 130 minutes; Rated PG; May release.

CAST

Daddy Warbucks	Albert Finney
Miss Hannigan	Carol Burnett
Lily	Bernadette Peters
Grace Farrell	Ann Reinking
Rooster	Tim Curry
Annie	Aileen Quinn
Punjab	Geoffrey Holder
Asp	Roger Minami

Orphans:

Molly	Toni Ann Gisondi
Pepper	Rosanne Sorrentino
Tessie	Lara Berk
Kate	April Lerman
Duffy	Lucie Stewart
July	Robin Ignico
FDR	Edward Herrmann
Eleanor Roosevelt	Lois DeBanzie
Bert Healy	Peter Marshall
Boylan Sisters	Loni Ackerman, Murphy Cross, Nancy Sinclair
Drake	I. M. Hobson
Mrs. Pugh	Lu Leonard
Mrs. Greer	Mavis Ray
Annette	Pam Blair
Celette	Colleen Zenk
Saunders	Victor Griffin
Frick	Jerome Collamore
Frack	Jon Richards
Photographer	Wayne Cilento
Weasel	Ken Swofford
Pound Man	Larry Hankin
Bundles	Irving Metzman
Mrs. McKracky	Angela Martin
Spike	Kurtis Epper Sanders

and Liz Marsh, Danielle Miller, Lisa Kieldrup, Angela Lee, Tina Maria Caspary, Julie Whitman, Jan Mackie, Shawnee Smith, Mandy Peterson, Jamie Flowers, Cherie Michan, Janet Marie Jones, Linda Saputo, Sonja Haney, Kari Baca, Victoria Hartman, Bob M. Porter, Gerald E. Brutsche, Jophery Brown, The Big Apple Circus

Roger Minami, Ann Reinking, Geoffrey Holder Above: Bernadette Peters, Tim Curry, Carol Burnett Top Left (C) and Below: Aileen Quinn Top Right: Carol Burnett, Aileen Quinn, Ann Reinking
©Columbia

Ann Reinking, Aileen Quinn, Albert Finney
Top: (L) Albert Finney, Aileen Quinn (R) Lois DeBanzie, Finney, Quinn, Edward Hermann

E.T. THE EXTRA-TERRESTRIAL

(UNIVERSAL) Producers, Steven Spielberg, Kathleen Kennedy; Director, Steven Spielberg; Associate Producer, Screenplay, Melissa Mathison; Music, John Williams; Photography, Allen Daviau; Designer, James D. Bissell; Editor, Carol Littleton; Assistant Directors, Katy Emde, Daniel Attias; E. T. created by Carlo Rambaldi; Costumes, Deborah Scott; In Technicolor and Dolby Stereo; 120 minutes; Rated PG: June release

CAST

Mary	Dee Wallace
Elliott	Henry Thomas
Keys	Peter Coyote
Michael	Robert Macnaughton
Gertie	Drew Barrymore
Greg	K. C. Martel
Steve	Sean Frye
Tyler	Tom Howell
Pretty Girl	Erika Eleniak
Schoolboy	David O'Dell
Science Teacher	Richard Swingler
Policeman	Frank Toth
Ultra Sound Man	Robert Barton
Van Man	Michael Darrell

Left: E.T.
© *Universal*

1982 Academy Awards for Best Original Score, Best Sound, Best Sound Editing, Best Visual Effects

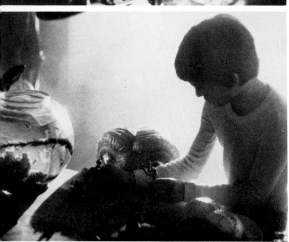

E.T., Henry Thomas

Drew Barrymore, E.T. Above: Henry Thomas, E.T.

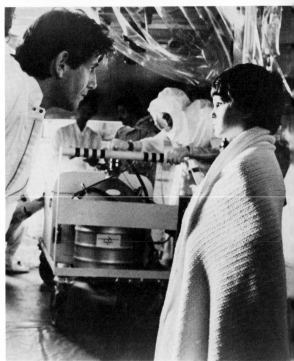

Henry Thomas Top: Peter Coyote, Henry Thomas, Dee Wallace

Robert Macnaughton (R) Top: Peter Coyote, Henry Thomas

AUTHOR! AUTHOR!

(20th CENTURY-FOX) Producer, Irwin Winkler; Director, Arthur Hiller; Screenplay, Israel Horovitz; Photography, Victor J. Kemper; Design, Gene Rudolf; Editor, William Reynolds; Music, Dave Grusin; Assistant Directors, Yudi Bennett, Mark McGann; Costumes, Gloria Gresham; Associate Producer, Dorothy Wilde; In TVC Lab Color; 110 minutes; Rated PG; June release.

CAST

Travalian	Al Pacino
Alice Detroit	Dyan Cannon
Gloria	Tuesday Weld
Kreplich	Alan King
Finestein	Bob Dishy
Patrick Dicker	Bob Elliott
Jackie Dicker	Ray Goulding
Igor	Eric Gurry
Bonnie	Elva Leff
Spike	B. J. Barie
Debbie	Ari Meyers
Geraldo	Benjamin H. Carlin
Roger Slessinger	Ken Sylk
Lt. Glass	James Tolkan
Officer Kapinsky	Tony Munafo
Oliver Cromwell	Reuben Singer
Fippsy Fippininni	Cosmo F. Allegretti
Ted Brawn	Kevin McClarnon
Mrs. Woo	Lori Tan Chinn
Seth Shapiro	Richard Belzer
J. J	Andre Gregory
Miss Knoph	Judy Graubart
Second Taxi Driver	Jaime Tirelli
Larry Kotzwinkle	Frederic Kimball

and Yudie Bank (Stranger), Denny Dillon (Woman), James Harder (Doorman), Margo Winkler (Millie), James Shaw (Eddie), Orlando Dole (Pimp), Jean-Pierre Stewart (Student), Doris Gramovot (Waitress) Rachael Horovitz (Young Lady), Matthew Horovitz (Drug Dealer), Julia Reardon (Girl Scout), Adam Winkler (Bystander), Florence Anglin (Bag Lady), Cristal Kim (Grunella), Chet Carlin (News Vender)

Al Pacino, Dyan Cannon

Top: Ben Carlin, B. J. Barie, Eric Gurry, Al Pacino, Ari Meyers, Elva Leff
©*20th Century-Fox*

Alan King, Al Pacino, Bob Dishy Top: (L) Tuesday Weld (R)
Al Pacino

BLADE RUNNER

(WARNER BROS.) Producer, Michael Deeley; Director, Ridley Scott; Screenplay, Hampton Fancher, David Peoples; Photography, Jordan Cronenweth; Design, Lawrence G. Paull; Associate Producer, Ivor Powell; Music, Vangelis; Editor, Terry Rawlings; Executive Producers, Brian Kelly, Hampton Fancher; Based on novel "Do Androids Dream of Electric Sheep" by Philip K. Dick; Assistant Directors, Newton Arnold, Peter Cornberg; Costumes, Charles Knode, Michael Kaplan; Art Director, David Snyder; In Panavision, Technicolor, Dolby Stereo; 114 minutes; Rated R; June release.

CAST

Deckard	Harrison Ford
Batty	Rutger Hauer
Rachael	Sean Young
Gaff	Edward James Olmos
Bryant	M. Emmet Walsh
Pris	Daryl Hannah
Sebastian	William Sanderson
Leon	Brion James
Tyrell	Joe Turkel
Zhora	Joanna Cassidy
Chew	James Hong
Holden	Morgan Paull
Bear	Kevin Thompson
Kaiser	John Edward Allen
Taffey Lewis	Hy Pyke
Cambodian Lady	Kimiro Hiroshige
Sushi Master	Robert Okazaki
Saleslady	Carolyn DeMirjian
Showgirl	Kelly Hine
Bartenders	Charles Knapp, Thomas Hutchinson, Leo Gorcey, Jr.
Barflies	Sharon Hesky, Rose Mascari
Policemen	Hiro Okazaki, Steve Pope, Robert Reiter

Left: Harrison Ford, and above with Sean Young
© *Warner Bros.*

Daryl Hannah, Rutger Hauer

Harrison Ford, Rutger Hauer Top: (L) Joanna Cassidy (R)
Harrison Ford Below: Rutger Hauer

FIREFOX

(WARNER BROS.) Producer-Director, Clint Eastwood; Screenplay, Alex Lasker, Wendell Wellman; Based on novel by Craig Thomas; Executive Producer, Fritz Manes; Photography, Bruce Surtees; Art Direction, John Graysmark, Elayne Ceder; Editors, Ferris Webster, Ron Spang; Music, Maurice Jarre; Associate Producer, Paul Hitchcock; Assistant Directors, Steve Perry, David Valdes; Special Effects, Robert Shepherd, Roger Dorney, Al Miller; In Panavision, DeLuxe Color, Dolby Stereo; 137 minutes; Rated PG; June release.

CAST

Mitchell Grant	Clint Eastwood
Kenneth Aubrey	Freddie Jones
Buckholz	David Huffman
Pavel Upenskoy	Warren Clarke
Semelovsky	Ronald Lacey
Colonel Kontarsky	Kenneth Colley
General Vladimirov	Klaus Lowitsch
Pyote Baranovich	Nigel Hawthorne
First Secretary	Stefan Schnabel
General Brown	Thomas Hill
Major Lanyev	Clive Merrison
Lt. Colonel Voskov	Kai Wulff
Natalia	Dimitra Arliss
Walters	Austin Willis
Captain Seerbacker	Michael Currie
Lt. Commander Fleischer	James Staley
General Rogers	Ward Costello
Air Marshall Kutuzov	Alan Tilvern
Dmitri Priabin	Oliver Cotton
William Saltonstall	Bernard Behrens
Admiral Curtin	Richard Derr
Major Dietz	Woody Eney
KGB Guard	Bernard Erhard
Police Inspector Tortyev	Hugh Fraser
KGB Official	David Gant
Customs Officer	John Grillo

and Czeslaw Grocholski, Barrie Houghton, Neil Hunt, Vincent J. Isaacs, Alexei Jawdokimov, Wolf Kahler, Eugene Lipinski, Phillip Littell, Curt Lowens, Lev Mailer, Fritz Manes, David Meyers, Alfredo Michelson, Zenno Nahayevsky, George Orrison, Tony Papenfuss, Oliver Pierre, Grisha Plotkin, George Pravda, John Ratzenberger, Alex Rodine, Lance Rosen, Eugene Scherer, Warrick Sims, Mike Spero, Malcolm Storry, Chris Winfield, John Yates, Alexander Zale, Igor Zatsepin, Konstantin Zlatev

Clint Eastwood Top: Clint Eastwood, Warren Clarke
© *Warner Bros.*

Clint Eastwood Above: Firefox
Top: David Huffman (L), Freddie Jones (R)

Clint Eastwood Above: Firefox

STAR TREK II: THE WRATH OF KHAN

(PARAMOUNT) Producer, Robert Sallin; Director, Nicholas Meyer; Screenplay, Jack B. Sowards; Story, Harve Bennett, Jack B. Sowards; Based on "Star Trek" created by Gene Roddenberry; Executive Producer, Harve Bennett; Photography, Gayne Rescher; Designer, Joseph R. Jennings; Editor, William P. Dornisch; Music, James Horner; In Panavision, Dolby Stereo and color; 113 minutes; Rated PG; June release.

CAST

Admiral Kirk	William Shatner
Mr. Spock	Leonard Nimoy
Dr. Leonard (Bones) McCoy	DeForest Kelley
Chief Engineer Montgomery Scott	James Doohan
Chekhov	Walter Koenig
Sulu	George Takei
Commander Uhura	Nichelle Nichols
Dr. Carol Marcus	Bibi Besch
David	Merritt Butrick
Terrell	Paul Winfield
Saavik	Kirstie Alley
Khan	Ricardo Montalban

Right Leonard Nimoy, Kirstie Alley
©*Paramount*

Merritt Butrick, Kirstie Alley

Ricardo Montalban Above: DeForest Kelley, Merritt Butrick, Bibi Besch, Kirstie Alley, William Shatner

George Takei, DeForest Kelley, Nichelle Nichols, Walter Koenig, William Shatner (seated) James Doohan, Kirstie Alley, Leonard Nimoy
Top: Ricardo Montalban, Walter Koenig, Paul Winfield

POLTERGEIST

(MGM/UA) Producers, Steven Spielberg, Frank Marshall; Director, Tobe Hooper; Screenplay, Steven Spielberg, Michael Grais, Mark Victor; Photography, Matthew F. Leonetti; Editor, Michael Kahn; Design, James H. Spencer; Assistant Director, Pat Kehoe; Associate Producer, Kathleen Kennedy; Music, Jerry Goldsmith; In Widescreen, Dolby Stereo and Metrocolor; 115 minutes; Rated PG; June release

CAST

Steve	Craig T. Nelson
Diane	JoBeth Williams
Dr. Lesh	Beatrice Straight
Dana	Dominique Dunne
Robbie	Oliver Robins
Carol Anne	Heather O'Rourke
Tangina	Zelda Rubinstein
Marty	Martin Casella
Ryan	Richard Lawson
Tuthill	Michael McManus
Mrs. Tuthill	Virginia Kiser
Teague	James Karen

Left: Heather O'Rourke, JoBeth Williams
©MGM/SLM

Dominique Dunne, JoBeth Williams, Craig T. Nelson, Oliver Robins

Heather O'Rourke Top: Martin Casella, Beatrice Straight, Richard Lawson

HANKY PANKY

(COLUMBIA) Producer, Martin Ransohoff; Director, Sidney Poitier; Associate Producers and Screenplay, Henry Rosenbaum, David Taylor; Executive Producer, Melville Tucker; Photography, Arthur Ornitz; Designer, Ben Edwards; Editor, Harry Keller; Music, Tom Scott; Costumes, Bernard Johnson; Assistant Director, Steve Barnett; Art Director, Christopher Nowak; In color; 110 minutes; Rated PG; June release.

CAST

Michael Jordon	Gene Wilder
Kate Hellman	Gilda Radner
Janet Dunn	Kathleen Quinlan
Ransom	Richard Widmark
Hiram Calder	Robert Prosky
Adrian Pruitt	Josef Sommer
Lacey	Johnny Sekka
Pilot	Jay O. Sanders
Dr. John Wolf	Sam Gray
Bus Driver	Johnny Brown
Stacy	Larry Bryggman
Pilot	Pat Corley
Anchorman	Bill Beutel
Cop at subway	Madison Arnold
Cab Driver	Nat Habib
Conferee	James Tolkan
Doorman	James Greene
Buck	Jay Garner
Calder Aide	Stephen D. Newman
Terrance Martin	Bill Moor
Mailman	Peter Boyden
Building Manager	Doris Belack
Club Members	Don Plumley, Anthony McKay
Bartender in club	Floyd Ennis
Clerk in club	David Snell
Manager in club	Donald Symington
Waiter in club	John Wylie

and Brad English, Richard Southern, Donna Fowler, David Froman, Edmond Genest, Peter Iacangelo, Arthur French, John Blood, Beau Starr, Frankie Faison, Larry Pine, Edwin McDonough, Brian Carney, Richard Russell Ramos, Bill Sadler, Victor Argo, Robert Buka, Craig Vandenburgh, Libi Staiger, Mildred Brion, John Greenwood, Gary Combs, Frank Ferrara

Kathleen Quinlan, Gene Wilder Above: Johnny Sekka, Wilder,
Jay O. Sanders

Top: Gilda Radner, Gene Wilder, Madison Arnold
Left: Wilder, Radner
©Columbia

GREASE 2

(PARAMOUNT) Producers, Robert Stigwood, Allan Carr; Direction and Choreography, Patricia Birch; Screenplay, Ken Finkleman; Suggested by characters created in Jim Jacobs and Warren Casey in "Grease"; Executive Producer, Bill Oakes; Photography, Frank Stanley; Designer, Gene Callahan; Editor, John F. Burnett; Music, Louis St. Louis; Associate Producer, Neil A. Machlis; In color; 115 minutes; Rated PG; June release.

CAST

Michael Carrington	Maxwell Caulfield
Stephanie Zinone	Michelle Pfeiffer
Dolores	Pamela Segall
Frenchy	Didi Conn
Ms. McGee	Eve Arden
Coach Calhoun	Sid Caesar
Blanche	Dody Goodman
Mr. Stuart	Tab Hunter
Mr. Spears	Dick Patterson
Miss Mason	Connie Stevens
T-Birds	Adrian Zmed, Christopher McDonald, Peter Frechette, Leif Green
Pink Ladies	Lorna Luft, Maureen Teefy, Alison Price, Pamela Segall

Right: Maxwell Caulfield, Michelle Pfeiffer **Below:** (L) Tab Hunter, Connie Stevens, Dody Goodman, Dick Patterson, Sid Caesar, Eve Arden (R) Maureen Teefy, Lorna Luft, Alison Price, Michelle Pfeiffer
©*Paramount*

Maxwell Caulfield, Leif Green, Adrian Zmed, Christopher McDonald, Peter Frechette

Maxwell Caulfield, Didi Conn

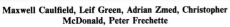

53

THE BEST LITTLE WHOREHOUSE IN TEXAS

(UNIVERSAL) Producers, Thomas L. Miller, Edward K. Milkis, Robert L. Boyett; Director, Colin Higgins; Screenplay, Larry L. King, Peter Masterson, Colin Higgins; Based on stage musical of same title; Co-Producer, Peter MacGregor-Scott; Photography, William A. Fraker; Design, Robert F. Boyle; Costumes, Theadora Van Runkle; Editors, Pembroke J. Herring, David Bretherton, Jack Hofstra, Nicholas Eliopoulos; Choreography, Tony Stevens; Music and Lyrics, Carol Hall; Additional Songs, Dolly Parton; Background Music, Patrick Williams; Art Director, Norman Newberry; Assistant Directors, Jack Frost Sanders, Jim Van Wyck, Emmitt-Leon O'Neil; Film Editor, Walt Hanneman; Assistant Producer, Dow Griffith; In Panavision and Technicolor; 114 minutes; Rated R; July release.

CAST

Sheriff	Burt Reynolds
Mona Stangely	Dolly Parton
Melvin	Dom DeLuise
Governor	Charles Durning
Deputy Fred	Jim Nabors
Senator Wingwood	Robert Mandan
Dulcie Mae	Lois Nettleton
Jewel	Theresa Merritt
Edsel	Noah Beery
Mayor	Raleigh Bond
C. J.	Barry Corbin
Mansel	Ken Magee
Rita	Mary Jo Catlett
Modene	Mary Louise Wilson
Himself	Howard K. Smith
Wulla Jean	Paula Shaw
Governor's Aide	Lee Ritchey
Governor's Secretary	Alice Drummond
Chicken Girl	Karyn Harrison
Privates Boy	Randy Bennett

Chicken Ranch Girls: Gail Benedict, Valerie Leigh Bixler, Leslie Cook, Carol Culver, Lorraine Fields, Trish Garland, Sandi Johnson, Lee Lund, Paula Lynn, Lily Mariye, Andrea Pike, Terrie M. Robinson, Jennifer Nairn-Smith, Terrie Treas, Melanie Winter. Aggies: Stephen Bray, Brian Bullard, Jeffrey Calhoun, Gary Chapman, John Dolf, David Engel, Ed Forsyth, Mark Fotopoulos, Michael Fullington, David Warren Gibson, Joe Hart, Jeffrey Hornaday, Patrick Maguire, Ted Marriot, Jerry Mitchell, Steven Moore, Douglas Robb, Kevin Ryan, Tim Topper, Marvin Tunney, Randy Val Cupp, Robert Warners. Dogettes: Robin Lynn Funk, Larry Kenton, Edie Lehmann, Mark McGee, Karen McLain, Benjamin Taylor, Arnetia Walker, Ty Whitney. Melvin's Crew: Robert Briscoe, John Walter Davis, Gregory Itzin, Timothy Stack, Larry B. Williams. Reporters: Robert Ginnaven, John Edson, Sharon Ammann, Claudette Gardner, Suzi McLaughlin

Left: Dolly Parton, Theresa Merritt Top: Dolly Parton and the Chicken Ranch girls
© Universal

Miss Mona's girls

Burt Reynolds, Lois Nettleton

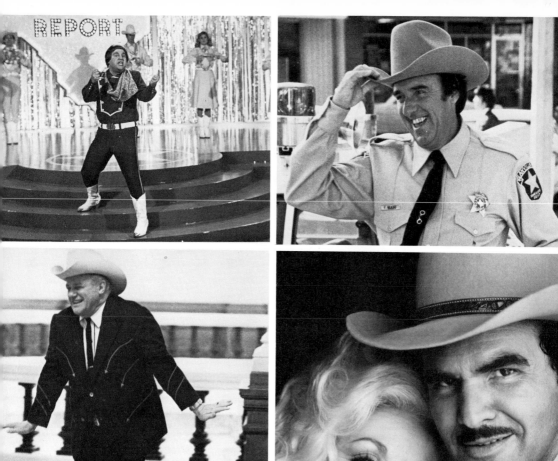

**Texas A & M football team Above: Charles Durning
Top: Dom DeLuise**

**Football team and Miss Mona's girls Above: Dolly Parton,
Burt Reynolds Top: Jim Nabors**

THE WORLD ACCORDING TO GARP

(WARNER BROS.) Producers, George Roy Hill, Robert L. Crawford; Director, George Roy Hill; Executive Producer, Patrick Kelley; Screenplay, Steve Tesich; Based on novel by John Irving; Photography, Miroslav Ondricek; Designer, Henry Bumstead; Editors, Ronald Roose, Stephen A. Rotter; Music adapted by David Shire; Costumes, Ann Roth; Assistant Directors, Alan Hopkins, Robert E. Warren; Art Director, Woods Mackintosh; Animation Sequence, John Canemaker; In Technicolor; 136 minutes; Rated PG; July release.

CAST

Garp	Robin Williams
Helen Holm	Mary Beth Hurt
Jenny Fields	Glenn Close
Roberta Muldoon	John Lithgow
Mr. Fields	Hume Cronyn
Mrs. Fields	Jessica Tandy
Hooker	Swoosie Kurtz
Young Garp	James McCall
John Wolfe	Peter Michael Goetz
Dean Bodger	George Ede
Michael Milton	Mark Soper
Duncan	Nathan Babcock
Walt	Ian MacGregor

and Warren Berlinger (Stew Percy), Susan Browning (Midge Percy), Brandan Maggart (Ernie Holm), Jenny Wright (Cushie), Brenda Currin (Pooh), Jillian Ross (Young Cushie), Laurie Robyn (Young Pooh), Victor Magnotta (1st Coach), Dominic A. Cecere (Opposing Coach), John Irving (Referee), Dan Goldman (Wrestler), Christopher Farr (Bosworth), Brett Littman (Zipper Boy), Brendon Roth (Infant Garp), Steven Krey (Babysitter), Al Cerullo, Jr. (Helicopter), Matthew C. Materazo, Deborah Watkins (Roof Stunt), Mark Sutton (Car Stunt), Amanda Plummer (Ellen James), Bette Henritze (Candidate), Jeanne DeBaer (Speaker), Ron Frazier (Stephen), Katherine Borowitz (Rachel), Isabell Monk (Woman with book), Edgard L. Mourino (Piano Stunt), John S. Corcoran (Man in tree), Tim Gallin (Freman), Kate McGregor-Stewart (Real Estate Lady), Sabrina Lee Moore (Babysitter), James Appleby (Stunt Pilot), Matthew Cowles (Speeding Plumber), Eve Gordon (Marge), David Fields (Infant Duncan), Ryan David (Duncan at 2), Kaiulani Lee (Chief Ellen Jamesian), Harris Laskawy (Randy), Lori Shelle (Laurel), Kath Reiter (Alice), Thomas Peter Daikos (Flying Baby Garp).

Robin Williams, Mary Beth Hurt Above: Mark Soper, Mary Beth Hurt

Top: Robin Williams, Swoosie Kurtz, Glenn Close
© *Warner Bros*

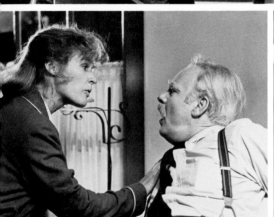

Robin Williams, Mary Beth Hurt Above: Glenn Close, George Ede Top: John Lithgow, Glenn Close, Robin Williams

Nathan Babcock, Robin Williams, Glenn Close Above: Jessica Tandy, Hume Cronyn

A MIDSUMMER NIGHT'S SEX COMEDY

(WARNER BROS.) Producer, Robert Greenhut; Direction and Screenplay, Woody Allen; Executive Producer, Charles H. Joffe; Photography, Gordon Willis; Designer, Mel Bourne; Costumes, Santo Loquasto; Editor, Susan E. Morse; Assistant Directors, Fredric B. Blankfein, Thomas Reilly, Anthony Gittelson; Associate Producer, Michael Peyser; Art Director, Speed Hopkins; A Jack Rollins and Charles H. Joffe Production in Technicolor; 88 minutes. Rated PG; July release.

CAST

Andrew	Woody Allen
Ariel	Mia Farrow
Leopold	Jose Ferrer
Dulcy	Julie Hagerty
Maxwell	Tony Roberts
Adrian	Mary Steenburgen
Student Foxx	Adam Redfield
Mr. Hayes	Moishe Rosenfeld
Mr. Thompson	Timothy Jenkins
Reynolds	Michael Higgins
Carstairs	Sol Frieder
Purvis	Boris Zoubok
Blint	Thomas Barbour
Mrs. Baker	Kate McGregor-Stewart

Left: Woody Allen, Mia Farrow
© *Warner Bros.*

Tony Roberts, Jose Ferrer, Mia Farrow, Julie Hagerty

Julie Hagerty, Tony Roberts, Jose Ferrer, Woody Allen, Mary Steenburgen
Top: Woody Allen, Mary Steenburgen

AN OFFICER AND A GENTLEMAN

(PARAMOUNT) Producer, Martin Elfand; Director, Taylor Hackford; Associate Producer-Screenplay, Douglas Day Stewart; Photography, Donald Thorin; Designer, Philip M. Jefferies; Editor, Peter Zinner; Music, Jack Nitzsche; Assistant Directors, David McGiffert, Pamela M. Eilerson; Art Director, John Cartwright; In Metrocolor; 126 minutes; Rated R; July release.

CAST

Zack Mayo	Richard Gere
Paula Pokrifki	Debra Winger
Sid Worley	David Keith
Byron Mayo	Robert Loggia
Lynette Pomeroy	Lisa Blount
Casey Seeger	Lisa Eilbacher
Sgt. Emil Foley	Louis Gossett, Jr.
Emiliano Della Serra	Tony Plana
Perryman	Harold Sylvester
Topper Daniels	David Caruso
Joe Pokrifki	Victor French
Esther Pokrifki	Grace Zabriskie
Young Zack	Tommy Petersen
Bunny	Mara Scott Wood
Schneider	David Greenfield
Donny	Dennis Rucker
Nellie Rufferwell	Jane Wilbur
Thraxton	Buck Welcher
Tom Worley	Vern Taylor
Betty Worley	Elizabeth Rogers
Drill Instructors	David R. Marshall, Gary C. Stillwell
Dilbert Dunker Instructor	Tee Dennard
Altitude Instructor	Norbert M. Murray
New Recruit	Daniel Tyler
Captain Graves	William Graves
Aerodynamics Instructor	Brian D. Ford
Air Officer Candidate	Keith J. Haar
Paula's Sisters	Pia Boyer, Danna Kiesel
Marvin Goatcher	Marvin Goatcher
Troy	John Laughlin
His Friend	Jeffrey P. Rondeau
Man in crowd	Michael Lee Bolger
Bartender	Mark L. Graves
Prostitutes	Meleesa Wyatt, Jo Anna Keane

Richard Gere, Debra Winger
Top: Richard Gere, Gerald Eyestone, Shannon Lynn, Keith J. Haar, David Keith, William Franklin, Louis Gossett, Jr. Left Center: Gossett, Gere, Keith

1982 Academy Awards for Best Supporting Actor (Louis Gossett, Jr.), Best Original Song (Up Where We Belong)
©*Paramount*

Richard Gere, Louis Gossett, Jr. Above: Lisa Blount,
David Keith

Richard Gere, David Keith Top: Gere, Debra Winger

TRON

(BUENA VISTA) Executive Producer, Ron Miller; Producer, Donald Kushner; Associate Producer, Harrison Ellenshaw; Direction and Screenplay, Steven Lisberger; Story, Steven Lisberger, Bonnie MacBird; Music, Wendy Carlos; Photography, Bruce Logan; Designer, Dean Edward Mitzner; Editor, Jeff Gourson; Assistant Directors, Lorin B. Salob, Lisa Marmon; Costumes, Elois Jennsen, Rosanna Norton; Art Directors, John Mansbridge, Al Roelofs; In Technicolor, Super Panavision, Dolby Stereo; 96 minutes; Rated PG; July release.

CAST

Kevin Flynn/Clu	Jeff Bridges
Alan Bradley/Tron	Bruce Boxleitner
Ed Dillinger/Sark	David Warner
Lora/Yori	Cindy Morgan
Dr. Walter Gibbs/Dumont	Barnard Hughes
Ram	Dan Shor
Crom	Peter Jurasik
Peter/Sark's Lieutenant	Tony Stephano
Warriors	Craig Chudy, Vince Deadrick
Expert Disc Warrior	Sam Schatz
Head Guard	Jackson Bostwick
Factory Guard	Dave Cass
Guards	Gerald Berns, Bob Neill, Ted White, Mark Stewart, Michael Sax, Tony Brubaker
Tank Commander	Charles Picerni
Tank Gunners	Pierre Vuilleumier, Erik Cord
Conscripts	Loyd Catlett, Michael J. Dudikoff II
Video Game Player	Richard Bruce Friedman
Video Game Cowboy	Loyd Catlett
Boys in arcade	Rick Feck, John Kenworthy

Left: Barnard Hughes
© Walt Disney Productions

Jeff Bridges, Cindy Morgan, Bruce Boxleitner

Don Shor, Jeff Bridges Above: Bruce Boxleitner   Jeff Bridges Top: Cindy Morgan, Jeff Bridges

Matt Dillon
Top: Emilio Estevez, Matt Dillon, Meg Tilly

TEX

(BUENA VISTA) Executive Producer, Ron Miller; Producer, Tim Zinnemann; Director, Tim Hunter; Screenplay, Charlie Haas, Tim Hunter; Based on novel by S. E. Hinton; Music, Pino Donaggio; Conductor, Natale Massara; Photography, Ric Waite; Designer, Jack T. Collis; Editor, Howard Smith; Assistant Directors, Tom Connors III, Christopher D. Miller; Art Director, John B. Mansbridge; In color; 103 minutes; Rated PG; August release.

CAST

Tex McCormick	Matt Dillon
Mason McCormick	Jim Metzler
Jamie Collins	Meg Tilly
Pop McCormick	Bill McKinney
Mrs. Johnson	Frances Lee McCain
Cole Collins	Ben Johnson
Johnny Collins	Emilio Estevez
Lem Peters	Phil Brock
Coach Jackson	Jack Thibeau
Hitchhiker	Zeljko Ivanek
Bob Collins	Tom Virtue
Connie	Pamela Ludwig

and Jeff Fleury (Roger), Suzanne Costallos (Fortune Teller), Marilyn Redfield (Ms. Carlson), Mark Arnott (Kelly), Jill Clark (Marcie), Sheryl Briedel (Lisa), Lisa Mirkin (Shelly), Rod Jones (Doctor) Richard Krause (Ride Operator), Don Harral (Doctor in hospital), Janine Burns (Nurse), Mark Huebner (Orderly), Ron Thulin (Anchorman), Mary Simons (Ms. Germanie), Francine Ringold (Reporter), Darren Cates, Wayne Dorris, Adam Hubbard (Kids), Robin Winters (Girl on bike), Lance Parkhill (Boy), Mike Coats (Dave) Charlie Haas (Lee), Larry Stallsworth (Patrolman), Scott Smith Eric Beckstrom (Bikers), S. E. Hinton (Mrs. Barnes), Coralie Hunter (Lukie)

Meg Tilly, Matt Dillon
Top: Matt Dillon, Jim Metzler

FAST TIMES AT RIDGEMONT HIGH

(UNIVERSAL) Producers, Art Linson, Irving Azoff; Director, Amy Heckerling; Screenplay, Cameron Crowe; Based on his book; Executive Producer, C. O. Erickson; Photography, Matthew R. Leonetti; Art Director, Dan Lomino; Editor, Eric Jenkins; Costumes, Marilyn Vance; Assistant Directors, Albert Shapiro, Marty Ewing, James Dillon; In Technicolor; 92 minutes; Rated R; August release.

CAST

Jeff Spicoli	Sean Penn
Stacy Hamilton	Jennifer Jason Leigh
Brad Hamilton	Judge Reinhold
Mike Damone	Robert Romanus
Mark "Rat" Ratner	Brian Backer
Linda Barrett	Phoebe Cates
Mr. Hand	Ray Walston
Arnold	Scott Thomson
Mr. Vargas	Vincent Schiavelli
Lisa	Amanda Wyss
Ron Johnson	D. W. Brown
Charles Jefferson	Forest Whitaker
Cindy	Kelli Maroney
Dennis Taylor	Tom Nolan
Pat Bernardo	Blair Ashleigh
Stoner Bud	Eric Stoltz
Jefferson's Brother	Stanley Davis, Jr.
Robber	James Russo
Greg	James Bershad
Brad's Bud	Nicholas Coppola
Vice Principal	Reginald H. Farmer
Stoner Bud	Anthony Edwards
Dina Phillips	Pamela Springsteen
Pirate King	Stuart Cornfeld
Businessman	Sonny Davis
Brad's Bud	Michael Wyle
Desmond	David F. Price
Curtis Spicoli	Patrick Brennan
Pizza Waitresses	Julie Guilmette, Shelly O'Neill

Stu Nahan (Himself), Duane Tucker (Dr. Brandt), Martin Brest (Dr. Miller), Douglas Brian Martin, Steven M. Martin (Twins), Taylor Negron (Himself), Kenny Lawrence, John Hollander, Ricky Redlich (Customers), Nancy Wilson (Girl in car), Virginia Peters (Waitress), Laurie Hendricks (Nurse), Lois Brandt (Mrs. O'-Rourke), Ellen Fenwick (Stacy's Mom), Cherie Effron, Suzanne Marie Fava (Girls), Lana Clarkson (Mrs. Vargas), Roy Holmer Wallack (Santa Claus), Ava Lazar, Lorie Sutton (Playmates).

Left: Sean Penn Top: Sean Penn, Ray Walston
© *Universal*

Robert Ramos, Brian Backer

Hallie Eckstein, Phoebe Cates, Jennifer Jason Leigh

TEMPEST

(COLUMBIA) Producer-Director, Paul Mazursky; Screenplay, Paul Mazursky, Leon Capetanos; Co-Producers, Steven Bernhardt, Pato Guzman; Photography, Donald McAlpine; Designer, Pato Guzman; Editor, Donn Cambern; Music, Stomu Yamashta; Costumes, Albert Wolsky; Assistant Director, Irby Smith; Art Director, Paul Eads; Choreographer, Gino Landi; In Metrocolor and Dolby Stereo; 140 minutes; Rated PG; August release.

CAST

Phillip	John Cassavetes
Antonia	Gena Rowlands
Aretha	Susan Sarandon
Alonzo	Vittorio Gassman
Kalibanos	Raul Julia
Miranda	Molly Ringwald
Freddy	Sam Robards
Phillip's Father	Paul Stewart
Trinc	Jackie Gayle
Sebastian	Anthony Holland
Harry Gondorf	Jerry Hardin
Dolores	Lucianne Buchanan
Greek Boat Captain	Vassilis Glezakos
Sailors	Sergio Nicolai, Luigi Laezza
Terry Bloomfield	Paul Mazursky
Betsy Bloomfield	Betsy Mazursky
Gabrielle	Carol Ficatier
Mackenzie	Peter Lombard
Doctor	Fred Pasternack
Nurses	Nadine Darling, Nina Kolment
Cynthia	Cynthia Harris
Paul	Paul Hecht
Mark	Mark Soper

and Murray Grand (Piano Player), John Marolakos (NY Cafe Owner), George Moscaidis (Athens Cafe Owner), Camille Lefko (Guard), Jerry Hewitt (Stuntman), Barry Mitchell (Woody Allen Lookalike), Al Cerullo (Pilot), Sheila Ozden (Belly Dancer), Nicos Mousoullis (Deck Hand), Evanthia Glezakou (Old Woman), Clint Chin (Steward), Stella Nastou (Secretary), Rudy Cherney (Man with pigeons), Thanasis Pagonis (Waiter)

Top: Gena Rowlands, John Cassavetes, Molly Ringwald Below: Raul Julia, Susan Sarandon, John Cassavetes, Molly Ringwald
©Columbia

Raul Julia, Molly Ringwald Top: Vittorio Gassman, Gena Rowlands Below: Ringwald, Sam Robards

FRIDAY THE 13th PART 3 IN 3D

(PARAMOUNT) Producer, Frank Mancuso, Jr.; Director, Steve Miner; Co-Producer, Tony Bishop; Photography, Gerald Feil; Editor, George Hively; Art Director, Robb Wilson King; Executive Producer, Lisa Barsamian; Music, Harry Manfredini; Associate Producer, Peter Schindler; 3D Supervisor, Martin Jay Sadoff; Screenplay, Martin Kitrosser, Carol Watson; Based on characters created by Victor Miller and Ron Kurz; In Panavision and Movielab Color; 96 minutes; Rated R; August release.

CAST

Chris Higgins	Dana Kimmell
Rick	Paul Kratka
Debbie	Tracie Savage
Andy	Jeffrey Roger
Vera	Catherine Park
Shelly	Larry Zerne
Chili	Rachel Howar
Chuck	David Katim
Jason	Richard Brooke
Fox	Gloria Charle
Cashier	Annie Gaybi
Edna	Cheri Maugan
Newscaster	Steve Mine
Loco	Kevin O'Bria
Ali	Nick Savag
Newswoman	Gianni Standaa
Harold	Steve Susskin
Mrs. Sanchez	Perla Walte
Abel	David Wile
State Troopers	Terry Ballard, Terence McCorr, Charlie Messenge

Dana Kimmell, Paul Kratka, Richard Brooker
Top: Cheri Maugans

Tracie Savage, Jeffrey Rogers Top: David Wiley (R)

EATING RAOUL

(20th CENTURY-FOX INTERNATIONAL CLASSICS/QUARTET FILMS) Producer, Anne Kimmel; Director, Paul Bartel; Screenplay, Richard Blackburn, Paul Bartel; Photography, Gary Thieltges; Editor, Alan Toomayan; Music, Arion Ober; In color; 87 minutes; Rated R; September release.

CAST

Mary Bland	Mary Woronov
Paul Bland	Paul Bartel
Raoul	Robert Beltran
Mr. Leech	Beck Henry
Mr. Kray	Richard Paul
Doris the Dominatrix	Susan Saiger

and Dan Barrows, Ralph Vrannen, Edie McClurg, Darcy Pulliam, Ed Begley, Jr., Hamilton Camp, John Paragon, Allan Rich, Don Steele, Richard Blackburn, Billy Curtis, Anna Mathias, John Shearin

Left: Robert Beltran
© *20th Century-Fox*

Paul Bartel, Mary Woronov

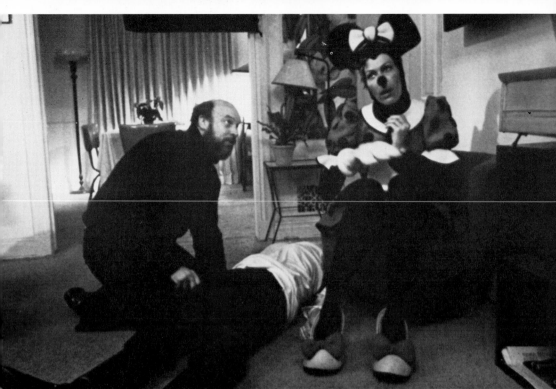

Paul Bartel, Mary Woronov (also above)

MY FAVORITE YEAR

(MGM/UA) Producer, Michael Gruskoff; Director, Richard Benjamin; Screenplay, Norman Steinberg, Dennis Palumbo; Story, Mr. Palumbo; Photography, Gerald Hirschfeld; Editor, Richard Chew; Music, Ralph Burns; Design, Charles Rosen; Costumes, May Routh; Associate Producer, Art Levinson; Assistant Director, William S. Beasley; In Metrocolor; 92 minutes; Rated PG; September release

CAST

Alan Swann	Peter O'Toole
Benjy Stone	Mark Linn-Baker
K. C. Downing	Jessica Harper
King Kaiser	Joseph Bologna
Sy Benson	Bill Macy
Belle Carroca	Lainie Kazan
Alice Miller	Anne DeSalvo
Herb Lee	Basil Hoffman
Uncle Morty	Lou Jacobi
Leo Silver	Adolph Green
Alfie Bumbacelli	Tony DiBenedetto
Myron Fein	George Wyner
Lil	Selma Diamond
Karl Rojeck	Cameron Mitchell

Left: Peter O'Toole, Lainie Kazan, Lou Jacobi, Mark Linn-Baker Top: Jessica Harper, Mark Linn-Baker
©MGM/UA

Anne de Salvo, Adolph Green, Joseph Bologna, Mark Linn-Baker, Bill Macy, Tony DiBenedetto, Peter O'Toole (prone)

Jessica Harper, Mark Linn-Baker, Peter O'Toole Left Center:
Joseph Bologna, Archie Hahn, John Welsh, Peter O'Toole,
Phil Bruns Top: Peter O'Toole (also Right)

73

SPLIT IMAGE

(ORION) Producer-Director, Ted Kotcheff; Screenplay, Scott Spencer, Robert Kaufman, Robert Mark Kamen; Story, Scott Spencer; Executive Producer, Jeff Young; Photography, Robert Jessup; Art Director, Jack Marty; Designer, Wolf Kroeger; Editor, Jay Kamen; Music, Bill Conti; Original Songs, Bill Conti, Will Jennings; Assistant Directors, Craig Huston, James M. Freitag; In Panavision and DeLuxe Color; A GAC Film Partners Enterprise; Originally titled "Captured"; Presented by PolyGram Pictures; 110 minutes; Rated R; October release.

CAST

Danny	Michael O'Keefe
Rebecca	Karen Allen
Kirklander	Peter Fonda
Pratt	James Woods
Diana	Elizabeth Ashley
Kevin	Brian Dennehy
Sean	Ronnie Scribner
Jane	Pamela Ludwig
Aaron	John Dukakis
Walter	Lee Montgomery
Gabriel	Michael Sacks
Judith	Deborah Rush
Jacob	Peter Horton
Collins	Ken Farmer
Hall	Cliff Stephens
Jerry	Brian Hinson
Gymnast	David Wallace
Big Wig	Kenneth Barry

and Robert A. Cowan, Herbert Kirkpatrick (Coaches), Christopher McCarty, Lee Ritchey (Sentries), Lynette Walden (Sexy Girl), Robert Hibbard (Cop), Scott Campbell (Barry), Melanie Strange (Debbie), David Tanner (Guitarist), Tom Rayhall (Sargent), Jeanne Evans (Newsboy's Mother), Irma Hall (Maid), Bill Engvall (Student), Peter Hans Sprague (Person), John Carroll, Haley McLane, Kelly Wimberly (Homelanders)

Right: Karen Allen, James Woods, Elizabeth Ashley Top: Peter Fonda, Karen Allen, Michael O'Keefe
© *Polygram Pictures*

Elizabeth Ashley, Brian Dennehy, Michael O'Keefe

Karen Allen, Michael O'Keefe

LOOKIN' TO GET OUT

(PARAMOUNT) Producer, Robert Schaffel; Director, Hal Ashby; Screenplay, Al Schwartz, Jon Voight; Executive Producer, Andrew Braunsberg; Associate Producer, Edward Teets; Photography, Haskell Wexler; Music, Johnny Mandel; Editor, Robert C. Jones; Designer, Robert Boyle; Assistant Directors, Charles Myers, Paul Moen; Art Director, James Schoppee; A North Star International/Voight-Schaffel production presented by Lorimar; In color; 106 minutes; Rated R; October release

CAST

Alex Kovac	Jon Voight
Patti Warner	Ann-Margret
Jerry Feldman	Burt Young
Smitty	Bert Remsen
Harry	Jude Farese
Joey	Allen Keller
Bernie Gold	Richard Bradford
Rusty (Redhaired Hooker)	Stacey Pickren
Lillian (Jerry's Ex-wife)	Samantha Harper
Harvey (Elevator Operator)	Fox Harris
Girl in Jeep	Marcheline Bertrand

and Roger Rook, Howard Gray, Bill Borsella, Henry Robinson (Poker Players), Sigmund Frohlich (Dealer), Steven E. Pelzer (Paul), Ruth Manning (Shannon), Don Lake (Alfred), Barbara Joyce Furman (Desk Assistant), Wiley Harker (Dr. Green), Barry Gootkind (Floorman), Howard Witt (Sid), Peter Lind Hayes, Mary Healy (Tourists), Siegfried and Roy (Magicians), Kris Kremo (Juggler), Angelina Jolie Voight (Tosh), Larry Alan Weisshart (Bellhop), Patrick O'Neill (Bartender), Frank Bella (Maitre D), Robert S. Aumen, Dick Padgette, Tony Hawkins, Lee Nickerson, Tony Hawkson, Michael DeLuna, Michael D. Misuraca, Joseph Miller, Gloria Manos, Pam Parmelli, Roberta Greenberg, Martha Sheehan, John Ortstadt, Myrtle Elizabeth Lolatte, Effie Karath, Cis Rundle, Peter Kulas, Bob Buckingham, Jim DeCloss, Ken Cohen, Don Caldwell, Ron Skurow, Steve Vincent, Danny Tucker, David Welch, Terry Fisher

Right: Ann-Margret, Angelina Jolie Voight, Jon Voight Top: Burt Young, Jon Voight, Bert Remsen
©*Paramount*

Jon Voight, Ann-Margret

Jon Voight, Burt Young

FIRST BLOOD

(ORION) Executive Producers, Mario Kassar, Andrew Vajna; Co-Executive Producer, Herb Nanas; Producer, Buzz Feitshans; Director, Ted Kotcheff; Screenplay, Michael Kozoll, William Sackheim, Q. Moonblood; Based on novel by David Morrell; Photography, Andrew Laszlo; Designer, Wolf Kroeger; Art Director, Stephane Reichel; Assistant Director, Craig Huston; Costumes, Tom Bronson; In Panavision, Dolby Stereo and color; 97 minutes; Rated R; October release

CAST

Rambo	Sylvester Stallone
Trautman	Richard Crenna
Teasle	Brian Dennehy
Mitch	David Caruso
Galt	Jack Starret
Balford	Michael Talbot
Shingleton	David Crowley
Ward	Chris Mulkey
Preston	Don Mackay
Lester	Alf Humphrey
Orval	John McLiam
Kern	Bill McKinney
Pilot	Chuck Tamburro
Cathcart	Bruce Barbour
Radio Operator	Craig Huston
Lt. Morgan	Patrick Stack
Boy	Dan Woznow
TV Reporter	Mike Winlaw
Attendant	Peter Lonstrup
Guardsmen	Raimund Stamm, Stephen Dimopoulos, Robert Metcalf
Hunters	Gary Hetherington, Alex Kliner, R. G. Miller

Sylvester Stallone
Top: Sylvester Stallone, Brian Dennehy

©*Anabasis N.V.*

Sylvester Stallone (also top)

Richard Crenna Top: Sylvester Stallone

48 HOURS

(PARAMOUNT) Producers, Lawrence Gordon, Joel Silver; Director, Walter Hill; Screenplay, Roger Spottiswoode, Walter Hill, Larry Gross, Steven E. de Souza; Executive Producer, D. Constantine Conte; Photography, Ric Waite; Designer, John Vallone; Editors, Freeman Davies, Mark Warner, Billy Weber; Music, James Horner; Costumes, Marilyn Kay Vance; Assistant Directors, David Sosna, Deborah A. Love; In Movielab Color and Dolby Stereo; 96 minutes; Rated R; November release.

CAST

Jack Cates	Nick Nolte
Reggie Hammond	Eddie Murphy
Elaine	Annette O'Toole
Haden	Frank McRae
Ganz	James Remar
Luther	David Patrick Kelly
Billy Bear	Sonny Landham
Kehoe	Brion James
Rosalie	Kerry Sherman
Algren	Jonathan Banks
Vanzant	James Keane
Frizzy	Tara King
Lisa	Greta Blackburn
Casey	Margot Rose
Sally	Denise Crosby
Candy	Olivia M. Brown
Young Cop	Todd Allen
Thin Cop	Bill Dearth
Big Cop	Ned Dowd
Old Cop	Jim Haynie
Detective	Jack Thibeau
Plainclothesman	Jon St. Elwood
Ruth	Clare Nono
Policewoman	Sandy Martin
Bob	Matt Landers
Cowboy Bartender	Peter Jason

and Bill Cross, Chris Mulkey (Cops), James Marcelino (Parking Attendant), Bennie Dobbins, Walter Scott, W. T. Zacha (Road Gang Guards), Begona Plaza (Indian Hooker), Loyd Catlett, B. G. Fisher, Reid Cruickshanks (Prison Guards), R. D. Call (Duty Sergeant), Brenda Venus, Gloria E. Gifford (Hookers), John Hauk (Henry), Clint Smith (Leroy), Nick Dimitri, John Dennis Johnston, Rock A. Walker, Dave Moordigian, J. Wesley Huston, Gary Pettinger, Marquerita Wallace, Angela Robinson, Jack Lightsy, Bob Yanez, Luis Contreras, Suzanne M. Regard, Ola Ray, Bjaye Turner

Left: Eddie Murphy, Nick Nolte (also top)
©Paramount

Annette O'Toole, Nick Nolte

Olivia Brown, Eddie Murphy

Nick Nolte Above: Eddie Murphy, James Remar Top: Sonny Landham, Kerry Sherman, James Remar

Peter Jason, Eddie Murphy Above: Murphy, Nick Nolte Top: Brenda Venus, Gloria Gifford, Murphy

Sean Connery, Betsy Brantley, and above with Lambert Wilson

FIVE DAYS ONE SUMMER

(WARNER BROS.) Producer-Director, Fred Zinnemann; Screenplay, Michael Austin; Based in part on "Maiden Maiden," a short story by Kay Boyle; Executive Producer, Peter Beale; Music, Elmer Bernstein; Photography, Giuseppe Rotunno; Designer, Willy Holt; Editor, Stuart Baird; Assistant Director, Tony Waye; Choreographer, D'Dee; Costumes, Emma Porteous; A Ladd Company release in Technicolor; 108 minutes; Rated PG; November release

CAST

Douglas	Sean Connery
Kate	Betsy Brantley
Johann	Lambert Wilson
Sarah	Jennifer Hilary
Kate's Mother	Isabel Dean
Brendel	Gerard Buhr
Jennifer Pierce	Anna Massey
Gillian Pierce	Sheila Reid
Dieter	Georges Claisse
His Wife	Kathy Marothy
Georg	Terry Kingley
Old Woman	Emilie Lihou
Martin	Alfred Schmidhauser
Van Royen	Jerry Brouwer
MacLean	Alexander John
Station Master	Robert Diet
Guide	Gunther Clemen
Horse Taxi Driver	Michael Burrel
Eva	Skil Kaiser-Passin
French Students	Marc Duret, Francois Caron, Benoist Ferreux

Top: Lambert Wilson, Betsy Brantley Left: Sheila Reid, Anna Massey, Sean Connery Right Center: Brantley, Connery, Wilson

© Warner Bros.

COME BACK TO THE 5 & DIME, JIMMY DEAN, JIMMY DEAN

(CINECOM INTERNATIONAL) Executive Producer, Giraud Chester; Producer, Scott Bushnell; Director, Robert Altman; Screenplay, Ed Graczyk based on his play of the same title; Photography, Pierre Mignot; Editor, Jason Rosenfield; Designer, David Gropman; A Sandcastle 5 production in color; 109 minutes; Not rated; November release.

CAST

Mona	Sandy Dennis
Sissy	Cher
Joanne	Karen Black
Juanita	Sudie Bond
Edna Louise	Marta Heflin
Stella May	Kathy Bates
Joe Qualley	Mark Patton
Martha	Caroline Aaron
Clarissa	Ruth Miller
Sue Ellen	Gena Ramsel
Phyllis Marie	Ann Risley
Alice Ann	Dianne Turley Travis

Right: Sandy Dennis, Cher, Karen Black Top: Karen Black, Cher, Sudie Bond
©*Cinecom International*

Kathy Bates, Marta Heflin

Sandy Dennis

THAT CHAMPIONSHIP SEASON

(CANNON FILMS) Producers, Menahem Golan, Yoram Globus; Direction and Screenplay, Jason Miller; Based on his Pulitzer Prize play; Photography, John Bailey; Editor, Richard Halsey; Music, Bill Conti; In color; 110 minutes; Rated R; December release

CAST

George Sitkowski	Bruce Dern
James Daley	Stacy Keach
Coach Delaney	Robert Mitchum
Tom Daley	Martin Sheen
Phil Romano	Paul Sorvino
Macken	Arthur Franz
Jacks	Michael Bernosky
Malley	Joseph Kelly
Cooney	James M. Langan
Marelli	Tony Santaniello
Harrison	William G. McAndrew
Sharmen	Barry Weiner
Newspaper Editor	Edward Cunningham
Nelson	Robert E. Shlesinger
Zookeeper	George Lowry
Heckler	Jim Sparkman

Left: Robert Mitchum
©Cannon

Paul Sorvino, Stacy Keach, Robert Mitchum, Bruce Dern, Martin Sheen

Bruce Dern, Paul Sorvino, Martin Sheen, Stacy Keach Above: Sheen, Robert Mitchum, Dern Top: Keach, Dern, Sheen

Bruce Dern, Robert Mitchum, Martin Sheen, Paul Sorvino Above: Sorvino, Stacy Keach Top: Sorvino, Mitchum

STILL OF THE NIGHT

(MGM-UA) Producer, Arlene Donovan; Direction and Screenplay, Robert Benton; Story, David Newman, Robert Benton; Associate Producers, Wolfgang Glattes, Kenneth Utt; Photography, Nestor Almendros; Designer, Mel Bourne; Costumes, Albert Wolsky; Music, John Kander; Editor, Jerry Greenberg; Assistant Directors, Wolfgang Glattes, Anthony Gittelson; Art Director, Michael Molly; Film Editor, Bill Pankow; In Technicolor; 91 minutes; Rated PG; December release

CAST

Sam Rice	Roy Scheider
Brooke Reynolds	Meryl Streep
Grace Rice	Jessica Tandy
Joseph Vitucci	Joe Grifasi
Gail Phillips	Sara Botsford
George Bynum	Josef Sommer
Heather Wilson	Rikke Borge
Murray Gordon	Irving Metzman
Mugger	Larry Joshua
Auctioneer	Tom Norton
Mr. Harris	Richmond Hoxie
Mr. Chang	Hyon Cho
Girl	Danielle Cusson
Night Watchman	John Bentley
Elevator Operator	George A. Tooks
Receptionist	Sigrunn Omark
Car Thief	Randy Jurgenson
Auction Spotters	Palmer Deane, William Major, Joseph Priestly, Will Rose
Auction Bidders	Arnold Glimcher, Jeffrey Hoffeld, Linda LeRoy Janklow, Elinor Klein, Susan Patricof

Meryl Streep, Roy Scheider

Top: Meryl Streep, Josef Sommer
©*MGM/UA*

Meryl Streep, Roy Scheider

TOOTSIE

(COLUMBIA) Producers, Sydney Pollack, Dick Richards; Director, Sydney Pollack; Screenplay, Larry Gelbart, Murray Schisgal; Story, Don McGuire, Larry Gelbart; Photography, Owen Roizman; Designer, Peter Larkin; Executive Producer, Charles Evans; Editors, Fredric Steinkamp, William Steinkamp; Music, Dave Grusin; Costumes, Ruth Morley; Assistant Directors, David McGiffert, Joseph Reidy; Original Songs, Alan and Marilyn Bergman (Lyrics), Dave Grusin (Music); Sung by Stephen Bishop; In Panavision and color; 116 minutes; Rated PG; December release

CAST

Michael Dorsey/Dorothy Michaels	Dustin Hoffman
Julie	Jessica Lange
Sandy	Teri Garr
Ron	Dabney Coleman
Les	Charles Durning
Jeff	Bill Murray
George Fields	Sydney Pollack
John Van Horn	George Gaynes
April	Geena Davis
Rita	Doris Belack
Jacqui	Ellen Foley
Rick	Peter Gatto
Jo	Lynne Thigpen
Phil Weintraub	Ronald L. Schwary
Mrs. Mallory	Debra Mooney
Amy	Amy Lawrence
Boy	Kenny Sinclair
Page	Susan Merson
Middle-aged Men	Michael Ryan, James Carruthers
Stage Hand	Robert D. Wilson
Middle-aged Woman	Estelle Getty
Linda	Christine Ebersole
Actors	Bernie Pollack, Sam Stoneburner
Salesgirl	Marjorie Lovett

and Willy Switkes (Man at cab), Gregory Camillucci (Maitre D'), Barbara Spiegel (Billie), Tony Craig (Joel), Walter Cline (Bartender), Suzanne von Schaack (Party Girl), Anne Shropshire (Mrs. Crawley), Pamela Lincoln (Secretary), Mary Donnet (Receptionist), Bernie Passeltiner (Mac), Mallory Jones, Patti Cohane (Girls), Murray Schisgal (Party Guest), Greg Gorman (Photographer), Anne Prager (Acting Student), John Carpenter, Bob Levine (Actors), Richard Whiting (Priest), Tom Mardirosian, Jim Jansen (Stage Managers), Richard Wirth (Mel), Gavin Reed (Director), Annie Korzen, Ibbits Warriner, Lois de Banzie, Stephen C. Prutting, Carole Holland (Autograph Hounds)

Left: Dustin Hoffman, Jessica Lange Top: Dustin Hoffman
©Columbia

1982 Academy Award for Best Supporting Actress (Jessica Lange)

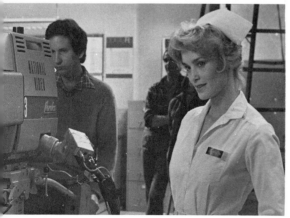

Jessica Lange

Teri Garr (C)

Dustin Hoffman, Dabney Coleman, George Gaynes Above: Hoffman, Charles Durning Top: Teri Garr, Dustin Hoffman

Sydney Pollack, Dustin Hoffman Above: Hoffman, George Gaynes, Top: Hoffman, Jessica Lange

HONKYTONK MAN

(WARNER BROS.) Producer-Director, Clint Eastwood; Executive Producer, Fritz Manes; Screenplay, Clancy Carlile from his novel; Photography, Bruce Surtees; Designer, Edward Carfagno; Editors, Ferris Webster, Michael Kelly, Joel Cox; Assistant Directors, Tony Brown, Tom Seidman; In Technicolor; 122 minutes; Rated PG; December release

CAST

Red Stovall	Clint Eastwood
Whit	Kyle Eastwood
Grandpa	John McIntire
Marlene	Alexa Kenin
Emmy	Verna Bloom
Virgil	Matt Clark
Arnspriger	Barry Corbin
Snuffy	Jerry Hardin
Highway Patrolman	Tim Thomerson
Dr. Hines	Macon McCalman
Henry Axle	Joe Regalbuto
Jim Bob	Gary Grubbs
Belle	Rebecca Clemons
Bob Wills	John Gimble
Flossie	Linda Hopkins
Lulu	Bette Ford
Junior	Jim Boelsen
Pooch	Tracey Walter
Miss Maud	Susan Peretz
Jack Wade	John Russell
Stubbs	Charles Cyphers
Smoky	Marty Robbins

and Ray Price, Shelly West, David Frizzell (Singers), Porter Wagoner (Dusty), Bob Ferrera, Tracy Shults, R. J. Ganzert, Hugh Warden, Kelsie Blades, Jim Ahart, Steve Autry, Peter Griggs, Julie Hoopman, Rozelle Gayle, Robert V. Barron, DeForest Covan, Lloyd Nelson, George Orrison, Glenn Wright, Frank Reinhard, Roy Jenson, Sherry Allurd, Gordon Terry, Tommy Alsup, Merle Travis, Robert D. Carver, Thomas Powels

Right: Clint Eastwood, Alexa Kenin Top: Kyle Eastwood, Clint Eastwood
© *Warner Bros.*

Clint Eastwood, Kyle Eastwood

Linda Hopkins, Clint Eastwood

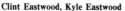

THE TOY

(COLUMBIA) Producer, Phil Feldman; Director, Richard Donner; Screenplay, Carol Sobieski; Photography, Laszlo Kovacs; Based on film by Francis Veber; Associate Producer, Margaret Booth; Music, Patrick Williams; Designer, Charles Harris; Editors, Richard Harris, Michael A. Stevenson; Assistant Directors, Bill Scott, Frank Bueno, Paul Moen; Costumes, Moss Mabry; A Rastar Film in color; 110 minutes; Rated PG; December release

CAST

Jack Brown	Richard Pryor
U. S. Bates	Jackie Gleason
Mr. Morehouse	Ned Beatty
Eric Bates	Scott Schwartz
Fancy Bates	Teresa Ganzel
Barkley	Wilfrid Hyde-White
Angela	Annazette Chase
Clifford	Tony King
O'Brien	Don Hood
Fraulein	Karen Leslie-Lyttle
Ruby Simpson	Virginia Capers
Geffran	B. J. Hopper
Honey Russell	Linda McCann
Senator Newcomb	Ray Spruell
District Attorney Russell	Stocker Fontelieu
Aerobics Class Leader	Stuart Baker-Bergen
Jack's Neighbor	Elbert Andre Patrick
Grand Dragon	Orwin Harvey
Clancy	Jim Clancy
Eugene Russell	Davis Hotard
Terry Gay	Debra Cole
Mrs. Newcomb	Marilyn Gleason
State Troopers	Steve Kahan, Paul Tuerpe
Klan Demonstrators	Jim Beyer, Tot Beyer
Drunk in jail	Robert M. Stevens
Morehouse's Secretary	Sally Birdsong
Chauffeur	Louis Weinberg
Bates' Secretary	Lucy Campbell Rowland
Man in carwash	Robert Cherry

and Robert Adams, Mark Bennett, John R. Wilson (Store Executives), Robert Costley, Robert Earle, Pauline Barcelona, Juan Coleman, Valerian Smith (Poker Players), Annie McGuire, Beverly Tagge, George Howard, Helen Howard (Party Guests), Bill Holliday, J. D. Martin, James Roddy (Police), Delana Renay Cole, Lewis Baker, LaMonica Matthews, Bruce Langley, Dawnis Kaye Smith, Santos Swing, Willie Swing (Ruby's Children)

Richard Pryor, Scott Schwartz Top Right: Ned Beatty, Pryor, Don Hood
©*Columbia*

Richard Pryor, Jackie Gleason Above: Teresa Ganzel, Gleason

FRANCES

(UNIVERSAL) Producer, Jonathan Sanger; Director, Graeme Clifford; Screenplay, Eric Bergren, Christopher DeVore, Nicholas Kazan; Co-Producer, Marie Yates; Photography, Laszlo Kovacs; Designer, Richard Sylbert; Editor, John Wright; Original Score, John Barry; Costumes, Patricia Norris; Associate Producer, Charles Mulvehill; Assistant Directors, Ed Milkovich, William Scott; Art Director, Ida Random; Set Designer, Emad Helmey; In Technicolor and Dolby Stereo; 141 minutes; Rated R; December release

CAST

Frances Farmer .... Jessica Lange
Harry York .... Sam Shepard
Lillian Farmer .... Kim Stanley
Ernest Farmer .... Bart Burns
and Jonathan Banks (Hitchhiker), Bonnie Bartlett (Stylist), James Brodhead (Sgt.), J. J. Chaback (Lady in hotel), Jordan Charney (Harold Clurman), Daniel Chodes (Director), Rod Colbin (Judge), Donald Craig (Ralph Edwards), Sarah Cunningham (Alma), Lee DeBroux (Director), Jeffrey DeMunn (Clifford Odets), Jack Fitzgerald (Clapper Man), Nancy Foy (Autograph Girl), Anne Haney (Hairdresser), Richard Hawkins (Bum), James Karen (Judge), Darrell Larson (Spy), Patricia Larson (Mrs. Hillier), Albert Lord (A.D.), Vincent Lucchesi (Arresting Sgt.), Jack Manning (Photographer), Gerald S. O'Loughlin (Doctor), Woodrow Parfrey (Dr. Doyle), Christopher Pennock (Dick), Rod Pilloud (Martoni), Larry Pines (Man on phone), John Randolph (Judge), Allan Rich (Bebe), Jack Riley (Barnes), David V. Schroeder (Lawyer), Helen Schustack (Wardrobe Mistress), Sandra Seacat (Drama Teacher), Charles Seaverns (Realtor), Lane Smith (Dr. Symington), Karin Strandjord (Connie), Andrew Winner (Firechief), Vern Taylor (Executive), Biff Yaeger (Cop), Keone Young (Doctor), Alexander Zale (Man in screening room)

Sam Shepard Top: Kim Stanley

Top: Jessica Lange
© *Universal*

Jessica Lange, also above (C) and Top with Sam Shepard   **Jessica Lange, Kim Stanley Above and Top: Jessica Lange**

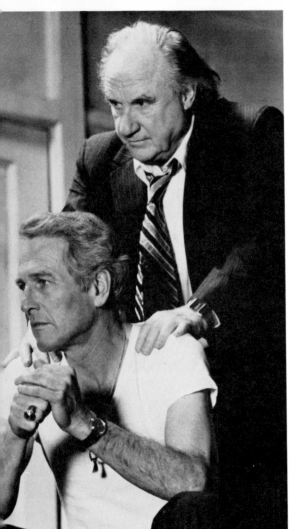

THE VERDICT

(20th CENTURY-FOX) Producers, Richard D. Zanuck, David Brown; Director, Sidney Lumet; Screenplay, David Mamet; Based on novel by Barry Reed; Executive Producer, Burtt Harris; Costumes, Anna Hill Johnstone; Designer, Edward Pisoni; Photography, Andrzej Bartkowiak; Editor, Peter Frank; Music, Johnny Mandel; Assistant Directors, Burtt Harris, Robert E. Warren; Art Director, John Kasarda; In Technicolor; 129 minutes; Rated R; December release

CAST

Frank Galvin	Paul Newman
Laura Fischer	Charlotte Rampling
Mickey Morrissey	Jack Warden
Ed Concannon	James Mason
Judge Hoyle	Milo O'Shea
Kaitlin Costello Price	Lindsay Crouse
Bishop Brophy	Edward Binns
Maureen Rooney	Julie Bovasso
Sally Doneghy	Roxanne Hart
Kevin Doneghy	James Handy
Dr. Towler	Wesley Addy
Dr. Thompson	Joe Seneca
Dr. Gruber	Lewis Stadlen
Joseph Alito	Kent Broadhurst
Billy	Colin Stinton
Jimmy the bartender	Burtt Harris
Young Priest	Scott Rhyne
Deborah Ann Kaye	Susan Benenson
Dr. Gruber's Nurse	Evelyn Moore
Dr. Gruber's Maid	Juanita Fleming
Bailiff	Jack Collard
Clerk	Ralph Douglas
Jury Foreman	Gregor Roy
Funeral Director	John Blood
Manager 2nd Funeral Parlor	Dick McGoldrick
Widow's Son	Edward Mason
Irish Nurses	Patty O'Brien, Maggie Task
Friedman	Joseph Bergman
Abrams	Herbert Rubens
John/Cigar Stand	J. P. Foley
Wheelchair Patient	Leib Lensky
Courthouse Lawyer	Clay Dear
Courthouse Guard	J. J. Clark
Waiter/Sheraton Bar	Greg Doucette
Sheraton Bartender	Tony LaFortezza
Sheraton Patrons	Marvin Beck, Herb Peterson

Left: Paul Newman, Jack Warden
© *20th Century-Fox*

Paul Newman, Charlotte Rampling

James Mason, Paul Newman

Milo O'Shea, James Mason, Paul Newman Left Center: Paul Newman, Joe Seneca
Top: Lindsay Crouse, James Mason Right: Paul Newman

SOPHIE'S CHOICE

(UNIVERSAL) Producers, Alan J. Pakula, Keith Barish; Direction and Screenplay, Alan J. Pakula; Based on novel by William Styron; Photography, Nestor Almendros; Designer, George Jenkins; Editor, Evan Lottman; Costumes, Albert Wolsky; Original Music, Marvin Hamlisch; Associate Producer, William C. Gerrity; Executive Producer, Martin Starger; Assistant Directors, Alex Hapsas, Joseph Ray; Art Director, John J. Moore; Presented by Lord Grade for ITC Entertainment; In Technicolor; 157 minutes; Rated R; December release

CAST

Sophie	Meryl Streep
Nathan	Kevin Kline
Stingo	Peter MacNicol
Narrator	Josef Sommer
In Brooklyn:	
Yetta	Rita Karin
Larry	Stephen D. Newman
Leslie Lapidus	Greta Turken
Morris Fink	Josh Mostel
Astrid Weinstein	Marcell Rosenblatt
Moishe Rosenblum	Moishe Rosenfeld
Lillian Grossman	Robin Bartlett
Polish Professor	Eugene Lipinski
Librarian	John Rothman
Dr. Blackstock	Joseph Leon
English Teacher	David Wohl
English Students	Nina Polan, Alexander Sirotin, Armand Dahan
Reporter	Joseph Tobin
Bellboy	Cortez Nance
In Poland:	
Rudolf Hoess	Gunther Maria Halmer
SS Doctor	Karlheinz Hackl
Frau Hoess	Ulli Fessl
Emmi Hoess	Melanie Pianka
Prisoner Housekeeper	Krystyna Karkowska
Wanda	Katharina Thalbach
Josef	Neddim Prohic
Sophie's Children	Jennifer Lawn, Adrian Kalitka
Hoess' Aide	Peter Wegenbreth
Female SS Guard	Vida Jerman
Sophie's Father	Ivo Pajer
Sophie as a child	Michaela Karacic

Meryl Streep, Kevin Kline

Top: Peter MacNicol, Meryl Streep, Kevin Kline
©Universal

1982 Academy Award for Best Actress (Meryl Streep)

Kevin Kline, Meryl Streep, Peter MacNicol Above: Kline, Streep Top: Kline, MacNicol

Meryl Streep, Kevin Kline Above: Streep, MacNicol Top: MacNicol, Greta Turken

BEST FRIENDS

(WARNER BROS.) Executive Producer, Joe Wizan; Producers, Norman Jewison, Patrick Palmer; Director, Norman Jewison; Screenplay, Valerie Curtin, Barry Levinson; Photography, Jordan Cronenweth; Editor, Don Zimmerman; Art Director, Joe Russo; Music, Michel Legrand; Costumes, Betsy Cox; Assistant Director, Win Phelps; 116 minutes; Rated PG; December release

CAST

Richard Babson	Burt Reynolds
Paula McCullen	Goldie Hawn
Eleanor McCullen	Jessica Tandy
Tim McCullen	Barnard Hughes
Ann Babson	Audra Lindley
Tom Babson	Kennan Wynn
Larry Weisman	Ron Silver
Nellie Ballou	Carol Locatell
Jorge Medina	Richard Libertini
Carol Brandon	Peggy Walton-Walker
Lyle Ballou	Noah Hathaway
Robbie Ballou	Mikey Martin

Top Left: Burt Reynolds, Audra Lindley, Goldie Hawn Below: Burt Reynolds, Jessica Tandy
© *Warner Bros.*

Barnard Hughes, Jessica Tandy, Burt Reynolds

Goldie Hawn, Audra Lindley Above: Hawn, Burt Reynolds

Gary Swanson, Season Eubley in "Vice Squad"
©Avco Embassy

Jeff Bridges, Bianca Jagger in "American Success"
©Columbia

VICE SQUAD (AVCO Embassy) Executive Producers, Sandy Howard, Bob Rehme, Frank Capra, Jr.; Producer, Brian Frankish; Director, Gary A. Sherman; Screenplay, Sandy Howard, Robert Vincent O'Neil, Kenneth Peters; Associate Producer, Frank Hildebrand; Photography, John Alcott; Assistant Directors, Bob Becker, Dick Espinoza; Designer, Lee Fischer; Editor, Roy Watts; Costumes, Bernadette O'Brien; In CFI Color; 97 minutes; Rated R; January release. CAST: Season Hubley (Princess), Gary Swanson (Tom), Wings Hauser (Ramrod), Pepe Serna (Pete), Beverly Todd (Louise), Joseph DiGiroloma (Kowalski), Maurice Emmanuel (Edwards), Wayne Hackett (Sorenson), Nina Blackwood (Ginger), Sudana Bobatoon (Dixie), Lydia Lei (Coco), Kelly Piper (Blue Chip), Kirstoffer Anders (Sgt. Brooks), Joseph Baroncini (Ted), Fred A. Berry (Dorsey), Tom Brent (Happy), Grand Bush (Black Pimp), Marilyn Coleman (Beatrice), Michael Ensign (Chauffeur), Nate Esformes (The John), Stacy Everly (Junkie), Clifford Frazier (Mace), Lyla Graham (Mrs. Cruikshank), Peter Harrell (Dude), Jonathan Haze (Dapper Man), Vincent J. Issac (Silky), Cyndi James-Reese (Black Whore), Ben Kronen (Elderly Man), Bob Laird, Doug Laird (Motorcycle Officers), Robert Miano (Sgt.), Richard Milholland (Driver), Vahan Mooseekian (Doctor), Mark Ness (Cab Driver), Stack Pierce (Rosco), Barbara Pilavin (Derelict), Donald Rawley (Gregory), David Ross (Officer), Stan Ross (Drunk), Cheryl Smith (White Whore), Hugo Stanger (Old Man at mansion), Arnold Turner (Boss Player), Nicole Volkoff (Lisa), Richard Wetzel (Fast Eddie), Ark Wong (Mr. Wong)

THE SEDUCTION (AVCO Embassy) Producers, Irwin Yablans, Bruce Cohn Curtis; Executive Producers, Joseph Wolf, Frank Capra, Jr., Chuck Russell; Direction and Screenplay, David Schmoeller; Associate Producer, Tom Curtis; Music, Lalo Schifrin; Editor, Tony DiMarco; Photography, Mac Ahlberg; Assistant Directors, Peter Manoogian, Betsy Magruder; In CFI Color; 104 minutes; Rated R; January release. CAST: Morgan Fairchild (Jamie), Michael Sarrazin (Brandon), Vince Edwards (Maxwell), Andrew Stevens (Derek), Colleen Camp (Robin), Kevin Brophy (Bobby), Wendy Smith Howard (Julie), Woodrow Parfrey (Salesman), Betty

Kean (Mrs. Caluso), Joanne Linville (Dr. Weston), Marri Mak (Lisa), Richard Reed (Floor Manager), Robert DeSimone (Photographer), Michael Griswold (Anchorman), Marilyn Staley (Newscaster), John Rose (Mrs. Wilson), Shailar Schmoeller (Ricky), Marilyn Wolf (Waitress), Jeffrey Richman (Technical Director), Kathryn Hart, Deborah Koppel (Teleprompter Girls)

AMERICAN SUCCESS (Columbia) January release. Carried in Volume 32 as "The American Success Company."

A STRANGER IS WATCHING (MGM/UA) Producer, Sidney Beckerman; Director, Sean S. Cunningham; Screenplay, Earl MacRauch, Victor Miller; Based on novel by Mary Higgins Clark; Photography, Barry Abrams; Editor, Susan E. Cunningham; Music, Lalo Schifrin; Associate Producer, Jack Grossberg; Art Director, Virginia Field; Assistant Directors, Jerry Leeds, Dan Eriksen; In Metrocolor; 92 minutes; Rated R; January release. CAST: Kate Mulgrew (Sharon), Rip Torn (Artie), James Naughton (Steve), Shawn von Schreiber (Julie), Barbara Baxley (Lally), Stephen Joyce (Detective), James Russo (Ronald)

EVILSPEAK (Moreno) Producers, Sylvio Tabet, Eric Weston; Director, Eric Weston; Screenplay, Joseph Garofalo, Eric Weston; Photography, Irv Goodnoff; Associate Producers, Gerald Hopman, H. Hal Harris; In color; 89 minutes; January release. CAST: Clint Howard, R. G. Armstrong, Joseph Cortese, Claude Earl Jones, Haywood Nelson, Don Stark, Charles Tyner, Lynn Hancock

DRIVE-IN MASSACRE (New American) Executive Producer, Martin W. Greenwald; Producer-Director, Stuart Segall; Screenplay, John Goff, Buck Flower; Photography, Kenneth Lloyd Gibb; Music, Lonjohn Productions; Assistant Director, Ken Dalton; In color; 78 minutes; Rated R; January release. CAST: Jake Barnes, Adam Lawrence, Douglas Gudbye, Newton Naushaus, Norman Sherlock, Valdesta

Michael Sarrazin, Morgan Fairchild in "The Seduction"
©Avco Embassy

Kate Mulgrew, Rip Torn, Shawn von Schreiber
in "A Stranger Is Watching" ©Heron Pro.

Tyne Daly, Mike Gomez, Kelly Ward, Daniel Valdez, Edward
James Olmos in "Zoot Suit"
©*Universal*

"Vernon, Florida"
©*New Yorker*

ZOOT SUIT (Universal) Producer, Peter Burrell; Executive Producer, Gordon Davidson; Direction and Screenplay, Luis Valdez; Based on his play of the same title; Photography, David Myers; Designer, Tom H. John; Editor, Jacqueline Cambas; Costumes, Yvonne Wood; Choreography, Patricia Birch; Music, Daniel Valdez, Shorty Rogers; Co-Producers, Kenneth Brecher, William P. Wingate; Associate Producer, Phillip Exparza; Assistant Directors, Win Phelps, Lisa Marmon; A Mark Taper Forum Presentation in color; 103 minutes; rated R; January release. CAST: Daniel Valdez (Henry Reyna), Edward James Olmos (El Pachuco), Charles Aidman (George), Tyne Daly (Alice), John Anderson (Judge), Abel Franco (Enrique), Mike Gomez (Joey), Alma Rose Martinez (Lupe), Frank McCarthy (Press), Lupe Ontiveros (Dolores), Ed Peck (Lt. Edwards), Robert Phalen (D.A.), Tony Plana (Rudy), Rose Portillo (Della), Marco Rodriguez (Smiley), Kelly Ward (Tommy), Helena Andreyko (Blondie), Bob Basso (Bailiff), Darlene Bryan (Little Blue), Bernadette Cologne (Legs), Miguel Delgado (Rafas), Roberta Delgado (Tillie), Anacani Echeverria, Bertha E. Oropeza, Candice L. Silva (Pachuca Vocalists), Carlos Garcia (Budda), Honey Garcia (Chola), James Hogan (Shore Patrol), Laura Leyva (Elena), Sal Lopez (Hobo), Luis Manuel (Cholo), Kim Miyori (Manchuka), Angela Moya (Bertha), Jeff Reynolds (P-Coat), Juan Rios (Crow), Greg Rosatti (Leatherneck), Nancy Salis (Bonita), Geno Silva (Galindo), Kurtwood Smith (Sgt. Smith), Dennis Stewart (Swabbie), Duke Stroud (Guard), Judy Susman (Sugarfoot), Jon Thomas (Ragman), Lewis Whitlock (Zooter), Antonette Yuskis (Guera), Robert Beltran (Lowrider), Alma Beltran (His Mother), Julio Medina (His Father), Socorro Valdez (His Girlfriend), Diane Rodriguez (Stenographer)

FOX STYLE KILLER (Aquarius) Producer, Paul R. Picard; Executive Producer, R. B. McGowen, Jr.; Director, Clyde Houston; Screenplay, Clyde Houston, Michael Fox; In CFI color; Rated R; 88 minutes; January release. CAST: Chuck Daniel, Juanita Moore, Denise Denise, Hank Rolike, Jovita Bush, Richard Lawson, Newell Alexander, Reuben Collins, John Taylor

BOSS LADY (Lima) Producer-Director, Chris Warfield; Screenplay, John Hayes; Music, Jack Stern; Editor, Meri McDonald; Photography, Elton Fuller; In color; 80 minutes; Rated R; January release. CAST: Claudia Smith, John Nuzzo, Candy Townsend, Fay Williams, Robert Atwood

POLITICS OF POISON (Cinema Ventures) Director, David Rabinovitch; In color; 60 minutes; Not rated; January release. A documentary focusing on the controversy in Humboldt County, California over the spraying of herbicides. Narrated by Michael Learned.

VERNON, FLORIDA (New Yorker) Producer-Director, Errol Morris; Photography, Ned Burgess; Editor, Brad Fuller; Music, Claude Register; In color; 60 minutes; Not rated; January release. CAST: Claude Register, Albert Bitterling, Henry Shipes, Snake Reynolds, Roscoe Collins, Coy Brock, Joe Payne, George Harris, Ray Cotton, Mr. and Mrs. J. W. Martin

IN OUR WATER (Film Forum) Producer-Director, Meg Switzgable; Associate Producer-Editor, Mona Davis; Photography, Barry Sonnenfeld, Robert Chappell, Dick Blofson, Ken Kelsh; Music, Jeffrey Berman; Not rated; 60 minutes; January release. A documentary on water pollution.

NEVER NEVER LAND (Sharp Features) Producer, Diane Baker; Director, Paul Annell; Screenplay, Marjorie L. Sigley; In color; Rated G; January release. CAST: Petula Clark, Cathleen Nesbitt, Anne Seymour, Michael J. Shannon

Mr. and Mrs. Fred Kaler in "In Our Water"
©*Film Forum*

Carla Tuten, Jackie Hall, Joanne Johnston in "Soldier Girls"
©*First Run*

Fred McCarren in "The Boogens"
©*Jensen Farley*

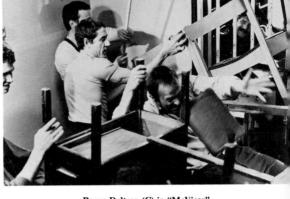

Roger Daltrey (C) in "McVicar"
©*Crown International*

THE BOOGENS (Jensen Farley) Producer, Charles E. Sellier, Jr.; Director, James L. Conway; Associate Producers, Bill Cornford, Cliff Osmond; Screenplay, David O'Malley, Bob Hunt; Story, Tom Chapman, David O'Malley; Music, Bob Summers; Costumes, Julie Staheli; Assistant Directors, Leon Dudevoir, Jerry Fleck; Assistant Producer, Carole Fontana; Editor, Jill Taggart; In color; 95 minutes; Rated R; January release. CAST: Rebecca Balding (Trish), Fred McCarren (Mark), Anne-Marie Martin (Jessica), Jeff Harlan (Roger), John Crawford (Brian), Med Flory (Dan), Jon Lormer (Blanchard), Peg Stewart (Victoria), Scott Wilkinson (Deputy), Marcia Reider (Martha)

MADMAN (Jensen Farley) Executive Producer, Sam Marion; Producer, Gary Sales; Screenplay and Direction, Joe Giannone; Music and Lyrics, Gary Sales; a Legend Lives Co. presentation in color; 89 minutes; Rated R; January release. CAST: Paul Ehlers (Madman), Alexis Dubin, Tony Fish, Harriet Bass, Seth Jones, Jan Claire, Alex Murphy, Jimmy Steele, Carl Fredericks, Michael Sullivan

SOLDIER GIRLS (First Run Features) Directed by Nicholas Broomfield and Joan Churchill; Photography, Joan Churchill; Editor, Nicholas Broomfield; In color; 87 minutes; Not rated; January release. A documentary about a platoon of women undergoing basic training at Fort Gordon, Ga., with Joann Johnson, Jackie Hall, Clara Alves, and sergeants Abing, Bertling, Taylor.

BUTTERFLY (Analysis) Producer-Director, Matt Cimber; Screenplay, John Goff, Matt Cimber; Based on novel by James M. Cain; Adapted by Matt Cimber; Executive Producer, Tino Barzie; Music, Ennio Morricone; Photography, Eddy van der Enden; Editor, Brent Schoenfeld; Assistant Director, Sanford Hampton; Art Director, Dave de Carlo; In color; 108 minutes; Rated R; February release. CAST: Stacy Keach (Jess), Pia Zadora (Kady), Orson Welles (Judge), Lois Nettleton (Belle), Edward Albert (Wash), James Franciscus (Moke), Stuart Whitman (Rev. Rivers), June Lockhart (Mrs. Gillespie), Ed McMahon (Mr. Gillespie), Paul Hampton (Norton), Buck Flower (Ed), Ann Dane (Janey), Greg Gault (Bridger), John

O'Connor White (Billy Roy), Peter Jason (Allen), Kim Ptak (Deputy), Leigh Christian (Saleslady), Dr. Abraham Rudnick (Court Stenographer), John Goff (Truck Driver), Dylan Urquidi (Danny)

McVICAR (Crown International) Producers, Bill Curbishley, Roy Baird, Roger Daltrey; Executive Producers, David Gideon Thomson, Jackie Curbishley; Director, Tom Clegg; Associate Producer, John Peverall; Music, Jeff Wayne; Photography, Vernon Layton; Assistant Directors, Barry Langley, Roy Stevens, Jerry Daly; Art Director, Brian Ackland-Snow; Editor, Peter Boyle; 111 minutes; Not rated; February release. CAST: Roger Daltrey (McVicar), Adam Faith (Probyn), Cheryl Campbell (Sheila), Steven Berkoff (Harrison), Brian Hall (Stokes), Jeremy Blake (Johnson), Leonard Gregory (Collins), Peter Jonfield (Harris), Anthony Trent (Tate), Matthew Scurfield (Jeffries), Joe Turner (Panda), Terence Stuart (Sid), Charlie Cork (Martin), Ronald Herdman (Nobby), Tony Haygarth (Rabies), Tony Rohr (Bootsie), Ralph Watson (Principal Officer E Wing), Richard Simpson (Douglas), Allan Mitchell (Jackson), Stanley Lloyd (Magistrate), Mikki Margorian (Secretary), James Marcus (Sewell), Georgina Hale (Kate), Anthony May (Billy), Malcolm Tierney (Frank), Raymond Skipp (Bimbo), Billy Murray (Joey), John Rolfe (Graham), Ricky Parkinson (Russell), David Beames (Policeman), Robert Walker (Co-driver), Jamie Foreman (Driver), Ian Hendry (Hitchens), Malcolm Terris (Principal Officer), Charles Cork, Paul Kember, Stephen Bent (Warders), Harry Fielder (Harry), Michael Feast (Cody)

THE KILLING OF AMERICA (Embassy) Produced and written by Leonard Schrader and Mataichiro Yamamoto; 90 minutes; Not rated; February release. A documentary examining the facts and images of violence and murder in the U.S.

DOCTOR JEKYLL'S DUNGEON OF DEATH (New American) Producer-Director, James Wood; Screenplay, James Mathers; Photography and Editing, James Wood; Music, Marty Allen; In color; 88 minutes; Rated R; February release. CAST: James Mathers (Dr. Jekyll), John Kearney, Tom Nicholson, Dawn Carver Kelly, Nadine Kalmes

Orson Welles in "Butterfly"
©*Analysis Films*

Alex Murphy, Harriet Bass, Jan Claire in "Madman"
©*Jensen Farley*

Peggy Lawson in "Dialogue with a Woman Departed"

Cherie Currie, Luca Bercovici in "Parasite"
© *Embassy*

SHANGHAI SHADOWS (Cinema Ventures) Producer-Director, David Rabinovitch; In color; 60 minutes; Not rated; February release; Narrated by Michael Learned. A documentary on the People's Republic of China.

THE LAST TASMANIAN (Cinema Ventures) Producer-Director, Tom Haydon; Written by Tom Haydon, Rhys Jones; Music, William Davies; Editor, Charles Rees; Narrated by Leo McKern; In color; 105 minutes; Not rated; February release. A documentary on the extermination of aborigines on the island of Tasmania.

DIALOGUE WITH A WOMAN DEPARTED (Film at the Public) Produced, directed, written, photographed and edited by Leo Hurwitz; 225 minutes; Not rated; February release. A documentary about the filmmaker's wife and co-worker Peggy Lawson, who died in 1971.

SWAMP THING (Embassy) Producers, Benjamin Melniker, Michael Uslan; Direction and Screenplay, Wes Craven; Photography, Robin Goodwin; Art Directors, David Nichols, Robb Wilson King; Editor, Richard Bracken; Music, Harry Manfredini; Assistant Directors, Todd Corman, Tony Cecere; Designer, Robb Wilson King; Costumes, Patricia Bolomet, Bennett Choate, Paul A. Simmons; In Technicolor; 92 minutes; Rated PG; March release. CAST: Louis Jourdan (Arcane), Adrienne Barbeau (Alice), Ray Wise (Dr. Holland), David Hess (Ferret), Nicholas Worth (Bruno), Don Knight (Ritter), Al Ruban (Charlie), Dick Durock (Swamp Thing), Ben Bates (Arcane Monster), Nannette Brown (Dr. Linda Holland), Reggie Batts (Jude), Mimi Meyer (Secretary), Karen Price (Messenger), Bill Erickson (Young Agent), Dov Gottesfeld (Commando), and Tommy Madden as Little Bruno

WASN'T THAT A TIME! (United Artists Classics) Producers, Jim Brown, George Stoney, Harold Leventhal; Director, Jim Brown; Written by Lee Hays; Editor, Paul Barnes; Photography, Jim Brown, Daniel Ducovny, Tom Hurwitz; Associate Producer, Ginger Turek; Assistant Directors, Sandy Smolan, Aldona Sabalis, Ed Cullen; In DuArt Color; 78 minutes; Rated PG; March release. a film about "The Weavers," a singing group that popularized folk music.

PARASITE (Embassy) Executive Producers, Joseph Wolf; Irwin Yablans; Producer-Director, Charles Band; Screenplay, Alan Adler, Michael Shoob, Frank Levering; Music, Richard Band; Special Effects, Stan Winston, James Kagel; Editor, Brad Arensman; Associate Producers, Richard Marcus, Michael Wolf; Photography, Mac Ahlberg; Art Director, Pamela B. Warner; Assistant Directors, Peter Manoogian, Betsy Magruder; Costumes, Lesley Lynn Nicholson; In Metrocolor and Stereovision; 85 minutes; Rated R; March release. CAST: Robert Glaudini (Dr. Paul Dean), Demi Moore (Patricia), Luca Bercovici (Ricus), James Davidson (Merchant), Al Fann (Collins), Tom Villard (Zeke), Scott Thomson (Chris), Cherie Currie (Dana), Vivian Blaine (Miss Dailey), James Cavan (Buddy), Joanelle Romero (Bo), Freddie Moore (Arn), Natalie May (Shell), Cheryl Smith (Captive Girl), Joel Miller (Punk)

CAT PEOPLE (Universal/RKO) Producer, Charles Fries; Director, Paul Schrader; Screenplay, Alan Ormsby; Based on story by DeWitt Bodeen; Executive Producer, Jerry Bruckheimer; Photography, John Bailey; Art Director, Edward Richardson; Editors, Bud Smith, Jacqueline Cambas; Music, Giorgio Moroder; Theme Lyrics written and performed by David Bowie; Special Effects, Albert Whitlock, Tom Burman, Assistant Directors, Michael F. Grillo, Stephen P. Dunn; Costumes, Daniel Paredes; In Technicolor and Dolby Stereo; 118 minutes; Rated R; March release. CAST: Nastassia Kinski (Irena Gallier), Malcolm McDowell (Paul Gallier), John Heard (Oliver), Annette O'Toole (Alice), Ruby Dee (Female), Ed Begley, Jr. (Joe), Scott Paulin (Bill), Frankie Faison (Det. Brandt), Ron Diamond (Det. Diamond), Lynn Lowry (Ruthie), John Larroquette (Bronte), Tessa Richarde (Billie), Patricia Perkins (Taxi Driver), Berry Berenson (Sandra), Fausto Barajas (Otis), John H. Fields (Manager Massage Parlor), Emery Hollier (Yeatman), Stephen Marshall (Moonie), Robert Pavlovitch (Ted), Julie Denney (Carol), Arione de Winter (Indian Village Mother), Francine Segal (Church Woman), Don Hood (Agent), David Showacre (Man in bar), Neva Gage (Cat-like Woman), Marisa Folse, Danelle Hand (Indian Girls), John C. Isbell (Police Officer), Roger Reid, Charles Joseph Konya, Jr., Marco St. John, Brett Alexander, Gregory Gatto, Terc Martinez, David Ross McCarty, Harold D. Hauss, James Deeth, Ray Wise, Jo Ann Dearing

Adrienne Barbeau, Reggie Batts in "Swamp Thing"
© *Embassy*

Nastassia Kinski, Malcolm McDowell in "Cat People"
© *Universal*

Cathryn Damon, Tim Choate, Wendy Fulton, Raymond Patterson in "First Time" ©*New Line*

Suzanne Weber, Pat Petersen in "Cold River" ©*Pacific International*

THE FIRST TIME (New Line Cinema) Executive Producers, Robert Shaye, Lawrence Loventhal; Producer, Sam Irvin; Associate Producer, Sara Risher; Director, Charlie Loventhal; Screenplay, Charlie Loventhal, Susan Weiser-Finley, W. Franklin Finley; A Goldmine Co. production in color; Rated R; March release. CAST: Tim Choate (Charlie), Krista Errickson (Dana), Marshall Efron (Rand), Wendy Fulton (Wendy), Raymond Patterson (Ron), Wallace Shawn (Goldfarb), Wendie Jo Sperber (Eileen), Cathryn Damon (Gloria), Jane Badler (Karen), Bradley Bliss (Melanie), Éva Charney (Polly), Bill Randolph (Rick), Rex Robbins (Leon), Robert Trebor (Joel)

THE ATOMIC CAFE (Archives Project) Produced and Directed by Kevin Rafferty, Jayne Loader, Pierce Rafferty; Editors, Jayne Loader, Kevin Rafferty; Music Coordinator, Rick Eaker; In color, black and white; 92 minutes; Not rated; March release. A pastiche of atomic bomb propaganda.

RICHARD PRYOR LIVE ON SUNSET STRIP (Columbia) Produced and written by Richard Pryor; Director, Joe Layton; Photography, Haskell Wexler; Designer, Michael Baugh; Editor, Sheldon Kahn; Assistant Director, Donald Yorkshire; Designer, Virginia Randolph; Costumes, Danielle Peredez; A Rastar Production in Metrocolor; 88 minutes; Rated R; March release. CAST: Richard Pryor at the Hollywood Palladium on two consecutive evenings.

CONAN THE BARBARIAN (Universal) Producers, Buzz Feitshans, Raffaella DeLaurentiis; Director, John Milius; Screenplay, John Milius, Oliver Stone; Executive Producers, D. Constantine Conte, Edward R. Pressman; Based on character created by Robert E. Howard; Photography, John Cabrera, Duke Callaghan; Designer, Ron Cobb; Editors, Fred Stafford, C. Timothy O'Meara; Music, Basil Poledouris; Costumes, John Bloomfield; Associate Producer, Edward Summer; Art Directors, Pierluigi Basile, Benjamin Fernandez; Assistant Director, Pepe Lopez Rodero; In Todd-AO and Technicolor; 129 minutes; Rated R; March release. CAST: Arnold Schwarzenegger (Conan), James Earl Jones (Thulsa Doom), Max von Sydow (King Osric), Sandahl Bergman (Valeria), Ben Davidson (Rexor), Cassandra Gaviola (Witch), Gerry Lopez (Subotai), Mako (Wizard), Valerie Quennessen (Princess), William Smith (Conan's

Father), Luis Barboo (Red Hair), Franco Columbo (Pictish Scout), Leslie Foldvary (Snake Girl), Gary Herman (Guard), Erick Holmey (Officer), Akio Mitamura (General), Nadiuska (Conan's Mother), Jorge Sanz (Young Conan), Jack Taylor (Priest), Sven Ole Thorsen (Thorgrim), Kiyoshi Yamasaki (Sword Master)

COLD RIVER (Pacific International) Produced, Directed and Written by Fred G. Sullivan; Executive Producers, Charles L. Ritchie, Jr., William A. Sweeney; Photography, Bil Godsey; Editor, John Carter; Music, Michael Gibson; Based on novel by William Judson; Song "Winter Nights": by Jim Wann, Michael Gibson; Sung by Cass Morgan; In color; 94 minutes; Rated PG; March release. CAST: Suzanne Weber (Lizzy), Pat Petersen (Tim), Richard Jaeckel (Mike), Robert Earl Jones (Trapper), Brad Sullivan (Reuben), Elizabeth Hubbard (Pauline), Augusta Dabney (Elizabeth), Adam Petroski (Seth), David Thomas (Senate Chairman), Wade Barnes (Senator), Deborah Beck (Reporter), Trent Gough (Minister), Robert Donley (Guide), Thomas Kubiak (Storekeeper), Mary Ellen Badger (Receptionist), Muriel Mason (Lady in wheelchair), Margo Lacy (Her Daughter), and Theodore C. Sweeney, Linda Videtti, Chris Curran, Ken Briell, Jan Naud

THE BEAST WITHIN (MGM/United Artists) Producers, Harvey Bernhard, Gabriel Katzka; Director, Philippe More; Story and Screenplay, Tom Holland; Based on novel by Edward Levy; Photography, Jack L. Richards; Editors, Robert Brown, Bert Lovitt; Music, Les Baxter; In Dolby Stereo, Panavision, and color; 98 minutes; Rated R; March release. CAST: Ronny Cox (Eli), Bibi Besch (Caroline), Paul Clemens (Michael), Don Gordon (Judge), R. G. Armstrong (Doc), Kitty Moffat (Amanda), L. Q. Jones (Sheriff), Logan Ramsey (Edwin), John Dennis Johnston (Horace), Luke Askew (Tom), Meshach Taylor (Deputy), Ron Soble (Tom)

BLOODSUCKING FREAKS (Troma) March release. Carried in Volume 28 as "The Incredible Torture Show."

Arnold Schwarzenegger, Sandahl Bergman in "Conan the Barbarian" ©*Universal*

"Richard Pryor Live on Sunset Strip" ©*Columbia*

Chuck Norris, Toni Kalem in "Silent Rage"
©*Columbia*

Phoebe Cates, Willie Aames in "Paradise"
©*Embassy*

JUST BEFORE DAWN (Picturemedia Limited) Producers, David Sheldon, Doro Vlado Hreljanovic; Director, Jeff Lieberman; Screenplay, Mark L. Arywitz, Gregg Irving; Based on story by Joseph Middleton; Music, Brad Fiedel; Executive Producers, Doro Vlado Hreljanovic, V. Paul Hreljanovic; In Panavision and Color; Rated R; March release. CAST: Chris Lemmon, Gregg Henry, Deborah Benson, Ralph Seymour, Jamie Rose, Mike Kellin, George Kennedy

10 VIOLENT WOMEN (New American) Producer-Director, Ted V. Mikels; Screenplay, Mr. Mikels, James Gordon White; Music, Nicholas Carras; In Eastmancolor; Presented by Joe Gage; 95 minutes; Rated R; March release. CAST: Sherri Vernon, Dixie Lauren, Georgia Morgan, Melodie Bell, Christina de Cattani

SILENT RAGE (Columbia) Producer, Anthony B. Unger; Director, Michael Miller; Screenplay, Joseph Fraley; Co-Producer, Andy Howard; Photography, Robert Jessup, Neil Roach; Art Director, Jack Marty; Editor, Richard C. Meyer; Music, Peter Bernstein, Mark Goldenberg; Associate Producer, Aaron Norris; Assistant Director, Robert P. Cohen, Alice West; In Metrocolor; 105 minutes; Rated R; April release. CAST: Chuck Norris (Dan), Ron Silver (Dr. Halman), Steven Keats (Dr. Spires),Toni Kalem (Alison), William Finley (Dr. Vaughn), Brian Libby (John), Stephen Furst (Charlie), Stephanie Dunnam (Nancy), Joyce Ingle (Mrs. Sims), Jay DePland (Bike Leader), Lillette Zoe Raley (Tatooed Mama), Mike Johnson, Linda Tatum, Kathy Lee, Desmond Dhooge, Joe Farago, John Barrett, Paula Selzer, Sandy Lang, Sonny Jones, Russel Higginbotham, Eddie Galt, David Andre Unger

SOUP FOR ONE (Warner Bros.) Producer, Marvin Worth; Direction and Screenplay, Jonathan Kaufer; Photography, Fred Schuler; Designer, Robert DeMora; Music, Nile Rodgers, Bernard Edwards, Johnny Mandel; Assistant Directors, Charles Okun, Thomas Reilly; In Technicolor; 87 minutes; Rated R; April release. CAST: Saul Rubinek (Allan), Marcia Strassman (Maria), Gerrit Graham (Brian), Teddy Pendergrass (Singer), Richard Libertini (Angelo), Andrea Martin (Seductress), Mordecai Lawner (Salesman), Lewis J. Stadlen (Allan's Father), Joanna Merlin (Allan's Mother), Christine Baranski, Ellen March, Maury Chaykin, Deborah Offner, Michael Jeter, Anna Deavere Smith, Laura Dean, Marley Friedman, Andrew Friedman, Jessica James, Kate Lynch, Suzzy Roche, Claudia Cron,

Cheri Jamison, Hilary Shapiro, Libby Boone, Catherine Lee Smith, Marisa Smith, Jamie Tirelli, Cristina San Juan, James Rebhorn, Ron Faber, Gloria Cromwell, Thomas Quinn, Rick Lieberman, Ellie Covan, Bo Rucker, Jack Chandler, Michael Pearlman, Lauren Sautner, Karen Werner, Maggie Jakobson, Max Gulack, William Cuellar, Mitchell Jason, Sherrie Bender, Kim Chan, Linda Ray, Lisa Parker, Merwin Goldsmith, Olivia K. Le'Aauanae

PARADISE (Embassy) Producers, Robert Lantos, Stephen J. Roth; Executive Producers, Bruce Mallen, Howard R. Lipson; Co-Producer, Wendy Grean; Direction and Screenplay, Stuart Gillard; Designer, Glaude Bonniere; Music, Paul Hoffert; Photography, Adam Greenberg; Costumes, Julie Ganton, Mary-Jane McCarty; Editor, Howard Terrill; Assistant Director, Jim Kaufman; In color; 100 minutes; Rated R; April release. CAST: Willie Aames (David), Phoebe Cates (Sarah), Richard Curnock (Geoffrey), Tuvia Tavi (The Jackal), Neil Vipond (Reverend), Aviva Marks (Rachel), Joseph Shiloach (Ahmed)

OUT OF THE BLUE (Discovery) Executive Producer, Paul Lewis; Director, Dennis Hopper; Screenplay, Leonard Yakir, Gary Jules Jouvenat; Photography, Marc Champion; Editor, Doris Dyck; Music, Tom Lavin; In color; Rated R; 94 minutes; April release. CAST: Linda Manz (CeBe), Sharon Farrell (Kathy), Dennis Hopper (Don), Raymond Burr (Brean), Don Gordon (Charlie)

BASKET CASE (Analysis) Producer, Edgar Ievins; Executive Producers, Arnie Bruck, Tom Kaye; Direction and Screenplay, Frank Henenlotter; Photography, Bruce Torbet; Editor, Frank Henenletter; Music, Gus Russo; In color; 90 minutes; Not rated; April release. CAST: Kevin Van Hentenryck (Duane), Terri Susan Smith (Sharon), Beverly Bonner (Casey), Robert Vogel (Hotel Manager), Diana Browne, Lloyd Pace, Bill Freeman (Doctors)

UNCENSORED CARTOONS (United Artists Classics) Compiled by Jerry Beck from Warner Brothers cartoons (mainly Merrie Melodies) originally produced by Leon Schlesinger; Animation Directors, Bob Clampett, Friz Freleng, Frank Tashlin, Chuck Jones, Tex Avery; Musical Director, Carl Stalling; In color; 73 minutes; Not rated; April release.

Gerrit Graham, Saul Rubinek in "Soup for One"
©*Warner Bros.*

Dennis Hopper, Sharon Farrell, Linda Manz in "Out of the Blue" ©*Discovery*

WARLORDS OF THE 21ST CENTURY (New World) formerly "Battletruck"; Producers, Lloyd Phillips, Rob Whitehouse; Director, Harley Cokliss; Screenplay, Irving Austin, Harley Cokliss, John Beech; Photography, Chris Menges; Editor, Michael Horton; Design, Gary Hansen; Art Director, Ron Highfield; Music, Kevin Peek; In color; 91 minutes; Rated PG; April release. CAST: Michael Beck (Hunter), Annie McEnroe (Corlie), James Wainwright (Straker), John Ratzenberger (Rusty), Randolph Powell (Judd), Bruno Lawrence (Willie), Diana Rowan (Charlene), John Bach (Bone)

THE SWORD AND THE SORCERER (Group I) Producers, Brandon Chase, Mariane Chase; Executive Producer, Robert S. Bremson; Director, Albert Pyun; Screenplay, Albert Pyun, Thomas Karnowski, John Stuckmeyer; Photography, Joseph Mangine; Editor, Marshall Harvey; Music, David Whittaker; Art Director, George Costello; In Dolby Stereo and color; 100 minutes; Rated R; April release. CAST: Lee Horsley (Talon), Kathleen Beller (Alana), Simon MacCorkindale (Mikah), George Maharis (Machelli), Richard Lynch (Cromwell), Richard Moll (Xusia), Anthony DeLongis (Rodrigo), Robert Tessier (Verdugo), Nina Van Pallandt (Maila), Anna Bjorn (Elizabeth)

PRANKS (New Image) Producer, Jeffrey Obrow; Directors, Jeffrey Obrow, Stephen Carpenter; Screenplay, Stephen Carpenter, Jeffrey Obrow, Stacey Giachino; Associate Producer, Stacey Giachino; Photography, Stephen Carpenter; Music, Chris Young; Assistant Director, John Hopkins; Editors, Jeffrey Obrow, Stephen Carpenter; Art Director, Charlotte Grant; In Getty Film Lab Color; 86 minutes; Rated R; April release. CAST: Laurie Lapinski (Joanne), Stephen Sachs (Craig), David Snow (Brian), Pamela Holland (Patti), Woody Ross (John), Dennis Ely (Bobby Lee), Jake Jones (Bill), Daphne Zuniga (Debbie), Richard Cowgill (Her Father), Kay Beth (Her Mother), Chandre (Alice), Robert Frederick (Tim), Chris Morrill (Jack), Jimmy Betz (Officer Lewis), Thomas Christian (Officer Dean), Billy Criswell (Rick), Robert Richardson, Chris Schroeder (Police)

PENITENTIARY II (MGM/UA) Produced, Directed and Written by James Fanaka; Photography, Steve Posey; Editor, James E. Nownes; Music, Jack W. Wheaton; In color; 109 minutes; Rated R; April release. CAST: Leon Isaac Kennedy (Too Sweet Gordon), Glynn Turman (Charles), Ernie Hudson (Half Dead), Mr. T (Himself), Peggy Blow (Ellen), Sephton Moody (Charles, Jr.), Donovan Womack (Jesse), Malik Carter (Seldom), Stan Kamber (Sam), Cepheus Jaxon (Do Dirty), Marvin Jones (Simp), Ebony Wright (Sugar), Eugenia Wright (Clarisse), Renn Woods (Nikki), Marci Thomas (Evelyn)

WHO SHALL LIVE AND WHO SHALL DIE (Kino International) Producers, James R. Kurth, Laurence Jarvik; Director, Laurence Jarvik; Photography, Reuben Aaronson; Editor, Mr. Jarvik; In color; 90 minutes; Not rated; April release. A documentary that examines the roles played by members of the U. S. Government and by American Jewish leaders in the efforts to save European Jews from extermination in Nazi concentration camps during World War II.

TOO FAR TO GO (Zoetrope) Producer, Chic Schultz; Executive Producer, Robert Geller; Associate Producer, David Kappes; Director, Fielder Cook; Screenplay, William Hanley; From stories by John Updike; Photography, Walter Lasally; Editor, Eric Albertson; Music, Elizabeth Swados; Art Director, Leon Munier; Assistant Director, Dwight Williams; In Technicolor; 100 minutes; Rated PG; April release. CAST: Blythe Danner (Joan), Michael Moriarty (Richard), Glenn Close (Rebecca), Ken Kercheval (Jack), Josef Sommer (Henry), Kathryn Walker (Marian), Doran Clark (Judith), Tim Holcomb (Richie), Margaret Schultz ("Bean"), Adam Storke (John), Thomas Hill (Psychiatrist)

SOGGY BOTTOM U.S.A. (Gaylord) Producer, Elmo Williams; Director, Ted Flicker; Screenplay, Eric Edson, Stephen C. Burnham, Joy N. Houck, Jr.; Story, Hal L. Harrison, Jr.; Music, Larry Cansler; Lyrics, John Stewart, Gary White; In color; Rated PG; April release. CAST: Ben Johnson, Anne Wedgeworth, Lois Nettleton, Dub Taylor, Anthony Zerbe, Jack Elam, P. J. Soles, Lane Smith, Don Johnson

HOSPITAL MASSACRE (Cannon) Producers, Menahem Golan, Yoram Globus; Director, Boaz Davidson; Screenplay, Marc Behm; Associate Producer, Christopher Pearce; Photography, Nicholas von Sternberg; Design, Jac McAnelly; Music, Arlon Ober; Assistant Directors, Steve McGlothen, Don Grenough; In color; Rated R; 90 minutes; April release. CAST: Barbi Benton (Susan), Chip Lucia (Harry), Jon Van Ness (Jack), John Warner Williams (Saxon), Gay Austin (Jacobs), Den Surles (Beam), Michael Frost (Ned), Karen Smith (Kitty), Marian Beeler, Elly Wold, Jonathan Moore, Tammy Simpson, Bill Errigo, Lanny Duncan, Thomas McClure, Beverly Hart, Jon Greene

Eugenia Wright, Leon Isaac Kennedy in "Penitentiary II"
©UA/MGM

MARK OF THE WITCH (Lone Star) Producers, Mary Davis, Tom Moore; Executive Producer, R. B. McGowen, Jr.; Director, Tom Moore; Screenplay, Mary Davis, Martha Peters; A Presidio Production in CFI Color; Rated R; 84 minutes; April release. CAST: Robert Elston, Anitra Walsh, Darryl Wells, Barbara Brownell, Jack Gardner, Marie Santell

PANDEMONIUM (MGM/UA) Executive Producer, Barry Krost; Producer, Doug Chapin; Director, Alfred Sole; Screenplay, Richard Whitley, Jaime Klein; Photography, Michel Hugo; Music, Dana Kaproff; Costumes, Roberta Weiner; Editor, Eric Jenkins; Design, Jack DeShields; Art Director, James Claytor; Assistant Directors, Ed Milkovich, Jack Clements; Associate Producers, Jaime Klein, Richard Whitley; In Panavision and Technicolor; 82 minutes; Rated PG; April release. CAST: Tom Smothers (Cooper), Debralee Scott (Sandy), Candy Azzara (Bambi), Suzanne Kent, Phil Hartmann, Michael Kless, David L. Lander, Bradley Lieberman, Victoria Carroll, Teri Landrum, Alix Elias, Ebbe Roe Smith, Randy Bennett, Miles Chapin, Marc McClure, Pat Ast, David Becker, Paul Reubens, John Paragon, Don McLeod, David McCharen, Richard C. Adams, Nancy Ryan, Jim Boeke, and special appearances by Gary Allen, Eve Arden, Kaye Ballard, Tab Hunter, Sydney Lassick, Edie McClurg, Jim McKrell, Lenny Montana, Donald O'Connor, Richard Romanus, Izabella Telezynska

DEATH VALLEY (Universal) Producer, Elliott Kastner; Director, Dick Richards; Co-Producer-Screenplay, Richard Rothstein; Co-Producer, Stanley Beck; Associate Producer, Stanley Mark; Photography, Stephen H. Burum; Art Director, Allen H. Jones; Editor, Joel E. Cox; Music, Dana Kaproff; Assistant Directors, Frank C. Beetson, Clark Paylow, Tad Devlin, William Braden; In Technicolor; 90 minutes; Rated R; May release. CAST: Paul LeMat (Mike), Catherine Hicks (Sally), Stephen McHattie (Hal), A. Wilford Brimley (Sheriff), Peter Billingsley (Billy), Edward Herrmann (Paul), Jack O'Leary (Earl), Mary Steelsmith (Baby Sitter), Gina Christian (R.V. Girl), Kirk I. Kiskella, Frank J. Cimorelli (R.V. Boys), Fred W. S. Newton (Outlaw), Arnold C. Waterman (Onlooker), J. P. S. Brown (Western Sheriff), Roy S. Gunsburg (Tour Guide), Glenn McCreedy (Stu), Merritt Holloway (Motel Clerk), Earl W. Smith, Allan Wood (Cronies)

Blythe Danner, Michael Moriarty in "Too Far to Go"
©Zoetrope

103

James Andronica, Michael Sarrazin, Tom Skerritt in "Fighting Back" © *Paramount*

FIGHTING BACK (Paramount) Producer, D. Constantine Conte; Director, Lewis Teague; Screenplay, Tom Hedley, David Z. Goodman; Associate Producer, Tom Hedley; Executive Producers, David Permut, Mark Travis; Co-Producers, David Lowe, Alex DeBenedetti; Photography, Franco DiGiacomo; Art Director, Robert Gundlach; Costumes, John Boxer; Music, Piero Piccioni; Editors, John J. Fitzstephens, Nicholas Smith; Assistant Directors, Jose Lopez Rodero, Ellen Rauch; Presented by Dino DeLaurentiis; In Technicolor; 98 minutes; Rated R; May release. CAST: Tom Skerritt (John), Patti LuPone (Lisa), Michael Sarrazin (Vince), Yaphet Kotto (Ivanhoe), David Rasche (Michael), Donna DeVarona (Sara), Gina DeAngelis (Vera), Jonathan Adam Sherman (Danny), Pat Cooper (Harry), Jim Lovelett (Tom), Joe Ragno (Mike), Sal Richards, (Bill), Frank Sivero (Frank), Lewis Van Bergen (Laz), Jim Moody (Lester), Peter Brocco (Donato), Patch MacKenzie (Lilly), Pete Richardson (Eldorado), Jean Erlich (Snowflake), Bob Ryan (Neighbor), George Manos (Carlo), Joseph R. Sicari (Salesman), Maurice Golchin (Mario), Maria Ferrer (Delfina), Robert Hitt (Centner), Sandrino Giglio (Mr. Moresco), Antoinette Iannelli (Mrs. Moresco), Earle Hyman (Police Chief), Mandel Kramer, Ted Ross, James Andronica, John Aquino, Richard Kuller, Dan Deitch, Alan Graf, Jean Laws, Bonny Palma, Vicki Giunta, Cynthia Howard, Mary Ann Thoeny, Josh Mostel, Tony Devon, G. James Reed, Dean Bennett, George Krafft, Ronald Maccone, Ralph Monaco, Brass Adams, Tony Munafo, Ettore Castellente, Maxine Green, Harold Rabinowitz, Lenny Del Genio, Melinda Marshall, Peter Dryden, Ronnie Skipper, Curtis McAllister, Zoya Leporska, Gregory Puriefoy, Verone Scruggs, Tim McLaughlin, Suellen Richmond, Michael Gleason, Andrew Edwards

FORBIDDEN WORLD (New World) Producer, Roger Corman; Co-Producer, Mary Ann Fisher; Director, Allan Holzman; Screenplay, Tim Curnen; Story, Jim Wynorski, R. J. Robertson; Photography, Tim Suhstedt; Editor, Allan Holzman; Music, Susan Justin; Design, Chris Horner, Robert Skotak; Art Directors, Joe Garrity, Wayne Springfield; Assistant Director, Mark Allan; In DeLuxe Color; 86 minutes; Rated R; May release. CAST: Jesse Vint (Mike), June Chadwick (Dr. Glaser), Dawn Dunlap (Tracy), Linden Chiles (Dr. Hauser), Fox Harris (Dr. Tinburgen), Raymond Oliver (Brian), Scott Paulin (Earl), Michael Bowen (Jimmy)

MAYA (Claridge) Producer, Antigua Domsa; Executive Producer, Omar Kacmarczyk; Director, Agust Agustsson; Screenplay, Beta Dominguez D., Joseph D. Rosevich; Editor, Ruth Schell; Photography, Oliver Wood; Music, Bika Reed, Don Salmon, Guacaran; In color; 104 minutes; Not rated; May release. CAST: Berta Dominguez D. (Maya), Joseph D. Rosevich (Martin), Luis Manuel (Juan), Valeria Richards (Valeria).

THE HOUSE WHERE EVIL DWELLS (MGM/UA) Producer, Martin B. Cohen; Director, Kevin Connor; Screenplay, Robert A. Suhosky; From novel by James W. Hardiman; Photography, Jacques Haitkin; Music, Ken Thorne; Art Director, Yoshikazu Sano; Editor, Barry Peters; In Technicolor; 88 minutes; Rated R; May release. CAST: Edward Albert (Ted), Susan George (Laura), Doug McClure (Alex), Amy Barrett (Amy), Mako Hattori (Otami), Toshiyuki Sasaki (Shugoro), Toshiya Maruyama (Masanori), Tsuyako Okajima (Witch), Henry Mitowa (Zen Monk)

SAVANNAH SMILES (Gold Coast) Producer, Clark L. Paylow; Director, Pierre DeMoro; Story-Screenplay, Mark Miller; Photography, Stephen W. Gray; Editor, Eva Ruggiero; Music, Ken Sutherland; Design, Charles Stewart; Art Director, Allen Terry; Associate Producer, Laurette DeMoro Gafferi; Assistant Director, Dennis White; In CFI Color; 107 minutes; Rated PG; May release. CAST: Mark Miller (Alvie), Donovan Scott (Boots), Bridgette Andersen (Savannah), Peter Graves (Dobbs), Chris Robinson (Driscoll), Michael Parks (Lt. Savage), Barbara Stanger (Joan), Pat Morita (Fr. O'Hara), Philip Abbott (Chief Pruitt), Fran Ryan (Wilma), John Fiedler (Clerk), Ray Anzalone (Greenblatt), Carol Wayne (Coreen)

GOIN' ALL THE WAY (Saturn International) Producer, Frank Rubin, Gary Gibbs; Director, Robert Freedman; Screenplay, Roger Stone, Jack Cooper, Music, Richard Hieronymus; In color; 85 minutes; Rated R; May release. CAST: Dan Waldman, Deborah Van Rhyn, Joshua Cadman, Sherie Miller, Joe Colligan, Sylvia Summers, Eileen Davidson

SAFARI 3000 (MGM/UA) Producers, Arthur Gardner, Jules V. Levy; Director, Harry Hurwitz; Story, Jules Levy, Arthur Gardner, Michael Harreschou; Screenplay, Michael Harreschou; Associate Producer, Robert Levy; Music, Ernest Gold; Photography, Adam Greenberg; Editor, Samuel E. Beetley; Art Director, Peter Williams; In Panavision and Technicolor; Rated PG; 92 minutes; May release. CAST: David Carradine (Eddie), Stockard Channing (J. J.), Christopher Lee (Count Borgia), Hamilton Camp (Feodor), Ian Yule (Freddie), Hugh Rouse (Hawthorne), Mary Ann Berold (Victoria), Peter J. Elliott (Stewart), Cocky Two Bull, Ben Masinga, James White, Mackson Ngobeni, Sam Williams, Fanyana H. Sidumo, Eric Flynn, Kerry Jordan, Albert Raphael, John Leslie, Ann Courtneidge, Anthony Fridjhon, Ian Hamilton, Anne Power, Eddie Stacey, Craig Gardner

DEATH SCREAMS (United Film) Producers, Chuck Ison, Ernest Bouskos; Director, David Nelson; Screenplay, Paul C. Elliott; Music, Dee Barton; In color; May release. CAST: Susan Kiger, Jody Kay, Martin Tucker, William T. Hicks, Jennifer Chase, Andria Savio, Monica Boston

ROARING FIRE (New Line) Executive Producer, N. J. Okada; Direction and Screenplay, Norry Suzuki; Action Sequences Director, Sonny Chiba; In color; Rated R; 92 minutes; May release. CAST: Sonny Chiba (Mr. Magic), Duke Sanada (Joji), Sue Shiomi (Chihiro), Abdullah the Butcher, Mickey Narita

THE HOUSE WHERE DEATH LIVES (New American) Producers, Alan Beattie, Peter Shanaberg; Director, Alan Beattie; Associate Producers, David Charles Thomas, Thomas Viertel; Photography, Stephen Posey; Music, Don Peake; Editor, Robert Leighton; Story, Alan Beattie, Jack Viertel; Executive Producer, John Cofrin; Screenplay, Jack Viertel; In Metrocolor; Rated R; 83 minutes; May release. CAST: Patricia Pearcy, David Hayward, John Dukakis, Joseph Cotten

BEACH HOUSE (New Line) Executive Producer, Sidney Abusch; Producer, Marino Amoruso; Director, John Gallagher; Screenplay, Marino Amoruso, John Gallagher; Photography, Peter Stein; Songs, Adam Roth; Score, C. P. Rith; Editors, Vidtor Kanefsky, John Bloomgarden; In TVC Color; 76 minutes; Rated PG; May release. CAST: Kathy McNeil (Cindy), Richard Duggan (Jimmy), Ileana Seidel (Cecile), John Cosola (Anthony), Spence Waugh (Kathy), Paul Anderson (Baby), Adam Roth (Googie), Chris Phillips (Nudge), Jonathan Paley (Drake), Al Wheatley (Marty), Marino Amoruso (Michael), Dana Nathan (Angela), Richard Warren (Frankie), Eddie Brill (Snooky), Bobby Amoruso, Regan Kennedy, Nancy Quinn, Maggie Page, Bev Bradford, Donna Cosola, John Amoruso

Phillip Abbott, Michael Parks, Peter Graves in "Savannah Smiles" © *Gold Coast*

T. K. Carter, Kurt Russell, Donald Moffat in "The Thing"
©*Universal*

Janet Julian, David Wallace in "Humongous"
©*Embassy*

THE THING (Universal) Producers, David Foster, Lawrence Turman; Director, John Carpenter; Screenplay, Bill Lancaster; Co-Producer, Stuart Cohen; Associate Producer, Larry France; Photography, Dean Cundey; Designer, John J. Lloyd; Special Makeup Effects, Rob Bettin; Editor, Todd Ramsay; Music, Ennie Morricone; Executive Producer, Wilbur Stark; Based on story "Who Goes There?" by John W. Campbell, Jr.; Art Director, Henry Larrecq; Assistant Director, Larry Franco; In Panavision, Technicolor, Dolby Stereo; 127 minutes; Rated R; June release. CAST: Kurt Russell (MacReady), A. Wilford Brimley (Blair), T. K. Carter (Nauls), David Clennon (Palmer), Keith David (Childs), Richard Dysart (Dr. Copper), Charles Hallahan (Norris), Peter Maloney (Bennings), Richard Masur (Clark), Donald Moffat (Garry), Joel Polis (Ruchs), Thomas Waites (Windows), Norbert Weisser (Norwegian), Larry France (Passenger with rifle), Nate Irwin (Helicopter Pilot), William Zeman (Pilot)

MEGAFORCE (20th Century-Fox) Producer, Albert S. Ruddy; Director, Hal Needham; Screenplay, James Whittaker, Albert S. Ruddy, Hal Needham, Andre Morgan; Based on story by Robert Kachler; Executive Producer, Raymond Chow; Photography, Michael Butler; Designer, Joel Schiller; Editors, Patrick Roark, S. Skip Schoolnik; Associate Producer, David Shamroy Hamburger; Music, Jerrold Immel; Assistant Director, Bill Coker; Art Director, Carol Wenger; Aerial Photography, David Butler; Music, Kevin Russell, Tod Howarth, Jonathan Cain; Lyrics, James McClarty; Performed by 707; Soundtrack on MCA Records and Tapes; In Technicolor, Panavision and Dolby Stereo; 99 minutes; Rated PG; June release. CAST: Barry Bostwick (Ace Hunter), Persis Khanbatta (Zara), Michael Beck (Dallas), Edward Mulhare (Byrne-White), George Furth (Eggstrom), Henry Silva (Guerera), Michael Kulcsar (Ivan), Ralph Wilcox (Zac), Evan Kim (Suki), Anthony Penya (Sixkiller), J. Victor Lopez (Lopez), Michael Carven (Anton), Bobby Bass (Motorcyclist), Samir Kamour (Aide), Youssef Merhi (Radio Operator), Roger Lowe (Chauffeur), Robert Fuller (Pilot), Ray Hill, Jr. (Commander)

KILL SQUAD (Summa Vista) Executive Producer, Ladd Rucker; Producers, Michael D. Lee, Patrick G. Donahue; Direction and Screenplay, Patrick G. Donahue; Photography, Christopher W. Strattan; Editor, Rick Yacco; Music, Joseph Conlan; Assistant Director, J. M. Hannan; Associate Producer, Maurice Sulkov; In color; 83 minutes; Rated R; June release. CAST: Jean Glaude, Jeff Risk, Jerry Johnson, Bill Cambra, Francisco Ramirez, Marc Sabin, Gary Fung, Alan Marcus, Cameron Mitchell

THE COMEBACK TRAIL (Rearguard) Producer-Director, Harry Hurwitz; Screenplay, Mr. Hurwitz, Roy Frumkes, Robert Winston; Photography, Victor Petrashevitz; Music, Igo Cantor; In color; 80 minutes; Not rated; June release. CAST: Chuck McCann (Enrico), Buster Crabbe (Duke), Robert Staats (Eddie), Jara Kahout (German Producer), Themselves: Henny Youngman, Irwin Corey, Hugh Hefner, Joe Franklin, Monti Rock 3rd

HUMONGOUS (Embassy) Producer, Anthony Kramreither; Director, Paul Lynch; Screenplay, William Gray; Photography, Brian Hebb; Editor, Nick Rotundo; Music, John Mills Cockell; In color; 97 minutes; Rated R; June release. CAST: Janet Julian (Sandy), David Wallace (Eric), Janet Baldwin (Carla), Joy Boushel (Donna), John Wildman (Nick), Layne Coleman (Bert), Shay Garner (Ida), Ed McFadyen (Parsons), Garry Robbins (Ida's Son)

TONIGHT FOR SURE (Kino International) Produced, Directed and Written by Francis Ford Coppola; Photography, Jack Hill; Music, Carmen Coppola; Design, Albert Locatelli, Barbara Cooper; Assistant Director, Frank Zuniga; In Eastmancolor; 69 minutes; Not rated; June release of a 1962 film. CAST: Don Kenney, Karl Schanzer, Virginia Gordon, Marli Renfro, Sandy Silver, Linda Gibson, Pat Brooks, Linda Lightfoot

THE SOLDIER (Embassy) Producer, Director, Screenplay, James Glickenhaus; Photography, Robert Baldwin; Music, Tangerine Dream; In Eastmancolor; 96 minutes; Rated R; June release. CAST: Ken Wahl (The Soldier), Klaus Kinski (Dracha), William Prince (U.S. President), Alberta Watson (Susan)

Persis Khambatta, Barry Bostwick in "Megaforce"
©*Northshore Investments*

Ken Wahl (without beret) in "The Soldier"
©*Embassy*

Sean Young, Michael McKean in "Young Doctors in Love"
©*ABC Motion Pictures*

Taylor Negron, Pamela Reed in "Young Doctors in Love"
©*ABC Motion Pictures*

SATAN'S MISTRESS (MPM) also "Dark Eyes," "Fury of the Succubus" and "Demon Rage." Produced and Written by James Polakof, Beverly Johnson; Director, James Polakof; Music, Roger Kellaway; In color; 90 minutes; Rated R; June release. CAST: Britt Ekland (Ann-Marie), Lana Wood (Lisa), Kabir Bedi (The Spirit), Don Galloway (Carl), John Carradine (Priest), Sherry Scott (Michele), Elise-Ann (Belline), Tom Hallick (Burt), Chris Polakof (Cissy), Howard Murphy (Beast)

YOUNG DOCTORS IN LOVE (20th Century-Fox) Producer, Jerry Bruckheimer; Executive Producer-Director, Garry Marshall; Screenplay, Michael Elias, Rich Eustis; Photography, Don Peterman; Designer, Polly Platt; Editor, Dov Hoenig; Music, Maurice Jarre; Associate Producers, Nick Abdo, Jeffrey Ganz; Assistant Directors, Michael F. Grillo, Stephen P. Dunn; Art Director, Tracy Bousman; In Metrocolor; 96 minutes; Rated R; July release. CAST: Michael McKean (Dr. Simon August), Sean Young (Dr. Stephanie Brody), Harry Dean Stanton (Dr. Oliver Ludwig), Patrick MacNee (Dr. Jacobs), Hector Elizondo (Angelo/Angela), Dabney Coleman (Dr. Prang), Pamela Reed (Norine Sprockett), Taylor Negron (Dr. Phil Burns), Saul Rubinek (Dr. Kurtzman), Patrick Collins (Dr. Rist), Ted McGinley (Dr. DeVol), Rick Overton (Dr. Flicker), Michael Richards (Malamud), Titos Vandis (Sal Bonafetti), Kyle T. Heffner (Dr. Litto), Crystal Bernard (Julie), Gary Friedkin (Dr. Chamberlain), Cameos by soap stars: John Beradino, Emily McLaughlin, Michael Damian, Steven Ford, Chris Robinson, Stuart Damon, Jamie Lyn Bauer, Tom Ligon, Kin Shriner, Janine Turner, Jackie Zeman and Mr. T, and nurses: Haunani Minn (Chang), Becky Gonzales (Perez), Lynne Marie Stewart (Thatcher), Esther Sutherland (Willa Mae), Ann Washington (Annie), Hillary Horan (Theresa), Coleen Maloney (Jones), Claudia Crown (Sanchez), Sonia Jennings (Nina), Kelly Moran (Skateboard)

BARBAROSA (Universal) Producer, Paul N. Lazarus III; Director, Fred Schepisi; Co-Producer-Screenplay, William D. Wittliff; Executive Producer, Martin Starger; Photography, Ian Baker; Editors, Don Zimmerman, David Ramirez; Music, Bruce Smeaton; Assistant

Directors, Tommy Thompson, Bill Cosentino; Designer, Don Woodruff; A Lord Grade presentation in color, Panavision, Todd AO; 90 minutes; Rated PG; July release. CAST: Willie Nelson (Barbarosa), Gary Busey (Karl), Isela Vega (Josephina), Gilbert Roland (Don Braulio), Danny De La Paz (Eduardo), Alma Martinez (Juanita), George Voskovec (Herman), Sharon Compton (Hilda), Howland Chamberlain (Emil), Harry Caesar (Sims), Wolf Muser (Floyd), Kai Wulff (Otto), Roberto Contreras (Cantina Owner), Luis Contreras (Angel), Itasco Wilson (Mattie), Robert Paul English (Horse Trader), Bruce Smith (Photographer), Sonia DeLeon (Old Whore), Joanelle Romero (Young Whore), Michael O'Rourke (Brother), Berkley H. Garrett (Bartender), Allison Wittliff (Emily), Juan Jose Martinez, Rene Luna, Christopher Garcia, Philip Pena, Jake Busey, Reid Wittliff, Bill Couch, Chuck Couch

ZAPPED! (Embassy) Producer, Jeffrey D. Apple; Director, Robert J. Rosenthal; Screenplay, Bruce Rubin, Robert J. Rosenthal; Executive Producers, Howard R. Schuster, Fran Schuster; Music, Charles Fox; Photography, Daniel Pearl; Associate Producers, Thomas Hammel, Jonathan Noah Krivine, Roger LaPage; Editors, Bob Bring, Robert Ferretti; Assistant Directors, Frank Capra III, K. C. Colwell, Stuart Neumann; Art Director, Boyd Willat; Lyrics, Steve Geyer; An Apple-Rose production in color; 96 minutes; Rated R; July release. CAST: Scott Baio (Barney), Willie Aames (Peyton), Robert Mandan (Walter), Felice Schachter (Bernadette), Scatman Crothers (Dexter Jones), Roger Bowen (Mr. Springboro), Marya Small (Mrs. Springboro), Greg Bradford (Robert), Hilary Beane (Corrine), Sue Ane Langdon (Rose), Heather Thomas (Jane), Hardy Keith (Roscoe), Curt Ayers (Art), Merritt Butrick (Cary), Jennifer Chaplin (Melissa), Irwin Keyes ("Too Mean"), Henry Ford Robinson (Umpire), Dick Balduzzi (Waiter), Bennett Liss (Croupier), Ron Deutsch (Larry), Ed Deezen (Sheldon), Bryan O'Byrne (Father Murray), Ed Bakey (Father Gallagher), Jan Leighton (Einstein), Lawanda Page (Mrs. Jones), Rosanne Katon (Donna), Sandy Serrano (Amy), Susan Ursitti (Debby), Corine Borher (Cindy), Michael Wainwright, Jason Hickman, Phil Gilbreth, Fred Grabert, Richard Paine, Holly Rutherford, Lisa LeCover, P. J. Martin, Kym Fisher, Mieke Lanter, Hyde Anderson, James Loren, Dale Lott, Lynn Seibel, Randy Patrick, Demetre Phillips, Joshua Daniel, Daniel Dayan

Gary Busey, Willie Nelson in "Barbarosa"
©*Universal*

Willie Aames, Felice Schachter, Scott Baio in "Zapped!"
©*Embassy*

Henry Winkler, Michael Keaton in "Night Shift"
©*Ladd Company*

Toshiro Mifune, Scott Glenn in "The Challenge"
©*Embassy*

NIGHT SHIFT (Warner Bros.) Producer, Brian Grazer; Director, Ron Howard; Screenplay, Lowell Ganz, Babaloo Mandel; Executive Producer, Don Kranze; Photography, James Crabe; Designer, Jack Collis; Editors, Robert J. Kern, Jr., Daniel P. Hanley, Mike Hill; Music, Burt Bacharach; Lyrics, Carole Bayer Sager; Assistant Directors, Jan Lloyd, Hans Beimler; Art Director, Pete Smith; Special Effects, Allen Hall; Ladd Company production in Technicolor and Dolby Stereo; 105 minutes; Rated R; July release. CAST: Henry Winkler (Chuck), Michael Keaton (Bill). Shelley Long (Belinda), Gina Hecht (Charlotte), Pat Corley (Edward), Bobby DiCicco (Leonard), Nita Talbot (Vivian), Basil Hoffman (Drollhauser), Tim Rossovich (Luke), Clint Howard (Jefferey), Joe Spinell (Manetti), Cheryl Carter (Tanya), Becky Gonzalez (Lupe), Corki Corman (Sylvia), Ildiko Jaid (Joyce), Ava Lazar (Sharon), Robbin Young, Ola Ray, Cassandra Gava, Mimi Lieber, Ashley Cox, Elizabeth Carder, Dawn Dunlap, Jeanne Mori, K. C. Winkler, Catherine Gilmour, Monique Gabriel, Jim Staahl, Barbara Ann Grimes, Richard Belzer, Badja Djola, Marc Flanagan, Beau Billingslea, Kevin R. Sullivan, Grand Bush, Julius Leflore, Floyd Levine, Reid Cruickshanks, Charles Fleisher, Tom Mahoney, Vincent Schiavelli, Jack Perkins, Jim Ritz, John Boyle, Brett Clark, Paul Kaufman, Joy Michael Vogelbacher, Hugo Napier, Tom Candela, Edward G. Betlow, Horace Long, Angelo Vignari, Kevin Costner, Rick Starr, Russell Forte, Jim Greenleaf, Jason Fitz-Gerald, Jeremy Lawrence, Shannen Doherty, The Solid Gold Dancers

RAW FORCE (American Panorama/Aquarius) Executive Producers, Rebecca Bella, Lawrence Woolner; Producer, Frank Johnson; Direction and Screenplay, Edward Murphy; Photography, Frank Johnson; Editor, Eric Lindemann; Music, Walter Murphy; Assistant Director, Barbara Greenwood; In CFI Color; 86 minutes; Rated R; July release. CAST: Cameron Mitchell (Captain), Geoff Binney (Mike), Jillian Kessner (Cookie), John Dresden (John), Jennifer Holmes (Ann), Hope Holiday (Hazel), Rey King (Chin), Vic Diaz (Monk)

THE CHALLENGE (Embassy) Producers, Robert L. Rosen, Ron Beckman; Director, John Frankenheimer; Screenplay, Richard Maxwell, John Sayles; Photography, Kozo Okazaki; Editor, John W. Wheeler; Music, Jerry Goldsmith; In color; 110 minutes; Rated R; July release. CAST: Scott Glenn (Rick), Toshiro Mifune (Yoshida), Donna Kei Benz (Akiko), Atsuo Nakamura (Hideo), Calvin Jung (Ando), Clyde Kusatsu (Go), Sab Shimono (Toshio), Kiyoako Nagai (Kubo), Kenta Fukasaku (Jiro), Shoga Shimada (Father of Yoshida), Yoshio Inaba (Instructor), Seiji Miyaguchi (Old Man), Miiko Taka (Yoshida's Wife)

THE SECRET OF N. I. M. H. (MGM/UA) Director, Don Bluth; Screenplay, Don Bluth, John Pomeroy, Gary Goldman; Based on "Mrs. Frisby and the Rats of N.I.M.H." by Robert C. O'Brien; Music, Gary Goldman; Editor, Jeffrey Patch; In Dolby Stereo and color; 82 minutes; Rated G; July release. An animated feature with the voices of Derek Jacobi (Nicodemus), Elizabeth Hartman (Mrs. Brisby), Arthur Malet (Ages), Dom DeLuise (Jeremy), Hermione Baddeley (Auntie Shrew), John Carradine (Great Owl), Peter Strauss (Justin), Paul Shenar (Jennar), Tom Hattan (Farmer Fitzgibbons), Shannen Doherty (Teresa), Wil Wheaton (Martin), Jodi Hicks (Cynthia), Ian Fried (Timmy)

CLASS OF 1984 (UFD) Executive Producers, Mark Lester, Merrie Lynn Ross; Producer, Arthur Kent; Director, Mark Lester; Screenplay, Mark Lester, John Saxton, Tom Holland; Story, Tom Holland; Photography, Albert Dunk; Music, Lalo Schifrin; "I Am the Future" performed by Alice Cooper; In color; 96 minutes; Rated R; August release. CAST: Perry King (Andy Norris), Merrie Lynn Ross (Diane Norris), Roddy McDowall (Terry Corrigan), Timothy Van Patten (Peter Stegman), Stefan Arngrim (Drugstore), Michael Fox (Arthur), Keith Knight (Barnyard), Lisa Langlois (Patsy), Neil Clifford (Fallon), Erin Flannery (Deneen), David Gardner (Morganthau)

DON'T GO IN THE WOODS ALONE (Seymour Borde) Producer-Director, James Bryan; Screenplay, Garth Eliassen; Music, H. Kingsley Thurber; Photography, Henry Zinman; Rated R; August release. CAST: Nick McClelland, James P. Hayden, Mary Gail Artz, Angie Brown, Tom Drury (Monster)

Mrs. Brisby and children in "The Secret of NIMH"
©*UA/MGM*

Timothy Van Patten (C) in "Class of 1984"
©*Guerrilla High Productions*

107

"Hey Good Lookin'" © *Warner Bros.*

Peter Gallagher, Daryl Hannah, Valerie Quennessen in
"Summer Lovers" © *Filmways*

HEY GOOD LOOKIN (Warner Bros.) Produced, Directed and
Written by Ralph Bakshi; Executive Producer, Ronald Kauffman;
Associate Producer, Lynne Betner; Editor, Donald W. Ernst; Music,
John Madara, Ric Sandler; In Technicolor; 86 minutes; Rated R;
August release. An animated film with Richard Romanus (Vinnie),
David Proval (Crazy), Jesse Welles (Eva), Tina Bowman (Rozzie),
Danny Wells, Bennie Massa, Gelsa Palao, Paul Roman, Larry
Bishop, Tabi Cooper (Stompers), Juno Dawson (Waitress), Shirley
Jo Finney (Chaplin), Martin Garner (Yonkel), Terry Haven (Alice),
Allen Joseph (Max), Philip M. Thomas (Chaplin), Frank de Kova
(Old Vinnie), Angelo Grisanti (Solly), Candy Candido (Sal), Ed
Peck (Italian Man), Lillian Adams, Mary Dean Lauria (Italian
Woman), Donna Ponterotto (Gelsa), Toni Basil (The Lockers Stag-
ing and Choreography)

THINGS ARE TOUGH ALL OVER (Columbia) Producer, How-
ard Brown; Direction, Thomas K. Avildsen; Screenplay, "Cheech"
Marin, Thomas Chong; Associate Producers, Shelby Chong, Debo-
rah Mannis; Original Music and Lyrics, Gaye Delorme; Designer,
Richard Tom Sawyer; Photography, Bobby Byrne; Editor, Dennis
Dolan; Assistant Directors, Pat Kehoe, Bob Roe; In Panavision and
color; 92 minutes; Rated R; August release. CAST: Richard
"Cheech" Marin (Mr. Slyman), Tommy Chong (Prince Habib), Mi-
chael Aragon (Cheech's Double), Toni Attell (Cocktail Waitress),
Mike Bacarella (Cop), Billy Beck (Pop), Don Bovingloh (Maitre D),
Richard Calhoun (Drummer), Jennifer Condos (Bass), John Cor-
rona (St. Louis Biker), David Couwlier (Man with tongue), Shelby
Fiddis, Rikki Marin (French Girls), Aaron Freeman (Cop), Mike
Friedman (Car Rental), Evelyn Guerrero (Donna), Maya Harman
(Belly Dancer), Vanaghan S. Housepian (Henchman), Lance Kinsey
(Plastic Surgeon), Irvin Koszewski (Chong's Double), Janice Ladik
(Mom in laundermat), Jay Lawson (Gas Station Attendant), Senta
Moses (Kid), Dorothy Neumann (Mom), John Paragon, Sandy
Weintraub (Red Carpet Men), Shabazz Perez (Man with toupe),
Gregory Polcyn (Busboy), Ben Powers (Pimp). Ernest Rayford III
John Tisdale (Car Wash Attendants), John Steadman (Oldtimer),
Rip Taylor (Himself), George Wallace (The Champ), Ruby Wax
(Patron), Diana Wild (Waitress), Farouk A. Zurond (Chauffeur)

SUMMER LOVERS (Orion) Producer, Mike Moder; Direction
and Screenplay, Randal Kleiser; Executive Producer, Joel Dean;
Editor, Robert Gordon; Designer, Bruce Weintraub; Original Score,
Basil Poledouris; In Dolby Stereo and Technicolor; 98 minutes;
Rated R; August release. CAST: Peter Gallagher (Michael), Daryl
Hannah (Cathy), Valerie Quennessen (Lina), Barbara Rush (Jean),
Carole Cook (Barbara), Hans Van Tongeren (Jan), Lydia Lenosi
(Aspa), Vladimiros Kiriakos (Yorghos), Carlos Rodriguez Ramos
(Cosmo), Henri Behar (Pjilippe), Rika Dialina (Monica), Andreas
Filipidis (Andreas), Peter Pye (Joe), Janis Benjamin (Trish)

SIX PACK (20th Century-Fox) Producer, Michael Trikilis; Director, Daniel Petrie; Screenplay, Mike Marvin, Alex Matter; Executive
Producers, Edward S. Feldman, Ted Witzer; Associate Producer,
Jack B. Bernstein; Photography, Mario Tosi; Designer, William J.
Creber; Editor, Rita Roland; Music, Charles Fox; Assistant Directors, Newton Arnold, Hope Goodwin, Ron Kinwald; In DeLuxe
Color; 110 minutes; Rated PG; August release. CAST: Kenny Rog-
ers (Brewster), Diane Lane (Breezy), Erin Gray (Lilah), Barry Cor-
bin (Sheriff), Terry Kiser (Terk), Bob Hannah (Diddler), Tom
Abernathy (Louis), Robbie Fleming (Little Harry), Anthony Mi-
chael Hall (Doc), Robby Still (Swifty), Benji Wilhoite (Steven),
Buddy Baker (Himself), Gary McGurrin (Hank), Charles Kahlen-
berg (Stan), Roy Tatum (Harley), Terry L. Beaver (Pensky), Bill
Ash (Old Man), Ernest Dixon (Clarence), Jay McMillan, Tim Bays
(Hippies), Jo Ahl (Deanna), Charlie Briggs, Warde Q. Butler, Jr.
(Stewards), Allison Bigger (Ludi), Tony Maniscalco, Bob Terhune,
Ross Guerrero, Jerry Campbell (Thugs), Barney Johnston (Jake),
Bill Gribble (Mechanic), Chuck Woolery, Chris Economaki (TV
Commentators), Jon Hayden (Rich Boy)

ALL BY MYSELF (Blackwood) Produced, Directed and Photographed by Christian Blackwood; Editor, Susan Ardo Berger; Associate Producer, David Schmerler; In color; 85 minutes; Not rated;
August release. A feature documentary about and with Eartha Kitt,
and guests Kitt McDonald, Cecil Gorey, Michael Smith, Joyce
Hauser, Allison Smith, Charles Strouse, Geoffrey Holder, Carmen
de Lavallade, Edward I. Koch, Joan Fontaine, Virginia Graham,
Joey Adams, Cindy Adams, Wayland Picard, Janet Oseroff, Harlem
World Dancers, Lovebug Starski, Chuck Leonard

Cheech, Chong, Shelby Fiddis, Rikki Marin in "Things Are
Tough All Over" © *Columbia*

Kenny Rogers (L) and new pit crew in "Six Pack"
© *20th Century-Fox*

Tanya Roberts, Josh Milrad, John Amos, Marc Singer in "Beastmaster" ©*MGM/UA*

Lawrence Monoson, Steve Antin, Geri Idol, Winifred Freedman in "The Last American Virgin" ©*Canon*

MOTHER LODE (Martin Shafer-Andrew Scheinman) Produced and Written by Fraser Clarke Heston; Executive Producer, Peter Snell; Director, Charlton Heston; Photography, Richard Leiterman; Design, Douglas Higgins; Editor, Eric Boyd Perkins; Music, Ken Wannberg; Associate Producer, Les Kimber; Art Directors, Michael Bolton, James H. Crow; An Agamemnon Films production in color; 101 minutes; Rated PG; August release. CAST: Charlton Heston (Silas McGee/Ian McGee), Nick Mancuso (Jean Dupre), Kim Basinger (Andrea Spalding), John Marley (Elijah), Dale Wilson (Gerard Elliot), Ricky Zantolas (George), Marie George (Elijah's Wife)

THE BEASTMASTER (MGM/UA) Producers, Paul Pepperman, Sylvio Tabet; Director, Don Coscarelli; Screenplay, Don Coscarelli, Paul Pepperman; Photography, John Alcott; Editor, Roy Watts; Music, Lee Holdridge; In Dolby Stereo and color; 120 minutes; Rated PG; August release. CAST: Marc Singer (Dar), Tanya Roberts (Kiri), Rip Torn (Maax), John Amos (Seth), Josh Milrad (Tal), Rod Loomis (Zed), Ben Hammer (Young Dar's Father), Ralph Strait (Sacco), Billy Jacoby (Young Dar)

CHILLY SCENES OF WINTER (United Artists Classics) formerly "Head Over Heels"; Producers, Mark Metcalf, Amy Robinson, Griffin Dunne; Direction and Screenplay, Joan Micklin Silver; Based on novel by Ann Beattie; Photography, Bobby Byrne; Music, Ken Lauber; Editor, Cynthia Scheider; Designer, Peter Jamison; In Metrocolor; 92 minutes; Rated PG; August release. CAST: John Heard (Charles), Mary Beth Hurt (Laura), Peter Riegert (Sam), Kenneth McMillan (Pete), Gloria Grahame (Clara), Nora Heflin (Betty), Jerry Hardin (Patterson), Tarah Nutter (Susan), Mark Metcalf (Ox), Allen Joseph (Blind Man), Frances Bay (Mrs. Delillo), Griffin Dunne (Dr. Mark), Alex Johnson (Elise), Ann Beattie (Waitress), Angela Phillips (Rebecca)

THE JUNKMAN (H. B. Halicki International) Produced, Directed and Written by H. B. Halicki; Executive Producer, Richard L. Muse; Photography, Tony Syslo; Editor, Warner E. Leighton; Assistant Director, Chip Giannettini; In DeLuxe Color; 96 minutes; Rated PG; August release. CAST: H. B. Halicki, Christopher Stone, Susan Shaw, Lang Jeffries, Hoyt Axton, George Barris, Lynda Day George, Freddy Cannon, The Belmonts

THE LAST AMERICAN VIRGIN (Cannon) Producers, Menahem Golan, Yoram Globus; Director, Boaz Davidson; Assistant Directors, Mark Allen, Eric Jewett; Photography, Adam Greenberg; Art Director, Jim Dultz; Editor, Bruria Davidson; In Dolby Stereo and color; 90 minutes; Rated R; September release. CAST: Lawrence Monoson (Gary), Diane Franklin (Karen), Steve Antin (Rick), Joe Rubbo (David), Louisa Moritz (Carmela), Brian Peck (Victor), Kimmy Robertson (Rose), Tessa Richarde (Brenda), Winifred Freedman (Millie), Gerri Idol (Roxanne), Sandy Sprung (Mother), Paul Keith (Father), Phil Rubenstein (Gino), Roberto Rodriguez (Paco), Blanche Rubin (Librarian), Michael Chieffo (Soda Jerk), Leslie Simms (Mrs. Applebaum), Harry Bugin (Doctor), Julianna McCarthy (Counselor), Mel Wells (Druggist), Sylvia Lawler (Assistant), Nancy Brock (Ruby), Lyla Graham (Mrs. Roswell), Mordo Dana (Jeweler), Robert Doran (Earl)

AMITYVILLE II: THE POSSESSION (Orion) Executive Producer, Bernard Williams; Producers, Ira N. Smith, Stephen R. Greenwald; Director, Damiano Damiani; Screenplay, Tommy Lee Wallace; From the book "Murder in Amityville" by Hans Holzer; Associate Producer, Jose Lopez Rodero; Photography, Franco DiGiacomo; Costumes, Bill Kellard; Designer, Pierluigi Basile; Art Director, Ray Recht; Editor, Sam O'Steen; Music, Lalo Schifrin; A Dino DeLaurentiis presentation in color; 104 minutes; Rated R; September release. CAST: Burt Young (Anthony Montelli), Rutanya Alda (Deloris Montelli), James Olson (Father Adamski), Jack Magner (Sonny), Diane Franklin (Patricia), Andrew Prine (Father Tom), Leonardo Cimino (Chancellor), Brent Katz (Mark), Erica Katz (Jan), Ted Ross (Attorney), Petra Lea (Mrs. Greer), Danny Aiello III (Movers), John Ring (Police Chief), Peter Radon (Cab Driver), Moses Gunn (Detective)

BURDEN OF DREAMS (Flower Films) Produced, Directed and Photographed by Les Blank; Sound Recording and Editing, Maureen Gosling; In English, Spanish, German and Portuguese with English subtitles; In color; 94 minutes; Not rated; September release. A documentary about German filmmaker Werner Herzog and his struggle to complete "Fitzcarraldo" on location in the Peruvian Amazon, with Werner Herzog, Klaus Kinski, Claudia Cardinale, the Campa, Machiguenga and Aguaruna tribes of the Peruvian Amazon, and the film crew of "Fitzcarraldo."

Moses Gunn, James Olson, Jack Magner in "Amityville II" ©*Dino DeLaurentiis*

Les Blank and extras in "Burden of Dreams"

JoBeth Williams, Robert Urich in "Endangered Species"
©MGM/UA

Eddie Albert, Luciano Pavarotti, Kathryn Harrold in "Yes, Giorgio" ©MGM/UA

HOMEWORK (Jensen Farley) Executive Producer, Robert L. Fenton; Producer-Director, James Beshears; Screenplay, Maurice Peterson, Don Saffran; Photography, Paul Goldsmith; Editor, Allen Persselin; Music, Tony Jones, Jim Wetzel; Assistant Director, Jeanie Field; In Movielab Color; 90 minutes; Rated R; September release. CAST: Joan Collins (Diana), Michael Morgan (Tommy), Shell Kepler (Lisa), Lanny Horn (Ralph), Erin Donovan (Sheila), Lee Purcell (Ms. Jackson), Renee Harris (Cookie), Mark Brown (Mix), Steve Gustafson (John), Carrie Snodgress (Dr. Delingua), Wings Hauser (Red Dog), Joy Michael (Diana at 16), and Mel Welles; Beverly Todd, John Romano, Ernestina Jackson, Bill Knight, Newell Alexander, DeeDee Downs, Howard Storm, Betty Thomas

ENDANGERED SPECIES (MGM/UA) Producer, Carolyn Pfeiffer; Director, Alan Rudolph; Screenplay, Alan Rudolph, John Binder; Story, Judson Klinger, Richard Woods; Photography, Paul Lohmann; Editor, Tom Walls; Music, Gary Wright; In color; 97 minutes; Rated R; September release. CAST: Robert Urich (Ruben), JoBeth Williams (Harriet), Paul Dooley (Joe), Hoyt Axton (Ben), Peter Coyote (Steele), Marin Kanter (Mackenzie), Gailard Sartain (Mayor), Dan Hedaya (Peck), Harry Carey, Jr. (Dr. Emmer), John Considine (Burnside), Margery Bond (Judy), Joseph G. Medalis (Lawyer), Patrick Houser (Chester), Alvin Crow (Deputy Wayne), Ned Dowd (Deputy Bobby), Kent Rizley (Deputy Ray), Heather Menzies (Susan), Michelle Davison (Mrs. Haskins), Henry G. Sanders (Dr. Ross), Vernon Weddle (Varney).

WAITRESS (Troma) originally "Soup to Nuts"; Producers, Lloyd Kaufman, Michael Herz; Directors, Samuel Weil, Michael Herz; Screenplay, Michael Stone, Charles Kaufman; Photography, Lloyd Kaufman; Editor, Dan Lowenthal; In color; 87 minutes; Rated R; September release. CAST: Carol Drake (Andrea), June Martin (Jennifer), Renata Maler (Lindsey), Jim Harris (Jerry), David Hunt (Bill), Anthony Sarrero (Moe), Ed Fenton (Bellerman), Augie Grompone (Pieball), Bonnie Horan (Mrs. Bellerman), Fred Salador (Cavendish), Wendy Stuart (His Assistant), Bill Kirksey (Alfred), Katya Colman (Mrs. Alfred)

VORTEX (B Movies) Direction, Screenplay, Editing, Scott B and Beth B; Photography, Steven Fierberg; Music, Adele Bertel, Richard Edson, Lydia Lunch, the Bs; In color; 90 minutes; Not rated; Sep-

tember release. CAST: James Russo (Anthony), Lydia Lunch (Angel), Bill Rice (Frederick), Ann Magnusen (Pamela), Brent Collins (Peter), Bill Corsair (John), Tom Webber (Ron), Haoui Montaug (Harry), Richard France (Therapist), Chris Strang (Tarman), Richard Prince (Vito), David Kennedy (Congressman White), Kal Eric (Bodyguard), Scott B (Carlo-Cop), Gideon Horowitz, Christof Kohlhofer (Doctors), Dani Johnson (Patient/Teletypist), Bill Landis, Andy Whyland (Patients)

YES, GIORGIO (MGM/UA) Producer, Peter Fetterman; Director, Franklin J. Schaffner; Screenplay, Norman Steinberg; Suggested by novel by Anne Piper; Photography, Fred J. Koenekamp; Editor, Michael F. Anderson; Music, Michael J. Lewis, John Williams and others; In Dolby Stereo and color; 111 minutes; Rated PG; September release. CAST: Luciano Pavarotti (Giorgio), Kathryn Harrold (Pamela), Eddie Albert (Henry), Paola Borboni (Sister Teresa), James Hong (Kwan), Beulah Quo (Mei Ling), Norman Steinberg (Dr. Barmen), Rod Colbin (Ted), Kathryn Fuller (Faye), Joseph Mascolo (Dominic), Karen Kondazian (Francesca), Leona Mitchell, Kurt Adler, Emerson Buckley (Themselves)

LIAR'S MOON (Crown International) Producer, Don P. Behrns; Director, David Fisher; Executive Producers, Billy Hanna, Vic Ramos; Screenplay, David Fisher from story by Janice Thompson and Billy Hanna; Photography, John Hora; Editor, Christopher Greenbury; In Metrocolor; 106 minutes; September release. CAST: Matt Dillon, Cindy Fisher, Christopher Connelly, Hoyt Axton, Yvonne DeCarlo, Maggie Blye, Susan Tyrrell, Broderick Crawford

BEACH GIRLS (Crown International) Executive Producer, Mark Tenser; Producer, Marilyn J. Tenser; Co-Producer, Michael D. Castle; Director, Pat Townsend; Screenplay, Patrick Duncan, Phil Groves; Photography, Michael Murphy; Editor, George Bowers; Music, Michael Lloyd; Performed by Arsenal; Assistant Director, Stephen Eshelman; Art Director, Kenneth Herzenroder; Costumes, Kristin Nelson; In DeLuxe Color; 91 minutes; September release. CAST: Debra Blee (Sarah), Val Kline (Ginger), Jeana Tomasina (Ducky), James Daughton (Scott), Adam Roarke (Uncle Carl), Dan Barrows, Herb Braha, Mary Jo Catlett, Fern Fitzgerald, Tessa Richarde, Judson Vaughn, George Kee Cheung, Channing Clarkson, Paul E. Richards, Bert Rosario, Jacqueline Jacobs

THE END OF AUGUST (Quartet) Executive Producer, Martin Jurow; Producers, Warren Jacobson, Sally Sharp; Director, Bob Graham; Screenplay, Eula Seaton, Leon Heller, Anna Thomas, Gregory Nava; Based on novel "The Awakening" by Kate Chopin; Music, Shirley Walker; Photography, Bob Elswit; Art Director, Joe Wertheimer; Editor, Jay Lash Cassidy; Associate Producer, Scott Rosenfelt; Assistant Directors, Robin Oliver, Jan Wieringa, Brenda Haverstock; Costumes, David Loveless, Bob Anton; In color; Rated PG; 100 minutes; September release. CAST: Sally Sharp (Edna), Lilia Skala (Mlle. Reisz), David Marshall Grant (Robert), Kathleen Widdoes (Adele), Paul Roebling (Leonce), Paul Shenar (Arobin), John McLiam (Colonel), Mark Linn-Baker (Victor), Patricia Barry (Mrs. Merriman), Roy Poole (Dr. Mandalet), Patricia Falkenhain (Mme. Lebrun), William Meisle (Alphonse), Miles Mutchler (Farival), Adrian Boyes (Raoul), Andrews Chambers (Etienne), Brown Wallace (Merriman), Jenna Worthen (Grandmother), Sally Maloney (Nurse), Robert Harper (Joe), Saundra Santiago (Mariequiuta)

Lilia Skala, Sally Sharp in "The End of August"
©Quartet

BABY DOLLS (Coast Films) Director, Mel Welles; Screenplay, Buck Flower, John Goff; In color; Rated R; September release. CAST: Leslie Ackerman, Sandy Serrano, Len Lesser, Mel Welles, Ron Ross, Speed Stearns, Linda Gary

DAN'S MOTEL Produced, Directed, Written, Photographed and Edited by Jerry R. Barrish; Music, Rick Burnley; Songs, Tallie Cochrane, Jerry R. Barrish; Associate Producer, Simon Edery; Assistant Director, George Berg; In Monaco Labs color; Not rated; 78 minutes; September release. CAST: George Berg, Jim Rudolph, Mary Catherine Wright, Evan Davis, Tallie Cochrane, Michael King, Patrick Wright, Jim Bowyer, Francesca Knittel-Bowyer, Sam David

BOXOFFICE Producers, Josef Bogdanovich, Bruce Chastain; Direction and Screenplay, Josef Bogdanovich; Photography, Eric Saarinen; Editors, Bonnie Kozek, Edward Salier; Music, Ornette Coleman; Art Director, Michael Erler; Associate Producers, Mary Sothman, Michael Murphy; Assistant Director, Jesse Wayne; In DeLuxe Color; Not rated; 93 minutes; September release. CAST: Robin Clarke (Peter), Monica Lewis (Francesca), Eddie Constantine (Hugh), Aldo Ray (Lew), Edie Adams (Carolyn), Carol Cortne (Eve), Peter Hurkos, Chuck Mitchell

HUMAN HIGHWAY Executive Producer, Elliot Rabinowitz; Producer, L. A. Johnson; Associate Producer, Jeanne Fields; Director, Bernard Shakey with Dean Stockwell; Screenplay, Shakey, Stockwell, Fields, Russ Tamblyn, James Beshears; Photography, David Myers; In color; Not rated; 90 minutes; September release. CAST: Neil Young (Lionel), Russ Tamblyn (Fred), Dean Stockwell (Otto), Dennis Hopper (Cracker), Charlotte Stewart (Charlotte), Sally Kirkland (Katherine), Geraldine Baron (Irene), Devo

WALTZ ACROSS TEXAS (Atlantic) Producer, Martin Jurow; Director, Ernest Day; Screenplay, Bill Svanoe; Photographer, Robert Elswit; Music, Steve Dorff; Title Song sung by Waylon Jennings; Original Story, Terry Jastrow, Anne Archer; An Aster Film production in color; 100 minutes; Rated PG; October release. CAST: Anne Archer, Terry Jastrow, Noah Beery, Mary Kay Place, Josh Taylor, Richard Farnsworth

FAST-WALKING (Pickman) Produced, Directed and Written by James B. Harris; Based on novel "The Rap" by Ernest Brawley; Music, Lalo Schifrin; Associate Producer, Richard McWhorter; Executive Producer, Joseph Harris; Photography, King Baggot; Editor, Douglas Stewart; Art Director, Richard Haman; Presented by Lorimar; In color; 115 minutes; Rated R; October release. CAST: James Woods (Fast-Walking Miniver), Im McIntire (Wasco), Kay Lenz (Moke), Robert Hooks (William Galliot), M. Emmet Walsh (Sgt. Sanger), Timothy Agoglia Carey (Bullet), Susan Tyrrell (Evie), Charles Weldon (Jackson), John Friedrich (Squeeze), Sandy Ward (Warden), Lance LeGault (Lt. Barnes), Deborah White (Elaine), Helen Page Camp (Lady in visitor's room), Sydney Lassick (Ted)

HAMMETT (Warner Bros.) Producers, Fred Roos, Ronald Colby, Don Guest; Director, Wim Wenders; Screenplay, Ross Thomas, Dennis O'Flaherty; Based on book by Joe Gores; Adaptation, Thomas Pope; Executive Producer, Francis Coppola; Photography, Philip Lathrop, Joseph Biroc; Designers, Dean Tavoularis, Eugene Lee; Music, John Barry; Associate Producer, Mona Skager; Editors, Barry Malkin, Marc Laub, Robert Q. Lovett, Randy Roberts; Costumes, Ruth Morley; Art Directors, Angelo Graham, Leon Erickson; Assistant Directors, David Valdez, Daniel Attias; An Orion/Zoetrope/Warner Bros. production in Technicolor and Dolby Stereo; 94 minutes; Rated PG; October release. CAST: Frederic Forrest (Hammett), Peter Boyle (Jimmy Ryan), Marilu Henner (Kit Conger/Sue Alabama), Roy Kinnear (English Eddie), Elisha Cook (Eli), Lydia Lei (Crystal), R. G. Armstrong (Lt. O'Mara), Richard Bradford (Det. Bradford), Michael Chow (Fong), David Patrick Kelly (Punk), Sylvia Sidney (Donaldina), Jack Nance (Gary), Elmer L. Kline (Doc Fallon), Royal Dano (Pops), Samuel Fuller (Old Man), Lloyd Kino (Barber), Fox Harris (News Vendor), Rose Wond (Laundress), Liz Roberson (Lady in library), Jean Francois Ferreol (Sailor), Alison Hong, Patricia Kong (Young Girls), Lisa Lu (Donaldina's Assistant), Andrew Winner (Guard), Kenji Shibuya (Bouncer), James Quinn (Guard)

James Woods, Kay Lenz in "Fast-Walking"
© *Pickman*

HALLOWEEN III: SEASON OF THE WITCH (Universal) Producers, Debra Hill, John Carpenter; Direction and Screenplay, Tommy Lee Wallace; Executive Producers, Irwin Yablans, Joseph Wolf; Photography, Dean Cundey; Designer, Peter Jamison; Associate Producer, Barry Bernardi; Music, John Carpenter, Alan Howarth; Editor, Millie Moore; Assistant Directors, Ron L. Wright, Scott Ira Thaler; Special Effects, Jon G. Belyeu; In Panavision and Technicolor; 96 minutes; Rated R; October release. CAST: Tom Atkins (Dr. Challis), Stacey Nelkin (Ellie), Dan O'Herlihy (Conal), Ralph Strait (Buddy), Michael Currie (Rafferty), Jadeen Barbor (Betty), Bradley Schachter (Little Buddy), Garn Stephens (Marge), Nancy Kyes (Linda), Jon Terry (Starker), Patrick Pankurst (Technician), Al Berry (Harry), Wendy Wessberg (Teddy), Dick Warlock (Assassin), Norman Merrill (Red), Michelle Walker (Bella), Joshua Miller (Willie), Essex Smith (Jones), Martin Cassidy (Watcher), Maidie Norman (Nurse), John MacBride (Sheriff), Loyd Catlett (Charlie), Paddi Edwards (Secretary), Jeffrey D. Henry, Michael W. Green (Technicians)

MONSIGNOR (20th Century-Fox) Producers, Frank Yablans, David Niven, Jr.; Director, Frank Perry; Screenplay, Abraham Polonsky, Wendell Mayes; Based on novel by Jack Alain Leger; Photography, Billy Williams; Design, John DeCuir; Editor, Peter E. Berger; Music, John Williams; Costumes, Theoni V. Aldredge; Associate Producer, Kurt Neumann; Assistant Director, Gianni Cozzo; Art Director, Stefano Ortolani; In Moviecam, Technovision, Deluxe Color; 122 minutes; Rated R; October release. CAST: Christopher Reeve (Flaherty), Genevieve Bujold (Clara), Fernando Rey (Santoni), Jason Miller (Appolini), Joe Cortese (Varese), Adolfo Celi (Vinci), Leonardo Cimino (Pope), Tomas Milian (Francisco), Robert J. Prosky (Bishop Walkman), Joe Pantoliano (Musso), Milena Vukotic (Sister Verna), Jan Danby (Lieutenant), Gregory Snegoff, Harrison Muller (Soldiers), David Mills (Major), Joe Spinell (Bride's Father), Ritza Brown (Maid of Honor), Loredana Grappasonni (Bride), Ettore Mattia (Pietro), Carolyn Russoff, Yanti Somer, Paolo Scalondro (Secretaries), Domenico Poli (Priest), Elio Bonadonna, Giovanni Bonadonna, Remo DeAngelis (Killers), Pamela Prati, Annie Papa, Stefania D'Amario (Girls), Michele Messina (Guard), Agnes Nobencourt, Tracy Bonbrest (Postulants), Francesco Angrisano (Priest)

Marilu Henner, Frederick Forrest in "Hammett"
© *Zoetrope*

MacKenzie Phillips, Amy Madigan in "Love Child"
©The Ladd Co.

Laurene Landon, Armand Assante in "I, the Jury"
©20th Century-Fox

LOVE CHILD (Ladd Company) Producer, Paul Maslansky; Director, Larry Peerce; Screenplay, Anne Gerard, Katherine Specktor; Story, Anne Gerard; Music, Charles Fox; Photography, Jim Pergola; Art Director, Don K. Ivey; Editor, Bob Wyman; Assistant Directors, David Whorf, Paul Rose; In color; 97 minutes; Rated R; October release. CAST: Amy Madigan (Terry Jean Moore), Beau Bridges (Jack), Mackenzie Phillips (J. J.), Albert Salmi (Capt. Ellis), Joanna Merlin (Mrs. Sturgis), Margaret Whitton (Jacki), Lewis Smith (Jesse), Dennis Lipscomb (Arthur), Anna Maria Horsford (Mara), Michael Shane (Judge Hare), Randy Dreyfuss (Striker), Rhea Pearlman (June), Juanita Mahone (Cecily), Richard Whiting (Judy Weston), Luis Avalos (Tony), Mary McCusker (Jeanette), Patrick Sullivan, Richard Liberty (Police), Jody Wilson (Sgt. Benson), William Leonard (Judge Powell), Madeline Kiggins (Guard), Matthew Peerce (Boy in car), Dara Murphy (Nancy), Candy Trabuco (Vanessa), Sarah Zinsser (Sarah), Cheryl King (Van Inmate), Pat Mann (Parker), Jack Stevens (Jack's Son), John Archie (Guard), Ellen Beck (Rabbit), Susan Batson (Brenda), Patricia Williams (Lida), Carole Russo (Evelyn), Jill-Rene Weissman (Stefanie), Terry Jean Moore (Amy), Zelda Patterson (Other Girl), Richard Hunsinger, Al Kiggins, Raymond Peters (Correctional Officers), Carol Chaput (Guard), Annette Foosaner (Woman in yard), Norma Davids (Bonnie), Ronne Mickey (Faith), Tame Connolly (Norma)

NATIONAL LAMPOON'S CLASS REUNION (20th Century-Fox) Producer, Matty Simmons; Director, Michael Miller; Screenplay, John Hughes; Co-Producers, Harmon Berns, Peter V. Herald; Photography, Phil Lathrop; Designer, Dean Edward Mitzner; Editors, Richard C. Meyer, Ann Mills; Costumes, Jean Pierre Dorleac; Original Music, Peter Bernstein, Mark Goldenberg; Title Song performed by Gary J. S. Bonds; Assistant Directors, Robert P. Cohen, Emmitt-Leon O'Neil, B. Thomas Seidman; Sets, Jack Taylor, Jr.; Choreographer, Rita Graham; In Dolby Stereo and Metrocolor; an ABC Motion Picture; 84 minutes; Rated R; October release. CAST: Gerrit Graham (Bob), Michael Lerner (Dr. Young), Fred McCarren (Gary), Miriam Flynn (Bunny), Stephen Furst (Hubert), Marya Small (Iris), Shelley Smith (Meredith), Zane Buzby (Delores), Jacklyn Zeman (Jane), Blackie Dammett (Walter), Barry Diamond (Chip), Art Evans (Carl), Marla Pennington (Mary Beth), Randolph Powell (Jeff), Misty Rowe (Cindy), Jim Staahl (Egon), Gary Hibbard

(Fritz), Anne Ramsey (Mrs. Tabazooki), Steve Tracy (Milt), Isabel West (Gloria), Diane Black, Wendy Goldman, Robin Eurich, Anyavel Glynn, Terry Green, Chris Hubbell, Timothy Phillips, Roger Hamilton Spotts, Rhonda Rivera, Christine Rutherford, Lynn Warfel

I, THE JURY (20th Century-Fox) Producer, Robert Solo; Director, Richard T. Heffron; Screenplay, Larry Cohen; Based on Mickey Spillane's novel; Executive Producers, Michael Leone, Andrew D. T. Pfeffer; Music, Bill Conti; Designer, Robert Gundlach; Editor, Garth Craven; Costumes, Celia Bryant; Associate Producer, Martin Hornstein; Assistant Directors, Jerry Shapiro, Henry Bronchtein; In color; 111 minutes; Rated R; October release. CAST: Armand Assante (Mark Hammer), Barbara Carrera (Dr. Charlotte Bennett), Alan King (Charles Kalecki), Laurene Landon (Velda), Geoffrey Lewis (Joe), Paul Sorvino (Det. Chambers), Judson Scott (Kenricks), Barry Snider (Romero), Julia Barr (Norma), Jessica James (Hilda), Frederick Downs (Jack), Mary Margaret Amato (Myrna), F. J. O'Neill (Goodwin), William Schilling (Lundee), Robert Sevra (Breslin), Don Pike (Evans), Timothy Myers (Blake), Lee Anne Harris, Lynette Harris (Twins)

Q: QUETZALCOATL (UFD) Original title "Winged Serpent"; Produced, Directed and Written by Larry Cohen; Executive Producers, Dan Sandburg, Richard di Bona; Associate Producer, Paul Kurta; Photography, Fred Murphy; Editor, Armand Lebowitz; Music, Robert O. Ragland; Special Visual Effects, David Allen, Randy Cook, Peter Kuran; In color; 100 minutes; Rated R; October release. CAST: Michael Moriarty (Jimmy), Candy Clark (Joan), David Carradine (Shepard), Richard Roundtree (Powell), James Dixon (Lt. Murray), Malachy McCourt (Commissioner), Fred J. Scollay (Capt. Fletcher), Peter Hock (Det. Clifford), Ron Cey (Det. Hoberman), Mary Louise Weller (Mrs. Pauley), Bruce Carradine (Victim), John Capodice (Doyle), Tony Page (Webb), Larkin Ford (Curator), Larry Pine (Professor), Eddie Jones (Watchman), Shelly Desai (Kahea), Lee Louis (Banyon), Fred Morsell, Ed Kovens (Robbers), Richard Duggan (Construction Worker), Jennifer Howard (Newscaster), David Shell (Attorney), Larry Silverstri, Gabriel Wohl, Peter Genovese (Police), Nancy Stafford (Eyewitness), Bobbi Burns (Sunbather)

"National Lampoon's Class Reunion"
©ABC Motion Pictures

David Carradine in "Q"
©United Film Distribution Co.

DOCUMENTEUR: AN EMOTION PICTURE (Cine-Tamaris) Directed and Written by Agnes Varda; Photography, Nurith Aviv, Moshe Levin, Tom Taplin, Bob Carr; Editors, Sabine Mamou; Bob Gould; In color; 65 minutes; Not rated; October release. CAST: Sabine Mamou (Emilie), Mathieu Demy (Martin), Tina Odom (Tina), Lisa Blok (Lisa), Tom Taplin (Tom), Charles Southwood (Man in white room), Fred and Kelly Ricker (Couple in motel), Chris Leplus, Barry Farrell, Andrew Meyer (Sound Crew)

JINXED (MGM/UA) Producer, Herb Jaffe; Director, Don Siegel; Executive Producer, Howard Jeffrey; Screenplay, Bert Blessing, David Newman; Story, Bert Blessing; Photography, Vilmos Zsigmond; Editor, Doug Steward; Music, Bruce Roberts, Miles Goodman; Design, Ted Haworth; Sets, Wally Graham, Julie Harmount; Costumes, Bob DeMora; Associate Producers, Carol Siegel, Joe Cavalier; Assistant Director, Dan McCauley; In Technicolor; 103 minutes; Rated R; October release. CAST: Bette Midler (Bonita), Ken Wahl (Willie), Rip Torn (Harold), Val Avery (Milt), Jack Elam (Otto), Benson Fong (Dr. Wing)

PSYCHO FROM TEXAS (New American) Producer-Director and Screenplay, Jim Feazell; Photography, Paul Hipp; Editor, Arjay; Music, Jaime Mendoza-Nava; Assistant Director, Marland Proctor; Associate Producer, Sherry Feazell; In Movielab Color; 89 minutes; Rated R; October release. Cast: John King III (Wheeler), Herschell Mays (Phillips), Tommy Lamey (Slick), Candy Dee (Connie), Janel Ling (Ellen), Juanne Bruno (Bertha), Reed Johnson (Steve), Jack Collins (Sheriff)

THE SLAYER (21st Century) Executive Producer, Lloyd N. Abrams; Producer, William R. Ewing; Director, J. S. Cardone; Screenplay, Cardone, Ewing; Photography, Karen Grossman; Editor, Edward Salier; Music, Robert Folk; Assistant Director, Peter Manonigan; In DeLuxe Color; 80 minutes; Rated R; October release. CAST: Sarah Kendall (Kay), Frederick Flynn (Eric), Carol Kottenbrook (Brooke), Alan McRae (David), Michael Holmes (Marsh), Carl Kraines (Slayer)

THE PERSONALS (New World) Producer, Patrick Wells; Direction, Screenplay, Peter Markle; Photography, Peter Markle, Greg Cummins; Editor, Stephen E. Rivkin; Executive Producers, Robert Melamed, William Melamed; Associate Producers, Bill Schoppert, Stephen E. Rivkin; Music, Will Sumner; In DuArt Color; 90 minutes; Rated PG; October release. CAST: Bill Schoppert (Bill), Karen Landrey (Adriene), Paul Eiding (Paul), Michael Laskin (David), Vicki Dakil (Shelly), Chris Forth (Jennifer), Patrick O'Brien (Jay)

ANDROID (New World) Producer, May Ann Fisher; Executive Producers, Rupert Harvey, Barry Opper; Director, Aaron Lipstadt; Screenplay, James Reigle, Don Opper; Idea, Will Reigle; Photography, Tim Suhrstedt; Associate Producer, R. J. Kizor; Editor, Andy Horvitch; Music, Don Preston; Art Director, K. C. Schelbel, Wayne Springfield; Assistant Director, Matia Karrell; In DeLuxe Color; 80 minutes; Rated R; October release. CAST: Klaus Kinski (Dr. Daniel), Brie Howard (Maggie), Norbert Weisser (Keller), Crofton Hardester (Mendes), Kendra Kirchner (Cassandra), Don Opper

THE LOVE BUTCHER (Mirror) Producers, Gary Williams, Micky Belski; Directors, Mikel Angel, Don Jones; Screenplay, Don Jones, James Evergreen; Photography, Don Jones, Austin McKinney; Editor, Robert Freeman; Music, Richard Hieronymous; In Technicolor and Techniscope; 83 minutes; Rated R; October release. CAST: Erik Stern (Caleb/Lester), Kay Neer (Florence), Jeremiah Beecher (Russell), Edward Roehm (Capt. Stark), Robin Sherwood (Sheila)

TRICK OR TREATS (Lone Star) Produced, directed, written, edited and photographed by Gary Graver; Co-producer, Glenn Jacobson; Executive Producers, Caruth C. Byrd, Lee Thornburg; Associate Producer, Hedi Dietz; Assistant Director, Miller Drake; In CFI Color; Rated R; 91 minutes; October release. CAST: Jacklyn Girous (Linda), Peter Jason (Malcolm), Chris Graver (Christopher), David Carradine (Richard), Carrie Snodgress (Joan), Jillian Kesner (Andrea), John Blyth Barrymore (Mad Doctor), Dan Pastorini, Tim Rossovich, Paul Bartel, J. L. Clark, Catherine Coulson, Maria Dillon, Jason Renard, Owen Orr, Allen Wisch, Nike Zachmanoglou

THE CONCRETE JUNGLE (Pentagon/Aquarius) Producer, Billy Fine; Executive Producers, Jay Schultz, Richard Feinberg; Associate Producer, Louis Paciocco; Director, Tom DeSimone; Screenplay, Alan J. Adler; Photography, Andrew W. Friend, Music, Joe Conlan; In color; 99 minutes; Rated R; October release. CAST: Jill St. John, Tracy Bregman, Barbara Luna, June Barrett, Peter Brown, Aimee Eccles, Sondra Currie

MURAL MURALS (Cine-Tamaris) Direction and Screenplay, Agnes Varda; Photography, Bernard Auroux, Tom Taplin, Alain Blaisdell, Tim Klenzie, Daniel Adams; Editors, Sabine Mamou, Bob Gould; In color; 80 minutes; Not rated; October release. CAST: Juliet Berto (Visitor)

Ken Wahl, Bette Midler in "Jinxed"
©*MGM/UA*

JEKYLL AND HYDE TOGETHER AGAIN (Paramount) Producer, Lawrence Gordon; Director, Jerry Belson; Screenplay, Monica Johnson, Harvey Miller, Jerry Belson, Michael Leeson; Inspired by novel of Robert Louis Stevenson; Executive Producer, Joel Silver; Photography, Philip Lathrop; Designer, Peter Wooley; Editor, Billy Weber; Music, Barry DeVorzon; Assistant Directors, Jerry Sobul, Ross Brown; Costumes, Marilyn Kay Vance; In Metrocolor; 87 minutes; Rated R; October release. CAST: Mark Blankfield (Jekyll/Hyde), Bess Armstrong (Mary), Krista Errickson (Ivy), Tim Thomerson (Dr. Lanyon), Michael McGuire (Dr. Carew), Neil Hunt (Queen), Cassandra Peterson (Busty Nurse), Jessica Nelson (Barbara), Peter Brocco (Hubert), Michael Klingher, Noelle North, David Murphy (Students), Mary McCusker (Patient), Liz Sheridan (Mrs. Larson), Alison Hong (Asian Girl), Walter Janowitz (Elderly Man), Belita Moreno (Nurse Gonzales), Leland Sun (Wong), George Wendy (Injured Man), Glen Chin (Sushi Chef), Dan Barrows (Customer), Virginia Wing (Mme. WooWoo), Jesse Goins (Dutch), Jack Collins (Baron), Michael Ensign (Announcer), John Dennis Johnston (Macho Kid), David Ruprecht (Brigham), Clarke Coleman (Box Boy), Sam Whipple (Produce Man), Nancy Lenehan (Mother), Barret Oliver (Child), Tony Cox, Selwyn Emerson Miller (Lawn Jockeys), Art LaFleur (Clockman), Bernadette Birkett (Mrs. Simpson), Lin Shaye (Nurse), Madelyn Cates (Helen), George Chakiris (Himself), Sheila Rogers, Gerald Saunderson Peters, Bud Davis, Jose Borcia, Maher Bouros, Kate Fitzmaurice, Howard George

BUGS BUNNY'S 3rd MOVIE: 1001 RABBIT TALES (Warner Bros.) Producer, Friz Freleng; Sequence Directors, David Detiege, Art Davis, Bill Perez; Voice Characterization, Mel Blanc, Shep Menken, Lennie Weinrib; Story, John Dunn, David Detiege, Friz Freleng; Music, Rob Walsh, Milt Franklyn, Bill Lava, Carl Stalling; Editor, Jim Champin; Design, Bob Givens, Thomas M. Yakutis; Animators, Warren Barchelder, Bob Bransford, Marcia Fertig, Terrence Lennon, Bob Matz, Norm McCabe, Tom Ray, Virgil Ross; Camera, Nick Vasu; In color; 90 minutes; Rated G; November release. A feature-length retrospective of Classic Cartoons

Mark Blankfield, Bess Armstrong in "Jekyll and Hyde
Together Again" ©*Paramount*

113

Gilda Radner, Dan Aykroyd in "It Came from Hollywood"
©*Paramount*

George Stover, Don Leifert in "Nightbeast"
©*Amazing Films*

NORMAN LOVES ROSE (Atlantic) Producers, Henri Safran, Basil Appleby; Direction and Screenplay, Henri Safran; Photography, Vince Monton; Music, Mike Perjanik; A Norman Films production in color; 98 minutes; Rated R; November release. CAST: Carol Kane, Tony Owen, Myra DeGroot, David Downer, Barry Otto, Sandy Gore, Warren Mitchell

IT CAME FROM HOLLYWOOD (Paramount) Producers, Susan Strausberg, Jeff Stein; Executive Producers-Directors, Malcolm Leo, Andrew Solt; Associate Producers, Susan F. Walker, Jim Milio; In color, black and white; 80 minutes; Rated PG; November release. CAST: Dan Aykroyd, John Candy, Cheech and Chong, Gilda Radner with sequences from almost 100 different previously released films

CREEPSHOW (Warner Bros.) Producer, Richard P. Rubinstein; Director, George A. Romero; Screenplay, Stephen King; Executive Producer, Salah M. Hassanein; Music, John Harrison; Photography, Michael Gornick; Associate Producer, David E. Vogel; Design, Cletus Anderson; Costumes, Barbara Anderson; Editors, Michael Spolan, Pasquale Buba, George A. Romero, Paul Hirsch; Assitant Directors, John Harrison, Carl Clifford; In Technicolor and Dolby Stereo; 122 minutes; Rated R; November release. CAST: Hal Holbrook (Henry), Adrienne Barbeau (Wilma), Fritz Weaver (Dexter), Leslie Nielsen (Richard), Carrie Nye (Sylvia), E. G. Marshall (Upson), Viveca Lindfors (Aunt Bedelia), Ed Harris (Hank), Ted Danson (Harry), Stephen King (Jordy), Warner Shook (Richard), Robert Harper (Charlie), Elizabeth Regan (Cass), Gaylen Ross (Becky), Jon Lormer (Nathan), Don Keefer (Janitor), Bingo O'Malley (Jordy's Dad), John Amplas (Corpse), David Early (White), Nann Mogg (Mrs. Danvers), Iva Jean Saraceni (Billy's Mother), Joe King (Billy), Christine Forrest (Tabitha), Chuck Aber (Richard Raymond), Cletus Anderson (Host), Katie Karlovitz (Maid), Peter Messer (Yarbro), Marty Schiff, Tom Savini (Garbage Men)

HEIDI'S SONG (Paramount) Producers, Joseph Barbera, William Hanna; Director, Robert Taylor; Screenplay, Joseph Barbera, Jameson Brewer, Robert Taylor; Based on novel by Johanna Spyri; Score, Hoyt S. Curtin; Songs, Sammy Cahn, Burton Lane; Associate Producer, Iwao Takamoto; Editor, Gregory V. Watson, Jr.; Supervising Animators, Hal Ambro, Charlie Downs; Art Director, Paul Julian; In color; 94 minutes; Rated G; November release. VOICES OF Lorne Greene (Grandfather), Sammy Davis, Jr. (Head Ratte), Margery Gray (Heidi), Michael Bell (Willie), Peter Cullen (Gruffle), Roger DeWitt (Peter), Richard Erdman (Herr Sessman), Fritz Feld (Sebastian), Pamelyn Ferdin (Klara), Joan Gerber (Fraulein Rottenmeier), Virginia Gregg (Aunt Dete), Janet Waldo (Tinette), Frank Walker (Schnoodle/Hootie), Mike Winslow (Mountain)

NIGHTBEAST (Amazing Films) Written, Directed and Edited by Don Dohler; Photography, Richard Geiwitz; Assistant Director, Larry Reichman; Music, Rob Walsh, Jeffrey Abrams, Arlon Ober, Leonard Rogowski; In color; 85 minutes; Rated R; November release. CAST: Tom Griffith (Sheriff Cinder), Jamie Zemarel (Jamie), Karin Kardian (Lisa), George Stover (Steven), Don Leifert (Drago), Anne Frith (Ruth), Eleanor Herman (Mary Jane), Richard Dyszel (Mayor), Greg Dohler (Greg), Kim Dohler (Kim), Monica Neff (Suzie), Glenn Barnes (Glenn), Rose Wolfe (Glenn's Girl), Richard Ruxton (Governor)

ASHES AND EMBERS (Mypheduh Films) Produced, Directed and Written by Haile Gerima; 120 minutes; Not rated; November release. CAST: John Anderson (Ned), Evelyn A. Blackwell (Grandma), Norman Blalock (Jim), Kathy Flewellen (Liza), Uwezo Flewellen (Kimathi), Barry Wiggins (Randolph)

DON'T CRY, IT'S ONLY THUNDER (Sanrio Communications) Producer, Walt deFarla; Director, Peter Werner; Screenplay, Paul Hensler; Photography, Don McAlpine; Editors, Jack Woods, Barbara Pokras; Music, Maurice Jarre; In color; 108 minutes; Rated PG; November release. CAST: Dennis Christopher (Brian), Susan Saint James (Katherine), Roger Aaron Brown (Moses), Robert Englund (Tripper), James Whitmore, Jr. (Maj. Flaherty), Lisa Lu (Sister Marie), Thu Thuy (Sister Hoa), Travis Swords (Allen), Mai Thi Lien (Ann), Truong Minh Hal (Duc), Ken Metcalfe (Capt. Morris), Marie Ashton (Peggy), Robert Howland (Bugsy), Paul Hensler (Dr. Goldman), Wynne Dieppe (Immigration Woman), Ronald Sully (Troy), Tom Joyner (Supply Sgt.), Ronald Orso (Michael)

Hal Holbrook, Fritz Weaver in "Creepshow"
©*Warner Bros.*

Dennis Christopher, Mai Thi Lien in "Don't Cry, It's Only Thunder" ©*Sanrio*

Leah Ayres, Brian Matthews in "The Burning"
©*Filmways*

Michele Michaels, Debra Delisio in "Slumberparty Massacre"
©*Santa Fe Productions*

THE BURNING (Filmways/Orien) Director, Tony Maylam; Screenplay, Peter Lawrence, Bob Weinstein; Story, Harvey Weinstein, Tony Maylam, Brad Grey; Photography, Harvey Harrison; Editor, Jack Sholder; Music, Rick Wakeman; In color; 90 minutes; Rated R; November release. Film Ventures used same title for a 1981 release that was changed to "Don't Go in the House." CAST: Shelley Bruce (Tiger), Brian Matthews (Todd), Leah Ayres (Michelle), Brian Backer (Alfred), Larry Joshua (Glazer), Jason Alexander (Dave), Ned Eisenberg (Eddy), Carrick Glenn (Sally), Carolyn Houlihan (Karen), Fisher Stevens (Woodstock), Lou David (Cropsy)

THE LAST UNICORN (Jensen Farley) Produced and Directed by Arthur Rankin, Jr., Jules Bass; Screenplay, Peter S. Beagle from his novel; Photography, Hiroyasu Omoto; Animators, Yoshiko Sasaki, Masahiro Yoshida, Kayoko Sakano, Fukuo Suzuki; Editor, Tornoko Kida; Music, Jimmy Webb; Presented by Lord Grade; In color; 88 minutes; Rated G; November release. An animated feature with the voices of Alan Arkin (Schmendrick), Jeff Bridges (Prince Lir), Mia Farrow (Last Unicorn/Lady Amalthea), Tammy Grimes (Molly), Robert Klein (Butterfly), Angela Lansbury (Mommy Fortuna), Christopher Lee (King Haggard), Keenan Wynn (Capt. Cully), Paul Frees (Talking Cat), Rene Auberjonois (Speaking Skull)

THE SLUMBERPARTY MASSACRE (Sante Fe) Producer-Director, Amy Jones; Screenplay, Rita Mae Brown; Photography, Steve Posey; Editor, Wendy Green; Music, Ralph Jones; In color; 78 minutes; Rated R; November release. CAST: Michele Michaelis (Trish), Robin Stille (Valerie), Michael Villela (Russ), Andre Honore (Jackie), Debra Deliso (Kim), Gina Mari (Diane), David Millbern (Jeff), Joe Johnson (Neil), Pamela Roylance (Coach Jana), Brinke Stevens (Linda), Rigg Kennedy (David), Howard Furgeson (Devereaux)

SMITHEREENS (New Line) Produced, Directed and Edited by Susan Seidelman; Screenplay, Ron Nystwaner, Susan Seidelman; Photography, Chirine El Khadem; Music, Glenn Mercer, Bill Million; In color; 90 minutes; Not rated; November release. CAST: Susan Berman (Wren), Brad Rinn (Paul), Richard Hell (Eric), Nada Despotovich (Cecile), Roger Jett (Billy), Kitty Summerall (Blonde), Robynne White (Landlady), D. J. O'Neill (Ed), Joel Rooks (Xerox Boss), Pamela Speed (Terry), Tom Cherwin (Mike)

DIARIES (Center for Public Cinema) Director, Ed Pincus; Editors, Ed Pincus, Moe Shore, Ann Schaetzel; 200 minutes; Not rated; November release. A documentary record of the life of Ed Pincus, his wife and two children from 1971 through 1976.

STREET MUSIC (Pacificon) Produced and Photographed by Richard Bowen; Director, Jenny Bowen; Art Director, Don De Fina; Editors, Lisa Fruchtman, Diana Pelligrini; Music, Ed Bogus, Judy Munson; In color; Not rated; 92 minutes; November release. CAST: Elizabeth Daily (Sadie), Larry Breeding (Eddie), Ned Glass (Sam), Marjorie Eaton (Mildred), W. F. Walker (Jasper), Miriam Phillips (Hattie), D'Alan Moss (Monroe), Sam Morford (Slim), John Romano (Potts), David Parr (Simmons)

ATRAPADOS/TRAPPED (Panorama) Produced, directed and photographed by Matthew Patrick; Story and Screenplay, Julio Torresoto; Co-producers, Matthew Irmas, Jan Santagata; Music, John Petersen, Daniel Licht, Cahunto Classico; Editor, Matsuo Kuhara; Design, Javier Torres; Art Director, Felix Cordero; In color; Not rated; 91 minutes; November release. CAST: Julio Torresoto, Sonia Vivas

PINK MOTEL (New Image) Executive Producer, Ed Elbert; Producer, M. James Kouf, Jr.; Director Mike MacFarland; Associate Producer, Bren Plaistowe; Assistant Director, George w. Perkins; Photography, Nicholas J. von Sternberg; Art Director, Chester Kaczenski; Editor, Earl Watson; Title Song, Michael Bunnell; Performed by Nile; Screenplay, M. James Kouf, Jr.; In color; 90 minutes; Rated R; November release. CAST: Slim Pickens (Roy), Phyllis Diller (Margaret), John Macchia (Skip), Cathryn Hartt (Charlene), Christopher Nelson (Max), Terri Berland (Marlene), Tony Longo (Mark), Cathy Sawyer-Young (Lola), Brad Cowgill (Larry), Heidi Holicker (Lisa), Squire Fridell (George), Andrea Howard (Tracy)

CONTRACT: KILL (New American) Producer, Edgar Oppenheimer; Director, Claude Mulot; Screenplay, Albert Kantof, Claude Mulot; In Eastmancolor; 86 minutes; Rated R; November release. CAST: Bruno Pradal, Patti D'Arbanville, Gabrielle Tinti, Eva Swan, Charles Southwood, Sydney Chaplin, Francoise Prevost

Roger Jett, Susan Berman, Richard Hell in "Smithereens"
©*New Line Cinema*

Phyllis Diller, Slim Pickens in "Pink Motel"
©*New Image*

115

Mary Tyler Moore, Katherine Healy, Dudley Moore in "Six Weeks" ©*Universal*

TIME WALKER (New World) Executive Producer, Robert Shafter; Producers, Dimitri Villard, Jason Williams; Director, Tom Kennedy; Screenplay, Karen Levitt, Tom Friedman; Photography, Robbie Greenberg; Music, Richard Band; In DeLuxe Color; 83 minutes; Rated PG; November release. CAST: Ben Murphy (Doug), Nina Axelrod (Susy), Kevin Brophy (Peter), James Karen (Wendell), Robert Random (Parker), Austin Stoker (Dr. Hayworth), Jason Williams (Jeff), Melissa Prophet, Sam Chew, Jr., Gerard Prendergast, Jack Olson

ONE DOWN TWO TO GO (Almi) Director-Producer, Fred Williamson; Screenplay, Jeff Williamson; Photography, James Lemmo; Editor, Daniel Loewenthal; Executive Producer, Robert Atwell; Associate Producers, Randy Jurgensen, Stan Wakerfield, David Moon; In Dolby Stereo and color; 84 minutes; Rated R; November release. CAST: Fred Williamson (Cal), Jim Brown (J), Jim Kelly (Chuck), Richard Roundtree (Ralph), Paula Sills (Teri), Laura Loftus (Sally), Tom Signorelli (Mario), Joe Spinell (Joe), Louis Neglia (Armando), Peter Dane (Rossi), Victoria Hale (Maria), Richard Noyce (Hank), John Guitz (Bob), Warrington Winters (Sheriff), Arthur Haggerty (Mojo), Irwin Litvack (Banker), Addison Greene (Pete), Dennis Singletary (Roy), John Dorish (Deputy), Robert Pastner (Slim), Patty O'Brien (Nurse)

JIMMY THE KID (New World) Producer, Ronald Jacobs; Director, Gary Nelson; Screenplay, Sam Bobrick; Based on novel by Donald E. Westlake; Assistant Director, Donald Roberts; Music, John Cameron; Executive Producers, Harry Evans Sloan, Lawrence L. Kuppin; In color; 85 minutes; Rated PG; November release. CAST: Gary Coleman (Jimmy), Paul LeMat (John), Dee Wallace (May), Don Adams (Harry), Walter Olkewicz (Andrew), Ruth Gordon (Bernice), Cleavon Little (Herb), Fay Hauser (Nina), Avery Schreiber (Dr. Stevens), Pat Morita (Maurice)

THE BOSS' SON (Lagoon) Direction and Screenplay, Bobby Roth; Not rated; March release. CAST: Asher Brauner (Bobby), Rita Moreno (Mother), Rudy Solari (Father), Michelle Davison (Black Woman), Henry G. Sanders (Truckdriver), Ritchie Havens (Dispatcher), James Darren

Jeff Bridges, Sally Field, James Caan in "Kiss Me Goodbye" ©*20th Century-Fox*

SIX WEEKS (Universal) Producers, Peter Guber, Jon Peters; Director, Tony Bill; Screenplay, David Seltzer; Based on novel by Fred Mustard Stewart; Photography, Michael D. Margulies; Art Director, Hilyard Brown; Editor, Stu Linder; Music composed and performed by Dudley Moore; Associate Producer, Hillary Anne Ripps; Assistant Directors, Michael Daves, Bob Doberty; Choreographer, Ann Ditchburn; Designer, Sandy Veneziano; A PolyGram Picture in Metrocolor; 107 minutes; Rated PG; December release. CAST: Dudley Moore (Patrick Dalton), Mary Tyler Moore (Charlotte Dreyfus), Katherine Healy (Nicole Dreyfus), Shannon Wilcox (Peg), Bill Calvert (Jeff), Joe Regalbuto (Bob), John Harkins (Arnold), Michael Ensign (Choreographer), Ann Ditchburn (Assistant Choreographer), Chea Collette (Ballet Instructor), Clement St. George (TV Interviewer), Joan Yale Edmundson (Interviewer), Gary Nulsen (Doctor), Martin Casella (Volunteer/Campaign Office), Darwyn Carson (Girl in office), Fausto Barajas (Man in office), Darrell Larson (Art Teacher), Frank Adamo, Frank Patton (Subway Passengers), Barbara Bradish (Cashier), Lloyd Wilson (Foreman), Laurel Page (Interviewer), and members of Ballet West.

KISS ME GOODBYE (20th Century-Fox) Producer-Director, Robert Mulligan; Screenplay, Charlie Peters; Photography, Donald Peterman; Designer, Philip M. Jefferies; Editor, Sheldon Kahn; Music, Ralph Burns; Assistant Directors, James Quinn, Carol Green; Choreography, Gene Castle; Art Director, John V. Cartwright; In DeLuxe Color; 101 minutes; Rated PG; December release. CAST: Sally Field (Kay), James Caan (Jolly), Jeff Bridges (Rupert), Paul Dooley (Kendall), Claire Trevor (Charlotte), Mildred Natwick (Mrs. Reilly), Dorothy Fielding (Emily), William Prince (Rev. Hollis), Maryedith Burrell (Mrs. Newman), Alan Haufrect (Mr. Newman), Stephen Elliott (Edgar), Michael Ensign (Billy), Edith Fields (Waitress), Lee Weaver (Mr. King), Gene Castle (Guest), Lyla Graham (Miss Wells), Christopher Graver (Little Boy), Bernadette Birkett (Mother), Barret Oliver (Little Boy), Robert Miano (Michael), Wolf Muser (Mark), Norman Alexander Gibbs (Roland), Adam Wade (Roscoe), Abraham Gordon (Workman), Vincent J. Isaac (Messenger), Jeffrey Lampert, Jude Farese (Movers)

AIRPLANE II: THE SEQUEL (Paramount) Producer, Howard W. Koch; Direction and Screenplay, Ken Finkleman; Photography, Joe Biroc; Designer, William Sandell; Editor, Dennis Virkler; Original Music, Elmer Bernstein; Additional Music, Richard Hazard; Assistant Directors, Jack F. Sanders, Pamela Eilerson, Susan J. Bernay; In Metrocolor; 85 minutes; Rated PG; December release. CAST: Sonny Bono (Joe), Lloyd Bridges (McCroskey), Raymond Burr (Judge), Chuck Connors (Sarge), John Dehner (Commissioner), Rip Torn (Kruger), Chad Everett (Simon), Peter Graves (Capt. Oveur), Julie Hagerty (Elaine), Robert Hays (Striker), Kent McCord (Unger), James A. Watson, Jr. (Dunn), William Shatner (Murdock), Stephen Stucker (Jacobs), John Vernon (Dr. Stone), Laurene London (Testa), Wendy Phillips (Mary), Jack Jones (Singer), Art Fleming (Himself), Frank Ashmore, Richard Jaeckel, John Hancock (Controllers), Al White (Witness), Lee Bryant (Mrs. Hammen), John Larch (Prosecuting Attorney), Oliver Robins (Jimmy), Louis Giambalvo (Witness), Stephen Stucker (Court Reporter), Leon Askin (Anchorman), Sandahl Bergman (Officer), James Noble (Father of Flanagan), Lee Patterson (Captain), Louise Sorel (Stella)

LAND OF LOOK BEHIND (Solo Man) Producer-Director, Alan Greenberg; Photography, Jorg Schmidt-Reitwein; Music, K. Leimer, Bob Marley, The Wailers; 90 minutes; In color; Not rated; December release. CAST: Gregory Isaacs, Louis Lepke, Mutabaruka

FORCED VENGEANCE (MGM/UA) Producer, John B. Bennett; Director, James Fargo; Screenplay, Franklin Thompson; Photography, Rexford Metz; Editor, Irving C. Rosenblum; Design, George B. Chan; Music, William Goldsetin; Assistant Directors, Stan Zabka, Patty Chan; In Metrocolor; 90 minutes; Rated R; December release. CAST: Chuck Norris (Josh), Mary Louise Weller (Claire), Camila Griggs (Joy), Michael Cavanaugh (Stan), David Opatoshu (Sam), Seiji Sakaguchi (Cam), Frank Michael Liu (David), Bob Minor (Leroy), Lloyd Kino (Inspector), Leigh Hamilton (Sally), Howard Caine (Milt), Robert Emhardt (Carl), Roger Behrstock (Ron), Jimmy Shaw (Inspector)

FORBIDDEN LESSONS (SRC Films) In color; 78 minutes; Rated R; December release. CAST: Lola Felice, Barbara Roy

MIDNIGHT (Independent-International) Executive Producers, Samuel Sherman, Daniel Kennis; Producer, Donald Redinger; Direction and Screenplay, John A. Russo from his novel; Photography, Paul McCullough; Music, Sound Castle; In Eastmancolor; Rated R; 91 minutes; December release. CAST: Lawrence Tierney (Bert), Melanie Verliin (Nancy), John Hall (Tom), Charles Jackson (Hank), Doris Hackney (Harriet), John Amplas (Abraham), Robin Walsh (Cynthia), David Marchick (Cyrus), Greg Besnak (Luke)

PROMISING NEW ACTORS OF 1982

KEVIN BACON

KATE CAPSHAW

GLENN CLOSE

ZELJKO IVANEK

KATE JACKSON

DAVID KEITH

EDDIE MURPHY

GILDA RADNER

118

ANN REINKING

EDWARD JAMES OLMOS

JOHN SHEA

MARCIA STRASSMAN

ACADEMY AWARDS FOR 1982

(Presented Monday, April 11, 1983)

BEST PICTURE OF 1982

GANDHI

(COLUMBIA) Producer-Director, Richard Attenborough; Screenplay, John Briley; Executive Producer, Michael Stanley-Evans; Photography, Billy Williams, Ronnie Taylor; Music, Ravi Shankar; Additional Music, George Fenton; Co-Producer, Rani Dube; Editor, John Bloom; Designer, Stuart Craig; Associate Producer, Suresh Jindal; Assistant Directors, David Tomblin, Steve Lanning, Roy Button, Kamal Swaroop; Costumes, John Mollo, Bhanu Athaiya; Art Directors, Ram Yedeker, Norman Dorme; Presented by International Film Investors, Goldcrest Films International, Indo-British Films, National Film Development Corp; In Panavision, Dolby Stereo and color; 200 minutes with intermission; Rated PG; December release.

CAST

Mahatma Gandhi	Ben Kingsley
Margaret Bourke-White	Candice Bergen
General Dyer	Edward Fox
Lord Irwin	John Gielgud
Judge Broomfield	Trevor Howard
The Viceroy	John Mills
Walker	Martin Sheen
Kasturba Gandhi	Rohini Hattangady
Charlie Andrews	Ian Charleson
General Smuts	Athol Fugard

and Gunter Maria Halmer (Herman Kallenbach), Saeed Jaffrey (Sardar Patel), Geraldine James (Mirabehn), Alyque Padamsee (Mohammed Ali Jinnah), Amrish Puri (Kahn), Roshan Seth (Pandit Nehru), Ian Bannen (Police Officer), Michael Bryant (Secretary), John Clements (Advocate General), Richard Griffiths (Collins), Nigel Hawthorne (Kinnoch), Bernard Hepton (G.O.C.), Michael Hordern (Sir George Hodge), Shreeram Lagoo (Prof. Gokhale), Om Puri (Nahari), Virendra Razdan (Maulana Azad), Richard Vernon (Sir Edward Gait), Harsh Nayyar (Nathuram Godse), Prabhakar Patankar (Prakash), Vijay Kahsyap (Apte), Nigam Prakash (Karkare), Supriya Pathak (Manu), Nina Gupta (Abha), Shane Rimmer (Commentator), Peter Harlowe (Lord Mountbatten), Anang Desai (J. B. Kripalani), Alok Nath (Tyeb Mohammed), Dean Gaspar (Singh), David Gant (Daniels), Daniel Day Lewis (Colin), Avis Bunnage (His Mother), Sunila Pradhan (Mrs. Motilal Nehru), Manohar Pitale (Shukla), Ernest Clark (Lord Hunter), Pankaj Mohan (Mahadev Desai), Bernard Horsfall (Gen. Edgar), Daleep Tahil (Zia), Terrence Hardiman (Ramsay MacDonald), Jane Myerson (Lady Mountbatten), John Vine (A.D.C. to Gen. Dyer)

Left: Rohini Hattangady (L), Ben Kingsley (R)
Above: Ben Kingsley (C)

Academy Awards for Best Picture, Best Actor (Ben Kingsley), Best Direction, Original Screenplay, Cinematography, Film Editing, Art Direction, Costume Design
©*Columbia*

Troops fire on crowd protesting British rule

Police charge protesting miners led by Gandhi

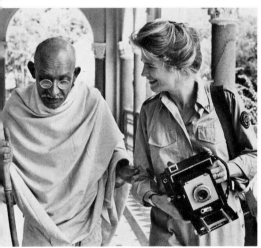

**Gandhi leads Salt March Above: Ben Kingsley, Candice
Bergen Top: Kingsley, Ian Charleson**

**Gandhi's funeral procession Above: Martin Sheen, Ben
Kingsley (also top)**

BEN KINGSLEY
in "Gandhi" © *Columbia*

1982 ACADEMY AWARD FOR BEST ACTOR

MERYL STREEP
in "Sophie's Choice" © *Universal*

1982 ACADEMY AWARD FOR BEST ACTRESS

LOUIS GOSSETT, JR.
in "An Officer and a Gentleman" © *Paramount*

1982 ACADEMY AWARD FOR BEST SUPPORTING ACTOR

JESSICA LANGE
in "Tootsie" © *Columbia*

1982 ACADEMY AWARD FOR BEST SUPPORTING ACTRESS

VOLVER A EMPEZAR
(To Begin Again)

(20th CENTURY-FOX INTERNATIONAL CLASSICS) Producer-Director, Jose Luis Garci; Screenplay, Jose Luis Garci, Angel Llorente; Photography, Manuel Rojas; Music, Johann Pachelbel, Cole Porter; Designer, Gil Parrondo; Executive Producers, Estaban Alenda, Angel Llorente; A Nickel Odeon, S. A. production in color; Spanish with English subtitles; 93 minutes. Rated PG; December release.

CAST

Albajara	Antonio Ferrandi
Elena	Encarna Pas
Roxiu	Jose Bodal
Gervasio Losada	Agustin Gonzale
Ernesto	Pablo Hoy
Carolina	Marta Fernandez Mur
Sabino	Pablo del Hoy

Encarna Paso, Antonio Ferrandis (also above right) Left Center: Antonio Ferrandis Top: Antonio Ferrandis, Encarna Paso
© *20th Century-Fox*

1982 ACADEMY AWARD FOR BEST FOREIGN-LANGUAGE FILM

JUST ANOTHER MISSING KID

(CANADIAN BROADCASTING CORP.) Producer-Director, John Zaritsky; Editor, Gord McClellan; Host, Ian Parker; Photography, John Griffin; Executive Producer, Glenn Sarty; Senior Producers, Ron Haggart, Brian Denike; Associate Producer, Brian Vallee; Additional Photography, Brian Hosking, Colin Allison, Edmund Long, Bill Carr; Sound, Richard France; Lighting, Don McElligott; Production Manager, David R. Tribe; Film Coordinator, Alex Powell; Film Research, Claire Weissman; Technical Producer, Merv Curley; Graphic Design, Bill Boyer; In color; 90 minutes; Not rated; December release. A documentary which exposes the glaring inefficiencies and failures of the American judicial system, and relates the frustrating search by the Wilson family for their missing son Eric who disappeared in 1978.

Eric Wilson ("missing kid") Top: Reporter Ian Parker
©CBC

1982 ACADEMY AWARD FOR BEST FEATURE DOCUMENTARY

127

Faye Dunaway	John Houseman	Ruth Gordon	Joel Grey	Audrey Hepburn	Cliff Roberts

PREVIOUS ACADEMY AWARD WINNERS

**(1) Best Picture, (2) Actor, (3) Actress, (4) Supporting Actor,
(5) Supporting Actress, (6) Director, (7) Special Award, (8) Best Foreign Language Film**

1927–28: (1) "Wings," (2) Emil Jannings in "The Way of All Flesh," (3) Janet Gaynor in "Seventh Heaven," (6) Frank Borzage for "Seventh Heaven," (7) Charles Chaplin.

1928–29: (1) "Broadway Melody," (2) Warner Baxter in "Old Arizona," (3) Mary Pickford in "Coquette," (6) Frank Lloyd for "The Divine Lady."

1929–30: (1) "All Quiet on the Western Front," (2) George Arliss in "Disraeli," (3) Norma Shearer in "The Divorcee," (6) Lewis Milestone for "All Quiet on the Western Front."

1930–31: (1) "Cimarron," (2) Lionel Barrymore in "A Free Soul," (3) Marie Dressler in "Min and Bill," (6) Norman Taurog for "Skippy."

1931–32: (1) "Grand Hotel," (2) Fredric March in "Dr. Jekyll and Mr. Hyde" tied with Wallace Beery in "The Champ," (3) Helen Hayes in "The Sin of Madelon Claudet," (6) Frank Borzage for "Bad Girl."

1932–33: (1) "Cavalcade," (2) Charles Laughton in "The Private Life of Henry VIII," (3) Katharine Hepburn in "Morning Glory," (6) Frank Lloyd for "Cavalcade."

1934: (1) "It Happened One Night," (2) Clark Gable in "It Happened One Night," (3) Claudette Colbert in "It Happened One Night," (6) Frank Capra for "It Happened One Night," (7) Shirley Temple.

1935: (1) "Mutiny on the Bounty," (2) Victor McLaglen in "The Informer," (3) Bette Davis in "Dangerous," (6) John Ford for "The Informer," (7) D. W. Griffith.

1936: (1) "The Great Ziegfeld," (2) Paul Muni in "The Story of Louis Pasteur," (3) Luise Rainer in "The Great Ziegfeld," (4) Walter Brennan in "Come and Get It," (5) Gale Sondergaard in "Anthony Adverse," (6) Frank Capra for "Mr. Deeds Goes to Town."

1937: (1) "The Life of Emile Zola," (2) Spencer Tracy in "Captains Courageous," (3) Luise Rainer in "The Good Earth," (4) Joseph Schildkraut in "The Life of Emile Zola," (5) Alice Brady in "In Old Chicago," (6) Leo McCarey for "The Awful Truth," (7) Mack Sennett, Edgar Bergen.

1938: (1) "You Can't Take It with You," (2) Spencer Tracy in "Boys' Town," (3) Bette Davis in "Jezebel," (4) Walter Brennan in "Kentucky," (5) Fay Bainter in "Jezebel," (6) Frank Capra for "You Can't Take It with You," (7) Deanna Durbin, Mickey Rooney, Harry M. Warner, Walt Disney.

1939: (1) "Gone with the Wind," (2) Robert Donat in "Goodbye, Mr. Chips," (3) Vivien Leigh in "Gone with the Wind," (4) Thomas Mitchell in "Stagecoach," (5) Hattie McDaniel in "Gone with the Wind," (6) Victor Fleming for "Gone with the Wind," (7) Douglas Fairbanks, Judy Garland.

1940: (1) "Rebecca," (2) James Stewart in "The Philadelphia Story," (3) Ginger Rogers in "Kitty Foyle," (4) Walter Brennan in "The Westerner," (5) Jane Darwell in "The Grapes of Wrath," (6) John Ford for "The Grapes of Wrath," (7) Bob Hope.

1941: (1) "How Green Was My Valley," (2) Gary Cooper in "Sergeant York," (3) Joan Fontaine in "Suspicion," (4) Donald Crisp in "How Green Was My Valley," (5) Mary Astor in "The Great Lie," (6) John Ford for "How Green Was My Valley," (7) Leopold Stokowski, Walt Disney.

1942: (1) "Mrs. Miniver," (2) James Cagney in "Yankee Doo Dandy," (3) Greer Garson in "Mrs. Miniver," (4) Van Heflin "Johnny Eager," (5) Teresa Wright in "Mrs. Miniver," (6) W liam Wyler for "Mrs. Miniver," (7) Charles Boyer, Noel Cowar

1943: (1) "Casablanca," (2) Paul Lukas in "Watch on the Rhine (3) Jennifer Jones in "The Song of Bernadette," (4) Charles C burn in "The More the Merrier," (5) Katina Paxinou in "F Whom the Bell Tolls," (6) Michael Curtiz for "Casablanca."

1944: (1) "Going My Way," (2) Bing Crosby in "Going M Way," (3) Ingrid Bergman in "Gaslight," (4) Barry Fitzgerald "Going My Way," (5) Ethel Barrymore in "None but the Lone Heart," (6) Leo McCarey for "Going My Way," (7) Margar O'Brien, Bob Hope.

1945: (1) "The Lost Weekend," (2) Ray Milland in "The Lo Weekend," (3) Joan Crawford in "Mildred Pierce," (4) Jam Dunn in "A Tree Grows in Brooklyn," (5) Anne Revere in "N tional Velvet," (6) Billy Wilder for "The Lost Weekend," (Walter Wanger, Peggy Ann Garner.

1946: (1) "The Best Years of Our Lives," (2) Fredric March "The Best Years of Our Lives," (3) Olivia de Havilland in " Each His Own," (4) Harold Russell in "The Best Years of O Lives," (5) Anne Baxter in "The Razor's Edge," (6) Willia Wyler for "The Best Years of Our Lives," (7) Laurence Olivi Harold Russell, Ernst Lubitsch, Claude Jarman, Jr.

1947: (1) "Gentleman's Agreement," (2) Ronald Colman in " Double Life," (3) Loretta Young in "The Farmer's Daughter (4) Edmund Gwenn in "Miracle On 34th Street," (5) Cele Holm in "Gentleman's Agreement," (6) Elia Kazan for "Ge tleman's Agreement," (7) James Baskette, (8) "Shoe Shine."

1948: (1) "Hamlet," (2) Laurence Olivier in "Hamlet," (3) Ja Wyman in "Johnny Belinda," (4) Walter Huston in "The Tre sure of the Sierra Madre," (5) Claire Trevor in "Key Largo," (John Huston for "The Treasure of the Sierra Madre," (7) Iv Jandl, Sid Grauman, Adolph Zukor, Walter Wanger, (8) "Mo sieur Vincent."

1949: (1) "All the King's Men," (2) Broderick Crawford in "A the King's Men," (3) Olivia de Havilland in "The Heiress." (Dean Jagger in "Twelve O'Clock High," (5) Mercedes McCa bridge in "All the King's Men," (6) Joseph L. Mankiewicz for " Letter to Three Wives," (7) Bobby Driscoll, Fred Astaire, Ce B. DeMille, Jean Hersholt, (8) "The Bicycle Thief."

1950: (1) "All about Eve," (2) Jose Ferrer in "Cyrano de Bergerac (3) Judy Holliday in "Born Yesterday," (4) George Sanders "All about Eve," (5) Josephine Hull in "Harvey," (6) Joseph Mankiewicz for "All about Eve," (7) George Murphy, Louis Mayer, (8) "The Walls of Malapaga."

1951: (1) "An American in Paris," (2) Humphrey Bogart in "T African Queen," (3) Vivien Leigh in "A Streetcar Named D sire," (4) Karl Malden in "A Streetcar Named Desire," (5) Ki Hunter in "A Streetcar Named Desire," (6) George Stevens f "A Place in the Sun," (7) Gene Kelly, (8) "Rashomon."

1952: (1) "The Greatest Show on Earth," (2) Gary Cooper "High Noon," (3) Shirley Booth in "Come Back, Little Sheba (4) Anthony Quinn in "Viva Zapata," (5) Gloria Grahame "The Bad and the Beautiful," (6) John Ford for "The Qui Man," (7) Joseph M. Schenck, Merian C. Cooper, Harold Lloy Bob Hope, George Alfred Mitchell, (8) "Forbidden Games."

1953: (1) "From Here to Eternity," (2) William Holden in "Stalag 17," (3) Audrey Hepburn in "Roman Holiday," (4) Frank Sinatra in "From Here to Eternity," (5) Donna Reed in "From Here to Eternity," (6) Fred Zinnemann for "From Here to Eternity," (7) Pete Smith, Joseph Breen.

1954: (1) "On the Waterfront," (2) Marlon Brando in "On the Waterfront," (3) Grace Kelly in "The Country Girl," (4) Edmond O'Brien in "The Barefoot Contessa," (5) Eva Marie Saint in "On the Waterfront," (6) Elia Kazan for "On the Waterfront," (7) Greta Garbo, Danny Kaye, Jon Whitely, Vincent Winter, (8) "Gate of Hell."

1955: (1) "Marty," (2) Ernest Borgnine in "Marty," (3) Anna Magnani in "The Rose Tattoo," (4) Jack Lemmon in "Mister Roberts," (5) Jo Van Fleet in "East of Eden," (6) Delbert Mann for "Marty," (8) "Samurai."

1956: (1) "Around the World in 80 Days," (2) Yul Brynner in "The King and I," (3) Ingrid Bergman in "Anastasia," (4) Anthony Quinn in "Lust for Life," (5) Dorothy Malone in "Written on the Wind," (6) George Stevens for "Giant," (7) Eddie Cantor, (8) "La Strada."

1957: (1) "The Bridge on the River Kwai," (2) Alec Guinness in "The Bridge on the River Kwai," (3) Joanne Woodward in "The Three Faces of Eve," (4) Red Buttons in "Sayonara," (5) Miyoshi Umeki in "Sayonara," (6) David Lean for "The Bridge on the River Kwai," (7) Charles Brackett, B. B. Kahane, Gilbert M. (Bronco Billy) Anderson, (8) "The Nights of Cabiria."

1958: (1) "Gigi," (2) David Niven in "Separate Tables," (3) Susan Hayward in "I Want to Live," (4) Burl Ives in "The Big Country," (5) Wendy Hiller in "Separate Tables," (6) Vincente Minnelli for "Gigi," (7) Maurice Chevalier, (8) "My Uncle."

1959: (1) "Ben-Hur," (2) Charlton Heston in "Ben-Hur," (3) Simone Signoret in "Room at the Top," (4) Hugh Griffith in "Ben-Hur," (5) Shelley Winters in "The Diary of Anne Frank," (6) William Wyler for "Ben-Hur," (7) Lee de Forest, Buster Keaton, (8) "Black Orpheus."

1960: (1) "The Apartment," (2) Burt Lancaster in "Elmer Gantry," (3) Elizabeth Taylor in "Butterfield 8," (4) Peter Ustinov in "Spartacus," (5) Shirley Jones in "Elmer Gantry," (6) Billy Wilder for "The Apartment," (7) Gary Cooper, Stan Laurel, Hayley Mills, (8) "The Virgin Spring."

1961: (1) "West Side Story," (2) Maximilian Schell in "Judgment at Nuremberg," (3) Sophia Loren in "Two Women," (4) George Chakiris in "West Side Story," (5) Rita Moreno in "West Side Story," (6) Robert Wise for "West Side Story," (7) Jerome Robbins, Fred L. Metzler, (8) "Through a Glass Darkly."

1962: (1) "Lawrence of Arabia," (2) Gregory Peck in "To Kill a Mockingbird," (3) Anne Bancroft in "The Miracle Worker," (4) Ed Begley in "Sweet Bird of Youth," (5) Patty Duke in "The Miracle Worker," (6) David Lean for "Lawrence of Arabia," (8) Sundays and Cybele."

1963: (1) "Tom Jones," (2) Sidney Poitier in "Lilies of the Field," (3) Patricia Neal in "Hud," (4) Melvyn Douglas in "Hud," (5) Margaret Rutherford in "The V.I.P.'s," (6) Tony Richardson for Tom Jones," (7) "8½."

1964: (1) "My Fair Lady," (2) Rex Harrison in "My Fair Lady," (3) Julie Andrews in "Mary Poppins," (4) Peter Ustinov in "Topkapi," (5) Lila Kedrova in "Zorba the Greek," (6) George Cukor for "My Fair Lady," (7) William Tuttle, (8) "Yesterday, Today and Tomorrow."

1965: (1) "The Sound of Music," (2) Lee Marvin in "Cat Ballou," (3) Julie Christie in "Darling," (4) Martin Balsam in "A Thousand Clowns," (5) Shelley Winters in "A Patch of Blue," (6) Robert Wise for "The Sound of Music," (7) Bob Hope, (8) "The Shop on Main Street."

1966: (1) "A Man for All Seasons," (2) Paul Scofield in "A Man for All Seasons," (3) Elizabeth Taylor in "Who's Afraid of Virginia Woolf?," (4) Walter Matthau in "The Fortune Cookie," (5) Sandy Dennis in "Who's Afraid of Virginia Woolf?," (6) Fred Zinnemann for "A Man for All Seasons," (8) "A Man and A Woman."

1967: (1) "In the Heat of the Night," (2) Rod Steiger in "In the Heat of the Night," (3) Katharine Hepburn in "Guess Who's Coming to Dinner," (4) George Kennedy in "Cool Hand Luke," (5) Estelle Parsons in "Bonnie and Clyde," (6) Mike Nichols for "The Graduate," (8) "Closely Watched Trains."

1968: (1) "Oliver!," (2) Cliff Robertson in "Charly," (3) Katharine Hepburn in "The Lion in Winter" tied with Barbra Streisand in "Funny Girl," (4) Jack Albertson in "The Subject Was Roses," (5) Ruth Gordon in "Rosemary's Baby," (6) Carol Reed for "Oliver!," (7) Onna White for "Oliver!" choreography, John Chambers for "Planet of the Apes" make-up, (8) "War and Peace."

1969: (1) "Midnight Cowboy," (2) John Wayne in "True Grit," (3) Maggie Smith in "The Prime of Miss Jean Brodie," (4) Gig Young in "They Shoot Horses, Don't They?," (5) Goldie Hawn in "Cactus Flower," (6) John Schlesinger for "Midnight Cowboy," (7) Cary Grant, (8) "Z."

1970: (1) "Patton," (2) George C. Scott in "Patton," (3) Glenda Jackson in "Women in Love," (4) John Mills in "Ryan's Daughter," (5) Helen Hayes in "Airport," (6) Franklin J. Schaffner for "Patton," (7) Lillian Gish, Orson Welles, (8) "Investigation of a Citizen above Suspicion."

1971: (1) "The French Connection," (2) Gene Hackman in "The French Connection," (3) Jane Fonda in "Klute," (4) Ben Johnson in "The Last Picture Show," (5) Cloris Leachman in "The Last Picture Show," (6) William Friedkin for "The French Connection," (7) Charles Chaplin, (8) "The Garden of the Finzi-Continis."

1972: (1) "The Godfather," (2) Marlon Brando in "The Godfather," (3) Liza Minnelli in "Cabaret," (4) Joel Grey in "Cabaret," (5) Eileen Heckart in "Butterflies Are Free," (6) Bob Fosse for "Cabaret," (7) Edward G. Robinson, (8) "The Discreet Charm of the Bourgeoisie."

1973: (1) "The Sting," (2) Jack Lemmon in "Save the Tiger," (3) Glenda Jackson in "A Touch of Class," (4) John Houseman in "The Paper Chase," (5) Tatum O'Neal in "Paper Moon," (6) George Roy Hill for "The Sting," (8) "Day for Night."

1974: (1) "The Godfather Part II," (2) Art Carney in "Harry and Tonto," (3) Ellen Burstyn in "Alice Doesn't Live Here Anymore," (4) Robert DeNiro in "The Godfather Part II," (5) Ingrid Bergman in "Murder on the Orient Express," (6) Francis Ford Coppola for "The Godfather Part II," (7) Howard Hawks, Jean Renoir, (8) "Amarcord."

1975: (1) "One Flew over the Cuckoo's Nest," (2) Jack Nicholson in "One Flew over the Cuckoo's Nest," (3) Louise Fletcher in "One Flew over the Cuckoo's Nest," (4) George Burns in "The Sunshine Boys," (5) Lee Grant in "Shampoo," (6) Milos Forman for "One Flew over the Cuckoo's Nest," (7) Mary Pickford, (8) "Dersu Uzala."

1976: (1) "Rocky," (2) Peter Finch in "Network," (3) Faye Dunaway in "Network," (4) Jason Robards in "All the President's Men," (5) Beatrice Straight in "Network," (6) John G. Avildsen for "Rocky," (8) "Black and White in Color."

1977: (1) "Annie Hall," (2) Richard Dreyfuss in "The Goodbye Girl," (3) Diane Keaton in "Annie Hall," (4) Jason Robards in "Julia," (5) Vanessa Redgrave in "Julia," (6) Woody Allen for "Annie Hall," (7) Maggie Booth (film editor), (8) "Madame Rosa."

1978: (1) "The Deer Hunter," (2) Jon Voight in "Coming Home," (3) Jane Fonda in "Coming Home," (4) Christopher Walken in "The Deer Hunter," (5) Maggie Smith in "California Suite," (6) Michael Cimino for "The Deer Hunter," (7) Laurence Olivier, King Vidor, (8) "Get Out Your Handkerchiefs."

1979: (1) "Kramer vs. Kramer," (2) Dustin Hoffman in "Kramer vs. Kramer," (3) Sally Field in "Norma Rae," (4) Melvyn Douglas in "Being There," (5) Meryl Streep in "Kramer vs. Kramer," (6) Robert Benton for "Kramer vs. Kramer," (7) Robert S. Benjamin, Hal Elias, Alec Guinness, (8) "The Tin Drum."

1980: (1) "Ordinary People," (2) Robert DeNiro in "Raging Bull," (3) Sissy Spacek in "Coal Miner's Daughter," (4) Timothy Hutton in "Ordinary People," (5) Mary Steenburgen in "Melvin and Howard," (6) Robert Redford for "Ordinary People," (7) Henry Fonda, (8) "Moscow Does Not Believe in Tears."

1981: (1) "Chariots of Fire," (2) Henry Fonda in "On Golden Pond," (3) Katharine Hepburn in "On Golden Pond," (4) John Gielgud in "Arthur," (5) Maureen Stapleton in "Reds," (6) Warren Beatty for "Reds," (7) Fuji Photo Film Co., (8) "Mephisto"

1982 FOREIGN FILMS

OPERA PRIMA

(NEW YORKER) Producer, Fernando Colomo; Director, Fernando Trueba; Screenplay, Oscar Ladoire, Fernando Trueba; Photography, Angel Luis Fernandez; Music, Fernando Ember; Editor, Miguel Angel Santamaria; Spanish with English subtitles; In color; 94 minutes; Not rated; January release.

CAST

Matias	Oscar Ladoire
Violeta	Paula Molina
Nicky	Luis Gonzalez-Regueral
Leon	Antonio Resines
Ana	Kitty Manver
Alejandro	Alejandro Serna
Zoila	Marisa Paredes
Warren Belch	David Thomson

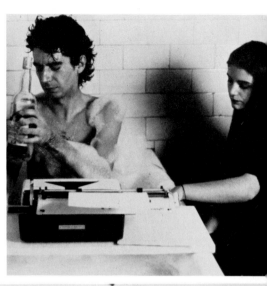

Right: Oscar Ladoire, Paula Molina
©*New Yorker*

David Thomson, Oscar Ladoire, Antonio Resines

Paula Molina, Luis Gonzalez-Regueral Top: Oscar Ladoire, Paula Molina

CIRCLE OF DECEIT

(UNITED ARTISTS CLASSICS) Producer, Eberhard Junkersdorf; Director, Volker Schlondorff; Screenplay, Volker Schlondorff, Jean-Claude Carriere, Margarethe von Trotta, Kai Hermann; From a novel by Nicolas Born; Photography, Igor Luther; Music, Maurice Jarre; Editor, Suzanne Baron; Sets, Bernd Lepel, Jacques Bufnoir; Costumes, Dagmar Niefind; Assistant Director, Regis Wargnier; Special Effects, Paul and Andre Trielli; A Franco-German Co-Production in Eastmancolor and Dolby Stereo; 108 minutes; Rated R; February release.

CAST

Georg Laschen	Bruno Ganz
Arianne Nassar	Hanna Schygulla
Rudnik	Jean Carmet
Hoffmann	Jerzy Skolimowski
Greta Laschen	Gila von Weitershausen
Berger	Peter Martin Urtel
John	John Munro
Excellence Joseph	Fouad Naim
Mrs. Joseph	Josette Khalil
Progressive Officer	Khaled el Saeid
Sister Brigitte	Sarah Salem
Cab Driver	Tafic Najem
Aicha	Magnia Fakhoury
Swedish Journalist	Jack Diagilaitas
Ahmed	Ghassan Mattar

Left: Hanna Schygulla
© *United Artists*

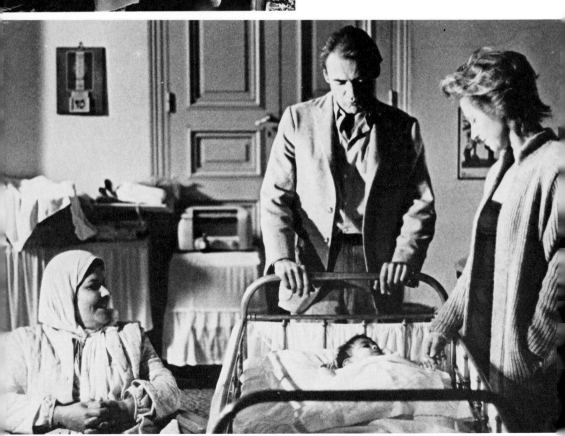

Bruno Ganz, Hanna Schygulla

Bruno Ganz, Hanna Schygulla Above: Jerzy Skolimowski (C)
Top: Ganz, Schygulla

Bruno Ganz

133

NIGHT CROSSING

(BUENA VISTA) Executive Producer, Ron Miller; Producer, Ton
Leetch; Associate Producer, Marc Stirdivant; Director, Delber
Mann; Screenplay, John McGreevey; Based on true story; Photogra
phy, Tony Imi; Designer, Rolf Zehetbauer; Music, Jerry Goldsmith
Editor, Gordon D. Brenner; Assistant Directors, Don Roberts, Do
French, Bettina Forg; In Technicolor and Dolby Stereo; 10(
minutes; Rated PG; February release.

CAST

The Strelzyks	
Peter	John Hur
Doris	Jane Alexande
Frank	Doug McKeo
Fitscher	Keith McKeo
The Wetzels	
Gunter	Beau Bridge
Petra	Glynnis O'Conno
Little Peter	Geoffrey Liesi
Andreas	Michael Liesi
The Kellers	
Josef	Ian Banne
Magda	Anne Stallybras
Lucas	Matthew Taylo
Major Koerner	Gunter Meisne
Schmolk	Klaus Lowitsc
Ziegler	Sky Dumon
Lt. Fehler	Jan Nikla
Doris' Mother	Kay Wals
Petra's Mother	Carola Hoh
Mrs. Roseler	Irene Prado
Pharmacist	Jan Paulus Biczyzck
Store Supervisor	Osman Raghe
First Store Clerk	Ursula Ludwi
Second Store Clerk	Jenny Thele
Shopper	Katharina Seyfert
Pilot	Gavin Jame

**Michael Liesek, Beau Bridges, Glynnis O'Connor, Geoffrey
Liesek**

**Top: Keith McKeon, Jane Alexander, John Hurt, Doug
McKeon**

© *Walt Disney Productions*

Doug McKeon, Jane Alexander, John Hurt Above: Alexander,
Glynnis O'Connor, Beau Bridges, Hurt Top: Alexander, Hurt

Jane Alexander, John Hurt

QUEST FOR FIRE

(20th CENTURY-FOX) Producers, John Kemeny, Denis Heroux Director, Jean-Jacques Annaud; Executive Producer, Michael Grus koff; Screenplay, Gerard Brach; Based on novel by J. H. Rosny, Sr Co-Producers, Jacques Dorfmann, Vera Belmont; Music, Philipp Sarde; Photography, Claude Agostini; Editor, Yves Langlois; Asso ciate Producers, Michael Moore, Claude Nedjar, Garth Thomas Designers, Brian Morris, Guy Comtois; Music performed by Lon don Symphony Orchestra with Peter Knight conducting; Creativ Makeup, Christopher Tucker; Costumes, John Hay, Penny Rose; A Canada-France Co-Production in Panavision, Dolby Stereo and Bellevue Pathe Color; 97 minutes; Rated R; February release

CAST

Naoh (Ulam) .... Everett McGi
Amoukar (Ulam)...Ron Perlma
Gaw (Ulam).. Nameer El-Kad
Ika (Ivaka)...Rae Dawn Chon

Left: Everett McGill, Nameer El-Kadi, Ron Perlman
©20th Century-Fox

Rae Dawn Chong, Everett McGill, Ron Perlman

PASSIONE D'AMORE

(PUTNAM SQUARE) Producer, Franco Committeri; Director, Ettore Scola; Screenplay, Ruggero Maccari, Ettore Scola; Based on story "Fosca" by Iginio Ugo Tarchetti; Photography, Claudio Ragona; Music, Armando Trovajoli; Editor, Raimondo Crociani; Art Director, Fiorenzo Senese; Costumes, Gabriella Pescucci; Assistant Director, Paolo Scola; In color; 117 minutes; Not rated; February release.

CAST

Giorgio Bacchetti	Bernard Giraudeau
Fosca	Valeria D'Obici
Clara	Laura Antonelli
Doctor	Jean-Louis Trintignant
Colonel	Massimo Girotti
Major Tarasso	Bernard Blier
Lt. Baggi	Gerardo Amato
Giorgio's Attendant	Sandro Ghiani
Capt. Rivolti	Alberto Incrocci
Fosca's Maid	Rosaria Schemmari
Colonel's Attendant	Francesco Piastra
Blond Lieutenant	Saverio Vallone
Clara's Husband	Franco Committeri

Bernard Giraudeau, Valeria d'Obici

Top: Bernard Giraudeau, Laura Antonelli
©*Putnam Square Films*

THE AMATEUR

(20th CENTURY-FOX) Producers, Joel B. Michaels, Garth H. Drabinsky; Director, Charles Jarrott; Screenplay, Robert Littell, Diana Maddox; Based on Mr. Littell's novel; Executive Producers, Mario Kassar, Andrew Vajna; Photography, John Coquillon; Designer, Trevor Williams; Editors, Stephan Fanfara, Richard Halsey; Music, Ken Wannberg; Assistant Director, Jon Anderson; Art Director, Richard Wilcox; Costumes, Suzanne Grace; A Balkan Film Productions Ltd. film in DeLuxe Color; 112 minutes; Rated R; February release

CAST

Charles Heller	John Savage
Prof. Lakos	Christopher Plummer
Elisabeth	Marthe Keller
Brewer	Arthur Hill
Schraeger	Nicholas Campbell
Rutledge	George Coe
Molton	John Marley
Kaplan	Jan Rubes
Anderson	Ed Lauter
Botaro	Miguel Fernandes
Rodzenko	Jan Triska
Porter	Graham Jarvis
Argus	Jacques Godin
Gretchen	Chapelle Jaffe
Sara	Lynne Griffin
Uncle Ludwig	Vladimir Valenta
Guide	Vlasta Vrana
Slater	Neil Dainard
Sharp-eyed Man	Lee Broker
Newscaster	Tedde Moore
Eva Lakos	Maruska Stankova
Clerk	Irena Mayeska
Terrorist	George Buza
U.S. Consul	George R. Robertson
CIA Security Guard	John Kerr
News Vendor	Guy Sanvido
Ambassador Neville	Robert Beatty
Chancellor	Walter Reyer
Vice Consul	Francois-Regis Klanfer

and Peter Wolsdorff (Gen. Felder), Henry Gomez (Master Sergeant), Erin Flannery (Waitress), Lisa Schrage, Susan Young (Teenagers), Tony Kramreither (TV Director), Paul Reymont (Technician) Aubrey Taylor (Doorman), Roman Chabursky (Busboy), Bob Lem (Nakamura), Fred Culik (Martin), Peter Langley (Demolition Expert), Harry Hornisch (Watcher), Helmut Graef (Taxi Driver), Zdenek Gruner (Czech Officer)

Right: Ed Lauter, John Savage Above: Marthe Keller, John Savage (also top)
©Balkan Films

Christopher Plummer

Marthe Keller, John Savage

THREE BROTHERS

(NEW WORLD) Direction and Screenplay, Francesco Rosi; Freely adapted from A. Platonov's "The Third Son"; Photography, Pasqualino DeSantis; Art Director, Andrea Crisanti; Costumes, Gabriella Pescucci; Editor, Ruggero Mastroianni; Music, Piero Piccioni; Song, Pino Daniele; Producers, Giorgio Nocella, Antonio Macri; In color; 113 minutes; Rated PG; February release.

CAST

Raffaele Giuranna .... Philippe Noiret
Donato Giuranna .... Charles Vanel
Nicola Giuranna .... Michele Placido
Rocco Giuranna/Young Donato .... Vittorio Mezzogiorno
Raffaele's Wife.. Andrea Ferreol
Giovanna .... Maddalena Crippa
Rosaria.. Sara Tafuri
Marta, the little girl ....Marta Zoffoli
Raffaele's Friend ....Tino Schipinzi
Young Donato's Wife .... Simonetta Stefanelli
First Judge..Pietro Biondi
Second Judge.. Ferdinando Greco
First Friend at bar .... Accursio DiLeo
Raffaele's Son .... Cosimo Milone
Second Friend at bar .... Luigi Infantino
The Brothers' Mother .... Gina Pontrelli
Nicola's Friend ....Girolamo Marzano
Friend at bar .... Ferdinando Murolo
Post Office Clerk .... Maria Antonia Capotorto
Friends at bar .... Francesco Capotorto, Cristofaro Chiapparino

©*New World*

DAS BOOT (The Boat)

(COLUMBIA) Executive Producers, Mark Damon, Edward R. Pressman, John W. Hyde; Co-Producer, Michael Bittins; Producer, Gunter Rohrbach; Direction and Screenplay, Wolfgang Petersen, Based on novel by Lothar-Gunther Buchheim; Photography, Jost Vacano; Music, Klaus Doldinger; Art Director, Gotz Weidner; Designer, Rolf Zehetbauer; Costumes, Monika Bauert; Special Effects, Karl Baumgartner; Assistant Director, Georg Borgel, Maria Antoinette Petersen; In Dolby Stereo and color; 150 minutes; Rated R; February release.

CAST

The Captain	Jurgen Prochnow
Lt. Werner/Correspondent	Herbert Gronemeyer
Chief Engineer	Klaus Wennemann
1st Lt/Number One	Hubertus Bengsch
2nd Lieutenant	Martin Semmelrogge
Chief Quartermaster	Bernd Tauber
Johann	Erwin Leder
Ullmann	Martin May
Hinrich	Heinz Honig
Chief Bosun	U. A. Ochsen
Ario	Claude-Oliver Rudolph
Pilgrim	Jan Fedder
Frenssen	Ralph Richter
Preacher	Joachim Bernhard
Schwalle	Oliver Stritzel
Bockstiegel	Konrad Becker
Dufte	Lutz Schnell
Bruckenwilli	Martin Hemme
Thomas Boxhammer	Roger Barth
Gunther Franke	Christian Bendomir
Norbert Fronwald	Albert Kraml
Jean-Claude Hoffmann	Peter Pathenis
Arno Kral	Christian Seipolt
Helmut Neumeier	Ferdinand Schaal
Wilhelm Pietsch	Rolf Weber
Dirk Salomon	Lothar Zajicek
Monique	Rita Cadillac
Thomsen	Otto Sander
Captain of the Weser	Gunter Lamprecht

Jurgen Prochnow, Herbert Gronemeyer
© *Columbia*

142

Klaus Wennemann, Jurgen Prochnow, Herbert Gronemeyer

THE TRAGEDY OF A RIDICULOUS MAN

(WARNER BROTHERS) Producer, Giovanni Bertolucci; Direction and Screenplay, Bernardo Bertolucci; Music, Ennio Morricone; Photography, Carlo DiPalma; Designer, Gianni Silvestri; Costumes, Lina Taviani; Assistant Directors, Antonio Gabrielli, Fiorella Infascelli; Editor, Cabriella Gristiani; A Ladd Company release in color; 118 minutes; Rated PG; February release.

CAST

Primo	Ugo Tognazzi
Barbara (his wife)	Anouk Aimee
Laura	Laura Morante
Adelfo	Victor Cavallo
Chiromant	Olimpia Carlisi
Marshal	Vittorio Caprioli
Colonel	Renato Salvatori
Giovanni (Primo's son)	Riki Tognazzi
Crossing Keeper	Don Backy
Magistrate	Cosimo Cinieri

Right: Ugo Tognazzi
© The Ladd Co.

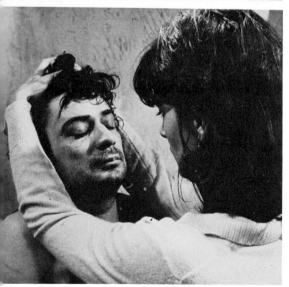

Victor Cavallo, Laura Morante Above: Ugo Tognazzi, Anouk Aimee

Ugo Tognazzi, Laura Morante, Riki Tognazzi, Anouk Aimee Above: Tognazzi, Aimee

THE CAT AND THE CANARY

(QUARTET) Producer, Richard Gordon; Director, Radley Metzger; Associate Producer, Ray Corbett; Photography, Alex Thomson; Designer, Anthony Pratt; Screenplay, Radley Metzger; Music, Steven Cagan; Editor, Roger Harrison; Assistant Director, Alan Carpenter; Based on play of same title by John Willard; In Technicolor; 98 minutes; Rated PG; February release.

CAST

Susan Sillsby	Honor Blackman
Paul Jones	Michael Callan
Hendricks	Edward Fox
Allison Crosby	Wendy Hiller
Cicily Young	Olivia Hussey
Mrs. Pleasant	Beatrix Lehmann
Annabelle West	Carol Lynley
Harry Blythe	Daniel Massey
Charlie Wilder	Peter McEnery
Cyrus West	Wilfrid Hyde-White

Right: Carol Lynley, Michael Callan
©*Quartet*

Daniel Massey, Wendy Hiller, Edward Fox

PORKY'S

(20th CENTURY-FOX) Producers, Don Carmody, Bob Clark; Direction and Screenplay, Bob Clark; Executive Producers, Harold Greenberg, Melvin Simon; Music, Carl Zittrer, Paul Zaza; Photography, Reginald H. Morris; Designer, Reuben Freed; Editor, Stan Cole; Associate Producer, Gary Goch; Assistant Directors, Ken Goch, Donald R. Brough; Costumes, Mary McLeod, Larry Wells; In color; 99 minutes; Rated R; March release.

CAST

Pee Wee	Dan Monahan
Billy	Mark Herrier
Tommy	Wyatt Knight
Mickey	Roger Wilson
Tim	Cyril O'Reilly
Meat	Tony Ganios
Wendy	Kaki Hunter
Honeywell	Kim Cattrall
Balbricker	Nancy Parsons
Brian Schwartz	Scott Colomby
Coach Brackett	Boyd Gaines
Coach Warren	Doug McGrath
Cherry Forever	Susan Clark
Ted Jarvis	Art Hindle
Cavanaugh	Wayne Maunder
Sheriff Wallace	Alex Karras
Porky	Chuck Mitchell
Mr. Carter	Eric Christmas
Coach Goodenough	Bill Hindman
Conklin	John Henry Redwood
Frank	Jack Mulcahy
Steve	Rod Ball
Cops	Julian Bird, Bill Fuller
Bartender	Will Knickerbocker
Ted's Partner	Bill Worman

and Ilse Earl (Mrs. Morris), Jill Whitlow (Mindy), Pat Lee (Stripper), Terry Guthrie (Miss Walker), Joanne Marsic (Waitress), Pete Conrad (Mule Train Driver), Butch Raymond, Gary Maas (Deputies), Cash Baron, Roger Womack, Charles Spadard (Bouncers), Lisa O'Reilly (Ginny), Allene Simmons (Jackie), Cathy Garpershak (Girl in shower), Jon Cecka (Highpockets), Don Daynard (Radio Announcer)

Left: Kim Cattrall, Boyd Gaines, Nancy Parsons Top: Mark Herrier, Tony Ganios, Roger Wilson, Wyatt Knight, Kaki Hunter, Dan Monahan
©*Simon Film Productions*

Mark Herrier, Wyatt Knight

Kaki Hunter (R)

Tony Ganios, Wyatt Knight, Cyril O'Reilly, Roger Wilson, Chuck Mitchell Top: Boyd Gaines, Mark Herrier, Scott Colomby, Wyatt Knight, Dan Monahan, Tony Ganios

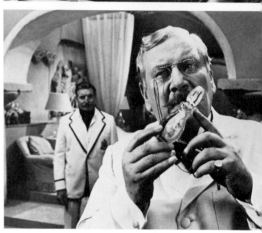

Jane Birkin, Nicholas Clay Above: Roddy McDowall, Denis
Quilley, Emily Hone Top: Peter Ustinov, Maggie Smith

EVIL UNDER THE SUN

(UNIVERSAL) Producers, John Brabourne, Richard Goodwin; Director, Guy Hamilton; Screenplay, Anthony Schaffer; Based on novel by Agatha Christie; Editor, Richard Marden; Designer, Elliot Scott; Costumes, Anthony Powell; Photography, Christopher Challis; Music, Cole Porter; Associate Producer, Michael-John Knatchbull; Assistant Director, Derek Cracknell; In Technicolor; 117 minutes; Rated PG; March release.

CAST

Hercule Poirot	Peter Ustinov
Sir Horace Blatt	Colin Blakely
Christine Redfern	Jane Birkin
Patrick Redfern	Nicholas Clay
Daphne Castle	Maggie Smith
Rex Brewster	Roddy McDowall
Myra Gardener	Sylvia Miles
Odell Gardener	James Mason
Kenneth Marshall	Denis Quilley
Arlena Marshall	Diana Rigg
Linda Marshall	Emily Hone
Police Sergeant	John Alderson
Police Inspector	Paul Antrim
Police Surgeon	Cyril Conway
Flewitt's Secretary	Barbara Hicks
Flewitt	Richard Vernon
Concierge	Robert Dorning
Gino	Dimitri Andreas

Top: James Mason, Sylvia Miles Below: Denis Quilley, Peter
Ustinov
© Universal

Peter Ustinov, Colin Blakely Top: Diana Rigg, Maggie Smith,
Denis Quilley

GREGORY'S GIRL

(SAMUEL GOLDWYN) Producers, Clive Parsons, Davina Belling; Direction and Screenplay, Bill Forsyth; Photography, Michael Coulter; Art Director, Adrienne Atkinson; Editor, John Gow; Music, Colin Tully; In color; 98 minutes; Rated PG; April release

CAST

Gregory	Gordon John Sinclair
Dorothy	Dee Hepburn
Headmaster	Chic Murray
Phil	Jake D'Arcy
Alec	Alex Norton
Alistair	John Bett
Andy	Robert Buchanan
Steve	William Greenlees
Charlie	Graham Thompson
Madeline	Allison Forster
Susan	Clare Grogan
Carol	Caroline Guthrie
Billy	Douglas Sannachan
Gregory's Dad	David Anderson
Eric	Alan Love

Left: Gordon John Sinclair
©Samuel Goldwyn Co.

Dee Hepburn, Gordon John Sinclair, Jake D'Arcy

Gordon John Sinclair (R) Top: (L & R) Dee Hepburn

GARDE A VUE (Under Suspicion)

(FRED BAKER) Producers, George Dancigers, Alexandre Mnouchkine; Director, Claude Miller; Adaptation, Claude Miller, Jean Herman; Based on novel "Brainwash" by John Wainright; Dialogue, Michel Audiard; Music, Georges Delerue; Assistant Director, Jean Pierre Vergne; Photography, Bruno Nuytten; Art Director, Lam Le; Costumes, Janine Fauvel; Editors, Albert Jurgenson, Catherine Dubeau; Set Designer, Eric Moulard; In color; 97 minutes; Not rated; April release.

CAST

Inspector Antoine Gallien	Lino Ventura
Jerome Martinaud	Michel Serrault
Chantal Martinaud	Romy Schneider
Inspector Marcel Belmont	Guy Marchand
Camille	Elsa Lunghini
Division Commissioner	Jean Claude Penchenat
Adami	Pierre Maguelon
Young Berthier	Mathieu Schiffman
Jabelain	Michel Such
Policemen	Patrick Depeyrrat, Yves Pignot
Young Policeman	Didier Agostini
Repair Truck Driver	Serge Malik
Arab	Mohammed Bekireche

Top: Michel Serrault, Elsa Lunghini Below: Michel Serrault
©Fred Baker

Lino Ventura, Michel Serrault Top: Romy Schneider

DEATHWATCH

(QUARTET) Producers, Gabriel Boustiani, Janine Rubeiz; Director, Bertrand Tavernier; Screenplay, Bertrand Tavernier, David Rayfiel; Based on novel "The Continuous Katherine Mortenhoe" by David Compton; Photography, Pierre-William Glenn; Music, Antoine Duhamel; Editors, Armand Psenay, Michael Ellis; Art Director, Tony Pratt; In Panavision and Fujicolor; 117 minutes; Rated R; April release.

CAST

Katherine Mortonhoe	Romy Schneider
Roddy	Harvey Keitel
Vincent Ferriman	Harry Dean Stanton
Tracey	Therese Liotard
Gerald Mortenhoe	Max von Sydow

Top: Max von Sydow, Romy Schneider (also below) Top Right: Romy Schneider, Harvey Keitel (and below)
©*Quartet*

Harvey Keitel

THE MEADOW

(NEW YORKER) Producer, Giuliani G. DeNegri; Direction and Screenplay, Paolo and Vittorio Taviani; Photography, Franco DiGiacomo; Editor, Roberto Perpignani; Art Director, Gianni Sbarra; Costumes, Lina Nerli Taviani, Renato Ventura; Choreography, Gino Landi; Music, Ennio Morricone; Italian with English subtitles; In color; 115 minutes; Not rated; April release.

CAST

Eugenia	Isabella Rossellini
Enzo	Michele Placido
Giovanni	Saverio Marconi
His Mother	Angela Goodwin
His Father	Giulio Brogi
Doctor	Remo Remotti
Stefano	Ermanno Taviani

and Miro Guidelli, Giuseppe Rocca, Francesca Taviani, Maria Toesca, Allesandra Toesca, Giovanni Bacciottini, Giacomo Pardini, Massimo Bertolaccini

Left: Isabella Rossellini
©*New Yorker*

Isabella Rossellini, Michele Placido

154

Isabella Rossellini, Saverio Marconi (also top left) Top Right:
Isabella Rossellini

Mel Gibson

THE ROAD WARRIOR

(WARNER BROS.) Producer, Byron Kennedy; Director, George Miller; Screenplay, Terry Hayes, George Miller, Brian Hannant; Assistant Directors, Brian Hannant, Patrick Clayton, Toivo Lember, Phil Hurst; Photography, Dean Semler; Costumes, Norma Moriceau; Art Director, Graham Walker; In Panavision, Dolby Stereo and color; 94 minutes; Rated R; April release; Original title "Mad Max II"

CAST

Max	Mel Gibson
Gyro Captain	Bruce Spence
Wez	Vernon Wells
Feral Kid	Emil Minty
Pappagallo	Mike Preston
Humungus	Kjell Nilsson
Warrior Woman	Virginia Hey
Curmudgeon	Syd Heylen
Big Rebecca	Moira Claux
Quiet Man	David Slingsby
Lusty Girl	Arkie Whiteley
Mechanic	Steve J. Spears
Toadie	Max Phipps
Farmer	William Zappa
Golden Youth	Jimmy Brown
Wounded Man	David Downer
Defiant Victim	Tyler Coppin
Broken Victim	Max Fairchild
Mechanic's Assistant	Kristoffer Greaves
Mohawk Biker with bearclaw	Guy Norris
Mohawk Biker	Tony Deary
Tent Lovers	Anne Jones, James McCardell
Young Woman	Kathleen McKay

Top: Mel Gibson
© *Warner Bros.*

Mel Gibson

DIVA

(UNITED ARTISTS CLASSICS) Producer, Irene Silberman; Director, Jean-Jacques Beineix; Screenplay, Jean-Jacques Beineix, Jean Van Hamme; From novel of Delacorta; Photography, Philippe Rousselot; Art Director, Hilton McConnico; Editors, Marie-Josephe Yoyotte, Monique Prim; Music, Vladimir Cosma; In color; 123 minutes; Not rated; April release.

CAST

Cynthia	Wilhelmenia Wiggins Fernandez
Jules	Frederic Andrei
Gorodish	Richard Bohringer
Alba	Thuy An Luu
Saporta	Jacques Fabbri
Nadia	Chantal Deruaz
Paula	Anny Romand
Weinstadt	Roland Bertin
L'Antillais	Gerard Darmon
Le Cure	Dominique Pinon
Krantz	Jean-Jacques Moreau
Zatopek	Patrick Floersheim

Left: Wilhelmenia Wiggins Fernandez
© *United Artists*

Thuy An Luu, Frederic Andrei

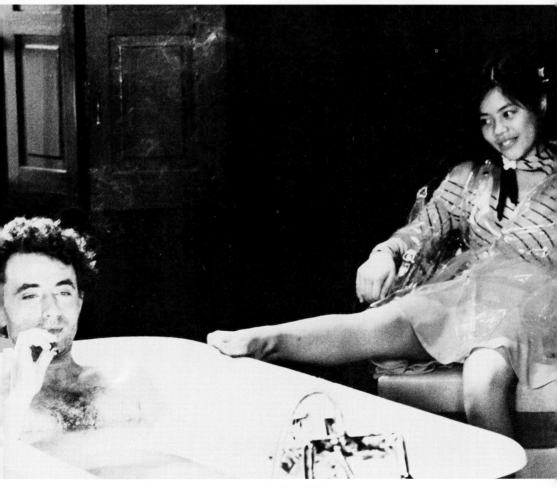

Richard Bohringer, Thuy An Luu Top: (L) Frederic Andrei,
Thuy An Luu (R) Frederic Andrei (R)

THE CHOSEN

(ANALYSIS) Executive Producer, Jonathan Bernstein; Producers, Edie and Ely Landau; Director, Jeremy Paul Kagan; Screenplay, Edwin Gordon; Based on novel by Chaim Potok; Music, Elmer Bernstein; Photography, Arthur Ornitz; Designer, Stuart Wurtzel; Associate Producer, Mel Howard; Costumes, Ruth Morley; Editor, David Garfield; In color; 108 minutes; Rated PG; April release.

CAST

Professor Malter .... Maximilian Schell
Reb Saunders .... Rod Steiger
Danny Saunders .... Robby Benson
Reuven Malter .... Barry Miller

Right: Maximilian Schell
© *20th Century-Fox*

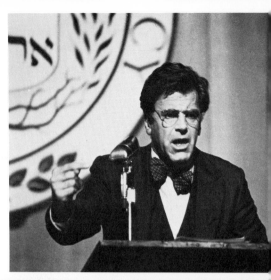

Robby Benson, Barry Miller

**Robby Benson, Barry Miller Top: Rod Steiger
(L), Robby Benson (R)**

SMASH PALACE

(ATLANTIC) Producer-Director, Roger Donaldson; Associate Producer, Larry Parr; Screenplay, Roger Donaldson, Peter Hansard, Bruno Lawrence; Photography, Graeme Cowley; Assistant Directors, Steve Locker Lampson, Susan Pointon; Art Director, Restor Griffiths; Editor, Mike Horton; In color; 95 minutes; Rated R; April release.

CAST

Al Shaw	Bruno Lawrence
Jacqui Shaw	Anna Jemison
Georgie Shaw	Greer Robson
Ray Foley	Keith Aberdein
"Tiny"	Des Kelly

Left: Bruno Lawrence
©*Atlantic*

Bruno Lawrence, Greer Robson, Anna Jemison

Bruno Lawrence, Greer Robson

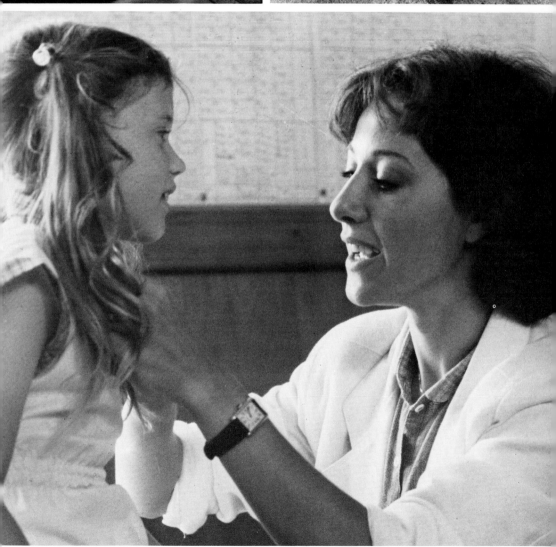

Greer Robson, Anna Jemison Top Left: Anna Jemison, Bruno Lawrence

LA VIE CONTINUE

(COLUMBIA) Producers, Lise Fayolle, Giorgio Silvagni; Director, Moshe Mizrahi; Screenplay, Moshe Mizrahi, Rachel Fabien; Photography, Yves Lafaye; Music, Georges Delerue; Art Director, Dominique Andre; A Triumph Films presentation; In color; 93 minutes; Rated PG; May release.

CAST

Jeanne	Annie Girardot
Pierre	Jean-Pierre Cassel
Max	Pierre Dux
Henri	Michel Aumont
Catherine	Giulia Salvatori
Elizabeth	Paulette Dubost
Philippe	Emmanuel Gayet
Jacquot	Rivera Andres

Right: Annie Girardot, Jean-Pierre Cassel
©Columbia

Giulia Salvatori, Annie Girardot Above: Pierre Dux, Annie Girardot

Emmanuel Gayet, Rivera Andres, Annie Girardot, Giulia Salvatori Above: Cassel, Girardot, Gayet

THE VULTURE

(NEW YORKER) Direction and Screenplay, Yaky Yosha; Based on chapters from "The Last Jew" by Yoram Kaniuk; Photography, Ilan Rozenberg; Art Director, Israel Wohlgalerenter; Editor, Anat Lubarsky; Hebrew with English subtitles; In color; 93 minutes; Not rated; May release (Israel 1981)

CAST

Boaz	Shraga Harpaz
Hasia	Hannah Maron
Hankin	Shimon Finkel
Yardena	Nitza Shaul
Noga	Andy Richman
Zvika	Ami Weinberg
Yasmin	Anat Atzmon
Uri's Mother	Ophelia Shtrahl
Zevik	Yoel Shar

Right: Andy Richman, Nitza Shaul
©*New Yorker*

Shraga Harpaz

Nitza Shaul

MARIANNE AND JULIANE

(NEW YORKER) Producer, Eberhard Junkersdorf; Direction and Screenplay, Margarethe von Trotta; Assistant Director, Helenka Hummel; Photography, Franz Rath; Editor, Dagmar Hirtz; Music, Nicolas Economou; Costumes, Monika Hasse, Jorge Jara; German with English subtitles; In color; 106 minutes; Not rated; May release (Germany 1981).

CAST

Marianne	Barbara Sukowa
Juliane	Jutta Lampe
Wolfgang	Rudiger Vogler
Sabine	Verenice Rudolph
Werner	Luc Bondy
Mother	Doris Schade
Father	Franz Rudnick
Juliane (at 17)	Ina Robinski
Marianne (at 16)	Julia Biedermann

Editors:

Helga	Ingeborg Weber
Carola	Carola Hembus
Margit	Margit Czenki
Wulfhild	Wulfhild Sydow
Anna	Anna Steinmann
Rolf	Rolf Schult
Juliane (at 6)	Barbara Paepcke
Marianne (at 5)	Rebecca Paepcke
Government Official	Karin Bremer
Teacher	Hannelore Minkus
Minister	Anton Rattinger
Karl (Marianne's friend)	Satan Deutscher
Her Other Friend	Michael Sellmann
Nurse	Lydia Billie
Lawyer	Wilbert Steinmann
Dieter	Christoph Parg

Jutta Lampe, Barbara Sukowa

Top: Barbara Sukowa, Jutta Lampe, Rudiger Vogler Left Center: Lampe, Verenice Rudolph
©*New Yorker*

166

LA FEMME ENFANT

YORKER) Direction and Screenplay, Raphaele Billetdoux; graphy, Alain Derobe; Designer, Renaud Sanson; Editor, ieve Winding; Assistant Director, Claire Lusseyran; Music, nir Cosma; French with English subtitles; In color; 100 es; Not rated; June release.

CAST

l	Klaus Kinski
eth	Penelope Palmer
ather	Michel Robin
Mother	Helene Surgere
rocer	Ary Auberge
riest	Georges Lucas

Right: Klaus Kinski, Penelope Palmer
©*New Yorker*

Michel Robin, Helene Surgere, Penelope Palmer

BOB LE FLAMBEUR
(Bob the Gambler)

(TRIUMPH) Produced, Directed and Written by Jean-Pierre Melville; Assistant Directors, Francois Gir, Guy Aurey, Yves-Andre Hubert; Dialogue, Auguste LeBreton; Photography, Henri Decae; Editor, Monique Bonnot; Art Directors, Jean-Pierre Melville, Claude Boxin; Music, Eddie Barclay, Jean Boyer; French with English subtitles; In black and white; 100 minutes; Not rated; June release (France 1956).

CAST

Anne	Isabel Corey
Bob Montagne	Roger Duchesne
Paolo	Daniel Cauchy
Inspector	Guy Decomble
Roger	Andre Garet
Jean	Claude Cerval
Suzanne	Colette Fleury
Marc	Gerard Buhr
Yvonne	Simone Paris

Left: Roger Duchesne
©*Columbia*

Roger Duchesne (C)

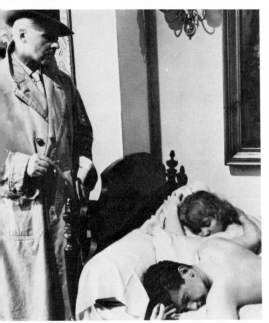

Roger Duchesne Top: (L) Roger Duchesne, Daniel Cauchy,
Isabel Corey (R) Isabel Corey

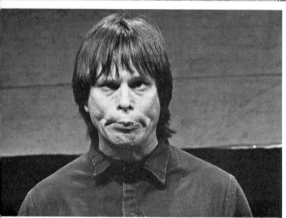

John Cleese Above: Terry Gilliam

MONTY PYTHON LIVE AT THE HOLLYWOOD BOWL

(COLUMBIA) Produced and Directed by Terry Hughes; Staged and Presented by Monty Python; Director, Ian MacNaughton; Executive Producers, George Harrison, Denis O'Brien; Co-Producer, James Rich, Jr.; Designers, John McGraw, John Miles; Editors, Julian Doyle, Jimmy B. Frazier; In color; 77 minutes; Rated R; June release. Performers; Graham Chapman, John Cleese, Terry Gilliam, Eric Idle, Terry Jones, Michael Palin, Neil Innes, Carole Cleveland

Above: Terry Gilliam, Michael Palin, Eric Idle, John Cleese
Top: Palin, Terry Jones, Idle, Graham Chapman,
Gilliam, Cleese
©Columbia

DEMON POND

(KINO INTERNATIONAL) Producers, Shigemi Sugisaki, Yukio Tomizawa, Kanji Nakagawa; Director, Masahiro Shinoda; Screenplay, Takeshi Tamura, Haruhiko Mimura; Story, Kyoka Izumi; Photography, Masao Kosugi, Noritaka Sakamoto; Art Directors, Kiyoshi Awazu, Setsu Asakura, Yuraka Yokoyama; Music, Isao Tomita; Editors, Zen Ikeda, Sachiko Yamaji; Assistant Director, Isao Kumagai; Assistant Producer, Seikichi Iiizumi; Choreography, Rui Takemura; In color; 123 minutes; Not rated; July release (Japan 1979).

CAST

Yuri/Princess Shirayuki	Tamasaburo Bando
Akira Hagiwara	Go Kato
Gakuen Yanazawa	Tsutomu Yamazaki
Nurse	Yatsuko Tanami
The Carp	Hisashi Igawa
The Crab	Fujio Tokita
Catfish Messenger	Norihei Miki
The Shadow/Yatabei the Bellkeeper	Jun Hamamura
The Camellia	Megumi Ishii
The Mackerel	Tadashi Furuta
Tiger Priest	Kazuo Sato
The Bone	Kai Ato
Diet Member	Ryunosuke Kaneda
Priest Shikami	Koji Nanbara
Yoju the Villager	Hatsuo Yamatani
His Wife	Maki Takayama
His Daughter	Yumi Nishigami
Village Assembly Leader	Toru Abe
Village Teacher	Shigeru Yazaki
Village Headman	Dai Kanai
Village Woman	Toshie Kobayashi
Denkichi	Juro Kara
Furosude Kotori	Hitoshi Ohmae
Old Woman	Fudeko Tanaka

Right: Tamasaburo Bando (C) and at top
© *Grange Communications*

Tsutomu Yamazaki

Go Kato, Tamasaburo Bando

LOLA

(UNITED ARTISTS CLASSICS) Producer, Horst Wendlandt; Director, Rainer Werner Fassbinder; Screenplay, Peter Marthesheimer, Pea Frohlich, Mr. Fassbinder; Photography, Xaver Schwarzenberger; Art Director, Rolf Zehefbauer; Music, Peer Raben; Editor, Juliane Lorenz; Costumes, Barbara Baum; German with English subtitles; In color; 114 minutes; Rated R; August release.

CAST

Lola	Barbara Sukowa
Von Bohm	Armin Mueller-Stahl
Schuckert	Mario Adorf
Esslin	Matthias Fuchs
Hettich	Helga Feddersen
Lola's Mother	Karin Baal
Wittich	Ivan Desny
Timmerding	Karl-Heinz von Hassel
Mrs. Fink	Sonia Neudorfer
Gigi	Elisabeth Volkmann
Volker	Hark Bohm
Mrs. Schuckert	Rosel Zech
Mrs. Volker	Isolde Barth
Susi	Cristine Kaufmann
Editor	Karsten Peters
TV Man	Nino Korda
Waiters	Raul Gimenez, Udo Kier
Demonstrators	Kary Baer, Rainer Will
Librarian	Andrea Keuer
Little Marie	Aurike Vigo
Pfortner	Herbert Steinmetz
G. I.	Gunther Kaufmann
Drunk	Helmut Petigk
Saleslady	Juliane Lorenz
Rahel	Marita Pleyer
Grandpa Berger	Maxim Oswarc

Barbara Sukowa (and at top left)

Barbara Sukowa, Armin Mueller-Stahl Top: Mario Adorf

PIAF—THE EARLY YEARS

(20th CENTURY-FOX INTERNATIONAL CLASSICS) Producer, Cy Feuer; Director, Guy Casaril; Associate Producer, Wilfrid Dodd; Screenplay, Guy Casaril, Francoise Ferley; Dialogue, Marc Behm; Adapted from the book "Piaf" by Simone Berteaut; Musical Numbers staged by Danny Daniels; Photography, Edmond Sechan; Art Director, Francois DeLamothe; Costumes, Rosine Delamare; Editor, Henry Taverna; Assistant Director, Michel Leroy; Presented by Moritz/Weissman Co. in Technicolor; French with English subtitles; 104 minutes; Rated PG; August release

CAST

Edith	Brigitte Ariel
Simone (Momone)	Pascale Christophe
Lucien Leplee	Guy Trejan
Raymond Asso	Pierre Vernier
Julien	Jacques Duby
Madeleine	Anouk Ferjac
Felix	Yvan Varco
Lulu	Sylvie Joly
Constantini	Michel Bedetti
Henri	Francois Dyrek

Top: Pascale Christophe, Brigitte Ariel (also below)
©*Moritz/Weissman*

Brigitte Ariel (also above)

LE BEAU MARIAGE
(The Well-Made Marriage)

(UNITED ARTISTS CLASSICS) Producers, Marbaret Menegoz, Les Films du Losange, Les Films Du Carrosse; Direction and Screenplay, Eric Rohmer; Photography, Bernard Lutic, Romain Winding, Nicolas Brunet; Editors, Cecile Decugis, Lisa Heredia; French with English subtitles; In color; 97 minutes; August release.

CAST

Sabine	Beatrice Romand
Edmond	Andre Dussollier
Simon	Feodor Atkine
Antique Dealer	Huguette Faget
Clarisse	Arielle Dombasle
Mother	Thamila Mezbah
Lise	Sophie Renoir
Frederic	Herve Duhamel
Nicolas	Pascal Greggory
The Bride	Virginie Thevenet
The Countess	Denise Bailly
Claude	Vincent Gauthier
Secretary	Anne Mercier
Client	Catherine Rethi
Traveler	Patrick Lambert

Right: Beatrice Romand, Andre Dusollier Below: Arielle Dombasle, Beatrice Romand
© *United Artists*

Andre Dusollier, Arielle Dombasle, Beatrice Romand Above: Dombasle, Romand

Beatrice Romand, Andre Dusollier

Jeremy Irons

MOONLIGHTING

(UNIVERSAL) Producers, Mark Shivas, Jerzy Skolimowski; Direction and Screenplay, Jerzy Skolimowski; Music, Stanley Myers; Associate Producer, Michael Guest; Assistant Directors, Peter Cotton, Nicholas Daubeny, Rod Lomax; Designer, Tony Woollard; Costumes, Jane Robinson; Editor, Barry Vince; In color; 97 minutes; Rated PG; September release.

CAST

Nowak	Jeremy Irons
Banaszak	Eugene Lipinski
Wolski	Jiri Stanislav
Kudaj	Eugeniusz Haczkiewicz

Top: Eugene Lipinski, Jeremy Irons, Eugeniuz Haczkiewics,
Jiri Stanislav
©Michael White

Eugeniuz Haczkiewicz, Jeremy Irons, Eugene Lipinski, Jiri
Stanislav Top: Jeremy Irons

SIBERIADE

(IFEX) Director, Andrei Mikhalkov-Konchalovsky; Screenplay, Valentin Yezhov, A. Mikhalkov-Konchalovsky; Photography, Levan Paatashvili; Editor, Valentina Koulaguine; Art Directors, Nikolai Dvigubsky, Alexander Adabashian; Music, Eduard Artemyev; Russian with English subtitles; 190 minutes with intermission; A Mosfilm production; In color; Not rated; September release (Russia 1979)

CAST

Afanasy Ustyuzhanin	Vladimir Samoilov
Nikolai Ustyuzhanin	Vitaly Solomin
Alexei Ustyuzhanin	Nikita Mikhalkov
Taya Solomina	Lyudmilla Gurchenko
Anastassia	Nathalia Andreitchenko
Yerofei Solomin	Yevgeny Perov
Spiridon Solomin	Sergei Shakurov
Philip Solomin	Igor Okhlupin
Taya (as a youth)	Yelena Koreneva
Alexei (as a youth)	Yevgeny Leonov-Gladyshev
Rodion Klimentov	Mikhail Kononov
Eternal Old Man	Pavel Kadochnikov
Yermolai	Nikolai Skorobogatov
Tofik Rustamov	Ruslan Mikaberidze
Fedor Nikolayevich	Vsevolod Larionov
Guryev	Konstantin Grieoryev

Left: Mikhail Kononov (C), Maxim Munzuk (R)
©*IFEX Films*

Liudmilla Gurchenko

Yevgeny Leonov-Gladyshev, and above with Vsevolod Larionov (R)

Yevgeny Leonov-Gladyshev, Yelena Koreneva Top: Nikita Mikhalkov, Liudmilla Gurchenko

Yevgeny Perov (R)

VERONIKA VOSS

(UNITED ARTISTS CLASSICS) Producer, Thomas Schuhly; Director, Rainer Werner Fassbinder; Screenplay, Peter Marthesheimer, Pea Frohlich; Photography, Xaver Schwarzenberger; Editor, Juliane Lorenz; Music, Peer Raben; German with English subtitles; In black and white; 105 minutes; Rated R; September release

CAST

Veronika Voss	Rosel Zech
Robert Krohn	Hilmar Thate
Henriette	Cornelia Froboess
Dr. Katz	Annemarie Duringer
Josefa	Doris Schade
Dr. Edel	Eric Schumann
Fat Film Producer	Peter Berling
G. I. Dealer	Gunther Kaufmann
Saleswoman	Sonia Neudorfer
Her Boss	Lilo Pempeit
Director 1	Volker Spengler
Director 2	Peter Zadek
Gardener	Herbert Steinmetz
Grete	Elisabeth Volkmann
Head Editor	Hans Wyprachtiger
Arztin	Tamara Kafka
Secretary	Juliane Lorenz
Kripobeamter	Dieter Schidor

Top and Below: Rosel Zech
© *United Artists Classics*

Rosel Zech, also above and top

180

L'ADOLESCENTE

(LANDMARK FILMS) Producer, Phillipe Dussart; Director, Jeanne Moreau; Screenplay, Henriette Jelinek, Jeanne Moreau; Photography, Pierre Gautard; Music, Phillipe Sarde; Editor, Albert Jurgenson; French with English subtitles; In color; 93 minutes; Rated R; September release (France 1979).

CAST

Marie	Laetitia Chauveau
Mamie	Simone Signoret
Eva	Edith Clever
Jean	Jacques Weber
Alexandre	Francis Huster

Right: Simone Signoret, Laetitia Chauveau
©*Landmark*

Laetitia Chauveau, Simone Signoret, Jacques Weber, Edith Clever Above: (L) Francis Huster, Edith Clever (R) Chauveau, Huster

FITZCARRALDO

(NEW WORLD PICTURES) Producers, Werner Herzog, Lucki Stipetic; Direction and Screenplay, Werner Herzog; Photography, Thomas Mauch; Music, Popol Vuh; Editor, Beate Mainka-Jellinghaus; Design, Henning von Gierke, Ulrich Bergfelder; Costumes, Gisela Storch; Assistant Director, Frederico Confaloni; In color; 157 minutes; Not rated; October release.

CAST

Brian Sweeney Fitzgerald/Fitzcarraldo	Klaus Kinski
Molly	Claudia Cardinale
Don Aquilino	Jose Lewgoy
Cholo the mechanic	Miguel Angel Fuentes
Captain Orinoco Paul	Paul Hittscher
Huerequeque the cook	Huerequeque Enrique Bohorquez
Station Master	Grande Othelo
Opera Manager	Peter Berling
Chief of the Campa Indians	David Perez Espinosa
Black Man at opera house	Milton Nascimento
Rubber Baron	Rui Polanah
Old Missionary	Salvador Godinez
Young Missionary	Dieter Milz
Notary	Bill Rose
Prison Guard	Leoncio Bueno

and the Ashininka-Campa Indians and their chiefs Miguel, Nicolas and Pascal Camaiteri Fernandez, the Campas Indians and their chief David Perez Espinosa, and the Machiguengas, also in the opera sequences were soloists Ceriano Luchetti, Costante Moret, Dimiter Petkov, Jean-Claude Dreyfuss, Mietta Sighele, Lourdes Magalhaes, Isabel Jimines de Cisneros, Liborio Simonella, Jesus Goiri, Christian Mantilla

Left: Klaus Kinski

Below: Claudia Cardinale (C)
©New World

Klaus Kinski

Claudia Cardinale

Klaus Kinski, Claudia Cardinale

SWEET HOURS

(NEW YORKER) Producer, Elias Querejeta; Direction and Screenplay, Carlos Saura; Photography, Teo Escamilla; Assistant Director, Francisco Javier Querejeta; Editor, Pablo G. Del Amo; Designer, Antonio Belizon; Spanish with English subtitles; In color; 105 minutes; Not rated; October release.

CAST

Juan	Inaki Aierra
Berta/Mother	Assumpta Serna
Uncle Pepe	Alvaro de Luna
Uncle Antonito	Jacques Lalande
Grandmother	Luisa Rodrigo
Maid	Alicia Sanchez
Aunt Pilar	Alicia Hermida
Juanico	Pablo Hernandez
Amparo	Marion Game
Pablo	Julien Thomast
Martita	Magdalena Garcia
Father	Pedro Sempson
Marta	Isabel Mestres
Painter	Antonio Saura
Sofi	Ofelia Angelica
Lucia	Clara Marin

Right: Assumpta Serna, Inaki Aierra

Below: Isabel Mestres, Clara Marin, Magdalena Garcia
©*New Yorker*

Inaki Aierra, Assumpta Serna
Above: Serna, Pablo Hernandez

Inaki Aierra, Pablo Hernandez, Assumpta Serna

NEST OF GENTRY

(CORINTH FILMS) Producer, Mosfilm Studios; Director, Andrei Konchalovski; Screenplay, A. Konchalovski, Valentin Yezhov; From Ivan Tugenev's novel "House of the Gentry"; Photography, Giorgi Rerberg; Music, Vichaslov Ovchinrikov; Editor, Andrei Konchalovski; Art Directors, A. Bolm, N. Dvigubsky, M. Romadin; Russian with English subtitles; In color; 106 minutes; Not rated; October release (Russia 1970).

CAST

Fyodor Lavretsky	Leonid Kulagin
Liza	Irina Kupchenko
Varvara Pavlovna	Beata Tyszkiewicz
Maria Dmitrievna	Tatiana Chernova
Panshin	Vlitinev Sergachov
Gedeonovsky	Vasili Merkuryev
Marfa Timofayevna	Maria Durasova
Prince Nelidov	Nikita Nikhalkov
Lenn	Alexander Kostomolotsky
Grishka	Sergei Nikonenko
Anton	V. Kochurikhin

Right: Leonid Kulagin, Irina Kupchenko
©Corinth Films

Leonid Kulagin, Beata Tyszkiewicz
Above: Irina Kupchenko, Kulagin

Leonid Kulagin

THE SENDER

(PARAMOUNT) Producer, Edward S. Feldman; Director, Roger Christian; Screenplay, Thomas Baum; Photography, Roger Pratt; Designer, Malcolm Middleton; Editor, Alan Strachan; Music, Trevor Jones; Associate Producers, J. C. Scott, John Comfort; Special Effects, Nick Allder; Assistant Director, Roger Simons; Art Directors, Steve Spence, Charles Bishop; Costumes, Shari Feldman, Ian Hickinbotham; In Dolby Stereo and Movielab Color; 92 minutes; Rated R; October release.

CAST

Gail Farmer	Kathryn Harrold
The Sender	Zeljko Ivanek
Jerolyn	Shirley Knight
Dr. Denman	Paul Freeman
The Messiah	Sean Hewitt
Dr. Hirsch	Harry Ditson
Dr. Erskine	Olivier Pierre
Young Girl	Tracy Harper
Viet Nam Veteran	Al Matthews
Nurse Jo	Marsha Hunt
Sheriff Prouty	Angus MacInnes
Nurse Reimbold	Jana Shelder
Dr. Warren	Monica Buferd
Computer Technician	Colin Bruce
Security Guard	Jerry Harte
TV Anchorwoman	Darcy Flynn

Left: Kathryn Harrold, Zeljko Ivanek
Top: Zeljko Ivanek (C)
©*Kingsmere Properties*

Zeljko Ivanek

Zeljko Ivanek

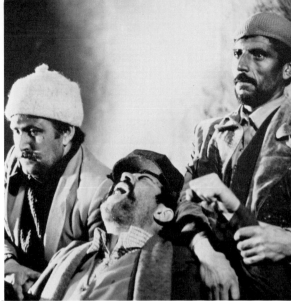

YOL
(The Trek of Life)

(TRIUMPH FILMS) Producers, Edi Hubschmid, K. L. Puldi; Director, Serif Goren; Screenplay, Yilmaz Guney; Editors, Yilmaz Guney, Elisabeth Waelchli; Photography, Erdogan Engin; Music, Sebastian Argol, Kendal; Turkish with English subtitles; In color; 111 minutes; Rated PG; October release.

CAST

Seyit Ali	Tarik Akan
Mehmet Salih	Halil Ergun
Omer	Necmettin Cobanoglu
Zine	Serif Sezer
Emine	Meral Orhousoy
Gulbahar	Semra Ucar
Mevlut	Hikmet Celik
Meral	Sevda Aktolga
Yusuf	Tuncay Akca

Top: Tarik Akan (C) Below: Akan and son
©*Columbia*

Tarik Akan and son Above: Akan, Serif Sezer

187

TIME STANDS STILL

(LIBRA) Producer, Mafilm-Budapest; Director, Peter Gother; Screenplay, Geza Beremenyi, Peter Gothar; Photography, Lajos Koital; Editor, Maria Nagy; Music, Gyorgy Seimeczi; In black and white and color; Hungarian with English subtitles; Not rated; 99 minutes; October release

CAST

Denes	Istvan Znamenak
Gabor	Henrik Pauer
Pierre	Sandor Soth
Vilmon	Peter Galfy
Magda	Aniko Ivan
Mother	Agi Kakassy
Father	Pal Hetenyi
Bodor	Lajos Oze

Top: Pal Hetenyi, Agi Kakassy
©*Libra Films*

Aniko Ivan (L)

Sandor Soth, Istvan Znamenak Top: Henrik Pauer, Aniko
Ivan, Sandor Soth, Istvan Znamenak

Istvan Znamenak, Aniko Ivan

THE MISSIONARY

(COLUMBIA) Producers, Neville C. Thompson, Michael Palin; Executive Producers, George Harrison, Denis O'Brien; Director, Richard Loncraine; Screenplay, Michael Palin; Photography, Peter Hannan; Art Director, Norman Garwood; Assistant Director, Gary White; Editor, Paul Green; Music, Mike Moran; Costumes, Shuna Harwood; A HandMade Films production in Panavision and color; 90 minutes; Rated R; November release.

CAST

Rev. Charles Fortescue	Michael Palin
Lady Ames	Maggie Smith
Lord Ames	Trevor Howard
The Bishop	Denholm Elliott
Slatterthwaite	Michael Hordern
Rev. Fitzbanks	Graham Crowden
Deborah	Phoebe Nicholls
Ada	Tricia George
Emmeline	Valerie Whittington
Limping Old Man	John Barrett
McEvoy	Peter Vaughan
Lady Fermly	Rosamund Greenwood
Lord Fermly	Roland Culver
Corbett	David Suchet
Gym Trainer	Derrick O'Connor
Parswell	Timothy Spall
Emily	Anne-Marie Marriott
Millicent	Janine Dutivitski
Portland	Julian Curry
Leicester	Charles McKeown
Maharajah	Ishaq Bux
Lord Quimby	Tony Steedman
Lady Quimby	Damaris Hayman
Sir Cyril Everidge	Frank Mills

and Dawn Archibald, Frances Barber, Debbie Bishop, Ceri Jackson, Janine Lesley, Sasha Mitchell, Francine Morgan, Sophie Thompson, Sally Watkins (Mission Girls), Tony Fawcett, Jaime Barr, Edward Bumstead (Boys at Mudflats), Neil Innes (Singer), David Leland, Hugh Fraser, Peter Bourke, Tilly Vosburgh, Arthur Howard, Hugh Walters, David Dixon, Anton Lesser, Yuseef Shah

Left: Michael Palin
©*Columbia*

Maggie Smith, Michael Palin, Michael Hordern

**Michael Palin, Maggie Smith Top Left: Denholm Elliott,
Michael Palin Right: Phoebe Nicholls**

SILENCE OF THE NORTH

(UNIVERSAL) Producer, Murray Shostak; Director, Allan Wintor
King; Screenplay, Patricia Louisiana Knop; Based on book of sam
title by Olive Fredrickson with Ben East; Co-Producer, Robert Bar
lis; Photography, Richard Leiterman; Designer, Bill Brodie; Edito
Arla Saare; Costumes, Olga Dimitrov; Music, Allan MacMilla
Assistant Director, Rob Lockwood; Art Directors, Susan Longmir
Gavin Mitchell, Alicia Keywan; In Panavision and color; Rated PC
94 minutes; November release

CAST

Olive Fredrickson	Ellen Bursty
Walter Reamer	Tom Skerr
John Fredrickson	Gordon Pinse
Little Olive Reamer	Jennifer McKinne
Vala Reamer	Donna Dobrijev
Lewis Reamer	Jeff Ban
Arthur Herriott	Colin Fc
Lea Goodwin	David Fc
John Goodwin	Richard Farre
Auctioneer	Larry Reynol
Young Man	Frank Turne
Young Woman	Ute Blunc
Billy	Thomas Hau

and Freddie Lang, Dennis Robinson, Robert Clothier, Brian Fu
tukian, Larry Musser, Leah Marie Hopkins, Ken Pogue, Ken Jame
Albert Angus, Frank Adamson, Murray Westgate, Kay Hawtre
Booth Savage, Lynn Mason Green, Graham McPherson, Chest
Robertson, Paul Verden, Sean Sullivan, Tom McEwen, Chapel
Jaffe, Tom Harvey, Ken Babb, Anna Freidman, Janet Amos, Fran
Gay, Peter Stefaniuk, George Myron

Ellen Burstyn, Tom Skerritt
Above and Top: Ellen Burstyn

Top: Tom Skerritt, Ellen Burstyn Below: Jeff Banks, Gordon
Pinsent, Burstyn
©*Universal*

TRAIL OF THE PINK PANTHER

(MGM/UA) Producers, Blake Edwards, Tony Adams; Director, Blake Edwards; Screenplay, Frank Waldman, Tom Waldman, Blake Edwards, Geoffrey Edwards; Story, Black Edwards; Based on characters created by David H. DePatie, Friz Freleng; Photography, Dick Bush; Editor, Alan Jones; Music, Henry Mancini; In Panavision and color; 97 minutes; December release; Out-takes and previously unused sequences from earlier "Pink Panther" films.

CAST

Inspector Clouseau	Peter Sellers
Sir Charles Litton	David Niven
Dreyfus	Herbert Lom
Clouseau Senior	Richard Mulligan
Marie Jouvet	Joanna Lumley
Lady Litton	Capucine
Bruno	Robert Loggia
Professor Balls	Harvey Korman
Cato	Burt Kwouk
Hercule	Graham Stark
Col. Bufoni	Peter Arne
Francois	Andre Maranne
Dr. Longet	Ronald Fraser
Quinlan	Leonard Rossiter
Commissioner Lasorde	Marne Maitland

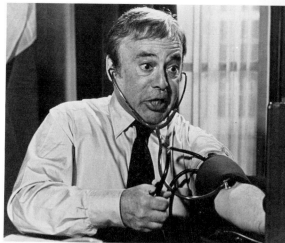

Right: Herbert Lom

Above: Peter Sellers, Harold Berens
©*United Artists*

Peter Sellers, Capucine

Joanna Lumley, Richard Mulligan

THE DARK CRYSTAL

(UNIVERSAL/AFD) Producers, Jim Henson, Gary Kurtz; Directors, Jim Henson, Frank Oz; Screenplay, David Odell; Story, Jim Henson; Executive Producer, David Lazer; Music, Trevor Jones; Conceptual Designer, Brian Froud; Production Designer, Harry Lange; Photography, Oswald Morris; Editor, Ralph Kemplen; Associate Producer, Bruce Sharman; Art Director, Charles Bishop; Choreography and Mime, Jean Pierre Amiel; Assistant Director, Dusty Symonds; In Technicolor, Panavision, Dolby Stereo; 97 minutes; Rated PG; December release.

CHARACTER PERFORMERS: Jen (Jim Henson), Kira (Kathryn Mullen), Aughra (Frank Oz), Fizzgig (Dave Goelz), Chamberlain (Frank Oz), General (Dave Goelz), High Priest (Jim Henson), Scientist (Steve Whitmire), Gourmand (Louise Gold), Ornamentalist (Brian Muehl), Historian (Bob Payne), Slave Master (Mike Quinn), Treasurer (Tim Rose), Urzah/Dying Master (Brian Muehl), Weaver (Jean Pierre Amiel), Cook (Hugh Spight), Numerologist (Robbie Barnett), Hunter (Swee Lim), Chanter (Simon Williamson), Scribe (Hus Levant), Alchemist (Toby Philpott), Healer (Dave Greenaway, Richard Slaughter)

CHARACTER VOICES: Jen (Stephen Garlick), Kira (Lisa Maxwell), Aughra (Billie Whitelaw), Fizzgig (Percy Edwards), Chamberlain (Barry Dennen), General (Michael Kilgarriff), High Priest/Dying Emperor (Jerry Nelson), Scientist (Steve Whitmire), Gourmand (Thick Wilson), Ornamentalist (Brian Muehl), Historian (John Baddeley), Slave Master (David Buck), Treasurer (Charles Collingwood), Dying Master (Brian Muehl), Urzah (Sean Barrett), Urskeks/Narrator (Joseph O'Conor)

Right: Jen, Mystic Master

Above: Jen, Kira

©ITC Entertainment

Skeksis Emperor, Chamberlain
Above: Jen visits Aughra's observatory

Kira and Jen
Above: Mystic

SEVEN SAMURAI

(LANDMARK FILMS) Producer, Shojiro Motoki; Director, Akira Kurosawa; Screenplay, Shinobu Hashimoto, Hideo Oguni, Akira Kurosawa; Photography, Asakazu Nakai; Music, Fumio Hayasaka; Art Director, So Matsuyama; Assistant Director, Hiromichi Horikawa; Japanese with English subtitles; In black and white; 208 minutes (original uncut version); Not rated; December release (Japan 1954)

CAST

Kambei, leader of samurai	Takashi Shimura
Kikuchiyo, would-be samurai	Toshiro Mifune
Kyuzo, swordsman	Seiji Miyaguchi
Katsushiro, young samurai	Ko Kimura
Shichiroji, Kambei's friend	Daisuke Kato
Heihachi, good-natured samurai	Minoru Chiaki
Gorobei, Wise warrior	Yoshio Inaba
Rikichi, militant villager	Yoshio Tsuchiya
Shino, village girl	Keiko Tsushima
Manzo, her father	Kamatari Fujiwara
Yohei, frightened villager	Bokuzen Hidari
Gisaku, village elder	Kuninori Kodo
Mosuke	Yoshio Kosugi
Gosaku	Keiji Sakakida
Peasant Woman	Fumiko Homma
Minstrel-Priest	Sojin Kamiyama
Grandfather	Toranosuke Ogawa
Husband	Yu Akitsu
Wife	Noriko Sengoku
Priest	Ichiro Chiba
Masterless Samurai	Gen Shimizu
Coolie	Jun Tatari
Vendor	Atsushi Watanabe

© *Landmark*

Toshiro Mifune, and above with Takashi Shimura (L)

Toshiro Mifune, Minoru Chiaki, Takashi Shimura (back), Isao Kimura, Daisuke Kato, Suiji Miyaguchi, Yoshio Inaba

COUP DE TORCHON
(CLEAN SLATE)

(BIOGRAPH/QUARTET/FRANK MORENO) Producer, Adolphe Viezzi; Director, Bertrand Tavernier; Screenplay, Jean Aurenche, Bertrand Tavernier; Based on novel "Pop. 1280" by Jir Thompson; Photography, Pierre William Glenn; Editor, Arman Psenny; Music Philippe Sarde; In color; 128 minutes; Not rated December release

CAST

Lucien	Philippe Noire
Rose	Isabelle Huppen
Le Peron/His Brother	Jean-Pierre Mariell
Huguette	Stephane Audra
Nono	Eddy Mitche
Chavasson	Guy Marchan
Anne	Irene Skoblin
Vanderbrouck	Michel Beaur
Priest	Jean Champio
Mercaillou	Victor Garrivie
Leonelli	Gerard Hernande
Fete Nat	Abdoulaye Dic
Paulo	Daniel Langle
Colonel	Francois Perr
Blind Man	Raymond Hermanti
Actor	Mamadou Diour
Friday	Samba Man

Jean-Pierre Marielle, Philippe Noiret, Stephane Audran,
Isabelle Huppert

Isabelle Huppert, Stephane Audran, Jean-Pierre Marielle Top:
(L) Philippe Noiret, Stephane Audran (R) Noiret, Isabelle
Huppert

Yasutaka Asahara (C), Minoru Sakurai (R) in "Muddy River"

Anthony Franciosa, Claudia Cardinale in "Careless"
©*Columbia*

MUDDY RIVER (Japan Film Center) Producer, Motoyasu Kumura; Director, Kohei Oguri; Screenplay, Takako Shigemori; From novel by Teru Miyamoto; Photography, Shohei Ando; Art Director, Akira Naito; Editor, Nobuo Ogawa; Music, Kuroudo Mori; 105 minutes; Not rated; January release. CAST: Nobutaka Asahara (Nobuo), Takahiro Tamura (His Father), Yumiko Fujita (His Mother), Minoru Sakurai (Kiichi), Makiko Shibata (His Sister), Mariko Kaga (Their Mother), Gannosuke Ashiya (Horse-car Man), Reiko Hatsune (Tobacco-shop Woman), Keizo Kanie (Policeman), Yoshitaka Nishiyawa (Guard), Taiji Tonoyama (Man on boat), Masako Yagi (Shinpei's former wife)

CARELESS ("Senilita") Director, Mauro Bolognini; Based on novel by Italo Svevo; Music, Peiro Piccioni; Photography, Armando Nannuzi; A Columbia Pictures release; In black and white; 110 minutes; Not rated; January release. CAST: Anthony Franciosa (Emilio), Claudia Cardinale (Angiolina), Betsy Blair (Amalia), Philippe Leroy (Stefano)

SISTERS or "THE BALANCE OF HAPPINESS" (Cinema 5) Executive Producer, Eberhard Junkersdorf; Director, Margarethe von Trotta; Screenplay, Ms. von Trotta, Martje Grohmann, Luisa Francia; Art Director, Winifried Henning; Editor, Annette Dorn; Photography, Franz Rath; Music, Konstantin Wecker; Costumes, Ingrid Zore; In color; 95 minutes; Not rated; January release. CAST: Jutta Lampe (Maria), Gudrun Gabriel (Anna), Jessica Fruh (Miriam), Rainer Delventha; (Maurice), Konstantin Wecker (Robert), Heinz Bennent (Munzinger), Agnes Fink (Mother), Fritz Lichtenhahn (Fritz), Guenther Scheutz (Professor), Barbara Sauerbaum (Maria as a child), Marie-Helene Diekmann (Anna as a child)

THE FORBIDDEN ACT (Lima) Producer, Akira Miura; Direction and Screenplay, Tatsumi Kumashiro; In color; Not rated; 78 minutes; January release. CAST: Aoi Nakajima, Sayuri Ichijo, Hiroko Isayama, Kazuko Shirakawa, Akira Takahashi

THE WITNESS (Libra) Direction and Screenplay, Peter Basco; Photography, Janos Zsombolyai; Music, Szabolcs Fenyes; In color; 110 minutes; Not rated; January release. CAST: Ferenc Kallai (Jozsef Pelikan), Lili Monori (Gizi, His Daughter), Zoltan Fabri (Zoltan), Lajos Oze (Comrade Virag), Bela Both (Gen. Bastya)

THE ALIEN'S PLACE (Icarus/Cinema Perspectives) Director, Rudolf van den Berg; Photography, Theo van de Sande; Dutch with English subtitles; 87 minutes; Not rated; January release. A documentary in which the filmmaker, a young Dutch Jew, examines his feelings about the State of Israel, Zionism, anti-Semitism, the Holocaust, and Palestinian demands for autonomy.

DAVID (Kino International) Producer, Joachim von Vietinghoff; Director, Peter Lilienthal; Screenplay, Peter Lilienthal, Jurek Becker, Ulla Zieman; From novel by Joel Konig; Photography, Al Ruban; Editor, Sieg un Jager; Music, Wojciech Kilar; German with English subtitles; In color; 106 minutes; Not rated; January release. CAST: Mario Fischel (David), Walter Taub (Rabbi Singer), Irene Vrkijan (Frau Singer), Torsten Henties (David as a child), Dominique Horwitz (Leo), Eva Mattes (Toni), Rudolf Sellner (Krell)

REVENGE OF THE SHOGUN WOMEN (21st Century) Producer, Frank Wong; Director, Mei Chung Chang; Screenplay, Lin Huang Kun, Terry Chambers; Photography, Zon Su Chang, Lorenz Somma; Editor, Niels Rasmussen; Music, Rob Walsh; In color and 3-D; 98 minutes; January release. CAST: Shisuen Leong, Shirley Han, PaiYing

THE BUSHIDO BLADE (Aquarius) Producer, Arthur Rankin, Jr.; Director, Tom Kotani; Screenplay, William Overgard; Photography, Shoji Ueda; Editor, Yoshitami Huroiwa; Editor, Anne V. Coates; Music, Maury Laws; In color; 92 minutes; Rated R; January release. CAST: Richard Boone (Col. Perry), Sonny Chiba (Prince Edo), Frank Converse (Capt. Hawk), Laura Gemser (Edo's Cousin), James Earl Jones (Harpooner), Mako (Friend), Toshiro Mifune (Commander), Timothy Murphy (Burr), Michael Starr (Johnson), Tetsuro Tamba (Lord Yamato), Mayumi Atano (Yuki)

LET THERE BE ROCK (Warner Bros.) formerly "AC/DC: Let There Be Rock." A High Speeds Production in color; Directed by Eric Dionysius, Eric Mistler; Photography, Jean Francis Gorde; Rated PG; 95 minutes; January release. CAST: Angus Young, Malcolm Young, Bon Scott, Phill Rudd, Cliff Williams

DEATH MASK OF THE NINJA (Essex) Director, Li Jackie Shao; In color; Rated R; January release. CAST: Joey Lee, Tiger Tung, Jon Chen, Nancy Lo

Lajos Oze, Ferenc Kallai in "The Witness"
©*Libra*

"Sisters"
©*Cinema 5*

Zbigniew Zapasiewicz, Ewa Dalkowska in "Without Anesthesia" ©*New Yorker*

Bud Cort, Kyra Nijinsky in "She Dances Alone" ©*Continental*

WITHOUT ANESTHESIA (New Yorker) also known as "Rough Treatment"; Director, Andrzej Wajda; Screenplay, Agnieszka Holland, Andrzej Wajda; Photography, Edward Klosinski; Music, Jerzy Derfel, Wojciech Mlynarski; Design, Allan Starski; Editor, Halina Prugar; Polish with English subtitles; In color; 131 minutes; February release. CAST: Zbigniew Zapasiewicz (Jerzy Michalowski), Ewa Dalkowska (Ewa Michalowska), Andrzej Seweryn (Jacek), Drystyna Janda (Agata), Emilia Krakowska (Wanda), Roman Wilhelmi (Bronski), Kazimierz Kaczor (Editor-in-chief), Iga Mayr (Ewa's Mother), Aleksandra Jasienska (Olenka), Marta Salinger (Gapcia), Stefania Iwinska (Maid), Halina Golanko (Ewa's Sister), Magda Teresa Wojcik (Jerzy's Lawyer), Danuta Balicka-Satanowska (Judge), Zygmunt Kestowicz (Secretary)

JOHN HEARTFIELD, PHOTOMONTAGIST (California Newsreel) Producer, British Film Institute; Director, Helmut Herbst; Written by Tom Fecht, Helmut Herbst, Eckhard Siepmann; Photography, Axel Brandt; Editor, Heidi Breitel; 63 minutes; Not rated; February release.

I HEARD IT THROUGH THE GRAPEVINE (Living Archives) by Dick Fontaine and Pat Hartley; Photography, Ivan Strasburg; Editor, Julian Ware; 95 minutes; Not rated; February release. CAST: James Baldwin, David Baldwin

SHE DANCES ALONE (Continental) Producers, Federico DeLaurentiis, Earle Mack; Director, Robert Dornhelm; Executive Producer, Marion Hunt; Screenplay, Paul Davids; Narration written by, Jon Bradshaw; Editor, Tina Frese; Photography, Karl Kofler; Music, Gustavo Santaolalla; Title Song, Bruce Roberts; Sung by Bud Cort; In color; 87 minutes; Not rated; February release. CAST: Kyra Nijinsky (Herself), Bud Cort (Director), Patrick Dupond (Dancer), Max von Sydow (Voice of Nijinsky), Walter Kent (Psychiatrist), Sauncey LeSueur (Little Kyra), Rosine Bena (Ballerina), Jeanette Etheridge (Girlfriend), Franco DeAlto (Patient in Hospital), Laura Hoover (Little Ballerina)

THE BOTTOM·LINE/ON AURA TOUT VU! (Silverstein) Producer, Alan Poire; Director, Georges Lautner; Screenplay, Francis Veber; Photography, Maurice Fellous; Music, Philippe Sarde; French with English subtitles; In color; 93 minutes; Rated R; February release. CAST: Pierre Richard ((Francois), Miou-Miou (Christine), Jean-Pierre Marielle (Morlock), Renee Saint-Cyr (Mme. Ferroni), Gerard Jugnot, Savine Azema, Gerard Chambre, Jean Luisi, Henri Guybet

SLEEPING DOGS (Sator) Producer-Director, Roger Donaldson; Screenplay, Ian Mune, Arthur Baysting; Story, Karl Stead; Photography, Michael Seresin; Editor, Ian John; Music, Murray Grindlay, David Calder, Mathew Brown; In color; 107 minutes; Not rated; February release. CAST: Melissa Donaldson (Melissa), Sam Neill (Smith), Bernard Keams (Prime Minister), Raf Irving (Reporter), Cass Donaldson (Cass), Nevan Rowe (Gloria), Ian Mune (Bullen), Don Selwyn (Taupiri), Ian Watkin (Dudley), Tommy Tinirau (Old Maori), Bill Johnson (Cousins), Roger Oakley (Assassin Leader), Clyde Scott (Jesperson), Dorothy McKegg (Gloria's Mother), Tony Groser (Gloria's Father), Bernard Moody (Man at wharf), Davina Whitehouse (Elsie), Bill Juliff (Burton), Warren Oates (Willoughby)

RAGING DRAGON (Bedford Entertainment) In color; Not rated; 92 minutes; February release. CAST: Bruce Chung, Bill Kuo, Ching Chen, Len Chow, Lee Tang

25 FIREMAN'S STREET (Unifilm) Produced by Budapest Studios; Direction and Screenplay, Istvan Szabo; Photography, Sandor Sara; Music, Zdenko Tamassy; In Eastmancolor; 97 minutes; Not rated; March release. CAST: Rita Bekes (Mrs. Gaskoy), Lucyna Winnicka (Maria), Peter Muller (Janos, her husband), Andras Balint (Andris), Mari Szemes (Julika), Agi Meszaros (Aranka), Margit Makay (Maria's Mother), Karoly Kovacs (Maria's Father)

LOVE AND LIES (International Film Exchange/Sovexport Film) Director, Ilya Frez; Screenplay and Story, G. Shcherbakova, I. Frez; Photography, G. Tutonov; Music, A. Rybnikov; In color; 90 minutes; Not rated; March release. CAST: Tanya Akaiuta (Katya), Nikita Mikhailovsky (Roman), E. Solovei (Tanya), I. Miroschichenko (Lucy), L. Fedoseyeva-Shukshina (Vera), A. Filozov (Kostyn), T. Pelteer (Grandmother), R. Nifontova (Tanya's Mother), E. Gerenimov (Volodyha), A. Filatov (Misha), V. Kurkov (Sasha)

GRADUATE FIRST/Passe Ton Bac D'Abord (New Yorker) Producer, Les Films du Livradois; Direction and Screenplay, Maurice Pialat; Photography, Pierre William Glenn, Jean Paul Janssen; Editors, Corinne Lazare, Patrice Grisolet, Anne Saint Macary, Stephanie Granel; Assistant Directors, Patrick Grandperret, Emmanuel Clot, Jean Marie Duhard; Music, Patrick Juvet; Performed by Les Freres Lacki; French with English subtitles; In color; 85 minutes; Not rated; March release. CAST: Sabine Haudepin (Elisabeth), Philippe Marlaud (Phillippe), Annik Alane (Mother), Michel Caron (Father), Christian Bouillette (Old Man), Jean-Francois Adam (Teacher), Bernard Tronczyk (Bernard), Patrick Lepczynski (Patrick), Agnes Makowiak (Agnes), Patrick Playez (Rocky), Charline Pourre (Charline), Muriel Lacroix (Muriel), Frederique Cerbonnet (Frederique), Fabienne Neuville (Elisabeth's Sister), Patrice Pisula (Patrice), Aline Fayard (In cafe), Pierre Barski (Babar), Valerie Chassigneux (Valerie), Cathy Gallet (Cathy), Patrice Kubiak (Patrice), Geordes Vimart (Baju), Stanislawa Tronczyk (Bernard's Mother), Josephine Lepczynski (Patrick's Mother), Francois Lepczynski (Patrick's Father), Andre Bitoun (Man in Rolls)

Tanya Akaiuta, Nikita Mikhailovsky in "Love and Lies"
©*IFE*

199

"The Power of Men Is the Patience of Women"
©*Iris Films*

THE POWER OF MEN IS THE PATIENCE OF WOMEN (Iris) Producer, Sphinx Films; Direction and Screenplay, Cristina Perincioli; Photography, Katia Forbert Petersen; Music, Flying Lesbians; Producer, Marianne Gassner; Editor, Helga Schnurre; In color; 76 minutes; Not rated; March release. CAST: Elisabeth Walinski, Eberhard Feik, Dora Kurten, Christa Gehrmann, Hilde Hessmann, Barbara Stanek

PABLO PICASSO: THE LEGACY OF A GENIUS (Blackwood) Producer-Director, Michael Blackwood; Associate Director-Editor, Phyllis Chinlund; Photography, Mead Hunt; In color; 90 minutes; March release. Interviews with Robert Rosenblum, Dominique Bozo, Clement Greenberg, Roland Penrose, Henry Moore, Francoise Gilot, David Hockney, Roy Lichtenstein, Anthony Caro, Matta, George Segal, Elaine de Kooning, Howard Hodgkin, Jennifer Bartlett, Claude Viallat, Pierre Buraglio, Dominique Thiolat, Gerhard Richter, Eduardo Chillida, Shirley Jaffe, Claude Picasso, Maia Picasso

SPECIAL TREATMENT (New Yorker) Executive Producers, Milan Zmukic, Dan Tana; Direction, Goran Paskaljevick; Screenplay, G. Paskaljevic, Dusan Kovacevic, Filip David; Photography, Aleksander Petkovic; Editor, Olga Skrigin; Designer, Dragoljub Ivkov; Serbo-Croatian with English subtitles; In color; 94 minutes; Not rated; March release. CAST: Ljuba Tadic (Dr. Ilich), Milena Dravic (Katja), Dusica Zegarac (Jelena), Danilo Stojkovic (Stevo), Petar Kralj (Marko), Milan Srdoc (Old Man), Radmila Zivkovic (Mila), Bora Todorovic (Rada), Predrag Bijelic (Dejan), Bata Zivojinovic (Brewery Director), Pavle Vuisic (Director's Father), Janez Vrhovec (Hospital Director)

THE SAVAGE HUNT OF KING STAKH (IFEX) Producer, Byelorusfilm USSR; Director, Valery Rubinchik; Screenplay, Vladimir Korotkevich, Valery Rubinchik; Photography, Tatyana Loginova; Design, Alexander Chertovich; Music, Evgeny Glebov; In color; 112 minutes; Not rated; March release. CAST: Boris Plotnikov (Andrei), Elena Dimitrova (Nadezhda), Albert Filozov (Steward), Boris Khmelnitzkij (Ales), Roman Filippov (Gryn), Valentina Chendrikova (Widow), Igor Kluss (Rygor), Vladimir Fedorov (Midget)

William Shatner, Lee Grant in "Visiting Hours"
©*Filmplan Intnl.*

HIM AND ME (Film Forum) Directed, written, photographed and edited by James Benning; Produced by ZDF German Television; 88 minutes; Not rated; March release. A narrative film about one man's journey through the American landscape since 1950 with Rebecca Pauly, Art Schade.

VISITING HOURS (20th Century-Fox) Executive Producers, Pierre David, Victor Solnicki; Producer, Claude Heroux; Director, Jean Claude Lord; Screenplay, Brian Taggert; Photography, Rene Verzier; Music, Jonathan Goldsmith; Editors, Jean Claude Lord, Lise Thouin; Art Director, Michel Proulx; Assistant Director, Julian Marks; Costumes, Delphine White; A Filmplan International production in color; 105 minutes; Rated R; March release. CAST: Michael Ironside (Colt), Lee Grant (Deborah), Linda Purl (Sheila), William Shatner (Gary), Lenore Zann (Lisa), Harvey Atkin (Vinnie), Helen Hughes (Louise), Michael J. Reynolds (Porter), Kirsten Bishopric (Denise), Debra Kirschenbaum (Connie), Elizabeth Leigh Milne (Patricia), Maureen McRae (Elizabeth), Dustin Waln (Hawker), Neil Affleck (Officer), Damir Andrei (Paramedic), Dorothy Barker (Sally), Steve Bettcher (Anesthetist), Walker Boone, Richard Briere (Police), Terrance P. Coady (Security Officer), Dora Dainton (Mrs. Corrigan), Sylvie Desbois (Desk Nurse), Tali Fischer (Bridget)

A WEEK'S VACATION (Biograph International) Director, Bertrand Tavernier; Screenplay, B. Tavernier, Colo Tavernier, Marie-Francoise Hans; Photography, Pierre William Glenn; Editor, Armand Psenny; Music, Pierre Papadiamandis; French with English subtitles; In Eastmancolor; 102 minutes; Not rated; March release (Paris 1980). CAST: Nathalie Baye (Laurence), Gerard Lanvin (Pierre), Michel Galabru (Mancheron), Philippe Noiret (Descombes), Philippe Leotard (Sabouret), Flore Fitzgerlad (Anne), Jean Daste (Father), Marie-Louise Ebeli (Mother)

AMIN: THE RISE AND FALL (International Film Marketing/Twin Continental) formerly "The Rise and Fall of Idi Amin"; Director-Producer, Sharad Patel; Photography, Harvey Harrison; Editor, Keith Palmer; In color; 101 minutes; Rated R; March release. CAST: Joseph Olita (Idi Amin), Geoffrey Keen (British Commissioner), Denis Hills (Himself), Leonard Trolley (Bob Astles), Andre Maranne (French Ambassador), Diane Mercer (His Wife), Tony Sibbald (Canadian Commissioner), Thomas Baptiste (Dr. Oloya), Louis Mahoney (Freedom Fighter), Ka Vundla (Malyamungu), Sophie Kind (French Ambassador's Daughter), Marlene Dogherty (Mrs. Dora Bloch)

CHRISTIANE F. (New World) Producers, Bernd Eichinger, Hans Weth; Director, Ulrich Edel; Screenplay, Herman Weigel; Photography, Justus Pankau, Jurgen Jurges; Editor, Jane Seitz; Music, David Bowie; Juergen Knieper; In color; 124 minutes; Not rated; German with English subtitles; March release. CAST: Natja Brunkhorst (Christiane F.), Thomas Haustein (Detiev), Jens Kuphal (Axel), Reiner Wolk (Leiche), Jan Georg Effler (Bernd), Christiane Reicheit (Babsi), Daniela Jaeger (Kessi), Kerstin Richter (Stella), Peggy Bussleck (Puppi), Kerstin Malessa (Tina), Bernhard Janson (Milan), Catherine Schabeck (Linda), Andre Fuhrmann (Atze), Lutz Hemmerling (Blenenstich), Uwe Diderich (Klaus), Lothar Chamski (Rolf), Stanislaus Solotar (Max), Christiane Lechle (Christiane's Mother), Ellen Esser (Kessi's Mother), David Bowie (Himself)

COMMENT CA VA? Producers, Sonimage, Institut Nationale du Audiovisuel, Bela Productions; Directors, Jean-Luc Godard, Anne-Marie Mieville; In French without subtitles; 78 minutes; Not rated; March release. CAST: Anne-Marie Mieville (Odette)

THE GREAT WHITE (Film Ventures) Producers, Maurizio Amati, Ugo Tucci; Director, Enzo G. Castellari; Screenplay, Marc Princi; Music, Morton Stevens; Associate Producer, Sandro Amati; An Edmondo Amati Film presented by Edward L. Montora in color; Rated PG; March release; CAST: James Franciscus, Vic Morrow, Joshua Sinclair, Timothy Brent, Chuck Kaufman, Thomas Moore, Joyce Lee

DRAGON ON FIRE (Trans-Continental) In color; Rated R; March release. Starring Dragon Lee

FINAL ASSIGNMENT (Almi Cinema 5) Producer, Lawrence Hertzog; Director, Paul Almond; Screenplay, Marc Rosen; a Persephone Production in color; Rated PG; 82 minutes; March release. CAST: Genevieve Bujold (Nicole), Michael York (Lyosha), Burgess Meredith (Zak), Colleen Dewhurst (Ulanov)

RED DUST/POLVO ROJO (Unifilm) Producer, Ricardo Avila; Direction and Screenplay, Jesus Diaz; Photography, Raul Rodriguez; Editor, Justo Vega; Music, Jose Maria Vitier; Assistant Director, Lazaro Burio; In color; 105 minutes; Not Rated; March release. STARRING Adolfo Llaurado, Rene De La Cruz

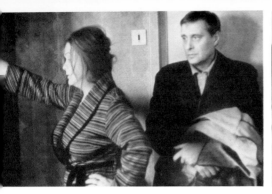

"Autumn Marathon"
©IFEX

Alexander Kalyagin, Eugenia Glushenko in "An Unfinished
Piece for Player Piano" ©Corinth

THE ARREST Producer, Serge Fradkoff; Direction and Screenplay, Raphael Rebibo; Photography, Maurice Fellous; Editor, Pierre Gillette; Music, Paul Micraki; 91 minutes; Not rated; April release. CAST: Bernard LeCoq (Erwin), Catherine Lachens (Lola), Francois Maistre (Chief), Fernand Berset (1st Person), Roland Amstutz (2nd Person), Jacques Rispal (Father), Pierre Nicole (Andre), Severine Bulard (Margot), Robert Schmid (Publisher), Paul Pasquier (Boss), Armen Godel (Intern), Philippe Menthe (Guard)

AN AUTUMN MARATHON (International Film Exchange) Producer, Mosfilm; Director, Georgi Danelia; Screenplay, Aleksandr Volodin; Photography, Sergei Vronsky; Russian with subtitles; In color; 90 minutes; Not rated; April release. CAST: Oleg Basilashvili (Andrei), Natalia Gundareva (Nina), Marina Neyelova (Alla), Yevgeny Leonov (Vasily)

BUDAPEST TALES (Hungarofilm) Producer, Hunnia Studio; Direction and Screenplay, Istvan Szabo; Photography, Sandor Sara; Music, Zdenko Tamassy; 91 minutes; Not rated; April release. CAST: Maya Komorowska, Agi Meszaros, Ildiko Bansagi, Andras Balint, Frantiszek Pieczka, Karoly Lovacs, Jozsef Madaras, Simon Surmiel, Zoltan Huszarik, Vilmos Kun, Sandor Halmagy, Rita Bekes

GRENDEL GRENDEL GRENDEL (Victorian) Producers, Phillip Adams, Alexander Stitt; Direction, Design, Screenplay and Lyrics, Alexander Stitt; Based on novel "Grendel" by John Gardner; Music, Bruce Smeaton; Animation Director, Frank Hellard; In color; 90 minutes; Not rated; April release. An animated film with Peter Ustinov, Keith Michell, Arthur Dignam, Julie McKenna

BUDO: GRAND MASTERS OF THE MARTIAL ARTS (Crown International) Executive Producer, Arthur Davis; Created and Produced by Hisao Masuda; Direction and Screenplay, Masayoshi Nemoto; Music, Stomy Yamashta; Photography, Ryo Yano, Yoshiski Kato; Editor, Koichi Atsumi; Narrator, Harry J. Quini; In color; 101 minutes; Rated PG; April release. A factual report on the Japanese fighting arts.

AN UNFINISHED PIECE FOR PLAYER PIANO (Corinth) Producer, Mosfilm Studio; Director, Nikita Mikhalkov; Screenplay, N. Mikhalkov, Alexander Adabashyan; from novel "Platonov" by Anton Chekhov; Photography, Pavel Lebeshev; Music, Eduard Artemyev; Russian with English subtitles; In color; 100 minutes; Not rated; April release. CAST: Alexander Kalyagin (Platonov), Elena Solovei (Sophia), Eugenia Glushenko (Sasha), Antonia Shuranova (Anna Petrovna), Yuri Bogatyrev (Sergei), Nikita Mikhalkov (Doctor), Oleg Tabakov (Shcherbuk), Pavel Kadochnikov (Glagolyev)

THE STUD FARM (New Yorker) Producers, Mafilm Objektiv, Dialog Studios; Direction and Screenplay, Andras Kovacs; Based on novel by Istvan Gall; Photography, Lajos Koltai; In Eastmancolor; 94 minutes; April release (Hungary 1978). CAST: Jozsef Madaras (Janos Buso), Ferenc Fabian (Matyas Buso), Sandor Horvath (Kristof Mathe), Karoly Sinka (Schobert), Ferenc Bacs (Bazsi), Levente Biro (Kabik), Andras Csibi (Aghy), Istvan Gyarmathy (Eor), Csongor Ferenczy (Baron), Andras Ambrus (Murom), Iren Bordan (Erzsi), Nandor Tomanek (Miksa Braun), Laszloa Horesnyi (Vizi)

DANCE CRAZE (Nu-Image) Producer, Gavrik Losey; Director, Joe Massot; Photography, Joe Dunton; Editor, Ben Rayner; Music, Clive Langer, Alan Winstanley; In color; 86 minutes; Not rated; April release (England 1980). The film focuses on the best of the British "Ska" bands: Bad Manners, The English Beat, The Bodysnatchers, Madness, The Selecter, The Specials.

TICKET OF NO RETURN (Public Cinema) formerly "Portrait of a Female Drunkard"; Producer, Marianne Gassner; Direction, Screenplay, Photography, Ulrike Ottinger; Assistant Director-Editor, Ila von Hasperg; Music Peer Raben; Costumes, Tabea Blumenschein; 108 minutes; Not rated; April release. (Berlin 1979). CAST: Tabea Blumenschein (She), Lutze (Drinker from the Zoo), Magdalena Montezuma (Social Question), Orpha Termin (Accurate Statistics), Monika von Cub (Common Sense), Paul Glauer (Dwarf), Nina Hagen (Chanteuse), Gunter Meisner (Willy the director), Kurt Raab (Head of the office), Volker Spengler (Transvestite), Zirkus Renz (Funambulist), The Destroyers (Helldrivers), Eddie Constantine, Mercedes Vostell, Wolf Vostell, Ginka Steinwachs (At the artists' table)

"The Stud Farm"
©New Yorker

"Ticket of No Return"

201

Paulo Cesar Pereio, Sonia Braga in "I Love You"
©*Atlantic*

Derek Thompson, Bob Hoskins, P. H. Moriarty in "The Long
Good Friday" ©*Embassy*

I LOVE YOU (Atlantic) Producer, Walter Clark; Direction and
Screenplay, Arnaldo Jabor; Photography, Murilo Salles; Editor,
Mair Tavares; Art Director, Marcos Weinstock; Music, Antonio
Carlos Jobim, Chico Buarque de Hollanda, Cesar Camargo Mari-
ano; Choreographer, Gerry Marotski; Costumes, Giovanna Vassalo,
Fernando Bodo; Assistant Directors, Gilberto Loureiro, Paulo
Sergio Almeida; A Flavia Film in color; 104 minutes; Not rated;
April release (Brazil 1981). CAST: Sonia Braga (Maria), Paulo Ce-
sar Pereio (Paulo), Vera Fischer (Barbara), Tarcisio Meira (Pilot),
Maria Lucia Dahl (Pilot's Wife), Regina Case (Shampoo Sales-
woman), Flavio Sao Thiago (Waldir the husband), Guaracy Ro-
drigues (Morgue Orderly), Sandro Soviatti (Taxi Driver), Vera
Abelha (Transvestite)

IF YOU COULD SEE WHAT I HEAR (Jensen Farley) Executive
Producers, Gene Corman, Dale Falconer; Producer-Director, Eric
Till; Co-Producer-Screenplay, Stuart Gillard; Based on book by
Tom Sullivan and Derek Gill; Photography, Harry Makin; Art Di-
rector, Gavin Mitchell; Music Co-ordinator, Eric Robertson; Songs,
Michael Lloyd; "You're the One" performed by Helen Reddy and
Tom Sullivan; Assistant Directors, David Shepherd, Richard
Flower; Editor, Eric Wrate; A Cypress Grove Films production in
color and Dolby Stereo; 103 minutes; Rated PG; April release.
CAST: Marc Singer (Tom Sullivan), R. H. Thomson (Will Sly),
Sarah Torgov (Patty), Shari Belafonte Harper (Heather), Douglas
Campbell (Porky), Helen Burns (Mrs. Ruxton), Harvey Atkin
(Bert), Barbara Gordon (Molly), Sharon Lewis (Helga), Lynda Ma-
son Greene (Sharon), Tony van Bridge (Dr. Wells), Jack Creley (Dr.
Franklin), Neil Dainard (Phil), Michael Tate (Dr. Jamieson), David
Gardner (Mr. Steffen), Noni Griffin (Mrs. Steffen), Adrienne Pocock
(Blythe), Hugh Webster (Sean)

ONE NIGHT STAND (Janus) Producers, Canadian Broadcasting
Corp., Allan King Associates; Director, Allan King; Screenplay,
Carol Bolt; Photography, Ken Gregg; In color; 93 minutes; Not
rated; April release. CAST: Chapelle Jaffe (Daisy), Brent Carver
(Rafe), Dinah Christie (Riva), Susan Hogan (Sharon), Mina E. Mina
(Honey), Len Doncheff (Cabbie), Robert Silverman (Nick), Pixie
Bigelow (Wife), Don Daynard (Bouncer)

**IT WAS NIGHT IN ROME/ERA NOTTE A ROMA (Joseph
Papp/FDM)** Director, Roberto Rossellini; Screenplay, Mr. Rossel-
lini, Sergio Amidie, Diego Fabri, Brunello Rondi; Photography,
Carlo Carlini; Editor, Roberto Cinquini; Music, Renzo Rossellini; In
Italian, Russian and German with English subtitles; 145 minutes;
Not rated; April release. CAST: Leo Genn (Pemberton), Giovanna
Ralli (Esperia), Sergei Bondarchuk (Fyodor), Hannes Messemer
(Von Kleist), Peter Baldwin (Bradley), George Tetarca (Tarcisio),
Renato Szlvatori (Renato)

THE LONG GOOD FRIDAY (Embassy) Producer, Barry Hanson;
Director, John Mackenzie; Screenplay, Barry Keeffe; Photography,
Phil Meheus; Editor, Mike Taylor; In color; 114 minutes; Rated R;
April release. CAST: Bob Hoskins (Harold), Helen Mirren (Victo-
ria), Eddie Constantine (Charlie), Dave King (Parky), Bryan Mar-
shall (Harris), George Coulouris (Gus), Derek Thompson (Jeff),
Bruce Alexander (Mac), Paul Barber (Errol), Pierce Brosnan (1st
Irishman), Charles Cork (Eric), Bill Cornelius (Pete), Stephen Davis
(Tony), Alan Devlin (Priest), Christopher Driscoll (Phil)

A SLAP IN THE FACE (IFEX) also known as "A Piece of the
Sky"; Producer, Armenfilm Studios; Director, Genrikh Malyan;
Screenplay, Stepan Aldzhedzhyan, Mr. Malyan; Based on story
"Blue Flowers" by Vaan Totovents; Photography, Sergei Israelyan;
Music, Tigran Mansuryan; Armenian with English subtitles; In
color; 90 minutes; Not rated; April release. CAST: Ashot Adamian
(Torik), Mger Mkrtchyan, Sofiko Chiarell, Galina Belyeyeva, Tigran
Voskonyan, Arsen Kuyumlan, Natalia Krachkovskaya

SILHOUETTES Producers, La Strada Productions, Claire Produc-
tions; Director, Giuseppe Murolo; Screenplay, George David Weiss,
Mr. Murolo, Russell Firestone; Photography, Roberto D'Ettorre
Piazzoli; Editor, Eugenio Alabiso; In color; 100 minutes; April re-
lease. CAST: George David Weiss (Paul), Susan Monts (Michele),
Kathryn Cordes (Caroline), Michael A. Pappalardo (Don), Gi-
useppe Murolo (Angelo), David Chase (Sid), Luciano Crovato
(Carlo), Tom Felleghy (Doctor), Fabrizio Guarducci (Street Artist),
Anna Terminiello (Mama Luna), Natalia de Capua (Music Student),
Mariella Russo (Salesclerk), Female Soccer Team

WEAPONS OF DEATH (Independent Artists) A Films International Picture in color; April release. Starring Eric Lee.

Marc Singer, Shari Belafonte Harper in "If You Could See
What I Hear" ©*Jensen Farley*

"A Slap in the Face"
©*IFEX*

Lex Goldsmith, Brett Marx, Louise Fletcher in "Lucky Star"
©*Pickman*

Veronica Lang, Graeme Blundell, Jeanie Drynan, John
Hargreaves in "Don's Party" ©*Satori*

THE LUCKY STAR (Pickman) Executive Producer, Andre Fleury; Producer, Claude Leger; Direction and Screenplay, Max Fischer; Associate Producer, Peiter Kroonenburg; Adaptation and Dialogue, Jack Rosenthal; Assistant Director, Pierre Magny; In color; 110 minutes; Rated PG, May release. CAST: Rod Steiger (Col. Gluck), Louise Fletcher (Loes Bakker), Lou Jacobi (Elia Goldberg), Brett Marx (David), Helen Hughes (Rose Goldberg), Yvon Dufour (Burgomaster), Jean Gascon (Priest), Isabelle Mejias (Marijke), Kalman Steinberg (Salomon), Guy L'Ecuyer (Antique Dealer), Johnny Krykamp (Kees), Peter Farber (Gendarme), Lex Goudsmith (Gendarme), Rijk DeGooyer (Gendarme), Hans Cornelis (Gestapo Men), Irene Kessler (Mrs. Stein), Tom Rack (Odd-job Man), Syd Libman (Rabbi), Fred DeGrote (Telephone Operator), Henry Gamer (Commissionaire)

URGH! A MUSIC WAR (Lorimar) Producer, Michael White; Director, Derek Burbidge; Creative Consultants, Mile and Ian Copeland; Associate Producer, Lyndall Hobbs; Assistant Director, Nigel Reed; Editors, Jim Alderton, Simon Milne; Art Work, Glen Habgood; In color and Dolby Stereo; 123 minutes; Rated R; May release. A documentary of 34 new bands which together form a complete picture of rock and roll at the start of the 1980's. Filmed in London, New York, California and France.

ONCE UPON A TIME (Janus) Producers, G. N. Lakshmipathy, K. N. Narayan; Director, Girish Karnad; Screenplay, Krishna Basrur, Girish Karnad; Dialogue, G. B. Joshi; Photography, A. K. Bir; In color; 156 minutes; Not rated; May release. CAST: Shankar Nag (Gandugali), Sunder Krishna Urs (Permadi), Akshata Rao (Savantri), Sushilendra (Hayakeshi), Alit Saldenha (Iraga), Rekha Sabnis (Permadi's Wife), Anil Thakkar (Kapardi), Vasant Rao (Maranayeka)

MEMOIRS OF A FRENCH WHORE (Aidart) Producer, Benjamin Simon; Director, Daniel Duval; Screenplay, Daniel Duval, Christopher Frank, Jeanne Cordelier; Based on "The Life" by Jeanne Cordelier; Photography, Michel Cenet; Art Director, Francois Chanut; Editor, Jean-Bernard Bonis; Music, Vladimir Kosma; In color; 100 minutes; Not rated; May release. CAST: Miou-Miou (Marie), Maria Schneider (Maloup), Daniel Duval (Gerard), Neil Arestrup (Andre)

AS IF IT WERE YESTERDAY (Almi Cinema 5) Producer-Director, Myriam Abramowicz, Esther Hoffenberg; Photography, Jean-Noel Gabran; Editor, Dominique Loreau; Music, Neige; French and Flemish with English subtitles; In color; 85 minutes; Not rated; May release. A documentary about Belgians who saved Jewish children during World War II.

DON'S PARTY (Satori) Producer, Philip Adams; Director, Bruce Beresford; Screenplay, David Williamson; Photography, Don McAlpine; Editor, William Anderson; Art Director, Rhoisin Harrison; Music, Leos Jan; In color; 90 minutes; Not rated; May release. CAST: John Hargreaves (Don), Jeanie Dryman (Kath), Graeme Blundell (Simon), Veronica Lang (Jody), Ray Barrett (Mal), Pat Bishop (Jenny), Graham Kennedy (Mack), Kit Taylor (Evan), Candy Raymond (Kerry), Harold Hopkins (Cooley), Clare Binney (Susan), John Gorton (Himself)

EIJANAIKA (Shochiku) Direction and Story, Shohei Imamura; Screenplay, Shohei Imamura, Ken Miuamoto; Photography, Masahisa Himeda; Japanese with English subtitles; In color; 151 minutes; Not rated; May release. CAST: Shigeru Izumiya (Genji), Kaori Mamoi (Ine), Ken Ogata (Furukawa), Masao Kusakari (Itoman), Shigeru Tsuyuguchi (Kirgo), Minori Terada (Ijuin), Yohei Kaono (Hara)

SUPER FUZZ (Embassy) Director, Sergio Corbucci; Screenplay, Mr. Corbucci, Sabatino Cluffini; Photography, Silvano Ippeliti; Editor, Eugenio Alabiso; In color; 97 minutes; Rated PG; May release. CAST: Terence Hill (Dave), Ernest Borgnine (Sgt. Dunlop), Joanne Dru (Rosy), Marc Lawrence (Torpedo), Julie Gordon (Evelyn), Lee Sandman (Police Chief), Herb Goldstein (Silvius), Don Sebastian (Dingo), Sal Borghese (Paradise Alley), Claudio Ruffini (Tragedy Row), Sergio Smacchi (Slot Machine)

THE SECRET POLICEMAN'S OTHER BALL (Miramax) Producers, Martin Lewis, Peter Walker; Director, Julien Temple; Photography, Oliver Stapleton; Editor, Geoff Hogg; In Dolby Stereo and color; 95 minutes; Rated R; May release. CAST: John Cleese, Graham Chapman, Michael Palin, Terry Jones, Peter Cook, Pamela Stephenson, Pete Townshend, Sting, Eric Clapton, Jeff Beck, Phil Collins

Maria Schneider, Miou-Miou in "Memoirs of a French
Whore" ©*United Artists*

"Once Upon A Time"
©*Janus*

203

Nicholas Clay, Sylvia Kristel in "Lady Chatterley's Lover"
©*Cannon Group*

James Caan in "Bolero"
©*Double 13*

RACE D'EP (Little Sisters) Director, Lionel Soukas; Screenplay, Nicole Deschaumes; Conceived by Mr. Soukas, Guy Hocquenghem; Photography, Jerome de Missolz, Mr. Hocquenghem; Editor, Lionel Soukas; French with English subtitles; In color; 95 minutes; Not rated; May release. CAST: Elizar von Effenterre (Baron), Giles Sandler (Client), Pierre Hahn (Hirschfeld), Yves Jacquemard, Jean Demilier, Jean Michel Senechal (His Assistants), Betty (Transexual), Claire Amiard, Adeline Andre (Secretaries), Michel Journiac, Jean Luc, Piotr Stanislas (SS), Hunks Clements (Pretty Blond), Peter Vlaspolder (Handsome Dark-haired Boy), Guy Hocquenghem (Queen), Piotr Stanislas (American)

IRACEMA (Embrafilme) Conceived, Directed and Photographed by Jorge Bodanzky with Orlando Senna and Wolf Gauer; Screenplay, Mr. Senna; Editor, Eva Grundmann; In color; 90 minutes; Not rated; May release. CAST: Edna de Cassia (Iracema), Paulo Cesar Pereio (Tiao)

THE THIRD MILLENNIUM (Embrafilme) By Jorge Bodanzky, Wolf Gauer; 90 minutes; Not rated; May release. The documentary record of the annual visit to his constituents by Senator Evandro Carreira who represents the State of Amazonas in the Brazilian Senate at Brasilia.

LADY CHATTERLEY'S LOVER (Cannon Group) Producers, Christopher Peerce, Andre Diaoui; Director, Just Jaeckin; Screenplay, Christopher Wicking, Just Jaeckin; Based on novel by D. H. Lawrence; Adaptation, Marc Behm; Music, Stanley Myers, Richard Harvey; Photography, Robert Fraisse; In color; 141 minutes; Rated R; May release. CAST: Sylvia Kristel (Lady Chatterley), Shane Briant (Sir Clifford Chatterley), Nicholas Clay (Gamekeeper), Ann Mitchell (Ivy), Elizabeth Spriggs (Lady Eva), Peter Bennett (Butler), Pascale Rivault (Hilda)

DR. BUTCHER M.D. (Aquarius) Producer, Gianfranco Couyoumdjian; Direction and Screenplay, Frank Martin; Music, Walter Sea; A Flora production presented by Terry Levene; In Technicolor; Rated R; 80 minutes; May release. CAST: Ian McCulloch (Peter), Alexandra Cole (Lori), Sherry Buchanan (Kelly), Peter O'Neal (George), Donald O'Brian (Dr. Abrera)

THE WORLD OF DRUNKEN MASTER (Marvin) Producer-Director, Joseph Kuo; Executive Producer, Susana Kuo; Screenplay, Tien Shan Hsi; Martial Instructor, Yuen Hsiang Jen; In color; Rated R; 90 minutes; May release. CAST: Jack Long, Simon Lee, Jeanie Chang, Mark Long, Long Fei, Long Ten Hsiang, Chen Hui Lou, Kan Te Man, Wang Yong Hsen, Wang Yu

THE SQUEEZE (Maverick International) Producer, Turi Vasile; Executive Producer, Raymond R. Homer; Director, Anthony M. Dawson (Antonio Margheriti); Screenplay, Simon O'Neil, Marc Princi, Paul Costello; Photography, Sergio D'Offizi; Editor, Robert Sterbini; Music, Paolo Vasile; Art Director, Francesco Bronzi, Hans Zillman; Costumes, Adrianna Berselli; Assistant Director, Ignazio Dolce; In Pacific Labs Color; Rated R; 100 minutes; May release. CAST: Lee Van Cleef (Chris), Karen Black (Clarisse), Edward Albert (Jeff), Lionel Stander (Sam), Robert Alda (Donati), Angelo Infanti (Inspector), Antonella Murgia (Jessica), Peter Carsten (Von Stratten)

THE UPPERCRUST (Cine-International) Producers, Peter Patzak, Richard Chase; Director, Peter Patzak; Screenplay, Helmut Zenker, Peter Patzak; Photography, Walter Kindler; Editor, Traube Gruber; In color; Not rated; 114 minutes; May release. CAST: Franz Buchrieser (Kommissar), Frank Gorshin (Harry), Lukas Resetarits (Ludwig), Pavel Landovsky (Jakob), Bibiana Zeller (Herta), Broderick Crawford (Mike), Ernst Konarek (Wolfgang), Nigel Davenport (Pigel), Fred Schaffer (Erwin), Maria Bill (Elfi), Joey Forman (Eddie)

THE FEARLESS JACKAL (Marvin) Producer, Jackel Chan; Director, Lei Chiu; Martial Art Directors, Tai Sai Ngan, Chan Siu Lang; 90 minutes; Rated R; May release. CAST: Philip Ko, Leung Ka Yan

BOLERO (Double 13) Produced, Directed and Written by Claude Lelouch; Photography, Jean Boffety; Editors, Hughes Darmois, Sophie Bhaud; Music, Francis Lai, Michel Legrand; Choreography, Maurice Bejart; In Dolby Stereo and color; 173 minutes; June release. CAST: James Caan (Glenn Sr. & Jr.), Robert Hossein (Simon Meyer/Robert Prat), Nicole Garcia (Anne), Geraldine Chaplin (Suzan/Sara Glenn), Daniel Olbrychski (Karl), Jacques Villeret (Jacques), Jorge Donn (Boris/Sergio), Rita Poelvoorde (Tatyana/Tanya), Evelyn Bouix (Evelyne/Edith), Macha Meril (Magda), Francis Huster (Francis), Raymond Pelegrin (Raymond), Jean-Claude Brialy (Director of Lidao), Fanny Dant (Veronique), Jean-Claude Bouttier (Philippe), Richard Bohringer (Richard), Nicole Croisille (Nicole)

Geraldine Chaplin, James Caan in "Bolero"
©*Double 13*

204

"Not A Love Story"
©ESMA

"One Wonderful Sunday"
©FDM

A DISTANT CRY FROM SPRING (Shochiku Films of America) Director, Yoji Yamada; Screenplay, Yoji Yamada, Yoshitaka Asama; Story, Mr. Yamada; Japanese with English subtitles; In color; 124 minutes; Not rated; June release. CAST: Ken Takakura (Kosaku Tajima), Chieko Baisho (Tamiko Kazami), Hidetaka Yoshioka (Takeshi Kazami)

SWEET WILLIAM (World Northal) Producer, Jeremy Watt; Director, Claude Whatham; Screenplay, Beryl Bainbridge; Based on novel by Miss Bainbridge; Photography, Les Young; Editor, Pete Coulson; In color; 90 minutes; Not rated; June release. CAST: Sam Waterston (William), Jenny Agutter (Ann), Anna Massey (Edna), Daphne Exenford (Mrs. Walton), Geraldine James (Pamela), Arthur Loew (Capt. Walton), Peter Dean (Roddy), Rachel Bell (Mrs. Kershaw), Tim Piggot-Smith (Gerald), Emma Bakhle (Daisy), Victoria Fairbrother (Sheila), Ivor Roberts (Uncle Walter), Joan Cooper (Aunt Bee)

NOT A LOVE STORY (Quartet) Producer, Dorothy Todd Henaut; Director, Bonnie Sherr Klein, Linda Lee Tracey; Associate Director-Editor, Anne Henderson; Photography, Pierre Letarte; Music, Ginette Bellavance; In color; 75 minutes; Not rated, June release. A documentary about pornography and its impact on women, with Linda Lee Tracey as its principal witness.

SERIE NOIRE (Gaumont) Producer, Maurice Bernart; Director, Alain Corneau; Screenplay and Adaptation, Georges Perec, Alain Corneau; Based on "A Hell of a Woman" by Jim Thompson; Photography, Pierre-William Glenn; Editor, Thierry Derocles; Music, Duke Ellington, Juan Tizol; In color; 110 minutes; French with English subtitles; June release (France 1979). CAST: Patrick Dewaere (Frank), Myriam Boyer (Jeanne), Marie Trintignant (Mona), Bernard Blier (Staplin), Jeanne Herviale (Aunt), Andreas Katsulas (Andreas), Charlie Farnel (Marcel), Jack Jourdan (Trainer), Samuel Mek (Boxer), Fernand Coquet (Hell's Angel)

THE SEVEN GRANDMASTERS (Marvin) Producer-Director, Joseph Kuo; Martial Arts Director, Ho Pin Yuen; Rated R; In color; 95 minutes; June release

ONE WONDERFUL SUNDAY (FDM) Director, Akira Kurosawa; Screenplay, Keinosuke Uekusa; Photography, Asakazu Nakai; Music, Tadashi Hattori; In color; 95 minutes; Japanese with English subtitles; Not rated; June release (Japan 1947). CAST: Isao Numazaki, Chieko, Nakakita, Ichiro Sugai, Midori Ariyama, Masao Shimizu

NOW...AFTER ALL THESE YEARS (Arthur Cantor) Produced and Directed by Harald Luders, Pavel Schnabel; German with English subtitles; In color; 60 minutes; Not rated; June release. A documentary about the Prussian village of Rhina and its former Jewish population.

FABIAN (United Artists Classics) Director, Wolf Gremm; Based on novel by Erich Kastner; In color; 116 minutes; German with English subtitles; Rated R; June release. CAST: Hans Peter Hallwachs (Fabian), Hermann Lause (Labude)

PINK FLOYD—THE WALL (MGM/UA) Producer, Alan Marshall; Director, Alan Parker; Screenplay, Roger Waters; Executive Producer, Stephen O'Rourke; Photography, Peter Biziou; Animation, Gerald Scarfe, Editor, Gerry Hambling; Design, Brian Morris; Art Directors, Chris Burke, Clinton Cavers; Associate Producer, Garth Thomas; Assistant Director, Ray Corbett; In Metrocolor, Dolby Stereo; 99 minutes; Rated R; June release. CAST: Bob Geldof (Pink), Christine Hargreaves (Mother), James Laurenson (Father), Eleanor David (Wife), Kevin McKeon (Young Pink), Bob Hoskins (Manager), David Bingham (Little Pink), Jenny Wright (American Groupie), Alex McAvoy (Teacher), Ellis Dale (Doctor), James Hazeldine (Lover), Ray Mort (Playground Father), Marjorie Mason (Teacher's Wife), Robert Bridges (American Doctor), Michael Ensign (Hotel Manager), Marie Passarelli (Spanish Maid), Winston Rose (Security Guard)

ALIEN CONTAMINATION (Cannon) Producer, Claudio Mancini; Director, Lewis Coates; Associate Producer, Ugo Valenti; Music, Goblin; In color; Rated R; 90 minutes; June release. CAST: Ian McCulloch, Louise Marleau, Marino Mase, Siegfried Rauch, Gisela Hahn

Hans-Peter Hallwachs, Hermann Lause in "Fabian"
©United Artists

Jenny Wright, Bob Geldof in "Pink Floyd ..."
©MGM/UA

LIGHTNING KUNG FU (East-West) In Widescreen and color; 91 minutes; Rated R; June release. CAST: John Li, Hung Kam-Bo, Cheung Ying, Fan Lin

DER WILLI BUSCH REPORT (Almi Cinema 5) Producer, Elke Haltaufderhelde; Directed, Edited and Written by Niklaus Schilling; Photography, Wolfgang Dickmann; In German with English subtitles; In color; 119 minutes; Not rated; July release. CAST: Tilo Pruckner (Willi Busch), Dorothea Moritz (Adelheld Busch), Kornelia Boje (Rosemarie), Karin Frey (Helga), Jenny Thelen (Anne), Hannes Kaetner (Sir Henry), Klaus Hoser (Arno), Hildegard Friese (Aunt), Wolfgang Gronebaum (Jupp), Horst Nowak (Animator), Karl Sibold (Rector), Hans-Jurgen Leuthen (Mayor)

THE DYBBUK Director, Stephen Szlachtycz; In Yiddish with English subtitles; 105 minutes; Not rated; July release. CAST: The Kaminska Jewish State Theatre of Poland

ZULU DAWN (New World) Producer, Nate Kohn; Director, Douglas Hickox; Screenplay, Cy Endfield, Anthony Storey; Story, Mr. Endfield; Photography, Ousami Rawl; Music, Elmer Bernstein; In color; 117 minutes; Rated PG; July release (England 1979). CAST: Burt Lancaster (Col. Curnford), Peter O'Toole (Lord Chelmsford), Simon Ward (Vereker), John Mills (Sir Henry Bartle Frere), Denholm Elliott (Col Pulleine), Bob Hoskins (Command Sgt. Major Williams), Nigel Davenport (Col. Hamilton), Michael Jayston (Col. Crealock), Ronald Lacey (Newman), Phil Daniels (Boy Pullen), Freddie Jones (Bishop Colenso), Anna Calder-Marshall (Fannie), Christopher Cazenove (Lt. Coghill), Ronald Pickup (Lt. Harford), Donald Pickering (Maj. Russell)

WORKERS '80 A documentary about the August 1980 negotiations in which Solidarity, the Polish trade union movement, won its extraordinary demands that briefly achieved independence for Poland's workers and promised to change the nature of the state. Directed by Andrzej Chodakowski and Andrzej Zalackowski; In black and white; English translation by Richard Lourie, Antoni Milosz; Narrated by Ted O'Brien; 90 minutes; Not rated; July release.

TO AN UNKNOWN GOD Producer, Elias Quereleta; Director, Jaime Chavarri; Screenplay, Elias Quereleta, Jaime Chavarri; Based on script by Francisco J. Lucio; Photography, Teo Escamilla; Editor, Pablo G. Del Amo; Music, Luis De Pablo; Spanish with English subtitles; 95 minutes; Not rated; July release. CAST: Hector Alteric (Jose), Javier Eloriaga (Miguel), Maria Rosa Salgada (Adela), Rosa Valenty (Clara), Angela Molina (Solidad), Margarita Mas (Solidad grown), Mercedes San Pietra (Mercedes), Jose Joaquin Goza (Pedro), Mirta Millen (Ana), Jose Pagan (Julio), Emilio Siegris

THE SWISS IN THE SPANISH CIVIL WAR (Film Forum) Producers, Richard Dindo, David Streiff; Directed, Written and Edited by Richard Dindo; Photography, Robert Gnant; Swiss German with English subtitles; 80 minutes; Not rated; July release. A documentary that interviews survivors of the Spanish Civil War.

LOVE AND FAITH OF OGIN (Toho) Producers, Tsuneyasu Matsumoto, Kyoko Oshima, Muneo Shimolo; Director, Kei Kumal; Screenplay, Yoshitaka Yorita; Story, Toko Kan; Photography, Kozo Okazaki; Editor, Tatsuji Nakashizu; Music, Akira Ikutube; Japanese with English subtitles; In color; 115 minutes; Not rated; July release. CAST: Takashi Shimura (Sen Rikyu), Ryoko Nakano (Ogin), Toshiro Mifune (Hideyoshi), Atsuo Nakamura (Soji Yamagami), Kichiemon Nakamura (Takayama), Eji Okada (Ankokuji), Akira Nishimura (Sojin)

FIGHTING DRAGON VS. THE DEADLY TIGER (Fury Films) Director, Pang Nim; In color; Rated R; July release. CAST: Bruce Liang, Yasuaki Kurada, Chen Lau, Carlos Macos, Maria Kasan

THE CRIPPLED MASTERS (New Line) Director, Joe Law; Fight Choreographer, Chen Mu Chuan; In color; 92 minutes; Rated R; July release. CAST: Frankie Shum, Jack Conn

GALAXY EXPRESS 999 (New World) Executive Producer, Chiaki Imada; Director, Taro Rin; Screenplay, Shiro Ishimori, Paul Grogan; Based on tv series by Leiji Matsumoto; Animation Director, Kazuo Komatsubara; Editors, Robert Kizer, Masaaki Hanai, Skip Schoolnik; Music, Nozumi Aoki; A Toei production in color; Rated PG; 91 minutes; July release. An animated film featuring the voices of Corey Burton, Fay McKay, Anthony Pope, Booker Bradshaw, Barry Seegar, B. J. Ward, William Woodson

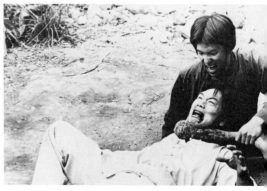

THE MAN WHO STOLE THE SUN (Kitty) Director, Kazuhiko Hasegawa; Screenplay, Leonard Schrader, Kazuhiko Hasegawa; Photography, Tatsuo Suzuki; Music, Takayuki Inoue; In color; Japanese with English subtitles; 147 minutes; Not rated; July release. CAST: Kenji Sawada (Makoto Kido), Bunta Sugawara (Yamashita), Kimiko Ikegami, Yutaka Mizutani, Toshiyuki Nishida

KING DICK (Aquarius) formerly "Little Dick the Mighty Midget"; Producer, Claudio Monti; Director, Cibba; Screenplay, Mr. Monti; Photography, Dino DeAngeli; Animation, Fabio Pacifico, Roberto Vital; Music, Claude Etie; Art Director, Guido Libratti; In color; 65 minutes; Not rated; July release (England 1973). An animated feature concerning the adventures of Little Dick, a midget.

SUMMER AFFAIR (Transvue) Producers, Nicholas Pomilia, Johnny Minervini; Direction and Screenplay, George S. Casorati; In color; Rated R; July release. CAST: Ornella Muti, Les Rannow, Abraham Gordon, Vicki Izay, Chris Avram, Marcy Marks, Louis Pistilli

BIRGITT HAAS MUST BE KILLED (Frank Moreno) Producers, Yves Gasser, Daniel Messere; Director, Laurent Heynemann; Adaptation and Screenplay, Pierre Fabre, Laurent Heynemann, Caroline Huppert; Photography, Jean-Francois Gondre; Music, Philippe Sarde; Editors, Armand Psenny, Jacques Comets; In color; 105 minutes; Not rated; August release. CAST: Philippe Noiret (Athanase), Jean Rochefort (Charles Philippe Bauman), Lisa Kreuzer (Birgitt), Bernard LeCoq (Colonna), Michel Beaune (Delaunay), Victor Garrivier (Nader), Maurice Teynac (Chamrode)

DRESS REHEARSAL (Munich Films) Producers, Laura Film, Thomas Schuhly; Direction and Screenplay by Werner Schroeter; French with English subtitles; 90 minutes; Not rated; August release. A documentary about the Nancy (France) Experimental Theatre Festival.

THE WOLVES/SHUSSHO IWAI (Public) Director, Hideo Gosha; Screenplay, Kei Tasaka; Photography, Kozo Okazaki; Art Director, Motoji Kojima; Music, Masaru Sato; Japanese with English subtitles; In color; Not rated; 131 minutes; August release. CAST: Tatsuya Nakadai (Seiji), Noboru Ando (Gunjiro), Toshio Kurosawa (Tsutomu), Komaki Kurihara (Niece), Kyoko Enami (Oyu), Isao Natsuyagi (Tetsunosuke)

THE JUDGE AND THE ASSASSIN (Libra) Director, Bertrand Tavernier; Screenplay, Bertrand Tavernier, Jean Aurenche; French with English subtitles; In color; 130 minutes; Not rated; August release. CAST: Philippe Noiret (Judge Rousseau), Michel Galabru (Sgt. Bouvier), Isabelle Huppert (Rose), Jean-Claude Brialy (Attorney), Renée Faure (Mme. Rousseau)

I AM A CAT (Toho) Director, Ken Ichikawa; Screenplay, Toshio Yasumi; From novel by Soseki Natsume; Photography, Kozo Okazaki; In color; Japanese with English subtitles; 116 minutes; Not rated; August release. CAST: Tatsuya Nakadi (Kushami), Mariko Okada (Mrs. Kaneda), Juzo Itami, Kuriko Namino, Nobuto Okamoto

THE LOVE SUICIDES AT SONEZAKI (Toho) Director, Yasuzo Masumura; Screenplay, Yoshio Shirasaka, Yasuzo Masumura; Based on tragedy written for Bunraku Puppet Theatre in 1703; Original Story, Monzaimon Chikamatsu; Editor, Tatsuji Nakashizu; Photography, Seitsuo Kobayashi; Music, Tatsudo Uzaki; In color; Japanese with English subtitles; 113 minutes; Not rated; August release (Japan 1977). CAST: Meiko Kaji, Tatsudo Uzaki, Hisashi Igawa, Sachiko Hidari, Isao Hashimoto, Moto Kimura, Jun Haiji, Sachiko Megura, Kazuyo Aoki, Takashi Iba

THE FAMILY (Public) Director, Karei Naru Ichikozo; Screenplay, Satsuo Yamamoto, Nabuo Yamada; Based on novel by Toyoko Yamazaki; Photography, Kozo Okazaki; Music, Masaru Sato; In color; Japanese with English subtitles; 210 minutes; Not rated; August release (Japan 1974). CAST: Tatsuya Nakadai (Son), Shin Saburi (Father), Kyoko Kagawa (Governess), Yumeji Tsukioka, Kinya Kitaoji

CANNIBALS IN THE STREETS (Almi Cinema 5) Producers, Maurizio Amati, Sandro Amati; Director, Anthony M. Dawson; Screenplay, Antonio Margheriti, Jimmy Gould; Story, Jimmy Gould; Photography, Fernando Arribas; Editor, G. Serralonga; Music, Alex Blonksteiner; Design, Walter Patriarca; Assistant Director, Joe Pullini; In color; 91 minutes; August release. CAST: John Saxon (Norman Hopper), Elizabeth Turner (Jane Hopper), John Morghen, Cindy Hamilton, Tony King, Wallace Wilkinson, Ray Williams, John Geroson, May Heatherley, Ronnie Sanders, Vic Perkins, Laura Dean

Hector Alterio, Ana Torrent in "The Nest"
©*Quartet*

THE NEST/EL NIDO (Quartet) Direction and Screenplay, Jaime De Arminan; Photography, Teo Escamilla; Editor, Jose Luis Matesanz; Set, Jean Claude Hoerner; Production Director, Manuel Perez; Costumes; Trini Ardura; Spanish with English subtitles; In color; 109 minutes; Rated PG; August release. CAST: Hector Alterio (Alejandro), Ana Torrent (Goyita), Luis Politti (Eladio), Agustin Gonzalez (Sargento), Patricia Adriani (Marisa), Maria Luisa Ponte (Amaro), Mercedes Alonso (Mercedes), Luisa Rodrigo (Gumer), Amparo Baro (Fuen)

UNDER THE FLAG OF THE RISING SUN (Toho) Producer, Shinsei Eigasha; Director, Kinji Fukasaku; Screenplay, Kaneto Shindo; Based on story by Shoji Yuki; Photography, Hiroshi Segawa; Music, Hikaru Hayashi; Editor, Keijchi Uraoka; Japanese with English titles; In color; 90 minutes; Not rated; August release (Japan 1972). CAST: Tetsuro Tamba (Katsuo), Sachiko Hidari (Sakie), Yumiko Fujita (Tomoko), Noboru Mitani (Terada), Paul Maki (Paul)

RETURN OF THE MASTER KILLER (World Northal) Producer, Sir Run Run Shaw; Director, LiuChia-Liang; A Shaw Brothers presentation in color; Rated R; August release. Starring Liu Chia Hui

THE CLUB (Roadshow) Producer, Matt Carroll; Director, Bruce Beresford; Screenplay, David Williamson; Associate Producer, Moya Iceton; Photography, Don McAlpine; Art Director, David Copping; Editor, William Anderson; Music, Mike Brady; In Panavision and color; Not rated; 99 minutes; August release. CAST: Jack Thompson (Laurie), Graham Kennedy (Ted), Frank Wilson (Jock), Harold Hopkins (Danny), John Howard (Geoff), Alan Cassell (Gerry), Maggie Doyle (Susy)

THE ASSOCIATE (Quartet) Producer, Magyar Productions; Director, Rene Gainville; Screenplay, Jean Claude Carriere, Rene Gainville; In color; 94 minutes; Not rated; August release. CAST: Michel Serrault, Claudine Auger, Catherine Alric, Judith Magre, Mathieu Carriere, Bernard Haller, Marco Perrin, Vadim Glowna

Michel Serrault, Claudine Auger in "The Associate"
©*Quartet*

Kristy McNichol, Christopher Atkins in "The Pirate Movie"
©*20th Century-Fox*

Pascale Rocard, Bernard Brieux in "The Rascals"
©*Quartet*

THE PIRATE MOVIE (20th Century-Fox) Producer, David Joseph; Director, Ken Annakin; Screenplay, Trevor Farrant; Based on "The Pirates of Penzance"; Photography, Robin Copping; Choreography, David Atkins; Editor, Kenneth W. Zemke; Costumes, Aphrodite Kondos; Original Songs, Terry Britten, Kit Hain, Sue Shifrin, Brian Robertson; In Dolby Stereo and color; 99 minutes; Rated PG; August release. CAST: Kristy McNichol (Mabel), Christopher Atkins (Frederic), Ted Hamilton (Pirate King), Bill Kerr (Major General), Maggie Kirkpatrick (Ruth), Garry McDonald (Sergeant-Inspector), Linda Nagle (Aphrodite), Kate Ferguson (Edith), Rhonda Burchmore (Kate), Catherine Lynch (Isabel), Chuck McKinney (Samuel), Marc Colombani (Dwarf Pirate), John Allansu (Chinese Captain)

LES TURLUPINS/THE RASCALS (Quartet) Executive Producer, Gilbert de Goldschmidt; Director, Bernard Revon; Screenplay, Mr. Revon, Didier Bouquet-Nadaud, Michel Zemer, Claude DeGivraya; Photography, Gerard de Battista; Music, Roland Romanelli; In color; French with English subtitles; 93 minutes; Rated R; September release. CAST: Bernard Brieux (Bernard), Thomas Chabrol (Didier), Pascale Rocard (Marie-Helene), Sebastien Drai-Dietrich (Vincent)

THE NIGHT OF THE SHOOTING STARS (United Artists Classics) Producer, Giuliani G. DeNegri; Directors, Paolo and Vittorio Taviani; Screenplay, the Tavianis, Giuliani G. DeNegri, Tonino Guerra; Photography, Franco di Giacomo; Editor, Roberto Perpignani; Music, Nicola Piovani; Italian with English subtitles; In color; 106 minutes; Not rated; September release. CAST: Omero Antonutti (Galvano), Margarita Lozano (Concetta), Claudio Bigagli (Corrado), Massimo Bonetti (Nicole), Norma Martelli (Ivana), Enrica Maria Modugno (Mara), Sabina Vannucchi (Rosanna), Dario Cantarelli (Priest), Sergio Dagliana (Olinto), Giuseppe Furia (Requiem), Paolo Hendel (Dilvo)

REPORTERS (Paris Films) Direction and Photography, Raymond Depardon; French with English subtitles; In color; 101 minutes; Not rated; September release. CAST: Jacques Chirae, Catherine Deneuve, Richard Gere, Francis Apesteguy, Jean-Luc Goddard, Gene Kelly, Valery Giscard d'Estaing, Francois Mitterand, Christina Onassis

THE TROUT (Triumph) Producer, Yves Rousset-Rouard; Executive Producer, Christian Ferry; Associate Producer, Patricia Losey; Director, Joseph Losey; Screenplay, Monique Lange, Joseph Losey; Based on novel "La Truite" by Roger Vailland; Dialogue, Monique Lange; Designer, Alexandre Trauner; Photography, Henri Alekan; Costumes, Annalisa Nasilli-Rocca; Editor, Marie Castro-Vasquez; Music, Richard Hartley; Assistant Director, Jean Achache; In Fuji Color; French with English subtitles; 105 minutes; Not rated; September release. CAST: Isabelle Huppert (Frederique), Jean-Pierre Cassel (Rambert), Jeanne Moreau (Lou), Daniel Olbrychski (Saint-Genis), Jacques Speisser (Galuchat), Isao Yamagata (Daigo), Lisette Malidor (Mariline), Jean-Paul Roussillon (Pere Verjon), Roland Bertin (Count), Craig Stevens (Carter), Ruggero Raimondi (Himself), Alexis Smith (Gloria), Lucas Delvaux (Young Employee), Pierre Forget (Frederique's Father), Ippo Fujikawa (Kumitaro), Yuko Kada (Akiko), Anne Francois (Hostess), Pascal Morand, Frederique Briel (Frederique's Friends)

LONELY HEART (Toho) Producers, Sai Ogura, Toshio Sakamoto; Director, Kon Ichikawa; Screenplay, Masaya Hidaka, Ikuko Oya, Kon Ichikawa; Based on Ed McBain's "Lady, Lady, I Did It!"; Photography, Kiyoshi Hasegawa; Editor, Teruko Tsuchiya; Music, Takahiro Ishikawa, Toru Okada; Japanese with English subtitles; In color; 106 minutes; Not rated; September release. CAST: Yutaka Mizutani (Murakami), Toshiyuki Nagashima (Kita), Rie Nakahara (Niwako), Eri Nagai (Shin), Rui Kuroda (Ben), Kei Tani (Noro), Etsuko Ichihara (Rui)

LETTER FROM SIBERIA (New Yorker) Director, Chris Marker; Photography, Sacha Vierny; Editor, Anne Sarraute; Music, Pierre Barbaud; 60 minutes; Not rated; September release. A documentary about Siberia with the voices of Catherine LeCouey, Henri Pichette, and commentary by Georges Rouquier

JOSEPHA (Triumph) Producers, Albina du Boisrouvray, Robert Amon; Direction and Screenplay, Christopher Frank; Based on his novel; In color; 146 minutes; Rated R; September release. CAST: Miou-Miou (Josepha), Claude Brasseur (Michel), Bruno Cremer (Regis)

Margarita Lozano, Omero Antonutti in "Night of the Shooting Stars" ©*United Artists*

Bruno Cremer, Miou-Miou, Claude Brasseur in "Josepha"
©*Columbia/Gaumont*

John Cassavetes in "The Incubus"
©*Film Ventures*

"Station"
©*Toho*

ON OUR LAND (November 29 Coalition) Producer-Director, Antonia Caccia; Executive Producer, Iain Bruce; An Octagon production; 60 minutes; Not rated; September release. A documentary on the present conditions of those Palestinians who remained after the creation of the state of Israel in 1948.

XICA (Embrafilme/Unifilm) Producer, Jarbas Barbosa; Director, Carlos Diegues; Screenplay, Carlos Diegues, Joao Felicio dos Santos; Photography, Jose Medeiros; Choreography, Marlene Silva; Editor, Mair Tavares; Music, Roberto Menescal, Jorge Ben; Portugese with English subtitles; In color; 117 minutes; Not rated; September release (Brazil 1976). CAST: Zeze Motta (Xica da Silva), Walmor Chagas (Joao) Altair Lima (Intendente), Elke Maravilha (Hortensia), Stepan Nercessian (Jose), Rodolfo Arena (Sargento-Mor), Jose Wilker (Conde), Marcus Vinicius (Teodoro), Joao Felicio dos Santos (Paroco), Dara Kocy (Zefina), Adalberto Silva (Cabeca), Julio Mackenzie (Raimundo), Luis Mota (Taverneiro), Beto Leao (Mathias), Paulo Padilha (Ourives), Baby Conceicao (Figena), Iara Jati (Tonha), Luis Felipe (Major)

THE INCUBUS (Film Ventures International) Producers, Marc Boyman, John M. Eckert; Director, John Hough; Screenplay, George Franklin; Based on novel by Ray Russell; Photography, Albert J. Dunk; Music, Stanley Myers; Designer, Edwin Watkins; Editor, George Appleby; In color; An Edward L. Montoro presentation; 90 minutes; Rated R; September release. CAST: John Cassavetes (Dr. Sam Cordell), John Ireland (Hank Walden), Kerrie Keane (Laura), Helen Hughes (Agatha), Duncan McIntosh (Tim), Erin Flannery (Jenny), Harvey Atkin (Joe)

BLOOD TIDE (21st Century) Executive Producer, John D. Schofield; Producer, Nico Mastorakis, Donald Langdon; Co-Producer, Brian Trenchard-Smith; Director, Richard Jefferies; Screenplay, Mr. Jefferies, Nico Mastorakis, Donald Langdon; Photography, Ari Stavrou; Editor, Robert Leighton; Music, Jerry Mosely; Assistant Director, Lakis Antonakes; In Technicolor; 82 minutes; Rated R; September release. CAST: James Earl Jones (Frye), Jose Ferrer (Nereus), Mary Louise Weller (Sherry), Martin Kove (Neil), Deborah Shelton (Madeline), Lydia Cornell (Barbara)

STATION (Toho) Producer, Juichi Tanaka; Director, Yasuo Furuhata; Screenplay, So Kuramoto; Photography, Daisaku Kumura; Editor, Nobuo Ogawa; Music, Ruydo Uzaki; Japanese with English subtitles; In color; 132 minutes; Not rated; September release. CAST: Ken Takarura (Eiji), Ishida Ayumi (Naoko), Ryo Ikebe (Detective), Setsuko Karasumaru (Suzuko), Jinoachi Nezu (Goro), Ryudo Uzaki (Yukio), Chieko Baisho (Kiriko), Tetsuya Takeda (Passenger), Hidji Otaki (Ala), Yuko Kotegawa (Fujiko)

LADIES AND GENTLEMEN THE FABULOUS STAINS (Paramount) Producer, Joe Roth; Executive Producer, Lou Lombardo; Director, Lou Adler; Screenplay, Rob Morton; Photography, Bruce Surtees; Editor, Tom Benko; Design, Leon Ericksen; Art Director, Graeme Murray; Assistant Director, Tommy Thompson; In color; Rated R; 87 minutes; October release. CAST: Diane Lane (Corinne), Ray Winstone (Billy), Peter Donat (Harley), David Clennon (Dave), John Lehne (Stu), Cynthia Sikes (Alicia), Laura Dern (Jessica), Marin Kanter (Tracy), Paul Cook (Danny), Steve Jones (Steve), Barry Ford (Lawnboy), John Fee Waybill (Lou), Christine Lahti (Aunt Linda), Janet Wright (Brenda), Vince Welnick (Jerry)

THE RETURN OF THE GRANDMASTERS (Marvin) Producer-Director, Joseph Kuo; Martial Arts Instructor, Wang Fu Chang; In color; Rated R; 90 minutes; October release. CAST: Jack Long, Jeanie Chang, Yuen Hsiao Tien, Simon Lee, Mark Long

VALENTINA (International Film Exchange) Producer, Mosfilm Studios; Direction and Screenplay, Gleb Panfilov; Photography, Leonid Kalashnikov; Art Director, Marksen Gaukhman-Sverdlov; Music, Vadim Bibergan; In color; Not rated; 100 minutes; October release. CAST: Rodion Nakhapetov, Inna Churikova, Yury Grebenshikov, Dasha Mikhailova, Sergei Koltakov, Larisa Udovichenko

THE DESTROYERS (World Northal) Producers, Sir Run Run Shaw, Mona Fong; Director, Chang Cheh; Screenplay, Yi Huang, Chang Cheh; In color; Rated R; October release. CAST: Sun Chien, Johnny Chang, Wang Li, Kuo Chue, Tai Ping

ROOTS OF EVIL (World Northal) Producer, Leo Remkes; Direction and Screenplay, Christian Anders; Music, Christian Anders; In color; Rated R; 85 minutes; October release. CAST: Christian Anders, Dunja Rajter, Deep Roy, Maribel Martin, Wolfgang Schutte

"The Incubus"
©*Film Ventures*

Dasha Mikhailova, Rodion Nakapetov in "Valentina"
©*IFEX*

209

Jurgen Arndt, Eva Mattes in "Celeste"
©*New Yorker*

Christopher Pate in "The Mango Tree"
©*Satori*

STALKER (Media Transactions) Director, Andrei Tarkovsky; Screenplay, Arkady, Boris Strugatzky; Based on their novel "Picnic by the Roadside"; Photography, Aleksandr Kniezhinsky; Russian with English subtitles; 160 minutes; Not rated; October release (Russia 1979). CAST: Aleksandr Kaidanovsky (Stalker), Nikolai Grinko (Scientist), Anatoli Solonitsin (Writer), Alice Friendlich (Stalker's Wife)

THE LIGHT AHEAD/FISHKE DER KRUMER (Carmel) Producer-Director, Edgar G. Ulmer; Screenplay, Chaver Pahver; Based on story by Mendele Mocher S'forim; Photography, J. Burgi Contner, Edward Hyland; Editor, Jack Kemp; Yiddish with English subtitles; 94 minutes; Not rated; October release (1939 film). CAST: Isidore Cashier (Mendele), Helen Beverly (Hodel), David Opatoshu (Fishke), Rosetta Bialis (Drapke), Tillie Rabinowitz (Neche), Anna Guskin (Gitl), Celia Budkin (Chaya), Jennie Cashier (Dube), Yudel Dubinsky (Isaac), Misha Fishson (Red), Leon Seidenberg (Alter), Wolf Mercur (Getsl the thief), Leon Shachter (Frechman), Wolf Goldfaden (Veker)

WHO? (Lorimar) Producer, Barry Levinson; Co-Producer, Kurt Berthold; Director, Screenplay, Jack Gould; From novel by Algis Budrys; Photography, Petrus Schlomp; Editor, Norman Wanstall; Music, John Cameron; Assistant Director, Sigi Rothemund; Art Director, Peter Scharff; In Eastmancolor; 93 minutes; Rated PG; October release. CAST: Elliott Gould (Sean), Trevor Howard (Col. Azarin), Joe Bova (Lucas), Ed Grover (Finchley), James Noble (Gen. Deptford), John Lehne (Haller), Kay Tornborg (Edith), Lyndon Brook (Dr. Barrister), Joy Garrett (Barbara), Ivan Desny (Gen. Sturmer), Alexander Allerson, Michael Lombard, John Stewart, Bruce Boa, Fred Vincent, Dan Sazarino, Craig McConnel, Herb Andress, Del Negro, Frank Schuller

JUSTICE OF THE DRAGON (Almi) Presented by Tomas Tang, Joseph Lai; Rated R; In color; 97 minutes; October release. CAST: Dragon Lee, Phoenix Kim, Philip Cheun

CARNIVAL (International Film Exchange) Producer, M. Gorky Central Studios; Director, T. Lioznova; Screenplay, A. Rodionova, T. Lioznova; In color; Not rated; 160 minutes with an intermission; October release. CAST: I. Muravyova, Y. Yakovlev, K. Luchko, A. Rumiantzeva

BY DESIGN (Atlantic) Producers, Beryl Fox, Werner Aellen; Executive Producers, Louis M. Silverstein, Douglas Leiterman; Director, Claude Jutra; Screenplay, Joe Wiesenfeld, Claude Jutra, David Eames; Photography, Jean Boffety; Music, Chico Hamilton; In color; Not rated; 90 minutes; October release. CAST: Patty Duke Astin, Sara Botsford, Saul Rubinek

AMOR BANDIDO/OUTLAW LOVE (Analysis) Producer, Luiz Carlos Barreto; Director, Bruno Barreto; Screenplay, Leopoldo Serran; Photography, Lauro Escorel Filho; Editor, Raimundo Higino; Music, Guto Graca Mello; In color; Portugese with English subtitles; 95 minutes; Not rated; October release. CAST: Paulo Gracindo (Galvae), Cristina Ache (Sandra), Paul Garnieri (Toninho), Ligia Diniz (Solange)

BONGO MAN Director, Stefan Paul; In color; 95 minutes; Not rated; October release. A report on the state of life in Jamaica with Jimmy Cliff and reggae.

CELESTE (New Yorker) Direction and Screenplay, Percy Adlon; Based on "Monsieur Proust" by Celeste Albaret; Photography, Jurgen Martin; German with English subtitles; 107 minutes; Not rated; October release. CAST: Eva Mattes (Celeste), Jurgen Arndt (Proust)

THE MANGO TREE (Satori) Producer, Michael Pate; Associate Producer, Michael Lake; Director, Kevin Dobson; Screenplay, Michael Pate; Photography, Brian Probyn; Editor, John Scott; Music, Marc Wilkinson; Art Director, Leslie Binns; Costumes, Pat Forster; In color; 93 minutes; Not rated; October release. CAST: Geraldine Fitzgerald (Grandma), Christopher Pate (Jamie), Robert Helpmann (Professor), Diane Craig (Miss Pringle), Gerard Kennedy (Preacher), Gloria Dawn (Pearl), Carol Burns (Maudie), Barry Pierce (Angus), Ben Gabriel (Wilkenshaw), Gerry Duggan (Scanlon), Jonathan Atherton (Stinker), Tony Bonner (Capt. Hinkler)

26 DAYS IN THE LIFE OF DOSTOYEVSKY (IFEX/SOVEXPORTFILM) Producer, Mosfilm Studios; Director, Alexander Zarkhi; Screenplay, Vladimir Vladimirov, Pavel Finn; Photography, Vladimir Klimov; In color; Not rated; 87 minutes; November release. CAST: Anatoly Solonitsin, Yevgenia Simonova, Eva Shikulska

Irina Maravyova, Yuri Yakoviev in "Carnival"
©*IFEX*

Anatoly Solonitsin in "26 Days in the Life of Dostoyevsky"
©*IFEX*

Bryan Brown, Judy Davis in "Winter of Our Dreams"
©Satori

Jo Kennedy, Ross O'Donovan in "Starstruck"
©Cinecom Intnl.

HEARTACHES Producers, Canadian Film Development Corp., Famous Players Ltd., Filmcorp Entertainment Finances Inc.; Director, Donald Shebib; Screenplay, Terence Heffernan; Photography, Vic Sarin; Editors, Gerry Hambling, Peter Boita; Music, Michael Martin; In color; 90 minutes; Not rated; November release. CAST: Margot Kidder (Rita), Annie Potts (Bonnie), Robert Carradine (Stanley), Winston Rekert (Marcello), George Touliatos (Mario), Guy Sanvido (Aldo), Arnie Achtman (Alvin), Michael Zeiniker (Andy), Jefferson Mappin (Willy), Maureen Fitzgerald (Anna), Albert Bernardo (Stefane)

WINTER OF OUR DREAMS (Satori) Producer, Richard Mason; Direction and Screenplay, John Duigen; Photography, Tom Cowen; Editor, Henry Dangar; Music, Sharon Calcraft; In color; 89 minutes; Not rated; November release. CAST: Judy Davis (Lou), Bryan Brown (Rob), Cathy Downes (Fretel), Baz Luhrmann (Pete), Peter Mochrie (Tim), Mervyn Drak (Mick), Margie McCrae (Lisa), Mercie Deane-Johns (Angela)

STARSTRUCK (Cinecom International) Producer, David Elfick, Richard Brennan; Director, Gillian Armstrong; Screenplay, Stephen MacLean; Photography, Russel Boyd; Editor, Nicholas Beauman; Choreographer, David Atkins; In Dolby Stereo and color; 102 minutes; Not rated; November release, CAST: Jo Kennedy (Jackie), Ross O'Donovan (Angus), Margo Lee (Pearl), Max Cullen (Reg), Pat Evison (Nana), John O'May (Terry), Dennis Miller (Lou), Norman Erskine (Hazza), Melissa Jaffer (Mrs. Booth), Philip Judd, Dwayne Hillman, Ian Gilroy (Swingers)

PRIVATES PM PARADE (HandMade) Producer, Simon Relph; Executive Producers, George Harrison, Denis O'Brien; Director, Michael Blakemore; Screenplay-Lyrics, Peter Nichols; Based on his play; Photography, Ian Wilson; Editor, Jim Clark; Music, Denis King; Design, Luciana; Art Directors, Michael White, Andrew Sanders; Assistant Director, Jake Wright; In color; Not rated; 100 minutes; November release. CAST: John Cleese (Maj. Flack), Denis Quilley (Capt. Dennis), Nicola Pagett (Sylvia), Patrick Pearson (Pvt. Flowers), Michael Elphick, Joe Melia

TO REMEMBER OR TO FORGET (IFEX/SOVEXPORT-FILM) Producer, Riga Studios; Director, Janis Streich; Screenplay, Oleg Rudnev; Photography, Harly Kukels; In color; Not rated; 89

minutes; November release. CAST: Ludmila Chursina, Girt Yakovlev, Dzidra Ritenberg, Maya Serzane, Anda Zaitse, Velta Straume, Regina Razuma, Eduart Pauls, Ivar Kelnyn

VASSILY AND VASSILISA (IFEX/SOVEXPORTFILM) Producer, Mosfilm Studios; Director, Irina Poplavskaya; Screenplay, Vassily Solovyov; Photography, Kadyrzhan Kydyraliev, Boris Sutotzky; In color; Not rated; 98 minutes; November release. CAST: Olga Ostroumova, Mikhail Kononov, Natalya Bondarchuk

THE BODYGUARD (IFEX/SOVESPORTFILM) Producer, Tajikfilm Studios; Direction and Screenplay, Ali Khamrayev; Photography, Leonid Kalashnikov, Yuri Klimenko, Vyacheslav Senin; Design, Shavkat Abdusalamov; In color; Not rated; 90 Minutes; November release. CAST: Alexander Kaidanovsky, Anatoli Solonitsyn, Shavkat Abdusalamov, Dilorom Alimova, Gulboston Tashbayeva, Abdugani Egamberdyev

PORTRAIT OF THE ARTIST'S WIFE (IFEX/SOVEXPORT-FILM) Producer, Mosfilm Studios; Director, Aleksandr Pankratov; Screenplay, Natalya Ryazantseva; Photography, Oleg Martynov; In color; Not rated; 90 minutes; November release. CAST: Sergei Shakurov, Valentina Telichkina, Nikita Mikhalkov

SEVERAL INTERVIEWS ON PERSONAL MATTERS (IFEX/SOVEXPORTFILM) Producer, Gruziyafilm Studios; Director, Lana Gogoberidze; Screenplay, Zaira Arsenishvili, Erlom Akhvlediani, Lana Gogoberidze; Photography, Nugzar Erkomaishvili; Design, Khristesia Lebanidze; Music, Giya Kancheli; In color; Not rated; 95 minutes; November release. CAST: Sofiko Chiaureli, Salome Kancheli, Ketevan Orakhelashvili, Ketevan Bochorishvili, Zhanri Lolashvili, Guya Badridze, Nana Mchedlidze

THE STEPPE (IFEX/SOVEXPORTFILM) Producer, Mosfilm Studios; Direction and Screenplay, Sergei Bondarchuk; Photography, Leonid Kalashnikov; In Widescreen and color; Not rated; 135 minutes; November release. CAST: Innokenty Smoktunovsky, Vladimir Sedov, Nikolai Trofimov, Sergei Bondarchuk, Ivan Lapikov, Georgy Burkov, Irina Skobtseva, Oleg Kuznetsov, Stanislav Lyubshin, Natalia Andreichenko

Valentina Telichkina, Nikita Mikhalkov in "Portrait of the Artist's Wife" ©IFEX

"To Remember or to Forget"
©IFEX

"My Death Should Be Blamed on Klava K."
©*IFEX*

Kerstin Tidelius, Carl-Axel Heiknert in "The Farewell"
©*Scandinavia Today*

GISELLE (21st Century) Executive Producer, Bernardo Goldszak; Producer, Carlo Mossy; Direction and Screenplay, Victor DiMello; Photography, Antonio Goncalves; Editor, Giuseppe Baldacconi; In color; Rated R; 89 minutes; November release. CAST: Alba Valeria (Giselle), Monique LaFond (Ana), Maria Lucia Dahl (Aidee), Carlo Mossy (Angelo), Nildo Parente (Luccini), Ricardo Faria (Sergino)

FUNERAL HOME (MPM) Executive Producer, Barry Allen; Producer-Director, William Fruet; Screenplay, Ida Nelson; Photography, Mark Irwin; Design, Susan Longmire, Roy Forge Smith; Editor, Ralph Brunjes; Music, Jerry Fielding; In color; Rated R; 93 minutes; November release. CAST: Lesleh Donaldson (Heather), Kay Hawtrey (Maude), Barry Morse (Davis), Dean Garbett (Rick), Stephen Miller (Billy), Harvey Atkin (Harry), Alf Humphries (Joe), Peggy Mahon (Florie), Doris Petrik (Ruby), Les Rubie (Sam), Bob Warners (Fred)

MY DEATH SHOULD BE BLAMED ON KLAVA K. (IFEX/-SOVEXPORTFILM) Directors, Nikolai Lebedev, Ernest Yasin; Screenplay, Mikhail Lvovsky; Photography, Valery Mironov; In color; Not rated; 80 minutes; November release. CAST: Nadezhda Gorshkova, Vladimir Sheveljkov, Liubov Polishuk, Veniamin Smekhov

TO THE STARS BY HARD WAYS (IFEX/SOVEXPORTFILM) Producer, Maxin Gorky Studio; Director, Richard Victorov; Screenplay, Kir Bulychev, Richard Victorov; Photography, Alexander Rybin; In color; Not rated; 148 minutes; November release. CAST: Yelena Metelkina, Nadezhda Sementsova, Vatslav Dvorzhetsky, Alexander Lazarev

THE TAKE-OFF (IFEX/SOVEXPORTFILM) Director, Savva Kulish; Screenplay, Oleg Osetinsky; Photography, Vladimir Klimov; Art Director, Vladimir Aronin; Music, Oleg Karavaichuk; In color; Not rated; 136 minutes; November release. CAST: Larisa Kadochnikova (Varvara), Albert Filozov (Panin), Yevgeny Yevtushenko (Tziolkovsky), Elena Finogenova (Liuba), Kirill Arbuzov (Ignaty), Vadim Aleksandrov (Tailor), Georgy Burkov (Rokotov)

TITLE SHOT (Cinepax) Producer, Rob Iveson; Executive Producer, Richard Gabourie; Screenplay, John Saxton; Story, Richard Gabourie; Photography, Henry Fiks; Editor, Ronald Sanders; Art Director, Karen Bromley; Music, Paul James Zaza; In color; Not rated; 96 minutes; November release. CAST: Tony Curtis (Frank Renzetti), Richard Gabourie (Blake), Susan Hogan (Sylvia), Allan Royal (Dunlop), Robert Delbert (Rufus), Natsuko Ohama (Terry), Jack Duffy (Green), Sean McCann (Grace), Taborah Johnson (Connie), Robert O'Ree (Iggy), Dennis Strong (Eddie)

HANDS OF LIGHTNING (Almi) An Asso Asia film in color and Cinemascope; Rated R; 93 minutes; November release. CAST: Wong Cheng Li, Jacky Lee, Sam Yuen, Stan Yuen, David Yuen

THE TREE OF KNOWLEDGE (Scandinavia Today) Director, Nils Malmros; Assistant Director, Soren Kjaer Nielsen; Screenplay, Nils Malmros, Fred Cryer; Photography, Jan Weincke; Editors, Merete Brusendorff, Janus Billeskov, Hannah Lowy; Costumes, Francoise Nicolet; In color; Not rated; 110 minutes; November release. CAST: Eva Gram Schjoldager, Jan Johansen, Line Arlien-Soborg, Marian Wendelbo, Gitte Iben Andersen, Lone Elliot, Astrid Holm Nielsen, Brian Theibel, Bo von der Lippe, Mavin Lysholm Jepsen, Morten Nautrup, Anders Oregard, Dan Rormand Brogger, Lars Spang Kjeldsen

THE FAREWELL (Scandinavia Today) Producer, Katinka Farago; Director, Tuija-Maija Nislanen; Assistant Director, Taisto Jalamo; Screenplay, Eija-Elina Bergholm, Vivica Bandler; Photography, Esa Vuorinen, Lasse Karlsson; Editor, Sylvia Ingemarsson; Art Directors, Anna Asp, Ulrika Rindegard; In Eastmancolor; Not rated; 90 minutes; November release. CAST: Carl-Axel Heiknert, Kerstin Tidelius, Sanna Hultman, Pirkko Nurmi, Lotta Larsson, Mimi Pollak, Gunnar Bjornstrand, Elina Salo, Berit Gustafsson, Maj-Lis Granlund, Bent Blomqvist, Stina Ekblad, Marianne Karlbeck-Straat

STEPPING OUT (Scandinavia Today) Director, Esben Hoilund Carlsen; Screenplay, Nils Schou; Photography, Dirk Bruel; Editor, Lizzie Weischenfeldt; Art Director, Karl-Otto Hedal; Music, Bent Fabricius-Bjerre; In color; Not rated; 104 minutes; November release. CAST: Solbjorg Hojfeldt, Kurt Dreyer, Ole Ernst, Ulf Pilgaard, Lisbeth Lundquist, Puk Schaufuss, Ove Sprogoe, Claus Nissen

"To the Stars by Hard Ways"
©*IFEX*

Solbjorg Hojfeldt, Kurt Dreyer in "Stepping Out"
©*Scandinavia Today*

Denholm Elliott, Joan Plowright, Sting in "Brimstone and Treacle" © *United Artists*

Johnny Yune, Ralph Mauro in "They Call Me Bruce?" © *Film Ventures*

ALONE IN THE DARK (New Line) Producer, Robert Shaye; Direction and Screenplay, Jack Sholder; Story, Jack Sholder, Robert Shaye, Michael Harpster; Photography, Joseph Mangine; Editor, Arline Garson; Music, Renato Serio; In Dolby Stereo and color; 92 minutes; Rated R; November release. CAST: Jack Palance (Hawkes), Donald Pleasence (Dr. Bain), Martin Landau (Preacher), Dwight Schultz (Don), Erland Van Lidth (Fatty), Lee Taylor-Allan (Toni), Deborah Hedwall (Nell), Philip Clark (Skagg-Smith), Elizabeth Ward (Lyla), Brent Jennings (Curtis), Gordon Watkins (Barnett), Carol Levy (Bunky), Keith Reddin (Billy)

BRIMSTONE AND TREACLE (United Artists Classics) Director, Richard Loncraine; Screenplay, Dennis Potter; Photography, Peter Hannon; Editor, Paul Green; Music, Police, Sting, Go-Gos; In Dolby Stereo and color; 85 minutes; Rated R; November release. CAST: Sting (Martin), Denholm Elliott (Tom), Joan Plowright (Norma), Suzanna Hamilton (Patricia), Dudley Sutton (Stroller), Mary MacLeod (Miss Heldsworth), Benjamin Whitrow (Businessman), Tim Preece (Clergyman)

THEY CALL ME BRUCE (Film Ventures International) Producer-Director, Elliott Hong; Photography, Robert Roth; Music, Tommy Vig; Associate Producer, Bob Gossom; Screenplay, David Randolph, Johnny Yune, Elliott Hong, Tim Clawson; Presented by Edward L. Montero; In color; 88 minutes; Rated PG; November release. CAST: Johnny Yune (Bruce), Margaux Hemingway (Karmen), Pam Huntington (Anita), Ralph Mauro (Freddy), Tony Brande (Boss of Bosses), Bill Capizzi (Lil Pete), Martin Azarow (Big Al)

FATHER SERGIUS (Corinth Films) Producer, Mosfilm Studios; Director, Screenplay, Igor Talankin; Based on novel by Leo Tolstoy; Photography, Georgi Rerberg, Anatoly Nikolayev; Design, Victor Petrov, Yuri Fomenko; Music, Shnitke; Russian with English subtitles; In color; 99 minutes; November release (USSR 1978). CAST: Sergei Bondarchuk (Prince Stepan Kasatsky/Father Sergius), Valentina Titova (Countess Mary), Vladislav Strzhelchik (Emperor Nicholas I), Ludmila Maksakova (Seductress), Alla Demidova (Pashenka), Irina Skobtseva (Lady at court ball)

EASY MONEY (IFEX/SOVEXPORTFILM) Producer, Mosfilm Studios; Direction and Screenplay, Evgeny Matveev; Photography, Leonid Kalashnikov; In color; Not rated; 86 minutes; November release. CAST: Liudmila Nilskaya, Elena Solovei, Aleksandr Mikhailov, Yuri Yakovlev, Pavel Kadochnikov, Leonid Kuravlev

A NEST IN THE WIND (IFEX/SOVEXPORTFILM) Producer, Tallinnfilm Studios; Director, Olav Nueland; Screenplay, Izakas Fridbergas, Grigory Kanovicus; Photography, Arvo Ikho; Design, Halia Klaar, Heikki Halla; Music, Lepo Sumera; In color; Not rated; 95 minutes; November release. CAST: Rudolf Allabert, Nelly Taar, Anne Maazik, Indrek Aavik, Tynu Kark

TWO CHAMPIONS OF DEATH (World Northal) Presented by the Shaw Brothers; Director, Chang Cheh; In color; Rated R; 105 minutes; November release. CAST: Lu Feng, Sun Chien, Kuo Chue, Chiang Sheng

EN TIERRE DE SANDINO/IN THE LAND OF THE SANDINISTAS (Young Filmmakers) Directed and Written by Jesus Diaz; Photography, Adriano Moreno, Guillermo Centeno; Editor, Justo Vega; Music, Leo Brouwer; In color; Not rated; 71 minutes; November release. A record of the historic moment of revolutionary transition in Nicaragua.

WITCH HUNT (Scandinavia Today) Director, Anja Breien; Executive Producer, Gunnar Svensrud; Assistant Director, Jan Olav Brynjulfsen; Screenplay, Anja Breien; Photography, Morten Skallerud; Designers, Ulf Axen, Hege Palm; Editor, Lars Magnus Hagstrom; In color; Not rated; 96 minutes; November release. CAST: Lil Terselius, Bjorn Skagestad, Anita Bjork, Erik Mork, Ella Hval, Mona Jacobsen, Espen Skjonberg, Eilif Armand, Jan Harstad, Lars Andreas Larsen, Cay Kristiansen, Jens Okking, Haege Juve, Lothar Lindtner Asser, Oddbjorn Hesjevoll

GOTTA RUN (Scandinavia Today) Director, Mikko Niskanen; Screenplay, Matti Ijas, Mikko Niskanen; Photography, Henrik Paersch; Editor, Tuula Mehtonen; Design, Matti Waskilampi; Music, Mikko Alatalo, Harri Rinne, Martti Luoma; Costumes, Maiju Veijalainen; In color; Not rated; 107 minutes; November release. CAST: Timo Toeikka, Tero Niva, Heikki Paavilainen, Sanna Majaniahti

Sergei Bondorchuk, Alla Demidova in "Father Sergius" © *Corinth*

Heikki Paavilainen, Timo Torikka, Tero Niva in "Gotta Run" © *Scandinavia Today*

Ronnaug Alten, Sunniva Lindekleiv in "Poor Ida"
©Scandinavia Today

Susanna Kall, Thommy Berggren in "Broken Sky"
©Scandinavia Today

THE EAGLE'S SHADOW (Cinematic) Producer, Ng See Yuen; Director, Yuen Woo Ping; Executive Producer, Cheng Chuan; Screenplay, Ng See Yuen; Photography, Chang Hai; Editor, Pan Hsiung Yoo; Presented by Serafim Karalexis; A Seasonal Film production in color and cinemascope; 90 minutes; Rated PG; November release. CAST: Jacky Chan, Juan Jan Lee, Simon Yuen, Roy Horan, Shih Tien, Chen Hsia, Wang Chiang, Louis Feng

FAT CHANCE (Summit Features) Directed by M. Summers; Presented by Doug Stampley and Gregory Earls; In color; 92 minutes; Not rated; November release. CAST: Franham Scott (Mike), January Stevens (Mary), Jack Aaron (Frank), Amy Steel (Alison), Robert Reynolds (Jackie), B. Constance Barry (Ethel), Peter Bogyo (Christopher), Nina David (Louisa), Sanford Seeger (Sal), Robert Gaus (Raymond)

FRUITS OF PASSION (Summit) Direction and Screenplay, Shuji Terayama; Based on novel "Return to the Chateau" by Pauline Reage; Narration and 'O' voice, Pauline Reage; Photography, Tatsuo Suzuki; Sets, Hiroshi Yamashita; Designs, Sawako Goda; Music, J. A. Seazer; Costumes, Kaisik Wong; Editor, Henri Colpi; Producers, Anatole Dauman, Hiroko Govaers; Associate Producers, Jacques-Henri Barratier, Philippe D'Argila; In Eastmancolor; 83 minutes; Not rated; November release. CAST: Klaus Kinski (Sir Stephen), Isabelle Illiers (O), Arielle Dombasle (Nathalie), Peter (Madame), Keiko Niitaka (Aisen), Sayoko Yamaguchi (Sakuya), Hitomi Takahashi (Byakuran), Miyuki Ono (Kasen), Akiko Suetsugu (Obana), Yuka Kamebuchi (Koken), Kenichi Nakamura (Young Man), Takeshi Wakamatsu (Caretaker), and voices of George Wilson (Narrator), Maria Meriko (Death)

HORROR PLANET (Almi) formerly "Inseminoid"; Executive Producer, Peter Schlesinger; Producers, Richard Gordon, David Speechley; Director, Norman J. Warren; Screenplay, Nick Maley, Gloria Maley; Photography, John Metcalfe; Editor, Peter Boyle; Music, John Scott; Assistant Director, Gary White; Design, Hayden Pearce; A Jupiter Films production presented by Sir Run Run Shaw; In Rank Color; 86 minutes; Rated R; November release. CAST: Judy Geeson (Sandy), Robin Clarke (Mark), Jennifer Ashley (Holly), Stephanie Beacham (Kate), Steven Grives, Barry Houghton, Rosalind Lloyd, Victoria Tennant, Trevor Thomas, Heather Wright, David Baxt, Dominic Jephcott

BROKEN SKY (Scandinavia Today) Executive Producer, Bert Sundberg; Photography, Lasse Bjorne, Bertil Rosengren, Lars Karlsson; Director, Ingrid Thulin; Art Director, Bengt Peters; Editor, Lasse Lundberg; Music, Bjorn Isfalt; In Fujicolor; Not rated; 96 minutes; November release. CAST: Susanna Kall, Thommy Berggren, Agneta Eckemyr, Margaretha Krook, Svea Holst, Fillie Lyckow, Karin Ericson, Christina Eriksson, Nike Lindstrom, Ernst, Gunther, Ola Strangeways, Axel Duberg, Olle Gronstedt, Anders Aberg

POOR IDA (Scandinavia Today) Director, Laila Mikkelsen; Executive Producer, Svein Johansen; Screenplay, Marit Paulsen from her novel "Liten Ida" in collaboration with Laila Mikkelsen; Photography Hans Welin, Kjell Vassdal; Editor, Peter Falck; Designer, Anders Barreus; In color; Not rated; 87 minutes; November release. CAST: Sunniva Lindekleiv, Howard Halvorsen, Lise Fjeldstad, Ellen Westerfjell, Roennaug Alten, Sverre Axelsen, Anne Toft Olsen, Sildur Solberg, Bernt Lindekleiv, Mette Lange-Nielsen, Runne Dybedahl

SALLY AND FREEDOM (Scandinavia Today) Executive Producer, Ingmar Bergman; Director, Gunnel Lindblom; Assistant Director, Pia Forsgren; Screenplay, Margareta Garpe, Gunnel Lindblom; Photography, Tony Forsberg, Lars Karlsson; Art Direction, Inger Pehrsson, Carina Dalunde; Editors, Sylvia Ingemarsson, Siv Lundgren; Music, Stefan Nilsson; In Eastmancolor; Not rated; 100 minutes; November release. CAST: Ewa Froling, Hans Wigren, Leif Ahrie, Gunnel Lindblom, Oscar Ljung, Gunn Wallgren, Svea Holst, Kim Anderzon, Susanne Lundquist, Liselotte Nilsson, Mona Lundgren, Iwa Boman, Margreth Weivers, Ulf Schonberg, Gerd Blomquist, Christian Berling, Peter Egge, Peder Falk, Sonja Hejdeman, Thomas Helander, Gulbin Basay, Semith Basay, Linda Kruger, Johanna Garpe, Stefan Nilsson

INTER NOS (Scandinavia Today) Direction and Screenplay, Hrafn Gunnlaugsson; Photography, Karl Oskarsson; Editor, Tibor Csontos; Art Director, Vilbor Aradottir; In color; Not rated; 100 minutes; November release. CAST: Benedikt Arnason, Margret Gunnlaugsdottir, Sirry Geirs

INSTRUCTORS OF DEATH (World Northal) Presented by Shaw Brothers; Director, Liu Chia-Liang; In color; Rated R; 110 minutes; December release. CAST: Liu Chia-Hui, Hui Ying-Hung, Mai Te-Lo

Ewa Froling, Hans Wigren in "Sally and Freedom"
©Scandinavia Today

"Inter Nos"
©Scandinavia Today

Viacheslav Esepov, Elena Koreneva in "Asya"
©Corinth

Krystyna Janda, John Gielgud in "The Orchestra Conductor"
©New Yorker

THE LADY ON THE BUS (Atlantic) Producer, Regina Films; Director, Neville d'Almeida; Screenplay, Nelson Rodriguez; Photography, Edson Santos; In color; 104 minutes; Rated R; December release. CAST: Sonia Braga, Nuno Leal Maia, Jorge Doria, Paulo Cesar Pereio

THE FIRST SWALLOW (Corinth) Producer, Gruziafilm; Director, Nana Mchedlidze; Screenplay, Levan Tchelidze, Nana Mchedlidze; Photography, Georgij Tchelidze; Editor, Nana Mchelidze; Music, Jansug Kakhidze; Art Director, Aliona Tarachwelidze; In color and Cinemascope; Georgian with English subtitles; 80 minutes; Not rated; December release. CAST: David Adashidze (Jason), Vasiko Nadaraya (Khvicha), Govram Lordkipanidze (Bejan), Anzor Kherkhadze (Wachtang), Iya Ninidze, Gulchina Didiani

ASYA (Corinth) Direction and Screenplay, Josef Heifitz; From novel by Ivan Turgenev; Photography, Heinrich Marajian; Music, Oleg Karavaichuk; Sets, Vladimir Svetozarov; Russian with English subtitles; In color; 97 minutes; Not rated; December release. CAST: Elena Koreneva (Asya), Viacheslav Esepov (N. N.), Igor Kostolevsky (Gagin)

THE GAMBLER (Corinth) Producer, Lenfilm USSR; Director, Alexei Batalov; Screenplay, M. Olshevsky; From novella by Fyodor Dostoyevsky; Photography, D. Meshkiyev; Music, O. Karavaichuk; Russian with English subtitles; In color; 99 minutes; Not rated; December release. CAST: Nikolai Burliayev (Alexei), Tatiana Ivanova (Paulina), Lyubov Dobrzhanskaya (Great Aunt), Vsevolod Kuznetsov (General), Jitka Zelenohorska (Blanche), Vassily Livanov (Des Grieux), Alexander Kaidanovsky (Astley)

LEAP INTO THE VOID (Summit) Direction and Story, Marco Bellocchio; Screenplay, Marco Bellocchio, Piero Natoli, Vincenzo Cerami; Photography, Beppe Lanci; Design, Amedeo Fago, Andrea Crisanti; Costumes, Lia Morandini; Music, Nicola Piovani; Editor, Roberto Perpignani; In Eastmancolor; 120 minutes; Not rated; December release. CAST: Michel Piccoli (Judge Ponticelli), Anouk Aimee (Marta Ponticelli), Michele Placido (Giovanni), Gisella Burinato (Anna), Antonio Piovanelli (Quasimodo), Anna Orso (Marilena), Giampaolo Saccarola (Insane Brother), Adriana Pecorelli (Sonia), Paola Ciampi (Ponticelli's Mother), Piergiorgio Bel-

locchio (Giorgio), Mario Prosperi, Enrico Bergier (Ponticelli's Brothers), Elisabeth Labi (Ponticelli's Fiancee), Mario Ravasio (Brother of Suicide), Gaetano Campisi, Marino Cenna (Actors), Lamberto Consani, Marina Sassi (Friends of Giovanni), Giancarlo Sammartano, Oreste Rotundo (Passersby), Remo Remotti (Thief), Rossano Weber (Fire-eater), Alessandro Antonucci, Daria Fago, Matteo Fago, Giovanni Frezza, Maria Pia Frezza (Ponticelli Children)

SARTRE PAR LUI-MEME/SARTRE BY HIMSELF (Film Forum) Producers, Pierre-Andre Boutang, Guy Seligmann; Directors, Alexandre Astruc, Michel Contat; Photography, Renato Berta; French with English subtitles; 190 minutes; Not rated; December release (France 1976). CAST: Jean-Paul Sartre, Simone de Beauvoir

THE ORCHESTRA CONDUCTOR (Public) Director, Andrzej Wajda; Screenplay, Andrzej Kijowski from conversations with Andrzei Markowski; Photography, Slawomir Idziak; Editor, Halina Prugar; Music, Beethoven; Polish with English subtitles; In color; 101 minutes; Not rated; December release. CAST: John Gielgud (Jan Lasocki), Krystyna Janda (Marta), Andrzej Seweryn (Adam)

BRITANNIA HOSPITAL (United Artists Classics) Producers, Davina Belling, Clive Parsons; Director, Lindsay Anderson; Screenplay, David Sherwin; Photography, Mike Fash; Editor, Michel Ellis; Art Director, Norris Spencer; Music, Alan Price; In Technicolor; 115 minutes; Rated R; December release. CAST: Leonard Rossiter (Potter), Graham Crowden (Millar), Malcolm McDowell (Mike), Joan Plowright (Phyllis), Jill Bennett (Macmillan), Marsha Hunt (Amanda), Frank Grimes (Fred)

MURDER BY PHONE (New World) Producers, Robert Cooper, Brian Walker; Director, Michael Anderson; Executive Producer, Stanley Colbert; Screenplay, John Kent Harrison, Michael Butler, Dennis Shryack; Music, John Barry; Photography, Reginald Morris; Associate Producer, Michael Hadley; In color; Rated R; 80 minutes; Formerly titled "Bells"; December release. CAST: Richard Chamberlain (Nat), John Houseman (Stanley), Sara Botsford (Ridley), Robin Gammell (Noah), Gary Reineke (Lt. Meara), Barry Morse (Waites)

MASKED AVENGERS (World Northal) A Shaw Brothers presentation in color; Rated R; 92 minutes; December release. No other credits available.

Marsha Hunt, Malcolm McDowell in "Britannia Hospital"
©United Artists

Sara Botsford, Richard Chamberlain in "Murder by Phone"
©New World

Willie
Aames

Karen
Allen

Richard
Attenborough

Adrienne
Barbeau

Scott
Baio

Karen
Black

BIOGRAPHICAL DATA

(Name, real name, place and date of birth, school attended)

AAMES, WILLIE (William Upton): 1961.

ABBOTT, DIAHNNE: NYC, 1945.

ABBOTT, JOHN: London, June 5, 1905.

ABEL, WALTER: St. Paul, MN, June 6, 1898. AADA.

ABRAHAM, F. MURRAY: Pittsburgh, PA, Oct. 24, 1939. UTx.

ADAMS, BROOKE: NYC, 1949. Dalton.

ADAMS, DON: NYC, 1927.

ADAMS, EDIE (Elizabeth Edith Enke): Kingston, PA, Apr. 16, 1929. Juilliard, Columbia.

ADAMS, JULIE (Betty May): Waterloo, Iowa, Oct. 17, 1928. Little Rock Jr. College.

ADAMS, MAUD (Maud Wikstrom): Lulea, Sweden.

ADDAMS, DAWN: Felixstowe, Suffolk, Eng., Sept. 21, 1930. RADA.

ADDY, WESLEY: Omaha, NB, Aug. 4, 1913. UCLA.

ADJANI, ISABELLE: Paris, 1955.

ADLER, LUTHER: NYC, May 4, 1903.

ADRIAN, IRIS (Iris Adrian Hostetter): Los Angeles, May 29, 1913.

AGAR, JOHN: Chicago, Jan. 31, 1921.

AGUTTER, JENNY: London, 1953.

AHERNE, BRIAN: Worcestershire, Eng., May 2, 1902. Malvern College, U. of London.

AIELLO, DANNY: June 20, 1935, NYC.

AIMEE, ANOUK: Paris, Apr. 27, 1934. Bauer-Therond.

AKINS, CLAUDE: Nelson, GA, May 25, 1936. Northwestern U.

ALBERGHETTI, ANNA MARIA: Pesaro, Italy, May 15, 1936.

ALBERT, EDDIE (Eddie Albert Heimberger): Rock Island, IL, Apr. 22, 1908. U. of Minn.

ALBERT, EDWARD: Los Angeles, Feb. 20, 1951. UCLA.

ALBRIGHT, LOLA: Akron, OH, July 20, 1925.

ALDA, ALAN: NYC, Jan. 28, 1936. Fordham.

ALDA, ROBERT (Alphonso D'Abruzzo): NYC, Feb. 26, 1914. NYU.

ALDERSON, BROOKE: Dallas, Tx.

ALEJANDRO, MIGUEL: NYC, Feb. 21, 1958.

ALEXANDER, JANE (Quigley): Boston, MA, Oct. 28, 1939. Sarah Lawrence.

ALLEN, KAREN: 1951.

ALLEN, NANCY: NYC 1950.

ALLEN, REX: Wilcox, AZ, Dec. 31, 1922.

ALLEN, STEVE: New York City, Dec. 26, 1921.

ALLEN, WOODY (Allen Stewart Konigsberg): Brooklyn, Dec. 1, 1935.

ALLYSON, JUNE (Ella Geisman): Westchester, NY, Oct. 7, 1917.

ALVARADO, TRINI: NYC, 1967.

AMECHE, DON (Dominic Amichi): Kenosha, WI, May 31, 1908.

AMES, ED: Boston, July 9, 1929.

AMES, LEON (Leon Wycoff): Portland, IN, Jan. 20, 1903.

AMOS, JOHN: Newark, NJ, Dec. 27, 1940. Colo. U.

ANDERSON, JUDITH: Adelaide, Australia, Feb. 10, 1898.

ANDERSON, MELODY: Canada 1955, Carlton U.

ANDERSON, MICHAEL, JR.: London, Eng., 1943.

ANDERSSON, BIBI: Stockholm, Nov. 11, 1935. Royal Dramatic Sch.

ANDES, KEITH: Ocean City, NJ, July 12, 1920. Temple U., Oxford.

ANDRESS, URSULA: Switz., Mar. 19, 1936.

ANDREWS, ANTHONY: London, 1948.

ANDREWS, DANA: Collins, MS, Jan. 1, 1909. Sam Houston Col.

ANDREWS, EDWARD: Griffin, GA, Oct. 9, 1914. U. VA.

ANDREWS, HARRY: Tonbridge, Kent, Eng., Nov. 10, 1911.

ANDREWS, JULIE (Julia Elizabeth Wells): Surrey, Eng., Oct. 1, 1935.

ANGEL, HEATHER: Oxford, Eng., Feb. 9, 1909. Wycombe Abbey.

ANN-MARGRET (Olsson): Valsjobyn, Sweden, Apr. 28, 1941. Northwestern U.

ANSARA, MICHAEL: Lowell, MA, Apr. 15, 1922. Pasadena Playhouse.

ANTHONY, TONY: Clarksburg, WV, Oct 16, 1937. Carnegie Tech.

ANTON, SUSAN: Yucaipa, CA. 1951. Bernardino Col.

ANTONELLI, LAURA: Pola, Italy.

ARCHER, JOHN (Ralph Bowman): Osceola, NB, May 8, 1915. USC.

ARDEN, EVE (Eunice Quedens): Mill Valley, CA, Apr. 30, 1912.

ARKIN, ALAN: NYC, Mar. 26, 1934. LACC.

ARNAZ, DESI: Santiago, Cuba, Mar. 2, 1915. Colegio de Dolores.

ARNAZ, DESI, JR.: Los Angeles, Jan. 19, 1953.

ARNAZ, LUCIE: Hollywood, July 17, 1951.

ARNESS, JAMES (Aurness): Minneapolis, MN, May 26, 1923. Beloit College.

ARTHUR, BEATRICE: NYC, May 13, 1926. New School.

ARTHUR, JEAN: NYC, Oct. 17, 1905.

ARTHUR, ROBERT (Robert Arthaud): Aberdeen, WA, June 18, 1925. U. Wash.

ASHLEY, ELIZABETH (Elizabeth Ann Cole): Ocala, FL, Aug. 30, 1939.

ASSANTE, ARMAND: NYC, Oct. 4, 1949. AADA.

ASTAIRE, FRED (Fred Austerlitz): Omaha, NB, May 10, 1899.

ASTIN, JOHN: Baltimore, MD, Mar. 30, 1930. U. Minn.

ASTIN, PATTY DUKE (see Patty Duke)

ASTOR, MARY (Lucile V. Langhanke): Quincy, IL, May 3, 1906. Kenwood-Loring School.

ATHERTON, WILLIAM: Orange, CT, July 30, 1947. Carnegie Tech.

ATKINS, CHRISTOPHER: Rye, NY, Feb. 21, 1961.

ATTENBOROUGH, RICHARD: Cambridge, Eng., Aug. 29, 1923. RADA.

AUBERJONOIS, RENE: NYC, June 1, 1940. Carnegie Tech.

AUDRAN, STEPHANE: Versailles, Fr., 1933.

AUGER, CLAUDINE: Paris, Apr. 26, 1942. Dramatic Cons.

AULIN, EWA: Stockholm, Sweden, Feb. 14, 1950.

AUMONT, JEAN PIERRE: Paris, Jan. 5, 1909. French Nat'l School of Drama.

AUTRY, GENE: Tioga, TX, Sept. 29, 1907.

AVALON, FRANKIE (Francis Thomas Avallone): Philadelphia, Sept. 18, 1939.

AYRES, LEW: Minneapolis, MN, Dec. 28, 1908.

AZNAVOUR, CHARLES (Varenagh Aznourian): Paris, May 22, 1924.

BACALL, LAUREN (Betty Perske): NYC, Sept. 16, 1924. AADA.

BACKUS, JIM: Cleveland, Ohio, Feb. 25, 1913. AADA.

BADDELEY, HERMIONE: Shropshire, Eng., Nov. 13, 1906. Margaret Morris School.

BAILEY, PEARL: Newport News, VA, March 29, 1918.

BAIN, BARBARA: Chicago, Sept. 13, 1934. U. Ill.

BAIO, SCOTT: Brooklyn, 1961.

BAKER, BLANCHE: NYC Dec. 20, 1956.

BAKER, CARROLL: Johnstown, PA, May 28, 1931. St. Petersburg Jr. College.

BAKER, DIANE: Hollywood, CA, Feb. 25, 1938. USC.

BALABAN, ROBERT: Chicago, Aug. 16, 1945. Colgate.

BALDWIN, ADAM: Chicago, Il. 1962.

BALIN, INA: Brooklyn, Nov. 12, 1937. NYU.

BALL, LUCILLE: Celaron, NY, Aug. 6, 1910. Chatauqua Musical Inst.

BALSAM, MARTIN: NYC, Nov. 4, 1919. Actors Studio.

BANCROFT, ANNE (Anna Maria Italiano): Bronx, NY, Sept. 17, 1931. AADA.

BANNEN, IAN: Airdrie, Scot., June 29, 1928.

BARDOT, BRIGITTE: Paris, Sept. 28, 1934.

BARRAULT, MARIE-CHRISTINE: Paris, 1946.

BARRETT, MAJEL (Hudec): Columbus, OH, Feb. 23. Western Reserve U.

BARRON, KEITH: Mexborough, Eng., Aug. 8, 1936. Sheffield Playhouse.

BARRY, GENE (Eugene Klass): NYC, June 14, 1921.

BARRYMORE, DREW: Los Angeles, Feb. 22, 1975.

BARRYMORE, JOHN BLYTH: Beverly Hills, CA, June 4, 1932. St. John's Military Academy.

BARTHOLOMEW, FREDDIE: London, Mar. 28, 1924.

BARYSHNIKOV, MIKHAIL: Riga, Latvia, Jan. 27, 1948.

BASEHART, RICHARD: Zanesville, OH, Aug. 31, 1914.

BATES, ALAN: Allestree, Derbyshire, Eng., Feb. 17, 1934. RADA.

BAXTER, ANNE: Michigan City, IN, May 7, 1923. Ervine School of Drama.

BAXTER, KEITH: South Wales, Apr. 29, 1933. RADA.

BEAL, JOHN (J. Alexander Bliedung): Joplin, MO, Aug. 13, 1909. Pa. U.

BEATTY, ROBERT: Hamilton, Ont., Can., Oct. 19, 1909. U. of Toronto.

BEATTY, WARREN: Richmond, VA, March 30, 1937.

BECK, MICHAEL: Horseshoe Lake, AR, 1948.

BEDELIA, BONNIE: NYC, Mar. 25, 1948. Hunter Col.

BEDI, KABIR: India, 1945.

BEERY, NOAH, JR.: NYC, Aug. 10, 1916. Harvard Military Academy.

BELAFONTE, HARRY: NYC, Mar. 1, 1927.

BELASCO, LEON: Odessa, Russia, Oct. 11, 1902.

BEL GEDDES, BARBARA: NYC, Oct. 31, 1922.

BELL, TOM: Liverpool, Eng., 1932.

BELLAMY, RALPH: Chicago, June 17, 1904.

BELLER, KATHLEEN: NYC, 1957.

BELMONDO, JEAN PAUL: Paris, Apr. 9, 1933.

BENEDICT, DIRK (Niewoehner): White Sulphur Springs, MT. March 1, 1945. Whitman Col.

BENJAMIN, RICHARD: NYC, May 22, 1938. Northwestern U.

BENNENT, DAVID: Lausanne, Sept. 9, 1966.

BENNETT, BRUCE (Herman Brix): Tacoma, WA, May 19, 1909. U. Wash.

BENNETT, JILL: Penang, Malay, Dec. 24, 1931.

BENNETT, JOAN: Palisades, NJ, Feb. 27, 1910. St. Margaret's School.

BENSON, ROBBY: Dallas, TX, Jan. 21, 1957.

BERENSON, MARISSA: NYC, Feb. 15, 1947.

BERGEN, CANDICE: Los Angeles, May 9, 1946. U. Pa.

BERGEN, POLLY: Knoxville, TN, July 14, 1930. Compton Jr. College.

BERGER, HELMUT: Salzburg, Aus., 1945.

BERGER, SENTA: Vienna, May 13, 1941. Vienna Sch. of Acting.

BERGER, WILLIAM: Austria, Jan. 20, 1928. Columbia.

BERGERAC, JACQUES: Biarritz, France, May 26, 1927. Paris U.

BERLE, MILTON (Milton Berlinger): NYC, July 12, 1908. Professional Children's School.

BERLIN, JEANNIE: Los Angeles, Nov. 1, 1949.

BERLINGER, WARREN: Brooklyn, Aug. 31, 1937. Columbia.

BERNARDI, HERSCHEL: NYC, 1923.

BERRI, CLAUDE (Langmann): Paris, July 1, 1934.

BERTO, JULIET: Grenoble, France, Jan. 1947.

BEST, JAMES: Corydon, IN, July 26, 1926.

BETTGER, LYLE: Philadelphia, Feb. 13, 1915. AADA.

BEYMER, RICHARD: Avoca, IA, Feb. 21, 1939.

BIEHN, MICHAEL: Ariz. 1957.

BIKEL, THEODORE: Vienna, May 2, 1924. RADA.

BIRNEY, DAVID: Washington, DC, Apr. 23, 1939. Dartmouth, UCLA.

BIRNEY, REED: Alexandria, Va., Sept. 11, 1954. Boston U.

BISHOP, JOEY (Joseph Abraham Gottlieb): Bronx, NY, Feb. 3, 1918.

BISHOP, JULIE (formerly Jacqueline Wells): Denver, CO, Aug. 30, 1917. Westlake School.

BISSET, JACQUELINE: Waybridge, Eng., Sept. 13, 1944.

BIXBY, BILL: San Francisco, Jan. 22, 1934. U. Cal.

BLACK, KAREN (Ziegler): Park Ridge, IL, July 1, 1942. Northwestern.

BLAINE, VIVIAN (Vivian Stapleton): Newark, NJ, Nov. 21, 1923.

BLAIR, BETSY (Betsy Boger): NYC, Dec. 11, 1923.

BLAIR, JANET (Martha Jane Lafferty): Blair, PA, Apr. 23, 1921.

BLAIR, LINDA: Westport, CT, 1959.

BLAKE, AMANDA (Beverly Louise Neill): Buffalo, NY, Feb. 20, 1921.

BLAKE, ROBERT (Michael Gubitosi): Nutley, NJ, Sept. 18, 1933.

BLAKELY, SUSAN: Frankfurt, Germany 1950. U. Tex.

BLAKLEY, RONEE: Stanley, ID, 1946. Stanford U.

BLOOM, CLAIRE: London, Feb. 15, 1931. Badminton School.

BLYTH, ANN: Mt. Kisco, NY, Aug. 16, 1928. New Wayburn Dramatic School.

BOCHNER, HART: Toronto, 1956. U San Diego.

BOGARDE, DIRK: London, Mar. 28, 1918. Glasgow & Univ. College.

BOLGER, RAY: Dorchester, MA, Jan. 10, 1903.

BOLKAN, FLORINDA (Florinda Soares Bulcao): Ceara, Brazil, Feb. 15, 1941.

BOND, DEREK: Glasgow, Scot., Jan. 26, 1920. Askes School.

BONO, SONNY (Salvatore): 1935.

BOONE, PAT: Jacksonville, FL, June 1, 1934. Columbia U.

BOOTH, SHIRLEY (Thelma Ford): NYC, Aug. 30, 1907.

BORGNINE, ERNEST (Borgnino): Hamden, CT, Jan. 24, 1918. Randall School.

BOTTOMS, JOSEPH: Santa Barbara, CA, 1954.

BOTTOMS, TIMOTHY: Santa Barbara, CA, Aug. 30, 1951.

BOULTING, INGRID: Transvaal, So. Africa, 1947.

BOVEE, LESLIE: Bend, OR, 1952.

BOWIE, DAVID: (David Robert Jones) Brixton, South London, Eng. Jan. 8, 1947.

BOWKER, JUDI: Shawford, Eng., Apr. 6, 1954.

BOXLEITNER, BRUCE: Elgin, Il., 1950.

BOYLE, PETER: Philadelphia, PA, 1937. LaSalle Col.

BRACKEN, EDDIE: NYC, Feb. 7, 1920. Professional Children's School.

BRADY, SCOTT (Jerry Tierney): Brooklyn, Sept. 13, 1924. Bliss-Hayden Dramatic School.

BRAGA, SONIA: Maringa, Brazil, 1951.

BRAND, NEVILLE: Kewanee, IL, Aug. 13, 1920.

BRANDO, JOCELYN: San Francisco, Nov. 18, 1919. Lake Forest College, AADA.

BRANDO, MARLON: Omaha, NB, Apr. 3, 1924. New School.

BRANDON, CLARK: NYC 1959.

BRANTLEY, BETSY: Rutherfordton, NC, 1955. London Central Sch. of Drama.

BRAZZI, ROSSANO: Bologna, Italy, Sept. 18, 1916. U. Florence.

BRIAN, DAVID: NYC, Aug. 5, 1914. CCNY.

| Raymond Burr | Rosalind Cash | Sid Caesar | Susan Clark | Jean-Pierre Cassel | Tyne Daly |

BRIDGES, BEAU: Los Angeles, Dec. 9, 1941. UCLA.

BRIDGES, JEFF: Los Angeles, Dec. 4, 1949.

BRIDGES, LLOYD: San Leandro, CA, Jan. 15, 1913.

BRISEBOIS, DANIELLE: Brooklyn, June 28, 1969.

BRITT, MAY: (Maybritt Wilkins): Sweden, March 22, 1936.

BRITTANY, MORGAN: (Suzanne Caputo): Los Angeles, 1954.

BRODIE, STEVE (Johnny Stevens): Eldorado, KS, Nov. 25, 1919.

BROLIN, JAMES: Los Angeles, July 18, 1940. UCLA.

BROMFIELD, JOHN (Farron Bromfield): South Bend, IN, June 11, 1922. St. Mary's College.

BRONSON, CHARLES (Buchinsky): Ehrenfield, PA, Nov. 3, 1920.

BROWN, BLAIR: Washington, DC, 1948; Pine Manor

BROWN, BRYAN: Panania, Aust., 1947.

BROWN, GEORG STANFORD: Havana, Cuba, June 24, 1943. AMDA.

BROWN, JAMES: Desdemona, TX, Mar. 22, 1920. Baylor U.

BROWN, JIM: St. Simons Island, NY, Feb. 17, 1935. Syracuse U.

BROWN, TOM: NYC, Jan. 6, 1913. Professional Children's School.

BROWNE, CORAL: Melbourne, Aust., July 23, 1913.

BROWNE, LESLIE: NYC, 1958.

BRYNNER, YUL: Sakhalin Island, Japan, July 11, 1915.

BUCHHOLZ, HORST: Berlin, Ger., Dec. 4, 1933. Ludwig Dramatic School.

BUETEL, JACK: Dallas, TX, Sept. 5, 1917.

BUJOLD, GENEVIEVE: Montreal, Can., July 1, 1942.

BURKE, PAUL: New Orleans, July 21, 1926. Pasadena Playhouse.

BURNETT, CAROL: San Antonio, TX, Apr. 26, 1933. UCLA.

BURNS, CATHERINE: NYC, Sept. 25, 1945. AADA.

BURNS, GEORGE (Nathan Birnbaum): NYC, Jan. 20, 1896.

BURR, RAYMOND: New Westminster, B.C., Can., May 21, 1917. Stanford, U. Cal., Columbia.

BURSTYN, ELLEN (Edna Rae Gillooly): Detroit, MI, Dec. 7, 1932.

BURTON, RICHARD (Richard Jenkins): Pontrhydyfen, S. Wales, Nov. 10, 1925. Oxford.

BUSEY, GARY: Tulsa, OK, 1944.

BUTTONS, RED (Aaron Chwatt): NYC, Feb. 5, 1919.

BUZZI, RUTH: Wequetequock, RI, July 24, 1936. Pasadena Playhouse.

BYGRAVES, MAX: London, Oct. 16, 1922. St. Joseph's School.

BYRNES, EDD: NYC, July 30, 1933. Haaren High.

CAAN, JAMES: Bronx, NY, Mar. 26, 1939.

CABOT, SUSAN: Boston, July 6, 1927.

CAESAR, SID: Yonkers, NY, Sept. 8, 1922.

CAGNEY, JAMES: NYC, July 17, 1899. Columbia.

CAGNEY, JEANNE: NYC, Mar. 25, 1919. Hunter.

CAINE, MICHAEL (Maurice Michelwhite): London, Mar. 14, 1933.

CAINE, SHAKIRA (Baksh): Guyana, Feb. 23, 1947. Indian Trust Col.

CALHOUN, RORY (Francis Timothy Durgin): Los Angeles, Aug. 8, 1922.

CALLAN, MICHAEL (Martin Calinieff): Philadelphia, Nov. 22, 1935.

CALVERT, PHYLLIS: London, Feb. 18, 1917. Margaret Morris School.

CALVET, CORRINE (Corrine Dibos): Paris, Apr. 30, 1929. U. Paris.

CAMERON, ROD (Rod Cox): Calgary, Alberta, Can., Dec. 7, 1912.

CAMP, COLLEEN: San Francisco, 1953.

CAMPBELL, GLEN: Delight, AR, Apr. 22, 1935.

CANALE, GIANNA MARIA: Reggio Calabria, Italy, Sept. 12.

CANNON, DYAN (Samille Diane Friesen): Tacoma, WA, Jan. 4, 1935.

CANOVA, JUDY: Jacksonville, FL, Nov. 20, 1916.

CANTU, DOLORES: 1957, San Antonio, TX.

CAPERS, VIRGINIA: Sumter, SC, 1925. Juilliard.

CAPSHAW, KATE: Ft. Worth, Tx. UMo.

CAPUCINE (Germaine Lefebvre): Toulon, France, Jan. 6, 1935.

CARA, IRENE: NYC, Mar. 18, 1958.

CARDINALE, CLAUDIA: Tunis, N. Africa, Apr. 15, 1939. College Paul Cambon.

CAREY, HARRY, JR.: Saugus, CA, May 16, 1921. Black Fox Military Academy.

CAREY, MACDONALD: Sioux City, IA, Mar. 15, 1913. U. of Wisc., U. Iowa.

CAREY, PHILIP: Hackensack, NJ, July 15, 1925. U. Miami.

CARMEN, JULIE: Mt. Vernon, NY, Apr. 4, 1954.

CARMICHAEL, IAN: Hull, Eng., June 18, 1920. Scarborough Col.

CARNE, JUDY (Joyce Botterill): Northampton, Eng., 1939. Bush-Davis Theatre School.

CARNEY, ART: Mt. Vernon, NY, Nov. 4, 1918.

CARON, LESLIE: Paris, July 1, 1931. Nat'l Conservatory, Paris.

CARPENTER, CARLETON: Bennington, VT, July 10, 1926. Northwestern.

CARR, VIKKI (Florence Cardona): July 19, 1942. San Fernando Col.

CARRADINE, DAVID: Hollywood, Dec. 8, 1936. San Francisco State.

CARRADINE, JOHN: NYC, Feb. 5, 1906.

CARRADINE, KEITH: San Mateo, CA, Aug. 8, 1951. Colo. State U.

CARRADINE, ROBERT: San Mateo, CA, 1954.

CARREL, DANY: Tourane, Indochina, Sept. 20, 1936. Marseilles Cons.

CARROLL, DIAHANN (Johnson): NYC, July 17, 1935. NYU.

CARROLL, MADELEINE: West Bromwich, Eng., Feb. 26, 1902. Birmingham U.

CARROLL, PAT: Shreveport, LA, May 5, 1927. Catholic U.

CARSON, JOHN DAVID: 1951, Calif. Valley Col.

CARSON, JOHNNY: Corning, IA, Oct. 23, 1925. U. of Neb.

CARSTEN, PETER (Ransenthaler): Weissenberg, Bavaria, Apr. 30, 1929. Munich Akademie.

CASH, ROSALIND: Atlantic City, NJ, Dec. 31, 1938. CCNY.

CASON, BARBARA: Memphis, TN, Nov. 15, 1933. U. Iowa.

CASS, PEGGY (Mary Margaret): Boston, May 21, 1925.

CASSAVETES, JOHN: NYC, Dec. 9, 1929. Colgate College, AADA.

CASSEL, JEAN-PIERRE: Paris, Oct. 27, 1932.

CASSIDY, DAVID: NYC, Apr. 12, 1950.

CASSIDY, JOANNA: Camden, NJ, 1944. Syracuse U.

CASTELLANO, RICHARD: Bronx, NY, Sept. 3, 1934.

CAULFIELD, JOAN: Orange, NJ, June 1, 1922. Columbia U.

CAVANI, LILIANA: Bologna, Italy, Jan. 12, 1937. U. Bologna.

CELI, ADOLFO: Sicily, July 27, 1922, Rome Academy.

CHAKIRIS, GEORGE: Norwood, OH, Sept. 16, 1933.

CHAMBERLAIN, RICHARD: Beverly Hills, CA, March 31, 1935. Pomona.

CHAMPION, MARGE: Los Angeles, Sept. 2, 1925.

CHANNING, CAROL: Seattle, Jan. 31, 1921. Bennington.

CHANNING, STOCKARD (Susan Stockard): NYC, 1944. Radcliffe.

CHAPIN, MILES: NYC, Dec. 6, 1954. HB Studio.

CHAPLIN, GERALDINE: Santa Monica, CA, July 31, 1944. Royal Ballet.

CHAPLIN, SYDNEY: Los Angeles, Mar. 31, 1926. Lawrenceville.

CHARISSE, CYD (Tula Ellice Finklea): Amarillo, TX, Mar. 3, 1922. Hollywood Professional School.

CHASE, CHEVY (Cornelius Crane Chase): NYC, 1943.

CHER (Cherlin Sarkesian): May 20, 1946, El Centro, CA.

CHIARI, WALTER: Verona, Italy, 1930.

CHRISTIAN, LINDA (Blanca Rosa Welter): Tampico, Mex., Nov. 13, 1923.

CHRISTIE, JULIE: Chukua, Assam, India, Apr. 14, 1941.

CHRISTOPHER, DENNIS (Carrelli): Philadelphia, PA, 1955. Temple U.

CHRISTOPHER, JORDAN: Youngstown, OH, Oct. 23, 1940. Kent State.

CILENTO, DIANE: Queensland, Australia, Oct. 5, 1933. AADA.

CLAPTON, ERIC: London, Mar. 30, 1945.

CLARK, DANE: NYC, Feb. 18, 1915. Cornell, Johns Hopkins U.

CLARK, DICK: Mt. Vernon, NY, Nov. 30, 1929. Syracuse U.

CLARK, MAE: Philadelphia, Aug. 16, 1910.

CLARK, PETULA: Epsom, England, Nov. 15, 1932.

CLARK, SUSAN: Sarnid, Ont., Can., Mar. 8. RADA

CLAYBURGH, JILL: NYC, Apr. 30, 1944. Sarah Lawrence.

CLERY, CORINNE: Italy, 1950.

CLOONEY, ROSEMARY: Maysville, KY, May 23, 1928.

COBURN, JAMES: Laurel, NB, Aug. 31, 1928. LACC.

COCA, IMOGENE: Philadelphia, Nov. 18, 1908.

COCO, JAMES: NYC, Mar. 21, 1929.

CODY, KATHLEEN: Bronx, NY, Oct. 30, 1953.

COLBERT, CLAUDETTE (Lily Chauchoin): Paris, Sept. 15, 1903. Art Students League.

COLE, GEORGE: London, Apr. 22, 1925.

COLEMAN, GARY: Zion, IL., 1968.

COLLINS, JOAN: London, May 23, 1933. Francis Holland School.

COLLINS, STEPHEN: Des Moines, IA, Oct. 1, 1947. Amherst.

COMER, ANJANETTE: Dawson, TX, Aug. 7, 1942. Baylor, Tex. U.

CONANT, OLIVER: NYC, Nov. 15, 1955. Dalton.

CONAWAY, JEFF: NYC, Oct. 5, 1950. NYC.

CONNERY, SEAN: Edinburgh, Scot., Aug. 25, 1930.

CONNORS, CHUCK (Kevin Joseph Connors): Brooklyn, Apr. 10, 1921. Seton Hall College.

CONNORS, MIKE (Krekor Ohanian): Fresno, CA, Aug. 15, 1925. UCLA.

CONRAD, WILLIAM: Louisville, KY, Sept. 27, 1920.

CONVERSE, FRANK: St. Louis, MO, May 22, 1938. Carnegie Tech.

CONVY, BERT: St. Louis, MO, July 23, 1935. UCLA.

CONWAY, KEVIN: NYC, May 29, 1942.

CONWAY, TIM (Thomas Daniel): Willoughby, OH, Dec. 15, 1933. Bowling Green State.

COOGAN, JACKIE: Los Angeles, Oct. 25, 1914. Villanova College.

COOK, ELISHA, JR.: San Francisco, Dec. 26, 1907. St. Albans.

COOPER, BEN: Hartford, CT, Sept. 30, 1932. Columbia U.

COOPER, JACKIE: Los Angeles, Sept. 15, 1921.

CORBETT, GRETCHEN: Portland, OR, Aug. 13, 1947. Carnegie Tech.

CORBY, ELLEN (Hansen): Racine, WI, June 13, 1913.

CORCORAN, DONNA: Quincy, MA, Sept. 29, 1942.

CORD, ALEX (Viespi): Floral Park, NY, Aug. 3, 1931. NYU, Actors Studio.

CORDAY, MARA (Marilyn Watts): Santa Monica, CA, Jan. 3, 1932.

COREY, JEFF: NYC, Aug. 10, 1914. Fagin School.

CORLAN, ANTHONY: Cork City, Ire., May 9, 1947. Birmingham School of Dramatic Arts.

CORLEY, AL: Missouri, 1956. Actors Studio.

CORNTHWAITE, ROBERT: Apr. 28, 1917. USC.

CORRI, ADRIENNE: Glasgow, Scot., Nov. 13, 1933. RADA.

CORTESA, VALENTINA: Milan, Italy, Jan. 1, 1925.

COSBY, BILL: Philadelphia, July 12, 1937. Temple U.

COSTER, NICOLAS: London, Dec. 3, 1934. Neighborhood Playhouse.

COTTEN, JOSEPH: Petersburg, VA, May 13, 1905.

COURTENAY, TOM: Hull, Eng., Feb. 25, 1937. RADA.

COURTLAND, JEROME: Knoxville, TN, Dec. 27, 1926.

CRABBE, BUSTER (LARRY) (Clarence Linden): Oakland, CA, Feb. 7, 1908. USC.

CRAIG, JAMES (James H. Meador): Nashville, TN, Feb. 4, 1912. Rice Inst.

CRAIG, MICHAEL: India, Jan. 27, 1929.

CRAIN, JEANNE: Barstow, CA, May 25, 1925.

CRAWFORD, BRODERICK: Philadelphia, Dec. 9, 1911.

CREMER, BRUNO: Paris, 1929.

CRENNA, RICHARD: Los Angeles, Nov. 30, 1926. USC.

CRISTAL, LINDA (Victoria Moya): Buenos Aires, Feb. 25, 1934.

CROSBY, HARRY: Los Angeles, CA, Aug. 8, 1958.

CROSBY, KATHRYN GRANT: (see Kathryn Grant)

CROSBY, MARY FRANCES: Calif., Sept. 14, 1959.

CROSS, BEN: London, 1948. RADA.

CROSS, MURPHY (Mary Jane): Laurelton, MD, June 22, 1950.

CROUSE, LINDSAY ANN: NYC, May 12, 1948. Radcliffe.

CROWLEY, PAT: Olyphant, PA, Sept. 17, 1932.

CRYSTAL, BILLY: NYC, 1948.

CULLUM, JOHN: Knoxville, TN, Mar. 2, 1930. U. Tenn.

CULP, ROBERT: Oakland, CA., Aug. 16, 1930. U. Wash.

CULVER, CALVIN: Canandaigua, NY, 1943.

CUMMINGS, CONSTANCE: Seattle, WA, May 15, 1910.

CUMMINGS, QUINN: Hollywood, Aug. 13, 1967.

CUMMINGS, ROBERT: Joplin, MO, June 9, 1910. Carnegie Tech.

CUMMINS, PEGGY: Prestatyn, N. Wales, Dec. 18, 1926. Alexandra School.

CURTIS, JAMIE LEE: Los Angeles, Ca., Nov. 21, 1958.

CURTIS, KEENE: Salt Lake City, UT, Feb. 15, 1925. U. Utah.

CURTIS, TONY (Bernard Schwartz): NYC, June 3, 1924.

CUSACK, CYRIL: Durban, S. Africa, Nov. 26, 1910. Univ. Col.

CUSHING, PETER: Kenley, Surrey, Eng., May 26, 1913.

DAHL, ARLENE: Minneapolis, Aug. 11, 1924. U. Minn.

DALLESANDRO, JOE: Pensacola, FL, Dec. 31, 1948.

DALTON, TIMOTHY: Wales, 1945. RADA.

DALTREY, ROGER: London, Mar. 1, 1945.

DALY, TYNE: NYC, 1947. AMDA.

DAMONE, VIC (Vito Farinola): Brooklyn, June 12, 1928.

D'ANGELO, BEVERLY: Columbus, OH., 1954.

DANIELS, WILLIAM: Bklyn, Mar. 31, 1927. Northwestern.

DANNER, BLYTHE: Philadelphia, PA. Bard Col.

DANO, ROYAL: NYC, Nov. 16, 1922. NYU.

DANTE, MICHAEL (Ralph Vitti): Stamford, CT, 1935. U. Miami.

DANTON, RAY: NYC, Sept. 19, 1931. Carnegie Tech.

DARBY, KIM: (Deborah Zerby): North Hollywood, CA, July 8, 1948.

DARCEL, DENISE (Denise Billecard): Paris, Sept. 8, 1925. U. Dijon.

DARREN, JAMES: Philadelphia, June 8, 1936. Stella Adler School.

DARRIEUX, DANIELLE: Bordeaux, France, May 1, 1917. Lycee LaTour.

| Robert Duvall | Shelley Duvall | Chad Everett | Morgan Fairchild | Peter Fonda | Teri Garr |

DA SILVA, HOWARD: Cleveland, OH, May 4, 1909. Carnegie Tech.

DAVIDSON, JOHN: Pittsburgh, Dec. 13, 1941. Denison U.

DAVIES, RUPERT: Liverpool, Eng., 1916.

DAVIS, BETTE: Lowell, MA, Apr. 5, 1908. John Murray Anderson Dramatic School.

DAVIS, BRAD: Fla., 1950. AADA.

DAVIS, MAC: Lubbock, TX, 1942.

DAVIS, NANCY (Anne Frances Robbins): NYC July 8, 1921, Smith Col.

DAVIS, OSSIE: Cogdell, GA, Dec. 18, 1917. Howard U.

DAVIS, SAMMY, JR.: NYC, Dec. 8, 1925.

DAY, DENNIS (Eugene Dennis McNulty): NYC, May 21, 1917. Manhattan College.

DAY, DORIS (Doris Kappelhoff): Cincinnati, Apr. 3, 1924.

DAY, LARAINE (Johnson): Roosevelt, UT, Oct. 13, 1917.

DAYAN, ASSEF: Israel, 1945. U. Jerusalem.

DEAN, JIMMY: Plainview, TX, Aug. 10, 1928.

DeCARLO, YVONNE (Peggy Yvonne Middleton): Vancouver, B.C., Can., Sept. 1, 1922. Vancouver School of Drama.

DEE, FRANCES: Los Angeles, Nov. 26, 1907. Chicago U.

DEE, JOEY (Joseph Di Nicola): Passaic, NJ, June 11, 1940. Patterson State College.

DEE, RUBY: Cleveland, OH, Oct. 27, 1924. Hunter Col.

DEE, SANDRA (Alexandra Zuck): Bayonne, NJ, Apr. 23, 1942.

DeFORE, DON: Cedar Rapids, IA, Aug. 25, 1917. U. Iowa.

DeHAVEN, GLORIA: Los Angeles, July 23, 1923.

DeHAVILLAND, OLIVIA: Tokyo, Japan, July 1, 1916. Notre Dame Convent School.

DELL, GABRIEL: Barbados, BWI, Oct. 7, 1930.

DELON, ALAIN: Sceaux, Fr., Nov. 8, 1935.

DELORME, DANIELE: Paris, Oct. 9, 1927. Sorbonne.

DEL RIO, DOLORES: (Dolores Ansunsolo): Durango, Mex., Aug. 3, 1905. St. Joseph's Convent.

DeLUISE, DOM: Brooklyn, Aug. 1, 1933. Tufts Col.

DEMAREST, WILLIAM: St. Paul, MN, Feb. 27, 1892.

DEMONGEOT, MYLENE: Nice, France, Sept. 29, 1938.

DENEUVE, CATHERINE: Paris, Oct. 22, 1943.

DeNIRO, ROBERT: NYC, Aug. 17, 1943. Stella Adler.

DENISON, MICHAEL: Doncaster, York, Eng., Nov. 1, 1915. Oxford.

DENNER, CHARLES: Tarnow, Poland, May 29, 1926.

DENNIS, SANDY: Hastings, NB, Apr. 27, 1937. Actors Studio.

DEPARDIEU, GERARD: Chateauroux, Fr., Dec. 27, 1948.

DEREK, BO (Mary Cathleen Collins): Long Beach, CA, 1957.

DEREK, JOHN: Hollywood, Aug. 12, 1926.

DERN, BRUCE: Chicago, June 4, 1936. U Pa.

DEWHURST, COLLEEN: Montreal, June 3, 1926. Lawrence U.

DEXTER, ANTHONY (Walter Reinhold Alfred Fleischmann): Talmadge, NB, Jan. 19, 1919. U. Iowa.

DeYOUNG, CLIFF: Los Angeles, CA, Feb. 12, 1945. Cal State.

DHIEGH, KHIGH: New Jersey, 1910.

DICKINSON, ANGIE: Kulm, ND, Sept. 30, 1932. Glendale College.

DIETRICH, MARLENE (Maria Magdalene von Losch): Berlin, Ger., Dec. 27, 1901. Berlin Music Academy.

DILLER, PHYLLIS: Lima, OH, July 17, 1917. Bluffton College.

DILLMAN, BRADFORD: San Francisco, Apr. 14, 1930. Yale.

DILLON, MATT: Larchmont, NY, Feb. 18, 1964. AADA.

DILLON, MELINDA: Hope, AR, Oct. 13, 1939. Goodman Theatre School.

DIVINE (Glenn): Baltimore, Md., 1946.

DOBSON, TAMARA: Baltimore, MD, 1947. Md. Inst. of Art.

DOMERGUE, FAITH: New Orleans, June 16, 1925.

DONAHUE, TROY (Merle Johnson): NYC, Jan. 27, 1937. Columbia U.

DONAT, PETER: Nova Scotia, Jan. 20, 1928. Yale.

DONNELL, JEFF (Jean Donnell): South Windham, ME, July 10, 1921. Yale Drama School.

DOOHAN, JAMES: Vancouver, BC, Mar. 3. Neighborhood Playhouse.

DOOLEY, PAUL: Parkersburg, WV, Feb. 22, 1928. U WV.

DORS, DIANA (Fluck): Swindon, Wilshire, Eng., Oct. 23, 1931. London Academy of Music.

D'ORSAY, FIFI: Montreal, Can., Apr. 16, 1904.

DOUGLAS, KIRK (Issur Danielovitch): Amsterdam, NY, Dec. 9, 1916. St. Lawrence U.

DOUGLAS, MICHAEL: Hollywood, Sept. 25, 1944. U. Cal.

DOURIF, BRAD: Huntington, WV, Mar. 18, 1950. Marshall U.

DOVE, BILLIE: NYC, May 14, 1904.

DOWN, LESLEY-ANN: London, Mar. 17, 1954.

DRAKE, BETSY: Paris, Sept. 11, 1923.

DRAKE, CHARLES (Charles Rupert): NYC, Oct. 2, 1914. Nichols College.

DREW, ELLEN (formerly Terry Ray): Kansas City, MO, Nov. 23, 1915.

DREYFUSS, RICHARD: Brooklyn, NY, 1947.

DRIVAS, ROBERT: Chicago, Oct. 7, 1938. U. Chi.

DRU, JOANNE (Joanne LaCock): Logan, WV, Jan. 31, 1923. John Robert Powers School.

DUBBINS, DON: Brooklyn, NY, June 28.

DUFF, HOWARD: Bremerton, WA, Nov. 24, 1917.

DUFFY, PATRICK: Montana, 1949. U Wash.

DUKE, PATTY: NYC, Dec. 14, 1946.

DULLEA, KEIR: Cleveland, NJ, May 30, 1936. Neighborhood Playhouse, SF State Col.

DUNAWAY, FAYE: Bascom, FL, Jan, 14, 1941. Fla. U.

DUNCAN, SANDY: Henderson, TX, Feb. 20, 1946. Len Morris Col.

DUNNE, IRENE: Louisville, KY, Dec. 20, 1898. Chicago College of Music.

DUNNOCK, MILDRED: Baltimore, Jan. 25, 1900. Johns Hopkins and Columbia U.

DUPEREY, ANNY: Paris, 1947.

DURBIN, DEANNA (Edna): Winnipeg, Can., Dec. 4, 1921.

DURNING, CHARLES: Highland Falls, NY, Feb. 28, 1933. NYU.

DUSSOLLIER, ANDRE: Annecy, France, Feb. 17, 1946.

DUVALL, ROBERT: San Diego, CA, 1930. Principia Col.

DUVALL, SHELLEY: Houston, TX, July 7, 1949.

EASTON, ROBERT: Milwaukee, Nov. 23, 1930. U. Texas.

EASTWOOD, CLINT: San Francisco, May 31, 1930. LACC.

EATON, SHIRLEY: London, 1937. Aida Foster School.

EBSEN, BUDDY (Christian, Jr.): Belleville, IL, Apr. 2, 1910. U. Fla.

ECKEMYR, AGNETA: Karlsborg, Swed., July 2. Actors Studio.

EDEN, BARBARA (Moorhead): Tucson, AZ, 1934.

EDWARDS, VINCE: NYC, July 9, 1928. AADA.

EGAN, RICHARD: San Francisco, July 29, 1923. Stanford U.

EGGAR, SAMANTHA: London, Mar. 5, 1939.

EICHHORN, LISA: Reading, PA, 1952. Queens Ont. U. RADA.

EKBERG, ANITA: Malmo, Sweden, Sept. 29, 1931.

EKLAND, BRITT: Stockholm, Swed., 1942.

ELIZONDO, HECTOR: NYC, Dec. 22, 1936.

ELLIOTT, DENHOLM: London, May 31, 1922. Malvern College.

ELLIOTT, SAM: Sacramento, CA, 1944. U. Ore.

ELY, RON (Ronald Pierce): Hereford, TX, June 21, 1938.

EMERSON, FAYE: Elizabeth, LA, July 8, 1917. San Diego State Col.

ERDMAN, RICHARD: Enid, OK, June 1, 1925.

ERICKSON, LEIF: Alameda, CA, Oct. 27, 1911. U. Calif.

ERICSON, JOHN: Dusseldorf, Ger., Sept. 25, 1926. AADA.

ESMOND, CARL: Vienna, June 14, 1906. U. Vienna.

EVANS, DALE (Francis Smith): Uvalde, TX, Oct. 31, 1912.

EVANS, GENE: Holbrook, AZ, July 11, 1922.

EVANS, LINDA (Evenstad): Conn., Nov. 19, 1943.

EVANS, MAURICE: Dorchester, Eng., June 3, 1901.

EVERETT, CHAD (Ray Cramton): South Bend, IN, June 11, 1936.

EWELL, TOM (Yewell Tompkins): Owensboro, KY, Apr. 29, 1909. U. Wisc.

FABARES, SHELLEY: Los Angeles, Jan. 19, 1944.

FABIAN (Fabian Forte): Philadelphia, Feb. 6, 1940.

FABRAY, NANETTE (Ruby Nanette Fabares): San Diego, Oct. 27, 1920.

FAIRBANKS, DOUGLAS JR.: NYC, Dec. 9, 1907. Collegiate School.

FAIRCHILD, MORGAN: (Patsy McClenny) Dallas, TX., 1950. UCLA.

FALK, PETER: NYC, Sept. 16, 1927. New School.

FARENTINO, JAMES: Brooklyn, Feb. 24, 1938. AADA.

FARINA, SANDY (Sandra Feldman): Newark, NJ, 1955.

FARR, DEREK: London, Feb. 7, 1912.

FARR, FELICIA: Westchester, NY, Oct. 4, 1932. Penn State Col.

FARRELL, CHARLES: Onset Bay, MA, Aug. 9, 1901. Boston U.

FARROW, MIA: Los Angeles, Feb. 9, 1945.

FAULKNER, GRAHAM: London, Sept. 26, 1947. Webber-Douglas.

FAWCETT, FARRAH: Texas, Feb. 2, 1947.

FAYE, ALICE (Ann Leppert): NYC, May 5, 1912.

FEINSTEIN, ALAN: NYC, Sept. 8, 1941.

FELDON, BARBARA (Hall): Pittsburgh, Mar. 12, 1941. Carnegie Tech.

FELLOWS, EDITH: Boston, May 20, 1923.

FERRELL, CONCHATA: Charleston, WV, Mar. 28, 1943. Marshall U.

FERRER, JOSE: Santurce, P.R., Jan. 8, 1909. Princeton U.

FERRER, MEL: Elberon, NJ, Aug. 25, 1917. Princeton U.

FERRIS, BARBARA: London, 1943.

FERZETTI, GABRIELE: Italy, 1927. Rome Acad. of Drama.

FIELD, SALLY: Pasadena, CA, Nov. 6, 1946.

FIGUEROA, RUBEN: NYC 1958.

FINNEY, ALBERT: Salford, Lancashire, Eng., May 9, 1936. RADA.

FIRTH, PETER: Bradford, Eng., Oct. 27, 1953.

FISHER, CARRIE: Los Angeles, CA, 1957. London Central School of Drama.

FISHER, EDDIE: Philadelphia, Aug. 10, 1928.

FITZGERALD, GERALDINE: Dublin, Ire., Nov. 24, 1914. Dublin Art School.

FLANNERY, SUSAN: Jersey City, NJ, July 31, 1943.

FLAVIN, JAMES: Portland, ME, May 14, 1906. West Point.

FLEMING, RHONDA (Marilyn Louis): Los Angeles, Aug. 10, 1922.

FLEMYNG, ROBERT: Liverpool, Eng., Jan. 3, 1912. Haileybury Col.

FLETCHER, LOUISE: Birmingham, AL, July 1934.

FOCH, NINA: Leyden, Holland, Apr. 20, 1924.

FOLDI, ERZSEBET: Queens, NY, 1967.

FONDA, JANE: NYC, Dec. 21, 1937. Vassar.

FONDA, PETER: NYC, Feb. 23, 1939. U. Omaha.

FONTAINE, JOAN: Tokyo, Japan, Oct. 22, 1917.

FORD, GLENN (Gwyllyn Samuel Newton Ford): Quebec, Can., May 1, 1916.

FORD, HARRISON: Chicago, IL, July 13, 1942. Ripon Col.

FOREST, MARK (Lou Degni): Brooklyn, Jan. 1933.

FORREST, STEVE: Huntsville, TX, Sept. 29, 1924. UCLA.

FORSLUND, CONNIE: San Diego, CA, June 19, 1950, NYU.

FORSTER, ROBERT (Foster, Jr.): Rochester, NY, July 13, 1941. Rochester U.

FORSYTHE, JOHN: Penn's Grove, NJ, Jan. 29, 1918.

FOSTER, JODIE: Bronx, NY, Nov. 19, 1962. Yale.

FOX, EDWARD: London, 1937, RADA.

FOX, JAMES: London, 1939.

FOXWORTH, ROBERT: Houston, TX, Nov. 1, 1941. Carnegie Tech.

FOXX, REDD: St. Louis, MO, Dec. 9, 1922.

FRANCIOSA, ANTHONY (Papaleo): NYC, Oct. 25, 1928.

FRANCIS, ANNE: Ossining, NY, Sept. 16, 1932.

FRANCIS, ARLENE (Arlene Kazanjian): Boston, Oct. 20, 1908. Finch School.

FRANCIS, CONNIE (Constance Franconero): Newark, NJ, Dec. 12, 1938.

FRANCISCUS, JAMES: Clayton, MO, Jan. 31, 1934. Yale.

FRANCKS, DON: Vancouver, Can., Feb. 28, 1932.

FRANK, JEFFREY: Jackson Heights, NY, 1965.

FRANKLIN, PAMELA: Tokyo, Feb. 4, 1950.

FRANZ, ARTHUR: Perth Amboy, NJ, Feb. 29, 1920. Blue Ridge College.

FRAZIER, SHEILA: NYC, 1949.

FREEMAN, AL, JR.: San Antonio, TX, 1934. CCLA.

FREEMAN, MONA: Baltimore, MD, June 9, 1926.

FREY, LEONARD: Brooklyn, Sept. 4, 1938, Neighborhood Playhouse.

FULLER, PENNY: Durham, NC, 1940. Northwestern U.

FURNEAUX, YVONNE: Lille, France, 1928. Oxford U.

GABEL, MARTIN: Philadelphia, June 19, 1912. AADA.

GABOR, EVA: Budapest, Hungary, Feb. 11, 1920.

GABOR, ZSA ZSA (Sari Gabor): Budapest, Hungary, Feb. 6, 1918.

GALLAGHER, PETER: Armonk, NY, 1956, Tufts U.

GAM, RITA: Pittsburgh, PA, Apr. 2, 1928.

GARBER, VICTOR: Montreal, Can., Mar. 16, 1949.

GARBO, GRETA (Greta Gustafson): Stockholm, Sweden, Sept. 18, 1905.

GARDENIA, VINCENT: Naples, Italy, Jan. 7, 1922.

GARDNER, AVA: Smithfield, NC, Dec. 24, 1922. Atlantic Christian College.

GARFIELD, ALLEN: Newark, NJ, Nov. 22, 1939. Actors Studio.

GARLAND, BEVERLY: Santa Cruz, CA, Oct. 17, 1930. Glendale Col.

GARNER, JAMES (James Baumgarner): Norman, OK, Apr. 7, 1928. Okla. U.

GARNER, PEGGY ANN: Canton, OH, Feb. 3, 1932.

GARR, TERI: Lakewood, OH, 1952.

GARRETT, BETTY: St. Joseph, MO, May 23, 1919. Annie Wright Seminary.

GARRISON, SEAN: NYC, Oct. 19, 1937.

GARSON, GREER: Ireland, Sept. 29, 1906.

GASSMAN, VITTORIO: Genoa, Italy, Sept. 1, 1922. Rome Academy of Dramatic Art.

GAVIN, JOHN: Los Angeles, Apr. 8, 1935. Stanford U.

GAYNOR, JANET: Philadelphia, Oct. 6, 1906.

GAYNOR, MITZI (Francesca Marlene Von Gerber): Chicago, Sept. 4, 1930.

Lillian   Moses
Gish   Gunn

Kathryn   Harry
Harrold   Hamlin

Mary Beth   David
Hurt   Huffman

GAZZARA, BEN: NYC, Aug. 28, 1930. Actors Studio.

GEARY, ANTHONY: Utah, 1948.

GEESON, JUDY: Arundel, Eng., Sept. 10, 1948. Corona.

GERARD, GIL: Little Rock, AR, 1940.

GERE, RICHARD: Philadelphia, PA, Aug. 29, 1949. U. Mass.

GERROLL, DANIEL: London, Oct. 16, 1951. Central.

GHOLSON, JULIE: Birmingham, AL, June 4, 1958.

GHOSTLEY, ALICE: Eve, MO, Aug. 14, 1926. Okla U.

GIANNINI, GIANCARLO: Spezia, Italy, Aug. 1, 1942. Rome Acad. of Drama.

GIBSON, MEL: Oneonta, NY., 1951. NIDA.

GIELGUD, JOHN: London, Apr. 14, 1904. RADA.

GILFORD, JACK: NYC, July 25.

GILLIS, ANNE (Alma O'Connor): Little Rock, AR, Feb. 12, 1927.

GILLMORE, MARGALO: London, May 31, 1897. AADA.

GILMORE, VIRGINIA (Sherman Poole): Del Monte, CA, July 26, 1919. U. Calif.

GINGOLD, HERMIONE: London, Dec. 9, 1897.

GISH, LILLIAN: Springfield, OH, Oct. 14, 1896.

GLASER, PAUL MICHAEL: Boston, MA, 1943. Boston U.

GLASS, RON: Evansville, IN, 1946.

GLEASON, JACKIE: Brooklyn, Feb. 26, 1916.

GLENN, SCOTT: Pittsburgh, PA, Jan. 26, 1942; William and Mary Col.

GODDARD, PAULETTE (Levy): Great Neck, NY, June 3, 1911.

GOLDBLUM, JEFF: Pittsburgh, PA, Oct. 22, 1952. Neighborhood Playhouse.

GOLDEN, ANNIE: NYC, 1952.

GONZALES-GONZALEZ, PEDRO: Aguilares, TX, Dec. 21, 1926.

GOODMAN, DODY: Columbus, OH, Oct. 28, 1915.

GORDON, GALE (Aldrich): NYC, Feb. 2, 1906.

GORDON, KEITH: NYC, Feb. 3, 1961.

GORDON, RUTH (Jones): Wollaston, MA, Oct. 30, 1896. AADA.

GORING, MARIUS: Newport, Isle of Wight, 1912. Cambridge, Old Vic.

GORMAN, CLIFF: Jamaica, NY, Oct. 13, 1936. NYU.

GORTNER, MARJOE: Long Beach, CA, 1944.

GOSSETT, LOUIS: Brooklyn, May 27, 1936. NYU.

GOULD, ELLIOTT (Goldstein): Brooklyn, Aug. 29, 1938. Columbia U.

GOULD, HAROLD: Schenectady, NY, Dec. 10, 1923. Cornell.

GOULET, ROBERT: Lawrence, MA, Nov. 26, 1933. Edmonton.

GRANGER, FARLEY: San Jose, CA, July 1, 1925.

GRANGER, STEWART (James Stewart): London, May 6, 1913. Webber-Douglas School of Acting.

GRANT, CARY (Archibald Alexander Leach): Bristol, Eng., Jan. 18, 1904.

GRANT, DAVID MARSHALL: Westport, CT, 1955. Yale.

GRANT, KATHRYN (Olive Grandstaff): Houston, TX, Nov. 25, 1933. UCLA.

GRANT, LEE: NYC, Oct. 31, 1930. Juilliard.

GRANVILLE, BONITA: NYC, Feb. 2, 1923.

GRAVES, PETER (Aurness): Minneapolis, Mar. 18, 1926. U. Minn.

GRAY, COLEEN (Doris Jensen): Staplehurst, NB, Oct. 23, 1922. Hamline U.

GRAY, LINDA: 1942.

GRAYSON, KATHRYN (Zelma Hedrick): Winston-Salem, NC, Feb. 9, 1922.

GREENE, ELLEN: NYC, Feb. 22. Ryder Col.

GREENE, LORNE: Ottawa, Can., Feb. 12, 1915. Queens U.

GREENE, RICHARD: Plymouth, Eng., Aug. 25, 1914. Cardinal Vaughn School.

GREENWOOD, JOAN: London, Mar. 4, 1919. RADA.

GREER, JANE: Washington, DC, Sept. 9, 1924.

GREER, MICHAEL: Galesburg, IL, Apr. 20, 1943.

GREY, JOEL (Katz): Cleveland, OH, Apr. 11, 1932.

GREY, VIRGINIA: Los Angeles, Mar. 22, 1917.

GRIEM, HELMUT: Hamburg, Ger. U. Hamburg.

GRIFFITH, ANDY: Mt. Airy, NC, June 1, 1926. UNC.

GRIFFITH, MELANIE: NYC, Aug. 9, 1957. Pierce Col.

GRIMES, GARY: San Francisco, June 2, 1955.

GRIMES, TAMMY: Lynn, MA, Jan. 30, 1934. Stephens Col.

GRIZZARD, GEORGE: Roanoke Rapids, NC, Apr. 1, 1928. UNC.

GRODIN, CHARLES: Pittsburgh, PA, Apr. 21, 1935.

GROH, DAVID: NYC, May 21, 1939. Brown U., LAMDA.

GUARDINO, HARRY: Brooklyn, Dec. 23, 1925. Haaren High.

GUINNESS, ALEC: London, Apr. 2, 1914. Pembroke Lodge School.

GUNN, MOSES: St. Louis, MO, Oct. 2, 1929. Tenn. State U.

GUTTENBERG, STEVEN: Brooklyn, NY, Aug. 1958. UCLA.

GWILLIM, DAVID: Plymouth, Eng., Dec. 15, 1948. RADA.

HACKETT, BUDDY (Leonard Hacker): Brooklyn, Aug. 31, 1924.

HACKETT, JOAN: NYC, May 1, 1939. Actors Studio.

HACKMAN, GENE: San Bernardino, CA, Jan. 30, 1931.

HADDON, DALE: Montreal, Can., May 26, 1949. Neighborhood Playhouse.

HAGMAN, LARRY (Hageman): Texas, 1939. Bard Col.

HALE, BARBARA: DeKalb, IL, Apr. 18, 1922. Chicago Academy of Fine Arts.

HALL, ALBERT: Boothton, AL, Nov. 10, 1937. Columbia.

HAMILL, MARK: Oakland, CA, Sept. 25, 1952. LACC.

HAMILTON, GEORGE: Memphis, TN, Aug. 12, 1939. Hackley.

HAMILTON, MARGARET: Cleveland, OH, Dec. 9, 1902. Hathaway-Brown School.

HAMILTON, NEIL: Lynn, MA, Sept. 9, 1899.

HAMLIN, HARRY: Pasadena, CA, 1952. Yale.

HAMPSHIRE, SUSAN: London, May 12, 1941.

HARDIN, TY (Orison Whipple Hungerford II): NYC, June 1, 1930.

HAREWOOD, DORIAN: Dayton, OH, Aug. 6. U Cinn.

HARMON, MARK: Los Angeles, CA, 1951; UCLA.

HARPER, VALERIE: Suffern, NY, Aug. 22, 1940.

HARRINGTON, PAT: NYC, Aug. 13, 1929. Fordham U.

HARRIS, BARBARA (Sandra Markowitz): Evanston, IL, 1937.

HARRIS, JULIE: Grosse Pointe, MI, Dec. 2, 1925. Yale Drama School.

HARRIS, RICHARD: Limerick, Ire., Oct. 1, 1930. London Acad.

HARRIS, ROSEMARY: Ashby, Eng., Sept. 19, 1930. RADA.

HARRISON, GREG: Catalina Island, CA, 1950; Actors Studio.

HARRISON, NOEL: London, Jan. 29, 1936.

HARRISON, REX: Huyton, Cheshire, Eng., Mar. 5, 1908.

HARROLD, KATHRYN: Tazewell, VA. 1950. Mills Col.

HARTMAN, DAVID: Pawtucket, RI, May 19, 1942. Duke U.

HARTMAN, ELIZABETH: Youngstown, OH, Dec. 23, 1941. Carnegie Tech.

HASSETT, MARILYN: Los Angeles, CA, 1949.

HAUER, RUTGER: Amsterdam, Hol. 1944.

HAVER, JUNE: Rock Island, IL, June 10, 1926.

HAVOC, JUNE (June Hovick): Seattle, WA, Nov. 8, 1916.

HAWN, GOLDIE: Washington, DC, Nov. 21, 1945.

HAYDEN, LINDA: Stanmore, Eng. Aida Foster School.

HAYDEN, STERLING (John Hamilton): Montclair, NJ, March 26, 1916.

HAYES, HELEN (Helen Brown): Washington, DC, Oct. 10, 1900. Sacred Heart Convent.

HAYS, ROBERT: San Diego, CA, 1948; SD State Col.

HAYWORTH, RITA (Margarita Cansino): NYC, Oct. 17, 1918.

HEARD, JOHN: Washington, DC, Mar. 7, 1946. Clark U.

HEATHERTON, JOEY: NYC, Sept. 14, 1944.

HECKART, EILEEN: Columbus, OH, Mar. 29, 1919. Ohio State U.

HEDISON, DAVID: Providence, RI, May 20, 1929. Brown U.

HEGYES, ROBERT: NJ, May 7, 1951.

HEMINGWAY, MARIEL: Nov. 1961.

HEMMINGS, DAVID: Guilford, Eng. Nov. 18, 1938.

HENDERSON, MARCIA: Andover, MA, July 22, 1932. AADA.

HENDRY, GLORIA: Jacksonville, FL, 1949.

HENNER, MARILU: NYC, Apr. 4, 1953.

HENREID, PAUL: Trieste, Jan. 10, 1908.

HENRY, BUCK (Zuckerman): NYC, 1931. Dartmouth.

HENRY, JUSTIN: Rye, NY, 1971.

HEPBURN, AUDREY: Brussels, Belgium, May 4, 1929.

HEPBURN, KATHARINE: Hartford, CT, Nov. 8, 1907. Bryn Mawr.

HERRMANN, EDWARD: Washington, DC, July 21, 1943. Bucknell, LAMDA.

HERSHEY, BARBARA: see Seagull, Barbara Hershey.

HESTON, CHARLTON: Evanston, IL, Oct. 4, 1922. Northwestern U.

HEWITT, MARTIN: Claremont, Ca, 1960; AADA.

HEYWOOD, ANNE (Violet Pretty): Birmingham, Eng., Dec. 11, 1932.

HICKMAN, DARRYL: Hollywood, CA, July 28, 1930. Loyola U.

HICKMAN, DWAYNE: Los Angeles, May 18, 1934. Loyola U.

HILL, ARTHUR: Saskatchewan, Can., Aug. 1, 1922. U. Brit. Col.

HILL, STEVEN: Seattle, WA, Feb. 24, 1922. U. Wash.

HILL, TERENCE (Mario Girotti): Venice, Italy, Mar. 29, 1941. U. Rome.

HILLER, WENDY: Bramhall, Cheshire, Eng., Aug. 15, 1912. Winceby House School.

HILLIARD, HARRIET: (see Harriet Hilliard Nelson)

HINGLE, PAT: Denver, CO, July 19, 1923. Tex. U.

HIRSCH, JUDD: NYC, Mar. 15, 1935. AADA.

HOFFMAN, DUSTIN: Los Angeles, Aug. 8, 1937. Pasadena Playhouse.

HOLBROOK, HAL (Harold): Cleveland, OH, Feb. 17, 1925. Denison.

HOLLIMAN, EARL: Tennasas Swamp, Delhi, LA, Sept. 11, 1928. UCLA.

HOLM, CELESTE: NYC, Apr. 29, 1919.

HOMEIER, SKIP (George Vincent Homeier): Chicago, Oct. 5, 1930. UCLA.

HOOKS, ROBERT: Washington, DC, Apr. 18, 1937. Temple.

HOPE, BOB: London, May 26, 1903.

HOPPER, DENNIS: Dodge City, KS, May 17, 1936.

HORNE, LENA: Brooklyn, June 30, 1917.

HORTON, ROBERT: Los Angeles, July 29, 1924. UCLA.

HOUGHTON, KATHARINE: Hartford, CT, Mar. 10, 1945. Sarah Lawrence.

HOUSEMAN, JOHN: Bucharest, Sept. 22, 1902.

HOUSER, JERRY: Los Angeles, July 14, 1952. Valley Jr. Col.

HOUSTON, DONALD: Tonypandy, Wales, 1924.

HOVEY, TIM: Los Angeles, June 19, 1945.

HOWARD, KEN: El Centro, CA, Mar. 28, 1944. Yale.

HOWARD, RON: Duncan, OK, Mar. 1, 1954. USC.

HOWARD, RONALD: Norwood, Eng., Apr. 7, 1918. Jesus College.

HOWARD, TREVOR: Kent, Eng., Sept. 29, 1916. RADA.

HOWELLS, URSULA: London, Sept. 17, 1922.

HOWES, SALLY ANN: London, July 20, 1930.

HUDDLESTON, MICHAEL: Roanoke, Va., AADA.

HUDSON, ROCK (Roy Scherer Fitzgerald): Winnetka, IL, Nov. 17, 1924.

HUFFMAN, DAVID: Berwin, IL, May 10, 1945.

HUGHES, BARNARD: Bedford Hills, NY, July 16, 1915. Manhattan Col.

HUGHES, KATHLEEN (Betty von Gerkan): Hollywood, CA, Nov. 14, 1928. UCLA.

HULCE, THOMAS: Plymouth, MI, Dec. 6, 1953. N.C.Sch. of Arts.

HUNNICUTT, GAYLE: Ft. Worth, TX, Feb. 6, 1943. UCLA.

HUNT, MARSHA: Chicago, Oct. 17, 1917.

HUNTER, KIM (Janet Cole): Detroit, Nov. 12, 1922.

HUNTER, TAB (Arthur Gelien): NYC, July 11, 1931.

HUPPERT, ISABELLE: Paris, Fr., Mar. 16, 1955.

HURT, MARY BETH (Supinger): Marshalltown, IA., 1948. NYU.

HURT, WILLIAM: Washington, D.C., Mar. 20, 1950. Tufts, Juilliard.

HUSSEY, RUTH: Providence, RI, Oct. 30, 1917. U. Mich.

HUSTON, JOHN: Nevada, MO, Aug. 5, 1906.

HUTTON, BETTY (Betty Thornberg): Battle Creek, MI, Feb. 26, 1921.

HUTTON, LAUREN (Mary): Charleston, SC, Nov. 17, 1943. Newcomb Col.

HUTTON, ROBERT (Winne): Kingston, NY, June 11, 1920. Blair Academy.

HUTTON, TIMOTHY: Malibu, CA, Aug. 16, 1960.

HYDE-WHITE, WILFRID: Gloucestershire, Eng., May 13, 1903. RADA.

HYER, MARTHA: Fort Worth, TX, Aug. 10, 1924. Northwestern U.

INGELS, MARTY: Brooklyn, NY, Mar. 9, 1936.

IRELAND, JOHN: Vancouver, B.C., Can., Jan. 30, 1914.

IVES, BURL: Hunt Township, IL, June 14, 1909. Charleston Ill. Teachers College.

JACKSON, ANNE: Alleghany, PA, Sept. 3, 1926. Neighborhood Playhouse.

JACKSON, GLENDA: Hoylake, Cheshire, Eng., May 9, 1936. RADA.

JACOBI, LOU: Toronto, Can., Dec. 28, 1913.

JACOBS, LAWRENCE-HILTON: Virgin Islands, 1954.

JACOBY, SCOTT: Chicago, Nov. 19, 1956.

JAECKEL, RICHARD: Long Beach, NY, Oct. 10, 1926.

JAFFE, SAM: NYC, Mar. 8, 1892.

JAGGER, DEAN: Lima, OH, Nov. 7, 1903. Wabash College.

JAGGER, MICK: July 26, 1943.

JAMES, CLIFTON: NYC, May 29, 1921. Ore. U.

JARMAN, CLAUDE, JR.: Nashville, TN, Sept. 27, 1934.

JASON, RICK: NYC, May 21, 1926. Madison.

JEAN, GLORIA (Gloria Jean Schoonover): Buffalo, NY, Apr. 14, 1927.

JEFFREYS, ANNE (Carmichael): Goldsboro, NC, Jan. 26, 1923. Anderson College.

JEFFRIES, LIONEL: London, 1927, RADA.

JERGENS, ADELE: Brooklyn, Nov. 26, 1922.

JETT, ROGER (Baker): Cumberland, Md., Oct. 2, 1946. AADA.

JOHN, ELTON: (Reginald Dwight) Middlesex, Eng., Mar. 25, 1947. RAM.

JOHNS, GLYNIS: Durban, S. Africa, Oct. 5, 1923.

JOHNSON, CELIA: Richmond, Surrey, Eng., Dec. 18, 1908. RADA.

Page   Shirley   Leon Isaac   Carol   Aron   Persis
Johnson   Jones   Kennedy   Kane   Kincaid   Khambatta

JOHNSON, PAGE: Welch, WV, Aug. 25, 1930. Ithaca.

JOHNSON, RAFER: Hillsboro, TX, Aug. 18, 1935. UCLA.

JOHNSON, RICHARD: Essex, Eng., 1927. RADA.

JOHNSON, ROBIN: Brooklyn, NY; May 29, 1964.

JOHNSON, VAN: Newport, RI, Aug. 28, 1916.

JONES, CAROLYN: Amarillo, TX, Apr. 28, 1933.

JONES, CHRISTOPHER: Jackson, TN, Aug. 18, 1941. Actors Studio.

JONES, DEAN: Morgan County, AL, Jan. 25, 1936. Ashburn College.

JONES, JACK: Bel-Air, CA, Jan. 14, 1938.

JONES, JAMES EARL: Arkabutla, MS, Jan 17, 1931. U. Mich.

JONES, JENNIFER (Phyllis Isley): Tulsa, OK, Mar. 2, 1919. AADA.

JONES, SAM J.: Chicago, IL, 1954.

JONES, SHIRLEY: Smithton, PA, March 31, 1934.

JONES, TOM (Thomas Jones Woodward): Pontypridd, Wales, June 7, 1940.

JONES, TOMMY LEE: San Saba, TX, Sept. 15, 1946. Harvard.

JORDAN, RICHARD: NYC, July 19, 1938. Harvard.

JOURDAN, LOUIS: Marseilles, France, June 18, 1920.

JULIA, RAUL: San Juan, PR, Mar. 9, 1940. U PR.

JURADO, KATY (Maria Christina Jurado Garcia): Guadalajara, Mex., 1927.

KAHN, MADELINE: Boston, MA, Sept. 29, 1942. Hofstra U.

KANE, CAROL: Cleveland, OH, 1952.

KAPLAN, JONATHAN: Paris, Nov. 25, 1947. NYU.

KATT, WILLIAM: Los Angeles, CA, 1955.

KAUFMANN, CHRISTINE: Lansdorf, Graz, Austria, Jan. 11, 1945.

KAYE, DANNY (David Daniel Kominski): Brooklyn, Jan. 18, 1913.

KAYE, STUBBY: NYC, Nov. 11, 1918.

KEACH, STACY: Savannah, GA, June 2, 1941. U. Cal., Yale.

KEATON, DIANE (Hall): Los Angeles, CA, Jan. 5, 1946. Neighborhood Playhouse.

KEATS, STEVEN: Bronx, NY, 1945.

KEDROVA, LILA: Greece, 1918.

KEEL, HOWARD (Harold Keel): Gillespie, IL, Apr. 13, 1919.

KEELER, RUBY (Ethel): Halifax, N.S., Aug. 25, 1909.

KEITH, BRIAN: Bayonne, NJ, Nov. 14, 1921.

KEITH, DAVID: Knoxville, Tn., 1954.

KELLER, MARTHE: Basel, Switz., 1945. Munich Stanislavsky Sch.

KELLERMAN, SALLY: Long Beach, CA, June 2, 1938. Actors Studio West.

KELLEY, DeFOREST: Atlanta, GA, Jan. 20, 1920.

KELLY, GENE: Pittsburgh, Aug. 23, 1912. U. Pittsburgh.

KELLY, JACK: Astoria, NY, Sept. 16, 1927. UCLA.

KELLY, NANCY: Lowell, MA, Mar. 25, 1921. Bentley School.

KEMP, JEREMY: Chesterfield, Eng., 1935, Central Sch.

KENNEDY, ARTHUR: Worcester, MA, Feb. 17, 1914. Carnegie Tech.

KENNEDY, GEORGE: NYC, Feb. 18, 1925.

KENNEDY, LEON ISAAC: Cleveland, Oh., 1949.

KERR, DEBORAH: Helensburg, Scot., Sept. 30, 1921. Smale Ballet School.

KERR, JOHN: NYC, Nov. 15, 1931. Harvard, Columbia.

KHAMBATTA, PERSIS: Bombay, Oct. 2, 1950.

KIDDER, MARGOT: Yellow Knife, Can., Oct. 17, 1948. UBC.

KIER, UDO: Germany, Oct. 14, 1944.

KILEY, RICHARD: Chicago, Mar. 31, 1922. Loyola.

KINCAID, ARON (Norman Neale Williams III): Los Angeles, June 15, 1943. UCLA.

KING, ALAN: (Irwin Kniberg): Brooklyn, Dec. 26, 1927.

KING, PERRY: Alliance, OH, Apr. 30. Yale.

KINGSLEY, BEN (Krishna Bhanji): Snaiton, Yorkshire, Eng., Dec. 31, 1943.

KINSKI, NASTASSIA: Germany, Jan. 24, 1960.

KITT, EARTHA: North, SC, Jan. 26, 1928.

KLEMPERER, WERNER: Cologne, Mar. 22, 1920.

KLUGMAN, JACK: Philadelphia, PA, Apr. 27, 1925. Carnegie Tech.

KNIGHT, ESMOND: East Sheen, Eng., May 4, 1906.

KNIGHT, SHIRLEY: Goessel, KS, July 5, 1937. Wichita U.

KNOWLES, PATRIC (Reginald Lawrence Knowles): Horsforth, Eng., Nov. 11, 1911.

KNOX, ALEXANDER: Strathroy, Ont., Can., Jan. 16, 1907.

KNOX, ELYSE: Hartford, CT, Dec. 14, 1917. Traphagen School.

KOENIG, WALTER: Chicago, IL, Sept. 14. UCLA.

KOHNER, SUSAN: Los Angeles, Nov. 11, 1936. U. Calif.

KORMAN, HARVEY: Chicago, IL, Feb. 15, 1927. Goodman.

KORVIN, CHARLES (Geza Korvin Karpathi): Czechoslovakia, Nov. 21. Sorbonne.

KOSLECK, MARTIN: Barkotzen, Ger., Mar. 24, 1907. Max Reinhardt School.

KOTTO, YAPHET: NYC, Nov. 15, 1937.

KREUGER, KURT: St. Moritz, Switz., July 23, 1917. U. London.

KRISTEL, SYLVIA: Holland, 1952.

KRISTOFFERSON, KRIS: Brownsville, TX, 1936, Pomona Col.

KRUGER, HARDY: Berlin, Ger., April. 12, 1928.

KULP, NANCY: Harrisburg, PA, 1921.

KUNTSMANN, DORIS: Hamburg, 1944.

KWAN, NANCY: Hong Kong, May 19, 1939. Royal Ballet.

LACY, JERRY: Sioux City, IA, Mar. 27, 1936. LACC.

LADD, CHERYL (Stoppelmoor): Huron, SD, July 12, 1951.

LADD, DIANE (Ladnier): Meridian, MS, Nov. 29, 1932. Tulane U.

LAHTI, CHRISTINE: Detroit, MI, Apr. 4, 1950; U Mich.

LAMARR, HEDY (Hedwig Kiesler): Vienna, Sept. 11, 1913.

LAMAS, LORENZO: Los Angeles, Jan. 1958.

LAMB, GIL: Minneapolis, June 14, 1906. U. Minn.

LAMOUR, DOROTHY: Dec. 10, 1914. Spence School.

LANCASTER, BURT: NYC, Nov. 2, 1913. NYU.

LANCHESTER, ELSA (Elsa Sullivan): London, Oct. 28, 1902.

LANDAU, MARTIN: Brooklyn, NY, 1931. Actors Studio.

LANDON, MICHAEL (Eugene Orowitz): Collingswood, NJ, Oct. 31, 1936. USC.

LANDRUM, TERI: Enid, OK., 1960.

LANE, ABBE: Brooklyn, Dec. 14, 1935.

LANE, DIANE: NYC, Jan. 1963.

| Lorenzo Lamas | Christine Lahti | Burt Lancaster | Diane Lane | Peter MacNicol | Linda Manz |

LANGAN, GLENN: Denver, CO, July 8, 1917.

LANGE, HOPE: Redding Ridge, CT, Nov. 28, 1933. Reed Col.

LANGE, JESSICA: Minnesota, Apr. 20, 1949. U. Minn.

LANGTON, PAUL: Salt Lake City, Apr. 17, 1913. Travers School of Theatre.

LANSBURY, ANGELA: London, Oct. 16, 1925. London Academy of Music.

LANSING, ROBERT (Brown): San Diego, CA, June 5, 1929.

LAURE, CAROLE: Montreal, Can., 1951.

LAURIE, PIPER (Rosetta Jacobs): Detroit, Jan. 22, 1932.

LAW, JOHN PHILLIP: Hollywood, Sept. 7, 1937. Neighborhood Playhouse, U. Hawaii.

LAWFORD, PETER: London, Sept. 7, 1923.

LAWRENCE, BARBARA: Carnegie, OK, Feb. 24, 1930. UCLA.

LAWRENCE, CAROL (Laraia): Melrose Park, IL, Sept. 5, 1935.

LAWRENCE, VICKI: Inglewood, CA, 1949.

LAWSON, LEIGH: Atherston, Eng., July 21, 1945. RADA.

LEACHMAN, CLORIS: Des Moines, IA, Apr. 30, 1930. Northwestern U.

LEAUD, JEAN-PIERRE: Paris, 1944.

LEDERER, FRANCIS: Karlin, Prague, Czech., Nov. 6, 1906.

LEE, CHRISTOPHER: London, May 27, 1922. Wellington College.

LEE, MARK: Australia, 1958.

LEE, MICHELE (Dusiak): Los Angeles, June 24, 1942. LACC.

LEIBMAN, RON: NYC, Oct. 11, 1937. Ohio Wesleyan.

LEIGH, JANET (Jeanette Helen Morrison): Merced, CA, July 6, 1926. College of Pacific.

LEMMON, JACK: Boston, Feb. 8, 1925. Harvard.

LENZ, RICK: Springfield, IL, Nov. 21, 1939. U. Mich.

LEONARD, SHELDON (Bershad): NYC, Feb. 22, 1907. Syracuse U.

LEROY, PHILIPPE: Paris, Oct. 15, 1930. U. Paris.

LESLIE, BETHEL: NYC, Aug. 3, 1929. Brearley School.

LESLIE, JOAN (Joan Brodell): Detroit, Jan. 26, 1925. St. Benedict's.

LESTER, MARK: Oxford, Eng., July 11, 1958.

LEWIS, JERRY: Newark, NJ, Mar. 16, 1926.

LIGON, TOM: New Orleans, LA, Sept. 10, 1945.

LILLIE, BEATRICE: Toronto, Can., May 29, 1898.

LINCOLN, ABBEY (Anna Marie Woolridge): Chicago, Aug. 6, 1930.

LINDFORS, VIVECA: Uppsala, Sweden, Dec. 29, 1920. Stockholm Royal Dramatic School.

LISI, VIRNA: Rome, 1938.

LITHGOW, JOHN: Rochester, NY, Oct. 19, 1945. Harvard.

LITTLE, CLEAVON: Chickasha, OK, June 1, 1939. San Diego State.

LOCKE, SONDRA: Shelbyville, TN, 1947.

LOCKHART, JUNE: NYC, June 25, 1925. Westlake School.

LOCKWOOD, GARY: Van Nuys, CA, Feb. 21, 1937.

LOCKWOOD, MARGARET: Karachi, Pakistan, Sept. 15, 1916. RADA.

LOLLOBRIGIDA, GINA: Subiaco, Italy, July 4, 1927. Rome Academy of Fine Arts.

LOM, HERBERT: Prague, Czechoslovakia, 1917. Prague U.

LOMEZ, CELINE: Montreal, Can., 1953.

LONDON, JULIE (Julie Peck): Santa Rosa, CA, Sept. 26, 1926.

LONOW, MARK: Brooklyn, N.Y.

LOPEZ, PERRY: NYC, July 22, 1931. NYU.

LORD, JACK (John Joseph Ryan): NYC, Dec. 30, 1928. NYU.

LOREN, SOPHIA: (Sofia Scicolone): Rome, Italy, Sept. 20, 1934.

LOUISE, TINA (Blacker): NYC, Feb. 11, 1934. Miami U.

LOVELACE, LINDA: Bryan, TX, 1952.

LOWITSCH, KLAUS: Berlin, Apr. 8, 1936. Vienna Academy.

LOY, MYRNA (Myrna Williams): Helena, MT, Aug. 2, 1905. Westlake School.

LUCAS, LISA: Arizona, 1961.

LULU: Glasglow, Scot., 1948.

LUND, JOHN: Rochester, NY, Feb. 6, 1913.

LUPINO, IDA: London, Feb. 4, 1916. RADA.

LYDON, JAMES: Harrington Park, NJ, May 30, 1923.

LYNLEY, CAROL (Jones): NYC, Feb. 13, 1942.

LYNN, JEFFREY: Auburn, MA, 1909. Bates College.

LYON, SUE: Davenport, IA, July 10, 1946.

LYONS, ROBERT F.: Albany, NY. AADA.

MacARTHUR, JAMES: Los Angeles, Dec. 8, 1937. Harvard.

MacGINNIS, NIALL: Dublin, Ire., Mar. 29, 1913. Dublin U.

MacGRAW, ALI: NYC, Apr. 1, 1938. Wellesley.

MacLAINE, SHIRLEY (Beatty): Richmond, VA, Apr. 24, 1934.

MacMAHON, ALINE: McKeesport, PA, May 3, 1899. Barnard College.

MacMURRAY, FRED: Kankakee, IL, Aug. 30, 1908. Carroll Col.

MacNEE, PATRICK: London, Feb. 1922.

MacNICOL, PETER: Dallas, Tx., Apr. 10. UMN.

MacRAE, GORDON: East Orange, NJ, Mar. 12, 1921.

MADISON, GUY (Robert Moseley): Bakersfield, CA, Jan. 19, 1922. Bakersfield Jr. College.

MAHARIS, GEORGE: Astoria, NY, Sept. 1, 1928. Actors Studio.

MAHONEY, JOCK (Jacques O'-Mahoney): Chicago, Feb. 7, 1919. U. of Iowa.

MAJORS, LEE: Wyandotte, MI, Apr. 23, 1940. E. Ky. State Col.

MAKEPEACE, CHRIS: Toronto, Can., 1964.

MALDEN, KARL (Mladen Sekulovich): Gary, IN, Mar. 22, 1914.

MALONE, DOROTHY: Chicago, Jan. 30, 1925. S. Methodist U.

MANN, KURT: Roslyn, NY, July 18, 1947.

MANZ, LINDA: NYC, 1961.

MARAIS, JEAN: Cherbourg, France, Dec. 11, 1913. St. Germain.

MARGO (Maria Marguerita Guadalupe Boldoay Castilla): Mexico City, May 10, 1917.

MARGOLIN, JANET: NYC, July 25, 1943. Walden School.

MARIN, JACQUES: Paris, Sept. 9, 1919. Conservatoire National.

MARINARO, ED: NYC 1951. Cornell.

MARSHALL, BRENDA (Ardis Anderson Gaines): Isle of Negros, P.I., Sept. 29, 1915. Texas State College.

MARSHALL, E. G.: Owatonna, MN, June 18, 1910. U. Minn.

MARSHALL, PENNY: Bronx, NY, Oct. 15, 1942. U. N. Mex.

MARSHALL, WILLIAM: Gary, IN, Aug. 19, 1924. NYU.

MARTIN, DEAN (Dino Crocetti): Steubenville, OH, June 17, 1917.

MARTIN, DEAN PAUL: Los Angeles, CA, 1952. UCLA.

| Jim Metzler | Mary Tyler Moore | Don Nute | Kate Nelligan | Michael O'Keefe | Glynnis O'Connor |

MARTIN, MARY: Weatherford, TX, Dec. 1, 1914. Ward-Belmont School.

MARTIN, STEVE: Waco, TX; 1946; UCLA.

MARTIN, TONY (Alfred Norris): Oakland, CA, Dec. 25, 1913. St. Mary's College.

MARVIN, LEE: NYC, Feb. 19, 1924.

MASON, JAMES: Huddersfield, Yorkshire, Eng., May 15, 1909. Cambridge.

MASON, MARSHA: St. Louis, MO, Apr. 3, 1942. Webster Col.

MASON, PAMELA (Pamela Kellino): Westgate, Eng., Mar. 10, 1918.

MASSEN, OSA: Copenhagen, Den., Jan. 13, 1916.

MASSEY, DANIEL: London, Oct. 10, 1933. Eton and King's Col.

MASSEY, RAYMOND: Toronto, Can., Aug. 30, 1896. Oxford.

MASTERSON, PETER: Angleton, TX, June 1, 1934. Rice U.

MASTROIANNI, MARCELLO: Fontana Liri, Italy, Sept. 28, 1924.

MATHESON, TIM: Glendale, Ca., Dec. 31, 1947. CalState.

MATTHAU, WALTER (Matuschanskayasky): NYC, Oct. 1, 1920.

MATTHEWS, BRIAN: Philadelphia, PA. Jan. 24, 1953. St. Olaf.

MATURE, VICTOR: Louisville, KY, Jan. 29, 1915.

MAY, ELAINE (Berlin): Philadelphia, Apr. 21, 1932.

MAYEHOFF, EDDIE: Baltimore, July 7. Yale.

MAYO, VIRGINIA: (Virginia Clara Jones): St. Louis, Mo; Nov. 30, 1920.

McCALLUM, DAVID: Scotland, Sept. 19, 1933. Chapman Coll.

McCAMBRIDGE, MERCEDES: Jolliet, IL, March 17, 1918. Mundelein College.

McCARTHY, KEVIN: Seattle, WA, Feb. 15, 1914. Minn. U.

McCLORY, SEAN: Dublin, Ire., March 8, 1924. U. Galway.

McCLURE, DOUG: Glendale, CA, May 11, 1935. UCLA.

McCOWEN, ALEC: Tunbridge Wells, Eng., May 26, 1925. RADA.

McCREA, JOEL: Los Angeles, Nov. 5, 1905. Pomona College.

McDERMOTT, HUGH: Edinburgh, Scot., Mar. 20, 1908.

McDOWALL, RODDY: London, Sept. 17, 1928. St. Joseph's.

McDOWELL, MALCOLM (Taylor): Leeds, Eng., June 15, 1943. LAMDA.

McENERY, PETER: Walsall, Eng., Feb. 21, 1940.

McFARLAND, SPANKY: Dallas, TX, 1936.

McGAVIN, DARREN: Spokane, WA, May 7, 1922. College of Pacific.

McGOVERN, ELIZABETH: Evanston, Il., July 18, 1961. Juilliard.

McGUIRE, BIFF: New Haven, CT, Oct. 25, 1926. Mass. State Col.

McGUIRE, DOROTHY: Omaha, NB, June 14, 1918.

McKAY, GARDNER: NYC, June 10, 1932. Cornell.

McKEE, LONETTE: Detroit, MI, 1954.

McKENNA, VIRGINIA: London, June 7, 1931.

McKEON, DOUG: New Jersey, 1966.

McKUEN, ROD: Oakland, CA, Apr. 29, 1933.

McLERIE, ALLYN ANN: Grand Mere, Can., Dec. 1, 1926.

McNAIR, BARBARA: Chicago, March 4, 1939. UCLA.

McNALLY, STEPHEN (Horace McNally): NYC, July 29, 1913. Fordham U.

McNICHOL, KRISTY: Los Angeles, CA, Sept. 11, 1962.

McQUEEN, BUTTERFLY: Tampa, FL, Jan. 8. 1911. UCLA.

MEADOWS, AUDREY Wuchang, China, 1919. St. Margaret's.

MEADOWS, JAYNE (formerly, Jayne Cotter): Wuchang, China, Sept. 27, 1920. St. Margaret's.

MEDWIN, MICHAEL: London, 1925. Instut Fischer.

MEEKER, RALPH (Ralph Rathgeber): Minneapolis, Nov. 21, 1920. Northwestern U.

MEKKA, EDDIE: Worcester, MA, 1932. Boston Cons.

MELATO, MARIANGELA: Milan, Italy, 1941. Milan Theatre Acad.

MELL, MARISA: Vienna, Austria, Feb. 25, 1939.

MERCADO, HECTOR JAIME: NYC, 1949. HB Studio.

MERCOURI, MELINA: Athens, Greece, Oct. 18, 1915.

MEREDITH, BURGESS: Cleveland, OH, Nov. 16, 1908. Amherst.

MEREDITH, LEE (Judi Lee Sauls): Oct., 1947. AADA.

MERKEL, UNA: Covington, KY, Dec. 10, 1903.

MERMAN, ETHEL (Ethel Zimmerman): Astoria, NY, Jan. 16, 1908.

MERRILL, DINA (Nedinia Hutton): NYC, Dec. 9, 1925. AADA.

MERRILL, GARY: Hartford, CT, Aug. 2, 1915. Bowdoin, Trinity.

METZLER, JIM: Oneonda, NY. Dartmouth Col.

MICHELL, KEITH: Adelaide, Aus., Dec. 1, 1926.

MIFUNE, TOSHIRO: Tsingtao, China, Apr. 1, 1920.

MILES, SARAH: Ingatestone, Eng., Dec. 31, 1941. RADA.

MILES, SYLVIA: NYC, Sept. 9, 1932.

MILES, VERA (Ralston): Boise City, OK, Aug. 23, 1929. UCLA.

MILFORD, PENELOPE: Winnetka, IL.

MILLAND, RAY (Reginald Truscott-Jones): Neath, Wales, Jan. 3, 1908. King's College.

MILLER, ANN (Lucille Ann Collier): Chireno, TX, Apr. 12, 1919. Lawler Professional School.

MILLER, BARRY: NYC 1958.

MILLER, JASON: Long Island City, NY, Apr. 22, 1939. Catholic U.

MILLER, LINDA: NYC, Sept. 16, 1942. Catholic U.

MILLER, MARVIN: St. Louis, July 18, 1913. Washington U.

MILLS, HAYLEY: London, Apr. 18, 1946. Elmhurst School.

MILLS, JOHN: Suffolk, Eng., Feb. 22, 1908.

MILNER, MARTIN: Detroit, MI, Dec. 28, 1931.

MIMIEUX, YVETTE: Los Angeles, Jan. 8, 1941. Hollywood High.

MINNELLI, LIZA: Los Angeles, Mar. 12, 1946.

MIOU-MIOU: Paris 1950.

MITCHELL, CAMERON: Dallastown, PA, Nov. 4, 1918. N.Y. Theatre School.

MITCHELL, JAMES: Sacramento, CA, Feb. 29, 1920. LACC.

MITCHUM, JAMES: Los Angeles, CA, May 8, 1941.

MITCHUM, ROBERT: Bridgeport, CT, Aug. 6, 1917.

MONTALBAN, RICARDO: Mexico City, Nov. 25, 1920.

MONTAND, YVES (Yves Montand Livi): Mansummano, Tuscany, Oct. 13, 1921.

MONTGOMERY, BELINDA: Winnipeg, Can., July 23, 1950.

MONTGOMERY, ELIZABETH: Los Angeles, Apr. 15, 1933. AADA.

MONTGOMERY, GEORGE (George Letz): Brady, MT, Aug. 29, 1916. U. Mont.

MOON, KEITH: London, Aug. 23, 1947.

MOOR, BILL: Toledo, OH, July 13, 1931. Northwestern.

MOORE, CONSTANCE: Sioux City, IA, Jan. 18, 1919.

MOORE, DICK: Los Angeles, Sept. 12, 1925.

MOORE, FRANK: Bay-de-Verde, Newfoundland, 1946.

MOORE, KIERON: County Cork, Ire., 1925. St. Mary's College.

MOORE, MARY TYLER: Brooklyn, Dec. 29, 1936.

MOORE, ROGER: London, Oct. 14, 1927. RADA.

MOORE, TERRY (Helen Koford): Los Angeles, Jan. 7, 1929.

MOREAU, JEANNE: Paris, Jan. 23, 1928.

MORENO, RITA (Rosita Alverio): Humacao, P.R., Dec. 11, 1931.

MORGAN, DENNIS (Stanley Morner): Prentice, WI, Dec. 10, 1910. Carroll College.

MORGAN, HARRY (HENRY) (Harry Bratsburg): Detroit, Apr. 10, 1915. U. Chicago.

MORGAN, MICHELE (Simone Roussel): Paris, Feb. 29, 1920. Paris Dramatic School.

MORIARTY, CATHY: Bronx, NY, 1961.

MORIARTY, MICHAEL: Detroit, MI, Apr. 5, 1941. Dartmouth.

MORISON, PATRICIA: NYC, 1915.

MORLEY, ROBERT: Wiltshire, Eng., May 26, 1908. RADA.

MORRIS, GREG: Cleveland, OH, 1934. Ohio State.

MORRIS, HOWARD: NYC, Sept. 4, 1919. NYU.

MORSE, DAVID: Hamilton, MA, 1953.

MORSE, ROBERT: Newton, MA, May 18, 1931.

MOSS, ARNOLD: NYC, Jan. 28, 1910. CCNY.

MULLIGAN, RICHARD: NYC, Nov. 13, 1932.

MURPHY, GEORGE: New Haven, CT, July 4, 1902. Yale.

MURPHY, MICHAEL: Los Angeles, CA, 1949.

MURRAY, BILL: Evanston, IL, Sept. 21, 1950; Regis Col.

MURRAY, DON: Hollywood, July 31, 1929. AADA.

MURRAY, KEN (Don Court): NYC, July 14, 1903.

MUSANTE, TONY: Bridgeport, CT, June 30, 1936. Oberlin Col.

NADER, GEORGE: Pasadena, CA, Oct. 19, 1921. Occidental College.

NAPIER, ALAN: Birmingham, Eng., Jan. 7, 1903. Birmingham University.

NATWICK, MILDRED: Baltimore, June 19, 1908. Bryn Mawr.

NAUGHTON, JAMES: Middletown, CT, Dec. 6, 1945. Yale.

NEAL, PATRICIA: Packard, KY, Jan. 20, 1926. Northwestern U.

NEFF, HILDEGARDE (Hildegard Knef): Ulm, Ger., Dec. 28, 1925. Berlin Art Academy.

NELL, NATHALIE: Paris, Oct. 1950.

NELLIGAN, KATE: London, Ont., Can., 1951. UToronto.

NELSON, BARRY (Robert Nielsen): Oakland, CA, 1920.

NELSON, DAVID: NYC, Oct. 24, 1936. USC.

NELSON, GENE (Gene Berg): Seattle, WA, Mar. 24, 1920.

NELSON, HARRIET HILLIARD (Peggy Lou Snyder): Des Moines, IA, July 18.

NELSON, LORI (Dixie Kay Nelson): Santa Fe, NM, Aug. 15, 1933.

NELSON, RICK (Eric Hilliard Nelson): Teaneck, NJ, May 8, 1940.

NEWHART, BOB: Chicago, IL, Sept. 5, 1929. Loyola U.

NEWLEY, ANTHONY: Hackney, London, Sept. 21, 1931.

NEWMAN, BARRY: Boston, MA, Mar. 26, 1938. Brandeis U.

NEWMAN, PAUL: Cleveland, OH, Jan. 26, 1925. Yale.

NEWMAR, JULIE (Newmeyer): Los Angeles, Aug. 16, 1935.

NEWTON-JOHN, OLIVIA: Cambridge, Eng., 1949.

NICHOLAS, PAUL: London, 1945.

NICHOLS, MIKE (Michael Igor Peschkowsky): Berlin, Nov. 6, 1931. U. Chicago.

NICHOLSON, JACK: Neptune, NJ, Apr. 22, 1937.

NICKERSON, DENISE: NYC, 1959.

NICOL, ALEX: Ossining, NY, Jan. 20, 1919. Actors Studio.

NIELSEN, LESLIE: Regina, Saskatchewan, Can., Feb. 11, 1926. Neighborhood Playhouse.

NIMOY, LEONARD: Boston, MA, Mar. 26, 1931. Boston Col., Antioch Col.

NIVEN, DAVID: Kirriemuir, Scot., Mar. 1, 1909. Sandhurst College.

NOLAN, LLOYD: San Francisco, Aug. 11, 1902. Stanford U.

NOLTE, NICK: Omaha, NB, 1941. Pasadena City Col.

NORRIS, CHRISTOPHER: NYC, Oct. 7, 1943. Lincoln Square Acad.

NORRIS, CHUCK: 1939, Oklahoma.

NORTH, HEATHER: Pasadena, CA, Dec. 13, 1950. Actors Workshop.

NORTH, SHEREE (Dawn Bethel): Los Angeles, Jan. 17, 1933. Hollywood High.

NORTON, KEN: Aug. 9, 1945.

NOVAK, KIM (Marilyn Novak): Chicago, Feb. 18, 1933. LACC.

NUREYEV, RUDOLF: Russia, Mar. 17, 1938.

NUTE, DON: Connellsville, PA, Mar. 13. Denver U.

NUYEN, FRANCE (Vannga): Marseilles, France, July 31, 1939. Beaux Arts School.

O'BRIAN, HUGH (Hugh J. Krampe): Rochester, NY, Apr. 19, 1928. Cincinnati U.

O'BRIEN, CLAY: Ray, AZ, May 6, 1961.

O'BRIEN, EDMOND: NYC, Sept. 10, 1915. Fordham, Neighborhood Playhouse.

O'BRIEN, MARGARET (Angela Maxine O'Brien): Los Angeles, Jan. 15, 1937.

O'BRIEN, PAT: Milwaukee, Nov. 11, 1899. Marquette U.

O'CONNELL, ARTHUR: NYC, Mar. 29, 1908. St. John's.

O'CONNOR, CARROLL: Bronx, NY, Aug. 2, 1925. Dublin National Univ.

O'CONNOR, DONALD: Chicago, Aug. 28, 1925.

O'CONNOR, GLYNNIS: NYC, Nov. 19, 1956. NYSU.

O'CONNOR, KEVIN: Honolulu, HI, May 7. U. Hi.

O'HANLON, GEORGE: Brooklyn, NY, Nov. 23, 1917.

O'HARA, MAUREEN (Maureen FitzSimons): Dublin, Ire., Aug. 17, 1920. Abbey School.

O'HERLIHY, DAN: Wexford, Ire., May 1, 1919. National U.

O'KEEFE, MICHAEL: Paulland, NJ, 1955, NYU, AADA.

OLIVIER, LAURENCE: Dorking, Eng., May 22, 1907. Oxford.

O'LOUGHLIN, GERALD S.: NYC, Dec. 23, 1921. U. Rochester.

OLSON, NANCY: Milwaukee, WI, July 14, 1928. UCLA.

O'NEAL, GRIFFIN: Los Angeles, 1965.

O'NEAL, PATRICK: Ocala, FL, Sept. 26, 1927. U. Fla.

O'NEAL, RON: Utica, NY, Sept. 1, 1937. Ohio State.

O'NEAL, RYAN: Los Angeles, Apr. 20, 1941.

O'NEAL, TATUM: Los Angeles, Nov. 5, 1963.

O'NEIL, TRICIA: Shreveport, LA, Mar. 11, 1945. Baylor U.

O'NEILL, JENNIFER: Rio de Janeiro, Feb. 20, 1949. Neighborhood Playhouse.

O'SULLIVAN, MAUREEN: Byle, Ire., May 17, 1911. Sacred Heart Convent.

O'TOOLE, ANNETTE: Houston, TX, 1953. UCLA

O'TOOLE, PETER: Connemara, Ireland, Aug. 2, 1932. RADA.

PACINO, AL: NYC, Apr. 25, 1940.

PAGE, GERALDINE: Kirksville, MO, Nov. 22, 1924. Goodman School.

PAGE, TONY (Anthony Vitiello): Bronx, NY, 1940.

PAGET, DEBRA (Debralee Griffin): Denver, Aug. 19, 1933.

PAIGE, JANIS (Donna Mae Jaden): Tacoma, WA, Sept. 16, 1922.

PALANCE, JACK (Walter Palanuik): Lattimer, PA, Feb. 18, 1920. UNC.

PALMER, BETSY: East Chicago, IN, Nov. 1, 1929. DePaul U.

PALMER, GREGG (Palmer Lee): San Francisco, Jan. 25, 1927. U. Utah.

PALMER, LILLI: Posen, Austria, May 24, 1914. Ilka Gruning School.

PAMPANINI, SILVANA: Rome, Sept. 25, 1925.

PAPAS, IRENE: Chiliomodion, Greece, Mar. 9, 1929.

| Michelle Pfeiffer | Sidney Poitier | Kathleen Quinlan | Richard Roundtree | Janice Rule | Michael Sarrazin |

PARKER, ELEANOR: Cedarville, OH, June 26, 1922. Pasadena Playhouse.

PARKER, FESS: Fort Worth, TX, Aug. 16, 1927. USC.

PARKER, JAMESON: 1947, Beloit Col.

PARKER, JEAN (Mae Green): Deer Lodge, MT, Aug. 11, 1912.

PARKER, SUZY (Cecelia Parker): San Antonio, TX, Oct. 28, 1933.

PARKER, WILLARD (Worster Van Eps): NYC, Feb. 5, 1912.

PARKINS, BARBARA: Vancouver, Can., May 22, 1943.

PARSONS, ESTELLE: Lynn, MA, Nov. 20, 1927. Boston U.

PARTON, DOLLY: Sevierville, TN, 1946.

PATRICK, DENNIS: Philadelphia, Mar. 14, 1918.

PATTERSON, LEE: Vancouver, Can., Mar. 31, 1929. Ontario Col.

PAVAN, MARISA (Marisa Pierangeli): Cagliari, Sardinia, June 19, 1932. Torquado Tasso College.

PEACH, MARY: Durban, S. Africa, 1934.

PEARSON, BEATRICE: Denison, TX, July 27, 1920.

PECK, GREGORY: La Jolla, CA, Apr. 5, 1916. U. Calif.

PELIKAN, LISA: Paris, July 12. Juilliard.

PEPPARD, GEORGE: Detroit, Oct. 1, 1928. Carnegie Tech.

PERKINS, ANTHONY: NYC, Apr. 14, 1932. Rollins College.

PERREAU, GIGI (Ghislaine): Los Angeles, Feb. 6, 1941.

PERRINE, VALERIE: Galveston, TX, Sept. 3, 1944. U. Ariz.

PESCOW, DONNA: Brooklyn, NY, 1954.

PETERS, BERNADETTE (Lazzara): Jamaica, NY, Feb. 28, 1948.

PETERS, BROCK: NYC, July 2, 1927. CCNY.

PETERS, JEAN (Elizabeth): Canton, OH, Oct. 15, 1926. Ohio State U.

PETTET, JOANNA: London, Nov. 16, 1944. Neighborhood Playhouse.

PFEIFFER, MICHELLE: Santa Ana, Ca., 1957.

PHILLIPS, MacKENZIE: Hollywood, CA, 1960.

PHILLIPS, MICHELLE (Holly Gilliam): NJ, June 4, 1944.

PICERNI, PAUL: NYC, Dec. 1, 1922. Loyola U.

PICKENS, SLIM (Louis Bert Lindley, Jr.): Kingsberg, CA, June 29, 1919.

PIDGEON, WALTER: East St. John, N.B., Can., Sept. 23, 1897.

PINE, PHILLIP: Hanford, CA, July 16, 1925. Actors' Lab.

PISIER, MARIE-FRANCE: Vietnam, May 10, 1944. U. Paris.

PLACE, MARY KAY: Port Arthur, TX, Sept., 1947. U. Tulsa.

PLAYTEN, ALICE: NYC, Aug. 28, 1947. NYU.

PLEASENCE, DONALD: Workshop, Eng., Oct. 5, 1919. Sheffield School.

PLESHETTE, SUZANNE: NYC, Jan. 31, 1937. Syracuse U.

PLUMMER, CHRISTOPHER: Toronto, Can., Dec. 13, 1927.

PODESTA, ROSSANA: Tripoli, June 20, 1934.

POITIER, SIDNEY: Miami, FL, Feb. 27, 1924.

POLITO, LINA: Naples, Italy, Aug. 11, 1954.

POLLARD, MICHAEL J. Pacific, NJ, May 30, 1939.

PORTER, ERIC: London, Apr. 8, 1928, Wimbledon Col.

POWELL, JANE (Suzanne Burce): Portland, OR, Apr. 1, 1928.

POWELL, ROBERT: London, June 1, 1944.

POWELL, WILLIAM: Pittsburgh, July 29, 1892. AADA.

POWER, TARYN: Los Angeles, CA, 1954.

POWERS, MALA (Mary Ellen): San Francisco, Dec. 29, 1921. UCLA.

PRENTISS, PAULA (Paula Ragusa): San Antonio, TX, Mar. 4, 1939. Northwestern U.

PRESLE, MICHELINE (Micheline Chassagne): Paris, Aug. 22, 1922. Rouleau Drama School.

PRESNELL, HARVE: Modesto, CA, Sept. 14, 1933. USC.

PRESTON, ROBERT (Robert Preston Meservey): Newton Highlands, MA, June 8, 1913. Pasadena Playhouse.

PRICE, VINCENT: St. Louis, May 27, 1911. Yale.

PRIMUS, BARRY: NYC, Feb. 16, 1938. CCNY.

PRINCE, WILLIAM: Nicholas, NY, Jan. 26, 1913. Cornell U.

PRINCIPAL, VICTORIA: Fukuoka, Japan, Mar. 3, 1950. Dade Jr. Col.

PROCHNOW, JURGEN: Germany, 1941.

PROVAL, DAVID: Brooklyn, NY, 1943.

PROVINE, DOROTHY: Deadwood, SD, Jan. 20, 1937. U. Wash.

PROWSE, JULIET: Bombay, India, Sept. 25, 1936.

PRYOR, RICHARD: Peoria, IL, Dec. 1, 1940.

PURCELL, LEE: Cherry Point, NC, June 15, 1947. Stephens.

PURCELL, NOEL: Dublin, Ire., Dec. 23, 1900. Irish Christian Brothers.

PURDOM, EDMUND: Welwyn Garden City, Eng., Dec. 19, 1924. St. Ignatius College.

PYLE, DENVER: Bethune, CO, 1920.

QUAYLE, ANTHONY: Lancashire, Eng., Sept. 7, 1913. Old Vic School.

QUINE, RICHARD: Detroit, MI, Nov. 12, 1920.

QUINLAN, KATHLEEN: Mill Valley, CA, Nov. 19, 1954.

QUINN, ANTHONY: Chihuahua, Mex., Apr. 21, 1915.

RAFFERTY, FRANCES: Sioux City, IA, June 16, 1922. UCLA.

RAFFIN, DEBORAH: Los Angeles, Mar. 13, 1953. Valley Col.

RAINES, ELLA (Ella Wallace): Snoqualmie Falls, WA, Aug. 6, 1921. U. Wash.

RAMPLING, CHARLOTTE: Surmer, Eng., Feb. 5, 1946. U. Madrid.

RAMSEY, LOGAN: Long Beach, CA, Mar. 21, 1921. St. Joseph.

RANDALL, TONY: Tulsa, OK, Feb. 26, 1920. Northwestern U.

RANDELL, RON: Sydney, Australia, Oct. 8, 1920. St. Mary's Col.

RASULALA, THALMUS (Jack Crowder): Miami, FL, Nov. 15, 1939. U. Redlands.

RAY, ALDO (Aldo DeRe): Pen Argyl, PA, Sept. 25, 1926. UCLA.

RAYE, MARTHA (Margie Yvonne Reed): Butte, MT, Aug. 27, 1916.

RAYMOND, GENE (Raymond Guion): NYC, Aug. 13, 1908.

REAGAN, RONALD: Tampico, IL, Feb. 6, 1911. Eureka College.

REASON, REX: Berlin, Ger., Nov. 30, 1928. Pasadena Playhouse.

REDDY, HELEN: Australia, Oct. 25, 1942.

REDFORD, ROBERT: Santa Monica, CA, Aug. 18, 1937. AADA.

REDGRAVE, CORIN: London, July 16, 1939.

REDGRAVE, LYNN: London, Mar. 8, 1943.

REDGRAVE, MICHAEL: Bristol, Eng., Mar. 20, 1908. Cambridge.

REDGRAVE, VANESSA: London, Jan. 30, 1937.

REDMAN, JOYCE: County Mayo, Ire., 1919. RADA.

REED, DONNA (Donna Mullenger): Denison, IA, Jan. 27, 1921. LACC.

REED, OLIVER: Wimbledon, Eng., Feb. 13, 1938.

REED, REX: Ft. Worth, TX, Oct. 2, 1939. LSU.

REEMS, HARRY (Herbert Streicher): Bronx, NY, 1947. U. Pittsburgh.

REEVE, CHRISTOPHER: NJ, Sept. 25, 1952. Cornell, Juilliard.

REEVES, STEVE: Glasgow, MT, Jan. 21, 1926.

REID, ELLIOTT: NYC, Jan. 16, 1920.

REINER, CARL: NYC, Mar. 20, 1922. Georgetown.

REINER, ROBERT: NYC, 1945. UCLA.

REMICK, LEE: Quincy, MA, Dec. 14, 1935. Barnard College.

RETTIG, TOMMY: Jackson Heights, NY, Dec. 10, 1941.

REVILL, CLIVE: Wellington, NZ, Apr. 18, 1930.

REY, FERNANDO: La Coruna, Spain, 1917.

REYNOLDS, BURT: Waycross, GA., Feb. 11, 1935. Fla. State U.

REYNOLDS, DEBBIE (Mary Frances Reynolds): El Paso, TX, Apr. 1, 1932.

REYNOLDS, MARJORIE: Buhl, ID, Aug. 12, 1921.

RHOADES, BARBARA: Poughkeepsie, NY, 1947.

RICH, IRENE: Buffalo, NY, Oct. 13, 1891. St. Margaret's School.

RICHARDS, JEFF (Richard Mansfield Taylor): Portland, OR, Nov. 1. USC.

RICHARDSON, RALPH: Cheltenham, Eng., Dec. 19, 1902.

RICKLES, DON: NYC, May 8, 1926. AADA.

RIEGERT, PETER: NYC Apr. 11, 1947; U Buffalo.

RIGG, DIANA: Doncaster, Eng., July 20, 1938. RADA.

RITTER, JOHN: Burbank, CA, 1949. U. S. Cal.

ROBARDS, JASON: Chicago, July 26, 1922. AADA.

ROBERTS, ERIC: Biloxi, MS, 1956. RADA.

ROBERTS, RALPH: Salisbury, NC, Aug. 17, 1922. UNC.

ROBERTS, TANYA: (Leigh) NYC 1965.

ROBERTS, TONY: NYC, Oct. 22, 1939. Northwestern U.

ROBERTSON, CLIFF: La Jolla, CA, Sept. 9, 1925. Antioch Col.

ROBERTSON, DALE: Oklahoma City, July 14, 1923.

ROBINSON, CHRIS: Nov. 5, 1938, West Palm Beach, FL. LACC.

ROBINSON, JAY: NYC, Apr. 14, 1930.

ROBINSON, ROGER: Seattle, WA, May 2, 1941. USC.

ROBSON, FLORA: South Shields, Eng., Mar. 28, 1902. RADA.

ROCHEFORT, JEAN: Paris, 1930.

ROGERS, CHARLES "BUDDY": Olathe, KS, Aug. 13, 1904. U. Kan.

ROGERS, GINGER (Virginia Katherine McMath): Independence, MO, July 16, 1911.

ROGERS, ROY (Leonard Slye): Cincinnati, Nov. 5, 1912.

ROGERS, WAYNE: Birmingham, AL, Apr. 7, 1933. Princeton.

ROLAND, GILBERT (Luis Antonio Damaso De Alonso): Juarez, Mex., Dec. 11, 1905.

ROLLINS, HOWARD E., Jr.: 1951, Baltimore, MD.

ROMAN, RUTH: Boston, Dec. 23, 1922. Bishop Lee Dramatic School.

ROME, SIDNE: Akron, OH. Carnegie-Mellon.

ROMERO, CESAR: NYC, Feb. 15, 1907. Collegiate School.

ROONEY, MICKEY (Joe Yule, Jr.): Brooklyn, Sept. 23, 1920.

ROSS, DIANA: Detroit, MI, Mar. 26, 1945.

ROSS, KATHARINE: Hollywood, Jan. 29, 1943. Santa Rosa Col.

ROSSELLINI, ISABELLA: Rome, June 18, 1952.

ROSSITER, LEONARD: Liverpool, Eng., Oct. 21, 1926.

ROUNDS, DAVID: Bronxville, NY, Oct. 9, 1938. Denison U.

ROUNDTREE, RICHARD: New Rochelle, NY, Sept. 7, 1942. Southern Ill.

ROWLANDS, GENA: Cambria, WI, June 19, 1936.

RUBIN, ANDREW: New Bedford, MA, June 22, 1946. AADA.

RUDD, PAUL: Boston, MA, May 15, 1940.

RULE, JANICE: Cincinnati, OH, Aug. 15, 1931.

RUPERT, MICHAEL: Denver, CO, Oct. 23, 1951. Pasadena Playhouse.

RUSH, BARBARA: Denver, CO, Jan. 4. 1929. U. Calif.

RUSSELL, JANE: Bemidji, MI, June 21, 1921. Max Reinhardt School.

RUSSELL, JOHN: Los Angeles, Jan. 3, 1921. U. Calif.

RUSSELL, KURT: Springfield, MA, March 17, 1951.

RUTHERFORD, ANN: Toronto, Can., Nov. 2, 1917.

RUYMEN, AYN: Brooklyn, July 18, 1947. HB Studio.

SACCHI, ROBERT: Bronx, NY, 1941; NYU.

SAINT, EVA MARIE: Newark, NJ, July 4, 1924. Bowling Green State U.

ST. JACQUES, RAYMOND (James Arthur Johnson): CT.

ST. JAMES, SUSAN (Suzie Jane Miller): Los Angeles, Aug. 14. Conn. Col.

ST. JOHN, BETTA: Hawthorne, CA, Nov. 26, 1929.

ST. JOHN, JILL (Jill Oppenheim): Los Angeles, Aug. 19, 1940.

SALDANA, THERESA: Brooklyn, NY, 1955.

SALMI, ALBERT: Coney Island, NY, 1925. Actors Studio.

SALT, JENNIFER: Los Angeles, Sept. 4, 1944. Sarah Lawrence Col.

SANDS, TOMMY: Chicago, Aug. 27, 1937.

SAN JUAN, OLGA: NYC, Mar. 16, 1927.

SARANDON, CHRIS: Beckley, WV, July 24, 1942. U. WVa., Catholic U.

SARANDON, SUSAN (Tomalin): NYC, Oct. 4, 1946. Catholic U.

SARGENT, RICHARD (Richard Cox): Carmel, CA, 1933. Stanford.

SARRAZIN, MICHAEL: Quebec City, Can., May 22, 1940.

SAVAGE, JOHN (Youngs): Long Island, NY, Aug. 25, 1949. AADA.

SAVALAS, TELLY (Aristotle): Garden City, NY, Jan. 21, 1925. Columbia.

SAVOY, TERESA ANN: London, July 18, 1955.

SAXON, JOHN (Carmen Orrico): Brooklyn, Aug. 5, 1935.

SCALIA, JACK: Bensonhurst, NY, 1951.

SCARWID, DIANA: Savannah, GA; AADA, Pace U.

SCHEIDER, ROY: Orange, NJ, Nov. 10, 1935. Franklin-Marshall.

SCHELL, MARIA: Vienna, Jan. 15, 1926.

SCHELL, MAXIMILIAN: Vienna, Dec. 8, 1930.

SCHNEIDER, MARIA: Paris, Mar. 27, 1952.

SCHRODER, RICKY: Staten Island, NY, Apr. 13, 1970.

SCHWARZENEGGER, ARNOLD: Austria, 1947.

SCOFIELD, PAUL: Hurstpierpoint, Eng., Jan. 21, 1922. London Mask Theatre School.

SCOTT, DEBRALEE: Elizabeth, NJ, Apr. 2.

SCOTT, GEORGE C.: Wise, VA, Oct. 18, 1927. U. Mo.

SCOTT, GORDON (Gordon M. Werschkul): Portland, OR, Aug. 3, 1927. Oregon U.

SCOTT, MARTHA: Jamesport, MO, Sept. 22, 1914. U. Mich.

SCOTT, RANDOLPH: Orange County, VA, Jan. 23, 1903. UNC.

SCOTT-TAYLOR, JONATHAN: Brazil, 1962.

SEAGULL, BARBARA HERSHEY (Herzstein): Hollywood, Feb. 5, 1948.

SEARS, HEATHER: London, 1935.

SECOMBE, HARRY: Swansea, Wales, Sept. 8, 1921.

SEGAL, GEORGE: NYC, Feb. 13, 1934. Columbia.

SELLARS, ELIZABETH: Glasgow, Scot., May 6, 1923.

SELWART, TONIO: Watenberg, Ger., June 9, 1906. Munich U.

SERNAS, JACQUES: Lithuania, July 30, 1925.

SEYLER, ATHENE (Athene Hannen): London, May 31, 1889.

SEYMOUR, ANNE: NYC, Sept. 11, 1909. American Laboratory Theatre.

SEYMOUR, JANE (Joyce Frankenberg): Hillingdon, Eng., Feb. 15, 1951.

SHARIF, OMAR (Michel Shalboub): Alexandria, Egypt, Apr. 10, 1932. Victoria Col.

SHARKEY, RAY: Brooklyn, NY, 1952; HB Studio.

SHATNER, WILLIAM: Montreal, Can., Mar. 22, 1931. McGill U.

SHAW, SEBASTIAN: Holt, Eng., May 29, 1905. Gresham School.

SHAW, STAN: Chicago, IL, 1952.

SHAWLEE, JOAN: Forest Hills, NY, Mar. 5, 1929.

SHAWN, DICK (Richard Shulefand): Buffalo, NY, Dec. 1, 1929. U. Miami.

229

| Andrew Stevens | Loretta Swit | George Takei | Kathleen Turner | James Victor | Brenda Vaccaro |

SHEARER, MOIRA: Dunfermline, Scot., Jan. 17, 1926. London Theatre School.

SHEARER, NORMA: Montreal, Can., Aug. 10, 1900.

SHEEN, MARTIN (Ramon Estevez): Dayton, OH, Aug. 3, 1940.

SHEFFIELD, JOHN: Pasadena, CA, Apr. 11, 1931. UCLA.

SHEPARD, SAM (Rogers): Ft. Sheridan, IL, Nov. 5, 1943.

SHEPHERD, CYBIL: Memphis, TN, Feb. 18, 1950. Hunter, NYU.

SHIELDS, BROOKE: NYC, May 31, 1965.

SHIRE, TALIA: Lake Success, NY. Yale.

SHORE, DINAH (Frances Rose Shore): Winchester, TN, Mar. 1, 1917. Vanderbilt U.

SHOWALTER, MAX (formerly Casey Adams): Caldwell, KS, June 2, 1917. Pasadena Playhouse.

SIDNEY, SYLVIA: NYC, Aug. 8, 1910. Theatre Guild School.

SIGNORET, SIMONE (Simone Kaminker): Wiesbaden, Ger., Mar. 25, 1921. Solange Sicard School.

SILVERS, PHIL (Philip Silversmith): Brooklyn, May 11, 1911.

SIMMONS, JEAN: London, Jan. 31, 1929. Aida Foster School.

SIMON, SIMONE: Marseilles, France, Apr. 23, 1910.

SIMPSON, O. J. (Orenthal James): San Francisco, CA, July 9, 1947. UCLA.

SINATRA, FRANK: Hoboken, NJ, Dec. 12, 1915.

SINDEN, DONALD: Plymouth, Eng., Oct. 9, 1923. Webber-Douglas.

SKALA, LILIA: Vienna; U. Dresden.

SKELTON, RED (Richard): Vincennes, IN, July 18, 1910.

SKERRITT, TOM: Detroit, MI, 1935. Wayne State U.

SLEZAK, WALTER: Vienna, Austria, May 3, 1902.

SMITH, ALEXIS: Penticton, Can., June 8, 1921. LACC.

SMITH, CHARLES MARTIN: Los Angeles, CA, 1954. CalState U.

SMITH, JOHN (Robert E. Van Orden): Los Angeles, Mar. 6, 1931. UCLA.

SMITH, KATE (Kathryn Elizabeth): Greenville, VA, May 1, 1909.

SMITH, KENT: NYC, Mar. 19, 1907. Harvard U.

SMITH, LOIS: Topeka, KS, Nov. 3, 1930. U. Wash.

SMITH, MAGGIE: Ilford, Eng., Dec. 28, 1934.

SMITH, ROGER: South Gate, CA, Dec. 18, 1932. U. Ariz.

SMITHERS, WILLIAM: Richmond, VA, July 10, 1927. Catholic U.

SNODGRESS, CARRIE: Chicago, Oct. 27, 1946. UNI.

SOLOMON, BRUCE: NYC, 1944. U. Miami, Wayne State U.

SOMERS, SUZANNE (Mahoney): San Bruno, CA, Oct. 16, 1946. Lone Mt. Col.

SOMMER, ELKE (Schletz): Berlin, Nov. 5, 1940.

SORDI, ALBERTO: Rome, Italy, 1919.

SORVINO, PAUL: NYC, 1939. AMDA.

SOTHERN, ANN (Harriet Lake): Valley City, ND, Jan. 22, 1907. Washington U.

SOUL, DAVID: Aug. 28, 1943.

SPACEK, SISSY: Quitman, TX, Dec. 25, 1949. Actors Studio.

SPENSER, JEREMY: Ceylon, 1937.

SPRINGER, GARY: NYC, July 29, 1954. Hunter Col.

STACK, ROBERT: Los Angeles, Jan. 13, 1919. USC.

STADLEN, LEWIS J.: Brooklyn, Mar. 7, 1947. Neighborhood Playhouse.

STAFFORD, NANCY: Ft. Lauderdale, FL.

STALLONE, SYLVESTER: NYC, 1946. U. Miami.

STAMP, TERENCE: London, 1940.

STANDER, LIONEL: NYC, Jan. 11, 1908. UNC.

STANG, ARNOLD: Chelsea, MA, Sept. 28, 1925.

STANLEY, KIM (Patricia Reid): Tularosa, NM, Feb. 11, 1925. U. Tex.

STANWYCK, BARBARA (Ruby Stevens): Brooklyn, July 16, 1907.

STAPLETON, JEAN: NYC, Jan. 19, 1923.

STAPLETON, MAUREEN: Troy, NY, June 21, 1925.

STEEL, ANTHONY: London, May 21, 1920. Cambridge.

STEELE, TOMMY: London, Dec. 17, 1936.

STEENBURGEN, MARY: Newport, AR, 1953. Neighborhood Playhouse.

STEIGER, ROD: Westhampton, NY, Apr. 14, 1925.

STERLING, JAN (Jane Sterling Adriance): NYC, Apr. 3, 1923. Fay Compton School.

STERLING, ROBERT (William Sterling Hart): Newcastle, PA, Nov. 13, 1917. U. Pittsburgh.

STERN, DANIEL: Bethesda, MD, 1957.

STEVENS, ANDREW: Memphis, TN, June 10, 1955.

STEVENS, CONNIE (Concetta Ann Ingolia): Brooklyn, Aug. 8, 1938. Hollywood Professional School.

STEVENS, KAYE (Catherine): Pittsburgh, July 21, 1933.

STEVENS, MARK (Richard): Cleveland, OH, Dec. 13, 1920.

STEVENS, STELLA (Estelle Eggleston): Hot Coffee, MS, Oct. 1, 1936.

STEVENSON, PARKER: CT, 1953.

STEWART, ALEXANDRA: Montreal, Can., June 10, 1939. Louvre.

STEWART, ELAINE: Montclair, NJ, May 31, 1929.

STEWART, JAMES: Indiana, PA, May 20, 1908. Princeton.

STEWART, MARTHA (Martha Haworth): Bardwell, KY, Oct. 7, 1922.

STIMSON, SARA: Helotes, TX, 1973.

STOCKWELL, DEAN: Hollywood, March 5, 1936.

STORM, GALE (Josephine Cottle): Bloomington, TX, Apr. 5, 1922.

STRAIGHT, BEATRICE: Old Westbury, NY, Aug. 2, 1916. Dartington Hall.

STRASBERG, SUSAN: NYC, May 22, 1938.

STRAUD, DON: Hawaii, 1943.

STRAUSS, PETER: NY, 1947.

STREEP, MERYL (Mary Louise): Basking Ridge, NJ, Sept. 22, 1950. Vassar, Yale.

STREISAND, BARBRA: Brooklyn, Apr. 24, 1942.

STRITCH, ELAINE: Detroit, MI, Feb. 2, 1925. Drama Workshop.

STRODE, WOODY: Los Angeles, 1914.

STRUTHERS, SALLY: Portland, OR, July 28, 1948. Pasadena Playhouse.

SULLIVAN, BARRY (Patrick Barry): NYC, Aug. 29, 1912. NYU.

SUTHERLAND, DONALD: St. John, New Brunswick, Can., July 17, 1934. U. Toronto.

SVENSON, BO: Goteborg, Swed., Feb. 13, 1941. UCLA.

SWEET, BLANCHE: Chicago, 1896.

SWINBURNE, NORA: Bath, Eng., July 24, 1902. RADA.

SWIT, LORETTA: Passaic, NJ, Nov. 4, AADA.

SYLVESTER, WILLIAM: Oakland, CA, Jan. 31, 1922. RADA.

SYMS, SYLVIA: London, June 1, 1934. Convent School.

TABORI, KRISTOFFER (Siegel): Los Angeles, Aug. 4, 1952.

TAKEI, GEORGE: Los Angeles, CA, Apr. 20. UCLA.

TALBOT, LYLE (Lysle Hollywood): Pittsburgh, Feb. 8, 1904.

TALBOT, NITA: NYC, Aug. 8, 1930. Irvine Studio School.

TAMBLYN, RUSS: Los Angeles, Dec. 30, 1934.

TANDY, JESSICA: London, June 7, 1909. Dame Owens' School.

TAYLOR, DON: Freeport, PA, Dec. 13, 1920. Penn State U.

TAYLOR, ELIZABETH: London, Feb. 27, 1932. Byron House School.

TAYLOR, KENT (Louis Weiss): Nashua, IA, May 11, 1906.

TAYLOR, ROD (Robert): Sydney, Aust., Jan. 11, 1929.

TAYLOR-YOUNG, LEIGH: Wash., DC, Jan. 25, 1945. Northwestern.

TEAGUE, ANTHONY SKOOTER: Jacksboro, TX, Jan. 4, 1940.

TEEFY, MAUREEN: Minneapolis, MN, 1954; Juilliard.

TEMPLE, SHIRLEY: Santa Monica, CA, Apr. 23, 1927.

TERRY-THOMAS (Thomas Terry Hoar Stevens): Finchley, London, July 14, 1911. Ardingly College.

TERZIEFF, LAURENT: Paris, June 25, 1935.

THACKER, RUSS: Washington, DC, June 23, 1946. Montgomery Col.

THAXTER, PHYLLIS: Portland, ME, Nov. 20, 1921. St. Genevieve.

THELEN, JODI: St. Cloud, Mn., 1963.

THOMAS, DANNY (Amos Jacobs): Deerfield, MI, Jan. 6, 1914.

THOMAS, MARLO (Margaret): Detroit, Nov. 21, 1938. USC.

THOMAS, PHILIP: Columbus, OH, May 26, 1949. Oakwood Col.

THOMAS, RICHARD: NYC, June 13, 1951. Columbia.

THOMPSON, JACK (John Payne): Sydney, Aus., 1940. U. Brisbane.

THOMPSON, MARSHALL: Peoria, IL, Nov. 27, 1925. Occidental.

THOMPSON, REX: NYC, Dec. 14, 1942.

THOMPSON, SADA: Des Moines, IA, Sept. 27, 1929. Carnegie Tech.

THULIN, INGRID: Solleftea, Sweden, Jan. 27, 1929. Royal Drama Theatre.

TICOTIN, RACHEL: Bronx, NY, 1958.

TIERNEY, GENE: Brooklyn, Nov. 20, 1920. Miss Farmer's School.

TIERNEY, LAWRENCE: Brooklyn, Mar. 15, 1919. Manhattan College.

TIFFIN, PAMELA (Wonso): Oklahoma City, Oct. 13, 1942.

TODD, RICHARD: Dublin, Ire., June 11, 1919. Shrewsbury School.

TOLO, MARILU: Rome, Italy, 1944.

TOMLIN, LILY: Detroit, MI, Sept. 1, 1939. Wayne State U.

TOPOL (Chaim Topol): Tel-Aviv, Israel, Sept. 9, 1935.

TORN, RIP: Temple, TX, Feb. 6, 1931. U. Tex.

TORRES, LIZ: NYC, 1947. NYU.

TOTTER, AUDREY: Joliet, IL, Dec. 20, 1918.

TRAVERS, BILL: Newcastle-on-Tyne, Eng., Jan. 3, 1922.

TRAVIS, RICHARD (William Justice): Carlsbad, NM, Apr. 17, 1913.

TRAVOLTA, JOEY: Englewood, NJ, 1952.

TRAVOLTA, JOHN: Englewood, NJ, Feb. 18, 1954.

TREMAYNE, LES: London, Apr. 16, 1913. Northwestern, Columbia, UCLA.

TREVOR, CLAIRE (Wemlinger): NYC, March 8, 1909.

TRINTIGNANT, JEAN-LOUIS: Pont-St. Esprit, France, Dec. 11, 1930. Dullin-Balachova Drama School.

TRUFFAUT, FRANCOIS: Paris, Feb. 6, 1932.

TRYON, TOM: Hartford, CT, Jan. 14, 1926. Yale.

TSOPEI, CORINNA: Athens, Greece, June 21, 1944.

TUCKER, FORREST: Plainfield, IN, Feb. 12, 1919. George Washington U.

TURNER, KATHLEEN: Springfield, MO., June 19, 1954. UMd.

TURNER, LANA (Julia Jean Mildred Frances Turner): Wallace, ID, Feb. 8, 1921.

TUSHINGHAM, RITA: Liverpool, Eng., 1940.

TUTIN, DOROTHY: London, Apr. 8, 1930.

TUTTLE, LURENE: Pleasant Lake, IN, Aug. 20, 1906. USC.

TWIGGY (Lesley Hornby): London, Sept. 19, 1949.

TYLER, BEVERLY (Beverly Jean Saul): Scranton, PA, July 5, 1928.

TYRRELL, SUSAN: San Francisco, 1946.

TYSON, CICELY: NYC, Dec. 19.

UGGAMS, LESLIE: NYC, May 25, 1943.

ULLMANN, LIV: Tokyo, Dec. 10, 1938. Webber-Douglas Acad.

USTINOV, PETER: London, Apr. 16, 1921. Westminster School.

VACCARO, BRENDA: Brooklyn, Nov. 18, 1939. Neighborhood Playhouse.

VALLEE, RUDY (Hubert): Island Pond, VT, July 28, 1901. Yale.

VALLI, ALIDA: Pola, Italy, May 31, 1921. Rome Academy of Drama.

VALLONE, RAF: Riogio, Italy, Feb. 17, 1916. Turin U.

VAN CLEEF, LEE: Somerville, NJ, Jan. 9, 1925.

VAN DE VEN, MONIQUE: Holland, 1957.

VAN DEVERE, TRISH (Patricia Dressel): Englewood Cliffs, NJ, Mar. 9, 1945. Ohio Wesleyan.

VAN DOREN, MAMIE (Joan Lucile Olander): Rowena, SD, Feb. 6, 1933.

VAN DYKE, DICK: West Plains, MO, Dec. 13, 1925.

VAN FLEET, JO: Oakland, CA, 1922.

VAN PATTEN, DICK: NYC, Dec. 9, 1928.

VAN PATTEN, JOYCE: NYC, Mar. 9, 1934.

VAUGHN, ROBERT: NYC, Nov. 22, 1932. USC.

VEGA, ISELA: Mexico, 1940.

VENNERA, CHICK: Herkimer, NY, Mar. 27, 1952. Pasadena Playhouse.

VENORA, DIANE: Hartford, Ct., 1952. Juilliard.

VENTURA, LINO: Parma, Italy, July 14, 1919.

VENUTA, BENAY: San Francisco, Jan. 27, 1911.

VERDON, GWEN: Culver City, CA, Jan. 13, 1925.

VEREEN, BEN: Miami, FL, Oct. 10, 1946.

VICTOR, JAMES: (Lincoln Rafael Peralta Diaz) Santiago, D.R., July 27, 1939. Haaren HS/NYC.

VILLECHAIZE, HERVE: Paris, Apr. 23, 1943.

VINCENT, JAN-MICHAEL: Denver, CO, July 15, 1944. Ventura.

VIOLET, ULTRA (Isabelle Collin-Dufresne): Grenoble, France.

VITALE, MILLY: Rome, Italy, July 16, 1938. Lycee Chateaubriand.

VOHS, JOAN: St. Albans, NY, July 30, 1931.

VOIGHT, JON: Yonkers, NY, Dec. 29, 1938. Catholic U.

VOLONTE, GIAN MARIA: Milan, Italy, Apr. 9, 1933.

VON SYDOW, MAX: Lund, Swed., July 10, 1929. Royal Drama Theatre.

WAGNER, LINDSAY: Los Angeles, June 22, 1949.

WAGNER, ROBERT: Detroit, Feb. 10, 1930.

WAHL, KEN: Chicago, IL, 1957.

WAITE, GENEVIEVE: South Africa, 1949.

WALKEN, CHRISTOPHER: Astoria, NY, Mar. 31, 1943. Hofstra.

WALKER, CLINT: Hartfold, IL, May 30, 1927. USC.

WALKER, NANCY (Ann Myrtle Swoyer): Philadelphia, May 10, 1921.

WALLACH, ELI: Brooklyn, Dec. 7, 1915. CCNY, U. Tex.

WALLACH, ROBERTA: NYC, Aug. 2, 1955.

WALLIS, SHANI: London, Apr. 5, 1941.

WALSTON, RAY: New Orleans, Nov. 22, 1917. Cleveland Playhouse.

WALTER, JESSICA: Brooklyn, NY, Jan. 31, 1940. Neighborhood Playhouse.

Jack Warden	Rachel Ward	Billy Dee Williams	Susannah York	Michael York	Mai Zetterling

WANAMAKER, SAM: Chicago, June 14, 1919. Drake.

WARD, BURT (Gervis): Los Angeles, July 6, 1945.

WARD, RACHEL: London, 1957.

WARD, SIMON: London, 1941.

WARDEN, JACK: Newark, NJ, Sept. 18, 1920.

WARNER, DAVID: Manchester, Eng., 1941. RADA.

WARREN, JENNIFER: NYC, Aug. 12, 1941. U. Wisc.

WARREN, LESLEY ANN: NYC, Aug. 16, 1946.

WARRICK, RUTH: St. Joseph, MO, June 29, 1915. U. Mo.

WASHBOURNE, MONA: Birmingham, Eng., Nov. 27, 1903.

WASHINGTON, DENZEL: Mt. Vernon, NY. Dec. 28, 1954. Fordham.

WASSON, CRAIG: Ontario, Or., Mar. 15, 1954. UOre.

WATERSTON, SAM: Cambridge, MA, Nov. 15, 1940. Yale.

WATLING, JACK: London, Jan. 13, 1923. Italia Conti School.

WATSON, DOUGLASS: Jackson, GA, Feb. 24, 1921. UNC.

WAYNE, DAVID (Wayne McKeehan): Travers City, MI, Jan. 30, 1914. Western Michigan State U.

WAYNE, PATRICK: Los Angeles, July 15, 1939. Loyola.

WEATHERS, CARL: New Orleans, La., 1948. Long Beach CC.

WEAVER, DENNIS: Joplin, MO, June 4, 1924. U. Okla.

WEAVER, MARJORIE: Crossville, TN, Mar. 2, 1913. Indiana U.

WEAVER, SIGOURNEY: NYC, 1949. Stanford, Yale.

WEBBER, ROBERT: Santa Ana, CA, Sept. 14, 1925. Compton Jr. Col.

WEDGEWORTH, ANN: Abilene, TX, Jan. 21. U. Tex.

WEISSMULLER, JOHNNY: Chicago, June 2, 1904. Chicago U.

WELCH, RAQUEL (Tejada): Chicago, Sept. 5, 1940.

WELD, TUESDAY (Susan): NYC, Aug. 27, 1943. Hollywood Professional School.

WELDON, JOAN: San Francisco, Aug. 5, 1933. San Francisco Conservatory.

WELLES, GWEN: NYC, Mar. 4.

WELLES, ORSON: Kenosha, WI, May 6, 1915. Todd School.

WERNER, OSKAR: Vienna, Nov. 13, 1922.

WESTON, JACK (Morris Weinstein): Cleveland, OH, Aug. 21, 1915.

WHITAKER, JOHNNY: Van Nuys, CA, Dec. 13. 1959.

WHITE, CAROL: London, Apr. 1, 1944.

WHITE, CHARLES: Perth Amboy, NJ, Aug. 29, 1920. Rutgers U.

WHITE, JESSE: Buffalo, NY, Jan. 3, 1919.

WHITMAN, STUART: San Francisco, Feb. 1, 1929. CCLA.

WHITMORE, JAMES: White Plains, NY, Oct. 1, 1921. Yale.

WHITNEY, GRACE LEE: Detroit, MI, Apr. 1, 1930.

WIDDOES, KATHLEEN: Wilmington, DE, Mar. 21, 1939.

WIDMARK, RICHARD: Sunrise, MN, Dec. 26, 1914. Lake Forest.

WILCOX-HORNE, COLIN: Highlands NC, Feb. 4, 1937. U. Tenn.

WILCOXON, HENRY: British West Indies, Sept. 8, 1905.

WILDE, CORNEL: NYC, Oct. 13, 1915. CCNY, Columbia.

WILDER, GENE (Jerome Silberman): Milwaukee, WI, June 11, 1935. U. Iowa.

WILLIAMS, BILLY DEE: NYC, Apr. 6, 1937.

WILLIAMS, CINDY: Van Nuys, CA, Aug. 22, 1947. LACC.

WILLIAMS, DICK A.: Chicago, IL, Aug. 9, 1938.

WILLIAMS, EMLYN: Mostyn, Wales, Nov. 26, 1905. Oxford.

WILLIAMS, ESTHER: Los Angeles, Aug. 8, 1921.

WILLIAMS, GRANT: NYC, Aug. 18, 1930. Queens College.

WILLIAMS, JOHN: Chalfont, Eng., Apr. 15, 1903. Lancing College.

WILLIAMS, TREAT (Richard): Rowayton, CT. 1952.

WILLIAMSON, FRED: Gary, IN, Mar. 5, 1938. Northwestern.

WILSON, DEMOND: NYC, Oct. 13, 1946. Hunter Col.

WILSON, FLIP (Clerow Wilson): Jersey City, NJ, Dec. 8, 1933.

WILSON, LAMBERT: Paris, 1959.

WILSON, NANCY: Chillicothe, OH, Feb. 20, 1937.

WILSON, SCOTT: Atlanta, GA, 1942.

WINDE, BEATRICE: Chicago, Jan. 6.

WINDOM, WILLIAM: NYC, Sept. 28, 1923. Williams Col.

WINDSOR, MARIE (Emily Marie Bertelson): Marysvale, UT, Dec. 11, 1924. Brigham Young U.

WINFIELD, PAUL: Los Angeles, 1940. UCLA.

WINKLER, HENRY: NYC, Oct. 30, 1945. Yale.

WINN, KITTY: Wash., D.C., 1944. Boston U.

WINTERS, JONATHAN: Dayton, OH, Nov. 11, 1925. Kenyon Col.

WINTERS, ROLAND: Boston, Nov. 22, 1904.

WINTERS, SHELLEY (Shirley Schrift): St. Louis, Aug. 18, 1922. Wayne U.

WINWOOD, ESTELLE: Kent, Eng., Jan. 24, 1883. Lyric Stage Academy.

WITHERS, GOOGIE: Karachi, India, Mar. 12, 1917. Italia Conti.

WITHERS, JANE: Atlanta, GA, 1926.

WOODLAWN, HOLLY (Harold Ajzenberg): Juana Diaz, PR, 1947.

WOODS, JAMES: Vernal, UT, Apr. 18, 1947. MIT.

WOODWARD, JOANNE: Thomasville, GA, Feb. 27, 1930. Neighborhood Playhouse.

WOOLAND, NORMAN: Dusseldorf, Ger., Mar. 16, 1910. Edward VI School.

WOPAT, TOM: Lodi, WI, 1950.

WORONOV, MARY: Brooklyn, Dec. 8, 1946. Cornell.

WRAY, FAY: Alberta, Can., Sept. 15, 1907.

WRIGHT, TERESA: NYC, Oct. 27, 1918.

WYATT, JANE: Campgaw, NJ, Aug. 10, 1911. Barnard College.

WYMAN, JANE (Sarah Jane Fulks): St. Joseph, MO, Jan. 4, 1914.

WYMORE, PATRICE: Miltonvale, KS, Dec. 17, 1926.

WYNN, KEENAN: NYC, July 27, 1916. St. John's.

WYNN, MAY (Donna Lee Hickey): NYC, Jan. 8, 1930.

WYNTER, DANA (Dagmar): London, June 8, 1927. Rhodes U.

YORK, DICK: Fort Wayne, IN, Sept. 4, 1928. De Paul U.

YORK, MICHAEL: Fulmer, Eng., Mar. 27, 1942. Oxford.

YORK, SUSANNAH: London, Jan. 9, 1941. RADA.

YOUNG, ALAN (Angus): North Shield, Eng., Nov. 19, 1919.

YOUNG, LORETTA (Gretchen): Salt Lake City, Jan. 6, 1912. Immaculate Heart College.

YOUNG, ROBERT: Chicago, Feb. 22, 1907.

ZACHARIAS, ANN: Stockholm, Sw., 1956.

ZADORA, PIA: Forest Hills, NY. 1954.

ZETTERLING, MAI: Sweden, May 27, 1925. Ordtuery Theatre School.

ZIMBALIST, EFREM, JR.: NYC, Nov. 30, 1918. Yale.

John
Alexander

Gregoire
Aslan

Alan
Badel

Beverly
Bayne

John
Belushi

Ingrid
Bergman

OBITUARIES

MABEL ALBERTSON, 81, film, stage and tv actress, died Sept. 28, 1982 of Alzheimer's disease in Santa Monica, Ca. Her film credits include "Mutiny on the Blackhawk," "She's Back on Broadway," "So This Is Love," "Forever, Darling," "The Long Hot Summer," "Home Before Dark," "Don't Give Up the Ship," "The Gazebo," "All in a Night's Work," "Period of Adjustment," "Barefoot in the Park," "Black Widow," "Ma and Pa Kettle at Waikiki," "Four Girls in Town," "A Fine Madness," "On a Clear Day You Can See Forever," "What's Up Doc?" She is probably best remembered for her tv roles in "Bewitched," "Tom Ewell Show" and "Those Whiting Girls." She was the sister of the late actor Jack Albertson. No reported survivors.

JOHN ALEXANDER, 85, Kentucky-born screen and stage actor, died July 13, 1982 at an Actors Fund Board meeting in NYC. His film credits include "Special Agent," "Petrified Forest," "Flowing Gold," "Mr. Skeffington," "Calling All Husbands," "The Doughgirls," "Arsenic and Old Lace," "The Horn Blows at Midnight," "Junior Miss," "A Tree Grows in Brooklyn," "It Shouldn't Happen to a Dog," "The Jolson Story," "Living in a Big Way," "New Orleans," "Cass Timberlane," "Where There's Life," "Summer Holiday," "The Night Has a Thousand Eyes," "Winchester 73," "Fancy Pants," "The Sleeping City," "The Model and the Marriage Broker," "The Marrying Kind," "Untamed Frontier," "The Muggers," "Pork Chop Hill," "No Name on the Bullet," "One Foot in Hell." He retired in 1962. No reported survivors.

GREGOIRE ASLAN, 73, Swiss-born Kridor Aslanian, character actor, died Jan. 8, 1982 of a heart attack while visiting in Cornwall, Eng. Among his screen credits are "Act of Love," "Red Inn," "Joe Macbeth," "Snorkel," "Windom's Way," "Roots of Heaven," "He Who Must Die," "Our Man in Havana," "Oasis," "Under Ten Flags," "King of Kings," "Call Me Genius," "The Devil at 4 O'Clock," "Happy Thieves," "Cleopatra,". "Lost Command," "Marco the Magnificent," "Bang Bang You're Dead," "The 25th Hour," "A Flea in Her Ear," "You Can't Win Them All." His widow survives.

ALAN BADEL, 58, British film and stage actor, died of a heart attack March 19, 1982 at his home in Chichester, Eng. During his career of over 40 years, his screen credits include "Salome," "Three Cases of Murder," "Will Any Gentleman?," "This Sporting Life," "Children of the Damned," "Arabesque," "Day of the Jackal," "The Stranger Left No Card," "Magic Fire," "Otley," "The Adventurers," "Young Mr. Pitt," "Where's Jack?," "Nijinsky." Surviving are his widow, and a daughter, actress Sarah Badel.

TOM BAKER, 42, U.S.-born screen and stage actor, died Sept. 2, 1982 of a drug overdose in NYC. His films include "I, A Man," "Beyond the Law," "Hallucination Generation," "All Together Now," "Angels Die Hard," "Rollercoaster," "American Hot Wax" and "Fyre." No reported survivors.

BEVERLY BAYNE, 87, Minneapolis-born stage and silent screen actress, died Aug. 18, 1982 in Scottsdale, Az. After her debut in "The Loan Shark," she appeared with Francis X. Bushman (her husband at the time) in a series of films, including "Diplomatic Service," "Social Quicksands," "Ladies World," and "Romeo and Juliet," and later in "Modern Marriage," "Age of Innocence," "Her Marriage Vow," "The Tenth Woman," "Passionate Youth," and her last in 1925, "Who Cares?" No reported survivors.

HUGH BEAUMONT, 72, Kansas-born film and tv actor, died of a heart attack May 14, 1982 while visiting his son in Munich, Ger. Credits include the Michael Shayne series, "South of Panama," "Right to the Heart," "Flight Lieutenant," "Fallen Sparrow," "Seventh Victim," "Blue Dahlia," "Last Outpost," "Phone Call from a Stranger," "Counterfeiters," "Second Chance," "Pier 23," "Night without Sleep," "Lost Continent," "Mississippi Gambler," "Mole People," "Night Passage," "Human Duplicators." He was best known for his tv role of the father in "Leave It to Beaver" series. Surviving are his widow, two sons, and a daughter.

JOHN BELUSHI, 33, Chicago-born tv and film comedian, died March 5, 1982 of a drug overdose in Hollywood, Ca. He had achieved great popularity on the tv series "Saturday Night Live" before making the films "Animal House," "The Blues Brothers," "1941," "Neighbors," "Goin' South," "Old Boyfriends" and "Continental Divide." He is survived by his widow, three brothers and a sister. Burial was on Martha's Vineyard, Ma.

BRENDA BENET, 36, Los Angeles-born film and tv actress, shot and killed herself in her West Los Angeles home on Apr. 7, 1982. She was best known for her regular appearances as Lee Williams Dumonde on the tv series "Days of Our Lives." She had been divorced from actors Paul Petersen and Bill Bixby.

MARJORIE BENNETT, 87, Australian-born screen, stage and tv actress, died of cancer June 14, 1982 in Hollywood. At the insistence of her sister, silent star Enid Bennett, she went to California and subsequently appeared in hundreds of pictures. Among her credits are "Monsieur Verdoux," "June Bride," "Perfect Strangers," "Limelight," "Young at Heart," "Autumn Leaves," "Sabrina," "Strange Intruder," "Rat Race," "Whatever Happened to Baby Jane?," "Saintly Sinners," "Promises Promises," "Mary Poppins," "Night Walker," "36 Hours," "Family Jewels," "Games," "Coogan's Bluff," "The Love God?," "Mother, Jugs and Speed," "Charley Varrick," She appeared frequently on tv in "Dobie Gillis," "December Bride," "Eve Arden Show," "Bob Cummings Show" and "Chips." Two nieces and three nephews survive.

INGRID BERGMAN, 67, Swedish-born three times Academy Award winning film and stage actress, died on her birthday Aug. 29, 1982 in London after a long battle against cancer. Her rare beauty and talent predestined her stardom and world-wide popularity. She received "Oscars" for "Gaslight" (1944), "Anastasia" (1956) and for best supporting actress in "Murder on the Orient Express" (1974). Other films include "Intermezzo" (her first U.S. film in 1939), "Adam Had Four Sons," "Dr. Jekyll and Mr. Hyde," "Casablanca," "Spellbound," "Saratoga Trunk," "Bells of St. Mary's," "Notorious," "Arch of Triumph," "Joan of Arc," "Under Capricorn," "The Surf," "Stromboli," "The Greatest Love," "Indiscreet," "Inn of the Sixth Happiness," "Goodbye Again," "The Visit," "The Yellow Rolls-Royce," "A Walk in the Spring Rain," "Cactus Flower" and "Autumn Sonata" (her last in 1978). Her last role was as Golda Meir on tv in "A Woman Called Golda." She had been married and divorced three times. Surviving are three daughters, Pia Lindstrom, Isabella and Ingrid Rossellini, and a son, Robertino Rossellini.

LARRY J. BLAKE, 68, character actor, died May 25, 1982 in Los Angeles. After his film debut in 1937 in "The Road Back," he appeared in such pictures as "The Jury's Secret," "Nurse from Brooklyn," "They Made Her a Spy," "Smash-Up," "Backlash," "Second Chance," "Lucky Stiff," "Holiday Affair," "Sunset Boulevard," "Winning Team," "High Noon," "Inside Detroit," "Earth vs the Flying Saucers," "The Love Bug," "Demon Seed" and "Time after Time." He appeared on tv's "Gunsmoke," "Adam 12," "Here's Lucy" and "Marcus Welby." His widow and a son survive.

233

| Virginia Bruce | Sue Carol | Hans Conreid | Robert Coote | Helmut Dantine | Ruth Donnelly |

RUDY BOND, 68, Philadelphia-born character actor on stage, screen and tv, died of a heart attack March 29, 1982 in Denver, Co., where he was rehearsing a play. His film credits include "With These Hands," "A Streetcar Named Desire," "Miss Sadie Thompson," "On the Waterfront," "Nightfall," "12 Angry Men," "Middle of the Night," "Mountain Road," "The Godfather," "The Taking of Pelham 1–2–3" and "The Rose." Surviving are his widow, a daughter, and two sons.

JAMES BRODERICK, 55, stage, film and tv actor, died of cancer Nov. 1, 1982 in New Haven, Ct. His screen credits include "Girl of the Night," "The Group," "Alice's Restaurant," "Dog Day Afternoon," and "The Taking of Pelham 1–2–3." On tv he appeared in "Brenner," "Family," "The Bold Ones," "Run for Your Life," "The F.B.I Story" and "Gunsmoke." Survivors include his widow, two daughters, and a son, actor Matthew Broderick.

VIRGINIA BRUCE, 72, Minneapolis-born Virginia Briggs, died Feb. 24, 1982 after a long illness in Woodland Hills, Ca. She began her film career in 1928 in "The Love Parade," subsequently becoming one of Hollywood's most popular leading ladies. Her credits include "Slightly Scarlet," "Safety in Numbers," "Miracle Man," "Sky Bride," "Winner Take All," "Downstairs," "Mighty Barnum," "Shadow of a Doubt," "Escapade," "Metropolitan," "Garden Murder Case," "The Great Ziegfeld," "Jane Eyre," "Born to Dance," "When Love Is Young," "Bad Man of Brimstone," "Arsene Lupin Returns," "Yellow Jack," "There Goes My Heart," "Let Freedom Ring," "Hired Wife," "Invisible Woman," "Butch Minds the Baby," "Pardon My Sarong," "Brazil," "The Night Has a Thousand Eyes," and "Strangers When We Meet." She had been married and divorced three times, her first husband was silent screen idol John Gilbert, by whom she had a daughter. A son by her second husband also survives.

VICTOR BUONO, 43, San Diego-born character actor on film, stage and tv, died Jan. 1, 1982 at his home in Apple Valley, Ca. After his "Oscar" nominated performance and screen debut in "Whatever Happened to Baby Jane?," he subsequently appeared in "Four for Texas," "The Strangler," "Robin and the 7 Hoods," "The Greatest Story Ever Told," "Hush, Hush, Sweet Charlotte," "Young Dillinger," "The Silencers," "Who's Minding the Mint?,' "Beneath the Planet of the Apes," "The Wrath of God," "Big Daddy," "Savage Season," "Arnold," and "Sam Marlowe, Private Eye." A brother and half-brother survive.

SUE CAROL, 73, nee Evelyn Lederer in Chicago, former actress, talent agent, and widow of Alan Ladd, died Feb. 4, 1982 from complications following a heart attack in Hollywood. Her film career began in 1927 and her credits include "Slaves of Beauty," "Soft Cushions," "The Cohens and the Kellys in Paris," "Skyscraper," "Walking Back," "Beau Broadway," "Air Circus," "Win That Girl," "Capt. Swagger," "Girls Gone Wild," "Why Leave Home," "Her Golden Calf," "She's My Weakness," "Dancing Sweeties," "Check and Double Check," "Graft," "In the Line of Duty," "Exalted Flapper," "Straightaway," and "A Doctor's Diary" (her last in 1937). She is survived by two daughters and two sons, all of whom are involved in the film industry.

TINA CARVER, 58, film and stage actress, died Feb. 18, 1982 in Everett, Wa. She had appeared in "A Bullet for Joey," "Inside Detroit," "Hell on Frisco Bay," "Uranium Boom," "A Cry in the Night," "The Man Who Turned to Stone," "From Hell It Came," "The Harder They Come" and "See How They Run." A daughter and two sons survive.

SARAH CHURCHILL, 67, stage and film actress, and daughter of the late Sir Winston Churchill, died Sept. 24, 1982 after a long illness in her native London. Her screen credits include "He Found a Star," "All Over the Town," "Royal Wedding," "Serious Charge," and "A Touch of Hell." There were no children from her three marriages. A sister survives.

HANS CONRIED, 66, Baltimore-born character actor on film, stage, radio and tv, died of a heart attack on Jan. 5, 1982 in Burbank, Ca. Among his near-100 film credits are "Dramatic School," "It's a Wonderful World," "Dulcy," "The Falcon Takes Over," "Nightmare," "Hitler's Children," "Journey into Fear," "A Lady Takes a Chance," "Crazy House," "Passage to Marseille," "My Friend Irma," "Nancy Goes to Rio," "Summer Stock," "5000 Fingers of Dr. T," "Davy Crockett," "The Birds and the Bees," "Bus Stop," "Jet Pilot," "Big Beat," "My Six Loves," "The Patsy," "Mrs. Parkington," "Oh God, Book II" and "The Cat from Outer Space." Surviving are his widow, two sons and two daughters.

ROBERT COOTE, 73, London-born tv, film and stage actor, died of a heart attack Nov. 25, 1982 in NYC. He made his Hollywood film debut in "Sally in Our Alley," followed by, among others, "Gunga Din," "Bad· Lands," "Nurse Edith Cavell," "Vigil in the Night," "Stairway to Heaven," "The Ghost and Mrs. Muir," "Forever Amber," "The Exile," "Berlin Express," "Three Musketeers," "Red Danube," "Soldiers Three," "Scaramouche," "The Merry Widow," "Prisoner of Zenda," "Commandos Strike at Dawn," "Othello," "The Swan," "The Constant Husband," "Merry Andrew," "The Horse's Mouth," "The Swinger," "The Cool Ones," "Prudence and the Pill," and "Theatre of Blood." A sister survives.

HELMUT DANTINE, 63, Vienna-born stage, screen and tv actor and producer, died of a heart attack May 5, 1982 in his home in Beverly Hills, Ca. After graduating from UCLA and Pasadena Playhouse, he made his film debut in "International Squadron," followed by "Mrs. Miniver," "Casablanca," "To Be or Not to Be," "The Pied Piper," "Edge of Darkness," "Mission to Moscow," "Northern Pursuit," "Mask of Dimitrious," "Passage to Marseille," "Hollywood Canteen," "Hotel Berlin," "Escape in the Desert," "Shadow of a Woman," "Call Me Madam," "Alexander the Great," "War and Peace," "Story of Mankind," "Hell on Devil's Island," "Fraulein," "Thundering Jets," "The Tempest," "Operation Crossbow," "The Killer Elite," "Tarzan the Apeman" (his last in 1981). Twice married and divorced, he is survived by a daughter and a son.

PATRICK DEWAERE, 35, ne Patrick Maurin, one of France's most popular actors, died from a self-inflicted gunshot on July 16, 1982 in his Paris home. After his film debut in 1970, his credits include "Going Places," "Lily Aime Moi," "The Best Way to Walk," "Get Out Your Handkerchiefs," "Coup de Tete," "A Bad Son," "Psy," "Beau-Pere," "Bottleneck," "Paco the Infallible," and "Paradise for All" (his last film). Surviving are his widow and a daughter.

DONALD DILLAWAY, 78, screen and stage actor, and talent agent, died Nov. 18, 1982 after a long illness in West Lake, Ca. He left NYC in 1930 to appear in "Cimarron," followed by "Min and Bill," "Body and Soul," "Young as You Feel," "Skyline," "Platinum Blonde," "She Wanted a Millionaire," "Cross Examination," "Pack Up Your Troubles," "Night Mayor," "Men Must Fight," "Mind Reader," "Little Giant," "Sing Sinner Sing," "I'm Still Alive," "The Magnificent Ambersons," "Over My Dead Body," "Amazon Quest," and "Sealed Cargo." His widow and two daughters survive.

RUTH DONNELLY, 86, stage and film comedienne, died Nov. 17, 1982 in NYC. Born in Trenton, NJ, she began her career at 17 as a chorus girl on Broadway, and her film career in 1927. Among her many credits are "Transatlantic," "Make Me a Star," "Blessed Event," "Hard to Handle," "Lily Turner," "Sing Sinner Sing," "Footlight Parade," "Bureau of Missing Persons," "Wonder Bar," "Heat Lightning," "Happiness Ahead," "Maybe It's Love," "Traveling Saleslady," "Hands Across the Table," "Song and Dance Man," "Mr. Deed Goes to Town," "Cain and Mabel," "A Slight Case of Murder," "Affairs of Annabel," "Annabel

| Tom Drake | Rainer Werner Fassbinder | Henry Fonda | Stanley Holloway | Victor Jory | Curt Jurgens |

Takes a Tour," "Mr. Smith Goes to Washington," "My Little Chickadee," "Model Wife," "You Belong to Me," "This Is the Army," "Thank Your Lucky Stars," "Pillow to Post," "The Bells of St. Mary's," "Cinderella Jones," "In Old Sacramento," "Cross My Heart," "Fighting Father Dunne," "The Snake Pit," "I'd Climb the Highest Mountain," "Wild Blue Yonder," "The Spoilers," "Autumn Leaves" and "Little Miss Broadway." She was the widow of Basil de Guichard. A sister survives.

TOM DRAKE, 63, ne Alfred Alderdice in Brooklyn, stage, screen and tv actor, died of lung cancer Aug. 11, 1982 in Torrance, Ca. After his 1940 film debut in "The Howards of Virginia," he appeared in "Two Girls and a Sailor," "Maisie Goes to Reno," "Mrs. Parkington," "Marriage Is a Private Affair," "The White Cliffs of Dover," "Meet Me in St. Louis," "This Man's Navy," "Green Years," "Courage of Lassie," "Cass Timberlane," "Master of Lassie," "Hills of Home," "Words and Music," "Mr. Belvedere Goes to College," "Disc Jockey," "FBI Girl," "Sangaree," "Raintree County," "Warlock," "The Sandpiper," "Johnny Reno," "The Singing Nun," "Alias a Gentleman," "Red Tomahawk," "Warkill," "The Spectre of Edgar Allan Poe" and "Savage Abduction" (his last in 1975). He was divorced from singer-actress Chris Curtis. A sister survives.

RAINER WERNER FASSBINDER, 36, prolific film maker, was found dead June 10, 1982 at the home of a friend in Munich, Ger. The probable cause of death was reported to be an accidental overdose of sleeping pills, cocaine and liquor. In addition to producing and directing, he also wrote plays and screenplays, and appeared as an actor in several of his films. Among his 41 feature pictures are "Love Is Colder Than Death" (his first), "Beware of a Holy Whore," "The Merchant of Four Seasons," "The Marriage of Maria Braun," "The Bitter Tears of Petra von Kant," "In a Year of 13 Moons," "The Third Generation," "Jail Bait," "Fox and His Friends" (in which he played the lead), "Effi Briest," "Ali: Fear Eats the Soul," "Mother Kusters Goes to Heaven," "Querelle," "Lili Marleen," "Chinese Roulette," "Wild Game" and "Lola." He was briefly married to actress Ingrid Caven. No reported survivors.

MARTY FELDMAN, 49, bulging-eyed London-born comedian, died of a massive heart attack Dec. 2, 1982 in Mexico City, immediately after completing the last day of shooting his role in the film "Yellowbeard." His career began in a comedy act and as a writer for tv and radio shows. U.S. film viewers became aware of him in "Young Frankenstein," followed by "Silent Movie," "The Adventures of Sherlock Holmes' Smarter Brother," "The Last Re-make of Beau Geste," "In God We Trust," "Sex with a Smile" and "Slapstick." He is survived by his widow and his mother. Burial was in Forest Lawn near his idol Buster Keaton.

NEIL FITZGERALD, 90, retired Ireland-born actor on stage, screen and tv, died June 15, 1982 in Princeton, NJ. After his film debut in 1935 in "The Informer," he appeared in "Bride of Frankenstein," "Charlie Chan in Shanghai," "Mary of Scotland," "The Plough and the Stars," "Parnell," "London by Night," "Arrest Bulldog Drummond," "Sergeant Madden," and "Mirage." He had been a regular performer on tv's "Edge of Night" and "Search for Tomorrow." No reported survivors.

HENRY FONDA, 77, Nebraska-born film, stage and tv actor, died of a chronic heart disease Aug. 12, 1982 in Los Angeles. After appearing in over 80 films, in 1982 he received his first "Oscar" for his performance in "On Golden Pond." Among his other credits beginning in 1935 with "The Farmer Takes a Wife," are "Trail of the Lonesome Pine," "You Only Live Once," "Wings of the Morning," "Jezebel," "Spawn of the North," "Jesse James," "Story of Alexander Graham Bell," "Young Mr. Lincoln," "Drums along the Mohawk," "Grapes of Wrath," "Chad Hanna," "Lady Eve," "The Male Animal," "Big Street," "Tales of Manhattan," "Immortal Sergeant," "Ox-Bow Inci-

dent," "Daisy Kenyon," "The Fugitive," "Fort Apache," "Mr. Roberts," "12 Angry Men," "My Darling Clementine," "The Best Man," "Advise and Consent," "Fail Safe," "Madigan," "The Boston Strangler," "Too Late the Hero." He is survived by his fifth wife, a daughter and son, actors Jane and Peter Fonda, and an adopted daughter Amy.

STANLEY HOLLOWAY, 91, London-born screen and stage actor, died Jan. 30, 1982 in Littlehampton, Sussex, Eng. He began his career as a song-and-dance man and comedian with hopes of becoming an opera star. His film roles began in 1921 and his credits include "The Co-Optimists," "Johnny in the Clouds," "Brief Encounter," "Wanted for Murder," "This Happy Breed," "Nicholas Nickleby," "Meet Me at Dawn," "Hamlet," "Passport to Pimlico," "The Lavendar Hill Mob," "Magic Box," "Tonight at 8:30," "Beggar's Opera," "In Harm's Way," "Operation Snafu," "Ten Little Indians," "Run a Crooked Mile." He was probably best known for his performance as Mr. Doolittle in the stage and film productions of "My Fair Lady." No reported survivors.

ULLA JACOBSSON, 53, Swedish-born film and stage actress, died Aug. 20, 1982 in Vienna of bone cancer. She began her career on stage in her native Gothenberg, and won international fame in the film "One Summer of Happiness," followed by "Smiles of a Summer Night," "Crime and Punsihment," "Love Is a Ball," "Zulu," "Heroes of Telemark." She is survived by her husband, an Austrian scientist.

DAME CELIA JOHNSON, 73, London-born actress on screen, stage and tv, died Apr. 26, 1982 after a stroke at her home in Nettlebed, Eng. In addition to her best known film, "Brief Encounter," she appeared in "In Which We Serve," "Randolph Family," "This Happy Breed," "The Astonished Heart," "I Believe in You," "The Captain's Paradise," "The Holly and the Ivy," "A Kid for Two Farthings," "Good Companions," "The Prime of Miss Jean Brodie." She was the widow of Peter Fleming and is survived by a son and two daughters.

VICTOR JORY, 79, versatile Alaska-born actor on film, stage, radio and tv, was found dead in his apartment in Santa Monica, Ca., on Feb. 12, 1982. His career in films spanned over 40 years and included over 70 pictures, in many of which he was the villain. Some of his roles were in "Second Hand Wife," "State Fair," "Pursued," "Madame DuBarry," "White Lies," "A Midsummer Night's Dream," "Mills of the Gods," "Escape from Devil's Island," "Too Tough to Kill," "Bulldog Drummond at Bay," "First Lady," "Tom Sawyer," "Wings of the Navy," "Dodge City," "Each Dawn I Die," "Gone with the Wind," "The Green Archer," "Girl from Havana," "Bad Men of Missouri," "Power of the Press," "The Kansan," "Loves of Carmen," "Canadian Pacific," "Highwayman," "Son of Ali Baba," "Man from the Alamo," "Valley of the Kings," "The Miracle Worker," "Jigsaw," "Mackenna's Gold," "Papillon." He is survived by a daughter, and a son Jon, artistic director of the Actors Theatre of Louisville, Ky., where he had participated in many productions.

CURT JURGENS, 66, Munich-born film and stage actor, died of an acute heart disease June 18, 1982 in Vienna. He had appeared in more than 160 pictures, including "Royal Waltz," "The Mozart Story," "The Enemy Below," "Inn of the Sixth Happiness," "The Last Waltz," "The Blue Angel," "House of Intrigue," "I Aim at the Stars," "Revolt of the Tartars," "Brainwashed," "The Longest Day," "Three-penny Opera," "Magnificent Sinner," "Disorder," "Lord Jim," "The Battle of Britain," "Legion of the Damned," "Hello and Goodbye," "And God Created Woman," "Nicholas and Alexandra," "The Spy who Loved Me." Surviving is his fifth wife, who carried out his wishes for a night funeral under torchlights.

Grace Kelly	Fernando Lamas	Paul Lynde	Patrick Magee	Isa Miranda	Vic Morrow

GRACE KELLY, Princess of Monaco, 52, Philadelphia-born former screen star, died in Monaco Sept. 14, 1982 of injuries after suffering a cerebral hemorrhage while driving her car on a treacherous mountain road in the Cote d'Azur region. The car plunged down a 45-foot embankment and burst into flames. Her film career began with "Fourteen Hours" in 1951 and was followed by "High Noon," "Mogambo," "Dial 'M' for Murder," "Rear Window," "The Country Girl" for which she received an "Oscar," "Green Fire," "Bridges at Toko-Ri," "To Catch a Thief," "The Swan" and "High Society." She retired from films in 1956 after her marriage to Prince Rainier III of Monaco. In addition to her husband, she is survived by a son, Prince Albert, and two daughters, Princess Caroline and Princess Stephanie. Interment was in Monaco's St. Nicholas Cathedral.

HENRY KING, 96, Virginia-born pioneer director, died in his sleep June 29, 1982 at his home in Toluca Lake, Ca. After appearing as a song and dance man, he became a movie actor, and drifted into directing after filling in for his director. He subsequently directed over 100 films (most for Fox), including "23½ Hours Leave," "The White Sister," "Tol'able David," "Seventh Day," "Sonny," "Bond Boy," "Fury," "Chad Hanna," "I'd Climb the Highest Mountain," "Wait Till the Sun Shines, Nellie," "Romola," "Stella Dallas," "The Winning of Barbara Worth," "Lightnin'," "State Fair," "Carolina," "Marie Galante," "Way Down East," "Lloyds of London," "Ramona," "Seventh Heaven," "In Old Chicago," "Alexander's Ragtime Band," "Jesse James," "Stanley and Livingstone," "Little Old New York," "A Yank in the R. A. F.," "Remember the Day," "The Black Swan," "Song of Bernadette," "Wilson," "A Bell for Adano," "Margie," "The Country Doctor," "Captain from Castille," "Prince of Foxes," "Twelve O'Clock High," "The Gunfighter," "David and Bathsheba," "Snows of Kilimanjaro," "The Sun Also Rises," "King of the Kyber Rifles," "Untamed," "Love Is a Many-Splendored Thing," "Carousel," "The Bravados," "Beloved Infidel" and "Tender Is the Night," his last in 1961. He was the last surviving founder of the Academy of Motion Picture Arts and Sciences, and organizer of its awards, the "Oscars." He is survived by his second wife, a daughter, and two sons.

FERNANDO LAMAS, 67, Argentina-born actor and director, died Oct. 8, 1982 of cancer in Los Angeles. After a successful career on stage and screen in Buenos Aires, he went to Hollywood in 1950, subsequently appearing in "Rich, Young and Pretty," "The Avengers," "Law and the Lady," "The Merry Widow," "The Girl Who Had Everything," "Dangerous When Wet," "Diamond Queen," "Sangaree," "Jivaro," "Rose Marie," "Gold Rush," "The Lost World," "Magic Fountain," "Duel of Fire," "Revenge of the Musketeers," "The Violent Ones," "Kill a Dragon," "Valley of Mystery," "Backtrack," "The Cheap Detective." He directed more than 60 segments for various tv series. Surviving are his fourth wife, actress-swimmer Esther Williams, and by previous marriages, two daughters, and a son, film and tv actor Lorenzo Lamas.

HARVEY LEMBECK, 58, Brooklyn-born character actor on screen, stage and tv, died of a heart ailment Jan. 5, 1982 in Los Angeles. After appearing on Broadway and tv, he moved to Hollywood where he had roles in such films as "You're in the Navy Now," "The Frogmen," "14 Hours," "Finders Keepers," "Just Across the Street," "Girls in the Night," "Stalag 17," "Mission over Korea," "The Command," "A View from the Bridge," "Beach Party," "Love with the Proper Stranger," "Unsinkable Molly Brown," "Pajama Party," "Beach Blanket Bingo," "Fireball 500," "The Spirit Is Willing," "Hello Down There" and "The Gong Show Movie." He is survived by his widow, a son, actor Michael Lembeck, and a daughter.

PAUL LYNDE, 55, Ohio-born stage, screen and tv actor, died of a massive heart attack Jan. 10, 1982 in his Beverly Hills home.

His film credits include "New Faces," "Son of Flubber," "Bye Bye Birdie," "Under the Yum-Yum Tree," "For Those Who Think Young," "Send Me No Flowers," "Beach Blanket Bingo," "The Glass Bottom Boat," "Silent Treatment," "How Sweet It Is," "The Villain." He was best known for his appearances on the long-running tv game show "Hollywood Squares." Two sisters survive.

PATRICK MAGEE, 58, Ireland-born stage and film actor, died of "natural causes" Aug. 14, 1982 in his London home. Screen credits include "The Young Racers," "Dementia 13," "The Servant," "Zulu," "Masque of the Red Death," "Persecution and Assassination of Marat/Sade," "The Birthday Party," "A Clockwork Orange," "Barry Lyndon." His widow and two children survive.

ISA MIRANDA, 77, one of Italy's leading actresses, died July 8, 1982 of an infected bone fracture in Rome. Her films include "As the Leaves," "Red Passport," "The Late Mathias Pascal," "The Lie of Nina Petrova," "Hotel Imperial," "Thou Art My Joy," "Between Two Worlds," "Adventure in Diamonds," "The Walls of Malapaga," "My Widow and I," "Seven Deadly Sins," "La Ronde," "Summertime," "What Price Murder," "Zaza," "Without Heaven," "Pact with the Devil," "Rasputin," "Defeat of Hannibal," "Rommel's Treasure," "The Empty Canvas," "The Yellow Rolls-Royce," "The Great Britain Train Robbery," "Shoes of the Fisherman," "A New World," "We'll Call Him Andrea," "Night Porter," and "Furnished Room." She was the widow of producer Alfredo Guarini. No reported survivors.

DOLORES MORAN, 56, film actress of the 1940's and 1950's, died Feb. 5, 1982 at Woodland Hills, Ca. Her credits include "Yankee Doodle Dandy," "The Hard Way," "Old Acquaintance," "To Have and Have Not," "Hollywood Canteen," "The Horn Blows at Mignight," "Too Young to Know," "The Man I Love," "Christmas Eve," "Johnny One-Eye," "Count the Hours," "The Silver Lode." She was divorced from producer Benedict Bogeaus. Her mother and her sister survive.

KENNETH MORE, 67, English film, stage and tv actor, died of Parkinson's disease July 12, 1982 in London. His screen roles were in such films as "Scott of the Antarctic," "Chance of a Lifetime," "No Highway in the Sky," "Clouded Yellow," "Galloping Major," "Island Rescue," "Brandy for the Parson," "Genevieve," "Yellow Balloon," "Doctor in the House," "Adventures of Sadie," "Deep Blue Sky," "Reach for the Sky," "Raising a Riot," "Admirable Crichton," "A Night to Remember," "Sink the Bismarck!," "The 39 Steps," "The Longest Day," "Dark of the Sun," "Oh, What a Lovely War!," "The Betrayal." He appeared in tv's "The Forsyte Saga" series. Surviving are his third wife, actress Angela Douglas, and two daughters.

VIC MORROW, 53, Bronx-born film, stage and tv actor, was killed July 23, 1982 when a helicopter crashed during the filming of a movie "The Twilight Zone," northwest of Los Angeles in the Saugus desert. He made his debut in 1955 in "The Blackboard Jungle," followed by "Survival," "Tribute to a Bad Man," "Men in War," "God's Little Acre," "Hell's Five Hours," "King Creole," "Cimarron," "Portrait of a Mobster," "Last Year at Malibu," "Posse from Hell," "Dead Watch," "A River of Diamonds," "The Bad News Bears," "How to Make It," "Dirty Mary, Crazy Larry," "Treasure of Matecumbe," "Funeral for an Assassin," "The Evictors." He was divorced from actress Barbara Turner. Two daughters survive.

JACK MULLANEY, 51, film and tv actor, died of a stroke June 27, 1982 in Hollywood. Among his credits are "Young Stranger," "Vintage," "Kiss Them for Me," "South Pacific," "Mr. Roberts," "All the Fine Young Cannibals," "Honeymoon Machine," "Seven Days in May," "Tickle Me," "Dr. Goldfoot and the Bikini Machine," "Spinout." On tv he had appeared in such series as "The Ann Sothern Show," "Ensign O'Toole," "It's About Time," "My Living Doll." No reported survivors.

Cathleen Nesbitt	Jay Novello	Warren Oates	Lee Patrick	Eleanor Powell	Romy Schneider

CATHLEEN NESBITT, 93, English actress of stage, tv and film, died of natural causes Aug. 2, 1982 in her London home. Among her 37 screen credits are "The Faithful Heart," "Mary Queen of Scots," "Criminal at Large," "Trouble Ahead," "The Passing of the Third Floor Back," "Beloved Vagabond," "Against the Tide," "Pygmalion," "Chamber of Horrors," "The Lamp Still Burns," "Man of Evil," "Nicholas Nickleby," "3 Coins in the Fountain," "Desiree," "Black Widow," "An Affair to Remember," "A Day at the Fair," "Separate Tables," "Parent Trap," "Men of Two Worlds," "The Trygon Factor," "Staircase," "Promise Her Anything," "Villain," "French Connection II," "Family Plot," "Julia" and "The Haunting of Julia." She appeared in over 40 tv productions, including the popular series "Upstairs Downstairs." A son and a daughter survive.

JAY NOVELLO, 78, screen and tv character actor, died of cancer Sept. 2, 1982 in North Hollywood, Ca. Of his many films, he was probably best known for the title role in "The Willie Sutton Story." Other credits include "Tenth Avenue Kid," "Calling All Marines," "They Met in Bombay," "Chicago Kid," "Kiss the Blood Off My Hands," "The Sniper," "Miracle of Our Lady of Fatima," "Iron Mistress," "Beneath the 12-Mile Reef," "Diamond Queen," "Mad Magician," "Son of Sinbad," "Lisbon," "Perfect Furlough," "Lost World," "Pocketful of Miracles," "A Very Special Favor," "Atlantis," "Art of Love," "Caper of the Golden Bulls," "Billy Bright." He was a regular on the tv series "McHale's Navy." He is survived by his widow and a daughter.

WARREN OATES, 52, Kentucky-born tv and film character actor, died of a heart attack Apr. 3, 1982 in his home in Hollywood Hills. His career began with the tv series "Have Gun, Will Travel," subsequently appearing in many other series, including "Stoney Burke." Among his film credits are "Up Periscope!," "Private Property," "Lover Come Back," "Hero's Island," "West of Montana," "Major Dundee," "The Rounders," "Return of the 7," "The Shooting," "Killer on a Horse," "In the Heat of the Night," "The Wild Bunch," "The Split," "Smith!," "Barquero," "Crooks and Coronets," "Trog," "Chandler," "Hired Hand," "Badlands," "Two-Lane Blacktop," "1941," "Tom Sawyer," "Dillinger," "Cockfighter," "The Brink's Job," "Stripes," "The Border," "Tough Enough" and "Blue Thunder." No reported survivors.

PHILIP OBER, 80, Alabama-born stage and screen character actor, died of lung cancer and heart failure Sept. 13, 1982 in Santa Monica, Ca. His film credits include "Secret Fury," "Never a Dull Moment," "The Magnificent Yankee," "Washington Story," "Come Back, Little Sheba," "The Clown," "From Here to Eternity," "About Mrs. Leslie," "Tammy and the Bachelor," "High Cost of Loving," "10 North Frederick," "The Mating Game," "North by Northwest," "Beloved Infidel," "Elmer Gantry," "The Ugly American," "The Brass Bottle," "The Ghost and Mr. Chicken," "Assignment to Kill," "The Facts of Life." In the late 1960's he retired from acting to join the U.S. Consular Service in Mexico. His third wife survives.

LEE PATRICK, stage, screen and tv actress, died in her Laguna Hills, Ca., home of a heart seizure Nov. 21, 1982, the day before her 71st birthday. She had just returned from a celebration in her native NYC. Among her many film credits are "Border Cafe," "Crashing Hollywood," "Night Spot," "The Sisters," "Strange Cargo," "Saturday's Children," "City of Conquest," "South of Suez," "Honeymoon for Three," "Footsteps in the Dark," "Million Dollar Baby," "The Smiling Ghost," "The Maltese Falcon," "In This Our Life," "Now, Voyager," "George Washington Slept Here," "A Night to Remember," "Jitterbugs," "Mrs. Parkington," "Keep Your Powder Dry," "See My Lawyer," "Over 21," "Mildred Pierce," "Mother Wore Tights," "Snake Pit," "Caged," "Fuller Brush Girl," "There's No Business Like Show Business," "Auntie Mame," "Pillow Talk," "Visit to a Small Planet," "Sum-

mer and Smoke," "Wives and Lovers," "New Interns," "The Black Bird." She also appeared in the tv series "Topper," and "Mr. Adams and Eve." Surviving is her husband of 45 years, Tom Wood.

BERNARD (BARNEY) PHILLIPS, 68, St. Louis-born character actor on radio, tv, stage and screen, died Aug. 17, 1982 in Los Angeles. Among his film credits are "Eight Iron Men," "Blueprint for Murder," "The Square Jungle," "Cry Terror," "The Decks Ran Red," "Ruby Gentry," "Julie," "All American," "Drango," "The Sand Pebbles," "Matti" and "Hijack." He was a regular on tv's "Dragnet" series for 13 years, and appeared on "Gunsmoke," "Trapper John" and "The Betty White Show." He is survived by his widow, former dancer-actress Marie DeForest.

ELEANOR POWELL, 69, Massachusetts-born tap-dancing star of stage and screen, died of cancer Feb. 11, 1982 at her home in Beverly Hills. Her film career began with "George White's Scandals of 1935," followed by "Broadway Melody of 1936," "Born to Dance," "Broadway Melody of 1938," "Rosalie," "Honolulu," "Broadway Melody of 1940," "Lady Be Good," "Ship Ahoy!," "I Dood It," "Thousands Cheer," "Sensations of 1945," "Duchess of Idaho." In 1943 she married actor Gleen Ford and retired from show business. They were divorced in 1959. A son, Peter Ford, survives.

ARTHUR RUBINSTEIN, 95, one of the greatest pianists of the century, died in his sleep Dec. 20, 1982 at his home in Geneva, Switz. After making his debut in Poland at 4, he continued to perform for his adoring public until his sight began to fail about five years before his death. During World War II he moved his family to Beverly Hills, Ca., became a U.S. citizen, and subsequently was ghosting at the piano for the stars in "I've Always Loved You," "Song of Love," "Night Song," and appeared himself in "Carnegie Hall," and "Of Men and Music." Surviving are his widow and four children, including actor John Rubinstein.

JOE SAWYER, 75, ne Joseph Sauers in Canada, screen and tv character actor, died of liver cancer Apr. 21, 1982 in Ashland, Or. After his film debut in 1931 in "Eskimo," he appeared in over 340 pictures, including "College Humor," "Frisco Kid," "Petrified Forest," "Walking Dead," "Pride of the Marines," "High Tension," "Black Legion," "San Quentin," "Tarzan's Revenge," "Stolen Heaven," "Gambling Ship," "Confessions of a Nazi Spy," "Union Pacific," "Roaring Twenties," "Grapes of Wrath," "Melody Ranch," "Sgt. York," "Belle Starr," "They Died with Their Boots On," "You're in the Army Now," "Let's Face It," "Brewster's Millions," "Gilda," "Deadline at Dawn," "Joe Palooka," "The Outlaw," "A Double Life," "If You Knew Susie," "Tanks a Million," "Fighting Father Dunne," "Lucky Stiff," "Traveling Saleswoman," "It Came from Outer Space," "Tucson," "Johnny Dark," "North to Alaska," "How the West Was Won." He was Sgt. O'Hara on tv's "Rin Tin Tin" series for 168 episodes. He is survived by three sons and a daughter.

ROMY SCHNEIDER, 43, Vienna-born stage and screen actress, died of cardiac arrest May 29, 1982 in Paris where she had been living since the 1960's. Among her more than 60 films, in a 30 year career, are "The Story of Vickie," "Scampolo," "Forever My Love," "Boccaccio '70," "The Trial," "Magnificent Sinner," "The Cardinal," "The Victors," "Good Neighbor Sam," "What's New Pussycat?," "Maedchen in Uniform," "10:30 P.M. Summer," "Triple Cross," "Otley," "The Pool," "Don't You Cry," "The Old Gun," "Dirty Hands," "That Most Important Thing: Love," "Mado," "A Woman at Her Window," "The Hero," "Cesar and Rosalie," "The Assassination of Trotsky," "Bloodline," "A Simple Story," "Clair de Femme," "Group Portrait with Lady," "La Passante du Sans-Souci." She was separated from her second husband, photographer Daniel Biasini. A daughter survives.

| Lee Strasberg | Jacques Tati | King Vidor | Charles Walters | Alan Webb | Jack Webb |

ROLFE SEDAN, 86, character actor on screen and tv, died Sept. 16, 1982 in his Pacific Palisades, Ca., home. His career spanned more than 60 years, beginning with silent films. Credits include "The Iron Mask," "Ritzie Rosie," "One Hysterical Night," "Sweethearts and Wives," "All the King's Horses," "Paris in Spring," "Anything Goes," "Bluebeard's Eighth Wife," "Stolen Heaven," "Under the Big Top," "Story of Vernon and Irene Castle," "Ninotchka," "Juarez and Maximilian," "Law of the Tropics," "Phantom of the Rue Morgue," "The World's Greatest Lover," "Young Frankenstein." No reported survivors.

RETA SHAW, 69, stage, screeen and tv actress, died Jan. 8, 1982 in Encino, Ca. She went from Broadway to Hollywood in 1955 to appear in "Picnic," subsequently playing roles in "Man Afraid," "Pajama Game," "The Lady Takes a Flyer," "All Mine to Give," "Pollyanna," "Sanctuary," "Bachelor in Paradise," "Mary Poppins," "Made in Paris," "The Ghost and Mr. Chicken," "Escape to Witch Mountain." A daughter and a sister survive.

LEIGH SNOWDEN, 51, Memphis-born retired actress, died of cancer May 11, 1982 in Los Angeles. Her film credits include "Kiss Me Deadly," "Francis in the Navy," "All That Heaven Allows," "Square Jungle," "Outside the Law," "The Creature Walks," "I've Lived Before," "Hot Red Rumble." She gave up her career in 1956 to marry accordionist Dick Contino. He and five children survive.

LEE STRASBERG, 80, died of a heart attack on Feb. 17, 1982. He was the father of method acting in America, teacher, artistic director of the Actors Studio, director, actor and a major influence in the world of theatre. At the age of 7 he emigrated to NYC from Poland with his family. His professional acting debut was in 1925 on Broadway. In 1975 he was persuaded to appear in the film "Godfather Part II," followed by roles in "Boardwalk," and "Going in Style." His third wife and four children survive, including actress Susan Strasberg.

JACQUES TATI, French actor, writer and director, died of a pulmonary embolism Nov. 5, 1982 in Paris. He created Hulot in "Mr. Hulot's Holiday" and his "Mon Oncle" won the 1958 "Oscar" for best foreign language film. His career began with minor roles in Paris theatres, but he became a screen actor in the early 1930's in short features. His popularity was assured with "Jour de Fete" in 1952, followed by "Playtime," and "Traffic." Surviving are his wife, a son and a daughter.

DAN TOBIN, 72, stage, screen and tv actor, died Nov. 26, 1982 in Santa Monica, Ca. His credits include "Stadium Murders," "Black Limelight," "Pittsburgh Kid," "Woman of the Year," "Undercurrent," "Bachelor and the Bobby-Soxer," "The Big Clock," "The Velvet Touch," "Sealed Verdict," "Miss Tatlock's Millions," "Dream Wife," "Catered Affair," "The Last Angry Man," "How to Succeed in Business," "The Love Bug Rides Again." For nine years he appeared on the "Perry Mason" tv series. His widow survives.

TOM TULLY, 85, Colorado-born character actor on stage, screen and tv, died after a long illness on Apr. 27, 1982 in Newport Beach, Ca. He left Broadway for Hollywood in 1943 subsequently appeared in many films, including "Mission to Moscow," "Northern Pursuit," "Destination Tokyo," "Secret Command," "Sign of the Cross," "I'll Be Seeing You," "The Unseen," "Kiss and Tell," "The Virginian," "Lady in the Lake," "Killer McCoy," "Intrigue," "June Bride," "Blood on the Moon," "Branded," "Lure of the Wilderness," "Turning Point," "Ruby Gentry," "Jazz Singer," "The Moon Is Blue," "The Caine Mutiny" for which he received an "Oscar" nomination, "Soldier of Fortune," "10 North Frederick," "The Carpetbaggers," "Coogan's Bluff," "Charley Varrick." He acted in several tv series. Surviving are his widow and children.

KING VIDOR, 88, Texas-born director of more than 50 feature films, died of a heart ailment Nov. 1, 1982 at his ranch in Paso Robles, Ca. In 1915 he went to Hollywood where he worked at many studio jobs before directing his first feature "The Turn in the Road." Subsequently his credits included "The Jack Knife Man," "Peg o' My Heart," "The Big Parade," "The Crowd," "The Patsy," "Show People," "Billy the Kid," "Street Scene," "The Champ," "Bird of Paradise," "Cynara," "Our Daily Bread," "So Red the Rose," "Texas Rangers," "Stella Dallas," "The Citadel," "Northwest Passage," "Comrade X," "Hallelujah," "H. M. Pulham, Esq.," "An American Romance," "Duel in the Sun," "The Fountainhead," "Beyond the Forest," "Lightning Strikes Twice," "Japanese War Bride," "Ruby Gentry," "War and Peace," "Solomon and Sheba," after which he retired in 1959. In 1979 he received a special Oscar for his lifetime achievements, after having been nominated five times previously for a directorial Oscar. He was married and divorced three times. Surviving are three daughters.

JIMMY WAKELY, 68, Arkansas-born country-western singer and actor, died of heart failure Sept. 23, 1982 in Mission Hills, Ca. He had appeared in over 30 films, including "Saga of Death Valley," "Tulsa Kid," "Twilight on the Trail," "Trail Blazing," "Silver Bullet," "Deep in the Heart of Texas," "Old Chisholm Trail," "Sundown Valley," "Cowboy Canteen," "West of the Alamo," "Moon over Montana," "Trail to Mexico," "Song of the Sierras," "Oklahoma Blues," "Gun Runner," "Across the Rio Grande," "Arrow in the Dust," "Silver Star." He is survived by his widow, a son and three daughters.

CHARLES WALTERS, 68, Pasadena-born director, former stage and screen actor, died of lung cancer Aug. 13, 1982 at his home in Malibu, Ca. After appearing on Broadway as a singer-dancer and actor, he became a dance director for a series of films before being signed as a full director at MGM. "Good News" was his first feature picture, followed by "Easter Parade," "Barkleys of Broadway," "Summer Stock," "Three Guys Named Mike," "Texas Carnival," "Belle of New York," "Lili," "Dangerous When Wet," "Torch Song," "Easy to Love," "The Glass Slipper," "The Tender Trap," "High Society," "Don't Go Near the Water," "Please Don't Eat the Daisies," "Two Loves," "Jumbo," "The Unsinkable Molly Brown," and "Walk, Don't Run" (his last in 1966). He also directed several tv shows, including "Here's Lucy." An adopted son survives.

ALAN WEBB, 75, English stage and film actor, died June 22, 1982 in Sussex, Eng. His film credits include "Challenge to Lassie," "The Third Secret," "The Pumpkin Eater," "King Rat," "Taming of the Shrew," "Falstaff: Chimes at Midnight," "Interlude," "Nicholas and Alexandra," "Entertaining Mr. Sloane" and "Women in Love." No reported survivors.

JACK WEBB, 62, California-born actor on radio, tv and screen, died of a heart attack on Dec. 23, 1982 in his Los Angeles home. His film credits include "He Walked by Night," "Dark City," "Sunset Boulevard," "The Men," "Halls of Montezuma," "Appointment with Danger," "You're in the Navy Now," "Dragnet," "Pete Kelly's Blues," "The D. I.," "30," "The Last Time I Saw Archie." His greatest success was achieved with his portrayal of Sgt. Joe Friday on the "Dragnet" radio and tv series. By 1973 he was producing five different tv series simultaneously: "Adam-12," "Emergency," "Escape," "Chase" and "Hec Ramsey." His fourth wife was with him when he died. Two daughters from a previous marriage also survive.

INDEX

240

252

253

254